Frederick Matthias
ALEXANDER

A FAMILY HISTORY

Young FM

Frederick Matthias ALEXANDER

A FAMILY HISTORY

J.A. Evans

Phillimore

2001

Published by
PHILLIMORE & CO. LTD.
Shopwyke Manor Barn, Chichester, West Sussex

ISBN 1 86077 178 5

Printed and bound in Great Britain by
Butler & Tanner Ltd.
Frome and London

To my parents
The late David Ivor Evans TD
and
Joan Alexander Evans

CONTENTS

LIST OF ILLUSTRATIONS

Frontispiece: Young FM

MAPS

FOREWORD

BY

MARJORY BARLOW

NIECE OF FREDERICK MATTHIAS ALEXANDER AND TEACHER OF THE TECHNIQUE

It is a pleasure to welcome this book. Jackie Evans has brought to life little known episodes in pioneer history which have resulted in the growth in a little over a hundred years of a great country.

The story she tells with honesty and attention to detail should interest many readers and not only those of the descendants of her characters. It is an account of courage and enterprise sustained against tremendous odds in a difficult and unfriendly environment.

I wish the book well and hope that it will achieve the wide circulation it deserves.

ACKNOWLEDGEMENTS

I could not have achieved this account without the assistance of a large number of people. In particular I wish to thank my cousin Jan Kelly of Launceston, Tasmania. She has undertaken Alexander research for over 20 years and we met during one of my visits to Tasmania in the mid-1980s. Without her support, encouragement, friendship and research this book would not have been possible. She has responded to all my questions with good humour and beavered away 'down under' to produce accurate information about the family in Tasmania. She is, like me, a great, great, grandchild of Matthias Alexander, senior; her great grandfather was Matthias, junior. Some of my other many relations in Tasmania have helped and assisted me in my project. Two brothers, the late Ken and the late Jim (Roy) Alexander, great grandsons of Matthias senior, were particularly kind and looked after me so well whenever I visited Wynyard. They took me around the area to visit many Alexander sites including Murdering Gully and the old Alexander Cemetery on Table Cape. They discovered stories about life in Wynyard in the early days, sent me books they thought would help me and Ken sent me a family photograph which I have included in this book. I shall always remember the Alexander party to celebrate the 100th anniversary of the lighthouse, held on Table Cape, and staying at Jim's house, Alexandria, on the site of the original Alexander settlement. I was particularly pleased when Ken arranged for me to meet Terry McKenna who remembered well my great grandfather Johnny. He was able to supply me with photographs and tell me about Johnny's life with the McKenna family. It was a pleasure to meet the late Mrs. Urban Alexander who spent all her married life in Burnie. She married Urban, grandchild of Matthias senior, in the very early part of the last century. Her memories of those days were fascinating. I also extend my thanks to the late Max Alexander, a great, great grandson of Matthias senior, and his widow Bev who helped me with my research and entertained me in their house in Wynyard. I am grateful to the late Anne Sligo in Melbourne and Desley Ruffin of Tasmania who are descended from Thomas Lewis and his wife Maria (née Davis). They provided me with important information about Maria and her first husband Thomas Brown which greatly helped my research. Desley Ruffin also sent me the photograph of Maria Davis.

My English family have given me tremendous support and help. In particular I wish to thank the late Joyce Alexander, my great aunt and widow of Beaumont, for allowing me to use all the Alexander material in her possession. This included FM's scrapbooks from Australia, a collection of letters and other papers. Secondly, I am most grateful to my aunt, Marjory Barlow, who has provided me with many letters and other details about the family. Additionally, she has kindly written the Foreword for this book. I am indebted to her for the hundreds of Alexander lessons she has given me in the past few years. She is a master of the Work and it is a privilege to be taught by her. Thirdly, I thank the late Marie and her sister the late Doreen, daughters of May Clelland (née Alexander) and Doreen's son John Laher who have added to my knowledge of the family and produced some interesting photographs. Fourthly, I have received support from the late Maxwell Alexander, AR's son, and his family and at Maxwell's special request I have included the picture of AR that he selected for the book. Fifthly, I was delighted to have the support of FM's son John Vicary who provided useful and interesting information along with a number of photographs. Lastly, I give a very special thanks to my mother without whose support and encouragement I am sure I would never have completed this account. She has read endless drafts of the text, searched through all her possessions for family information and accompanied me on the majority of my numerous overseas trips to walk in the footsteps of various Alexanders.

In America, I am grateful to the late Roy Alexander whose life-time hobby was family research. He wrote to me regularly for a number of years and provided me with most of the information about the Ramsbury Alexanders who crossed the Atlantic in the mid-1800s. Also I thank his nephew Cliff who has assisted me since Roy's death in 1988 and Roy's son, Joseph, who has permitted me to use two of his father's drawings and a church meeting pamphlet from the family archives. I am also indebted to Bonnie and Colbie Fredette, now in charge of a Nursing Home at the Whitney Homestead in Stow. I thank them for the very warm reception they gave us when we visited, for the information they supplied and sent on to me after the visit, and for permitting me to take photographs of the Homestead and the gardens. Lastly, I thank Missy Vineyard, an Alexander teacher, who has helped, encouraged and supported me in a number of ways and made available to me her typed copies of some of the handwritten Alexander papers.

To many Alexander teachers in this country I give my thanks. Of particular importance were, firstly, the late Margaret Goldie whose enthusiasm for this project was sometimes almost overwhelming. She gave me many Alexander papers and copies of a number of her books. Her copy of Judson Herrick's book on George Ellett Coghill published in 1948 was most valuable. Many years ago she had marked all the lines she thought of importance and relevance to Alexander's work. Whether or not she did this with FM I do not know but she was most anxious that some of these points be made in my book. It was not possible to include all the quotations she wanted so I was forced to make a selection. Although she saw the draft chapter containing the Coghill quotes she was too ill to make detailed comments. Therefore I accept full responsibility for the quotations used and thank the University of Chicago for permitting me to publish them. It is my greatest regret that I was unable to complete this book before Margaret Goldie died but I shall always remember my meetings with her. When she was still teaching in London we would meet at the Bonnington Hotel for tea and discuss Alexander matters. Later we would drink champagne during my many visits to her house in Richmond. She remembered the trip to, and her time in America so vividly and said that she was reduced to tears when she read my account of the journey.

The second Alexander teacher to whom I owe so much is Erika Whittaker. When she lived in Melbourne and we visited she always welcomed us with open arms. She came by bus and by foot to our hotel when the temperature was 104°F and she declared it too hot for my slightly younger mother, who was not used to these conditions, to venture outside. She accompanied us on our trips around the city taking us to the places where the various Alexanders lived and worked. She talked at length about her family and in particular her aunt, Ethel Webb, without whom it is unlikely that FM could have succeeded as he did. Now Erika has returned to Scotland she has given great support and like Margaret Goldie has provided the necessary enthusiasm to keep me at my task. Additionally, I thank her for the photographs that she has given me.

The third major contributor from the Alexander fraternity was Walter Carrington. I have spent many hours at the Carrington home in Lansdowne Road talking to Walter and his wife Dilys about FM and even more hours toiling through their extensive archives of Alexander material. Their support, help, encouragement, generosity and advice has been unstinting. They and the other teachers at Lansdowne Road have always made me so welcome, they have let me use their various teaching rooms and assisted me in finding documents. I thank them all and hope that the final result justifies their faith in me. I am most grateful to Walter for permitting me to use a number of photographs that Irene Tasker bequeathed to him.

The fourth teacher that I would like to thank is Elisabeth Walker who has allowed me to use information from her archives and has also provided support and encouragement.

There are many other people who are not Alexander teachers who have helped and assisted me throughout the time I have worked on this book but it would be invidious to attempt to mention them by name with one exception, that is Hilda Coates. She spent her childhood at Penhill and was living there with her parents when my great uncle bought the property. Her father, Arthur Rose, looked after FM's horses, cows and goats as well as the land and her mother Fanny worked in the house. Hilda, now a widow, still lives in the area and her memories of the Penhill days have provided valuable information. I am grateful to her for several photographs.

Although much of the information for this book has come from private collections, I have spent considerable time in various public depositories. All the staff at the record offices, libraries and museums have been helpful, friendly and efficient. In particular I thank the staff of the British Newspaper Library, Colindale; the Public Record Office, Chancery Lane (and latterly Kew); the Registry of Births, Marriages and Deaths at St Catherine's House and the Census Reading Rooms at Portugal Street (later in Chancery Lane, now both combined at the Family Records Centre in Myddelton Street, London); the Principle Registry of the Family Division, Somerset House (now High Holborn, London); the Corporation of London Record Office, Guildhall, London; the Greater London Record Office (now the Metropolitan Archives, Northampton Road, London); the Wiltshire and Swindon Record Office, Trowbridge, and I include John and Beryl Hurley who obtained many wills from this Record Office on my behalf; the Kent Record Office, Maidstone; the Bexley Local Studies and Archive Centre, Hall Place (now located at Bexley Central Library); the Froebel Archive for Childhood Studies at Roehampton; the Guildhall Library, London; the Foreign and Commonwealth Office Library, King Charles Street, London; the Bexleyheath Library and the Sidcup Library. Overseas, I am most grateful to the staff of the Archives Office of Tasmania, the Office of the Surveyor General, the Probate Registry, the State Library of Tasmania and the Lands Titles Office all in Hobart, the Launceston Reference Library, the

Queen Victoria Museum and Art Gallery, Launceston, Burnie Library, the Pioneer Village Museum, Burnie, the Australian Archives Office in Melbourne, Melbourne Library, and the Boston Library, Boston, Massachusetts. I thank the Queen Victoria Museum and Art Gallery in Launceston, the Pioneer Village Museum in Burnie, Portsmouth Central Library and the Kentish Times newspaper for allowing me to reproduce photographs from their collections.

I am grateful to all the authors who have permitted me to quote from their books. In particular I thank Barbara Croucher and Jill Chambers, both of whom have undertaken an enormous amount of research, Barbara into the history of Ramsbury and Jill into the Swing Riots. Allowing me to use their research to supplement my own has reduced the work required for two of the early chapters. Additionally, I thank Barbara for allowing me to use three of the photographs of Ramsbury that she used in her book *Ramsbury Then and Now*. In Australia, I thank Fuzzy Hearn for permitting me to use extracts from his book about Somerset in Tasmania. I extend my thanks to all the staff and unpaid helpers at the Society of Genealogists in London who have given me tremendous assistance over many years. The Society's very large collection has significantly helped in the production of this book. Similarly, I am grateful to the Church of Jesus Christ of Latter Day Saints in Exhibition Road, London for the courteous way they handled my enquiries.

In addition to the acknowledgements for permission to use photographs that I have already mentioned I am grateful to Valerie Little, Shirley Macaulay and the Society of Teachers of the Alexander Technique, London for their contributions. Lastly, I thank two of my RAF colleagues, Ruth Montague and Michael Webb, and my cousin Matthew Oakeley for reading my draft script and making editorial suggestions and John Gray, senior Alexander teacher at the Royal Academy of Dramatic Art, who has written the Legacy.

Although I have made strenuous efforts to trace the copyright holders of all the material used in this book in some cases I have failed and for this I apologise. Similarly I have been unable to contact a few of the photographers whose work I have used in this book. If any of these photographs are still within copyright I apologise to the photographers concerned.

I am most grateful to John Batchelor for the design and painting on the dust jacket.

J.A. EVANS
Sidcup

February 2001

INTRODUCTION

In 1988 I was asked to give a lecture to an International Alexander Technique Conference in Brighton about Frederick Matthias Alexander's background and history. This gave many Alexander teachers an insight into his early life and increased the interest of a number of teachers in his history. Some of these teachers wanted me to publish the talk but I was aware that considerably more research was required if I were to produce a coherent account. This was not possible as I was in full-time employment. After my retirement, I was persuaded to undertake more research with a view to publishing a book. It was felt by the Alexander family and a number of senior teachers that an accurate record of the background, family and life of Alexander was required. At the time many inaccurate articles, letters and books were circulating and producing a very biased view of Alexander and his family. I hope that this book will set the record straight and will interest a wider audience than already committed Alexandrians.

Throughout the book I have referred to Frederick Matthias Alexander as FM and his brother Albert Redden Alexander as AR. Within the family, Frederick was Fred and always known to me as Uncle Fred. In the early days some of his friends called him Alex while others like Robert Young called him Zan. To his early pupils he was Mr. Alexander but when he started the training course a less formal approach was considered appropriate. In the early 1930s it was not acceptable for a different generation to refer to their elders by their Christian name and so 'FM' was adopted. Similarly, Albert Redden, known within the family as Ab and later Doddy (certainly I remember him as Uncle Doddy), became 'AR'. For simplicity I have used a Christian name, usually the first one, for all other members of the family although this is not necessarily what they were commonly called.

My great uncles always referred to their teaching as the Work and this is how it is known today by the family. The expression was considered inappropriate at some now unknown stage, probably by the medical and other professional men who were writing about Alexander's work, and so the term Technique was introduced. I have used the term 'Work' and changed to 'Technique' at the approximate time it is thought to have occurred.

PART ONE

FREDERICK MATTHIAS ALEXANDER'S ANCESTORS FROM WILTSHIRE, ENGLAND TO TABLE CAPE, TASMANIA

WILTSHIRE.

English Miles.
1 2 3 4 5 6 7 8 9 10

Part of WILTSHIRE
locally situate in Berkshire.

REFERENCE to the HUNDREDS.

Malmesbury	1	Westbury	15
Chippenham	2	Swanborough	16
Bradford	3	Sth Damerham	17
Melksham	4	Warminster	18
Calne	5	Heytesbury	19
Potterne	} 6	Amesbury	20
Cannings		Mere	21
Highworth	7	Downton	22
Cricklade & Staple	8	Chalk	23
Kingsbridge	9	Dunworth	24
Elstub & Everley	8	Branch & Dole	25
Nth Damerham	10	Cawden &	} 26
Ramsbury	11	Cadworth	
Seidley	12	Underditch	27
Kinwardstone	13	Alderbury	28
Whorwelsdown	W	Frustfield	29

The Figures prefixed to the Towns denote the distance from London.

Longitude West 2° from Greenwich

Engd by Gray & Son.

Phillimore Atlas and Index of Parish Registers, ed. Cecil R. Humphery-Smith (2nd edn. 1995)

1

ALEXANDERS OF ENGLAND

The ploughman near at hand,
Whistles o'er the furrowed land,
And the milkmaid singeth blithe,
And the mower whets his scythe,
And every shepherd tells his tale
Under the hawthorne in the dale.

John Milton: *L'Allegro*

When the paternal grandfather of Frederick Matthias Alexander, Matthias Alexander, sailed with his brother, Joseph, to Australia in 1831, he left the village of his birth in southern England where some of his ancestors had lived for over 300 years. This village, known as Ramsbury, is in a valley in Wiltshire through which the river Kennet flows and is about five miles east of Marlborough. In 1831, there were 1,538 people living in the village and a total of 2,290 in the parish.[1]

A permanent settlement was established in Ramsbury in Saxon times, although neolithic and Bronze Age articles found in the area indicate that people were living in the vicinity many years before the Saxons arrived. Certainly the Romans came to the valley and there were a number of villa sites around Ramsbury and there may have been one in the centre of the village. Two Roman roads were located very close to the village. One, Ermine Way, crossed the northern part of the Ramsbury parish while the other, which connected Winchester and Wanborough, passed through the nearby village of Mildenhall. But it was the Saxons, who probably dominated the area from the middle of the sixth century, who developed the settlement at Ramsbury. The remains of a Saxon iron smelting forge were found in Ramsbury High Street some years ago and the Saxon cathedral, located in the centre of the village, was undoubtedly the largest building.[2] As the present Ramsbury church built on the same site dates from the 13th century, it is likely that the old cathedral was used until then. The Saxons cleared large areas of forest and developed a central farming system with the manor at the centre. They created villages about two to three miles apart avoiding the Roman roads and the ancient ridgeways which were considered dangerous as they were frequented by itinerant undesirables.[3]

Ramsbury with its plentiful supply of water and relatively gentle slopes provided good farming land. So once the trees in the immediate vicinity were removed the village began to prosper. By the time of the Domesday Survey in 1086, the manor of Ramsbury was the second largest in Wiltshire. The record referred to the hundred of Ramsbury and, so the

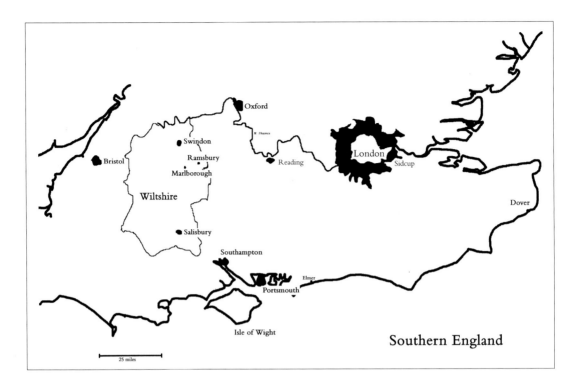

entry included two or maybe even three villages in addition to Ramsbury. However, as these other villages were mainly scrubby downland or woodland on clay that contained flints, undoubtedly the most valuable land was around the village of Ramsbury near the river Kennet.

The short entry of 1086, translated into modern English, stated:

> The Bishop (the Bishop of Salisbury) also holds Ramsbury. Before 1066 it paid tax for 90 hides. Land for 54 ploughs. Of this land 30 hides in lordship; 8 ploughs there; 9 slaves. 68 villagers and 43 smallholders who have 29 ploughs. Meadow, 80 acres; 10 mills which pay £6 30d; pasture 14 furlongs long and 5 furlongs wide; woodland 16 furlongs long and 4 furlong wide. Of this manor's land the priests hold 4 hides, Otbold 12 hides, Herbert 5 hides, Quintin 5 hides, the reeve's wife (the manor overseer) 1 hide; they have in lordship 11 ploughs; 31 smallholders with 6 ploughs. In Cricklade 5 burgesses who belong to this manor pay 5s. Value of the Bishop's lordship, £52 15s.; of what the others hold, £17 5s.[4]

A hide was a measure of land that would support one free family and dependants but varied in size depending on the locality. The exact size of a hide in Ramsbury is debatable. The land for ploughs is roughly estimated for Wiltshire as the 'number of plough teams of 8 oxen which could be employed if the land was fully exploited'.[5] The slaves belonging to the Bishop may have been descendants of the Celts who remained on the estate from Roman times but whether or not any of them were ancestors of the Alexanders is not known. Clearly, the bishopric had significantly reduced in size following the move of the Bishop to

Old Sarum in 1075 as all that remained of the Cathedral establishment was a small group of priests with 4 hides.[6] Bishop Herman, a foreigner from Flanders, had ruled Ramsbury from 1045 and united the sees of Sherborne and Ramsbury in 1058. The arrival of the Normans and their wish to reorganise the English Church led to the decision to move the united sees to Salisbury. This gave the church a new start in a place not hindered by Anglo-Saxon precedents or vested interests. Thus, the Normans could ensure that their ideas for secular cathedral government, at that time new to England, would be enacted. A new cathedral was built at Salisbury which was completed during the time of the new bishop, St Osmund, who was appointed in 1078.[7]

The bishops of Salisbury did not forget the manor in Ramsbury which was one of their larger ones, and for many years to come they visited regularly not only in the summer months of July and August but also in October to enjoy the game and often at Christmas. The game included pigeons which were apparently a great source of controversy between the bishop and the villagers because they ate so much corn. The bishop's palace or manor house was near the Kennet over which the bishops claimed exclusive fishing rights; the Kennet was famous for trout. Also, the bishop had a swannery. The house was surrounded by a large park which by 1458 contained about 400 deer and a rabbit warren.[8] Additionally, there was a considerable amount of land but by the end of the 14th century most of the manor demesne land was leased. This had resulted in the formation of other manors, namely Hilldrop, Littlecote and Axford, and a number of smaller estates.[9]

From the earliest times the tithes of Ramsbury belonged to the chapter of Salisbury but then they were passed to the prebend, the canon, of Ramsbury and by 1226 had a yearly value of 40 marks all of which it is assumed came from the parish.

> The prebendary was entitled to tithes of corn, wool and lambs from the whole parish and various other tithes and obligations some of which were given to the vicar of Ramsbury. In 1341 he had a manor house, 2 carucates, 12 acres of meadow, 30 acres of several pasture and feeding for 100 sheep, 40 acres of woodland, a mill, and lands held by villeins whose rents and works were worth 31s. 4d. a year.

Some two hundred years later the prebend was valued at £52.[10]

The Saxons had set up a common field system in Ramsbury and although this changed slowly over the years, it was not abolished until the Ramsbury Enclosure Act in 1778. Thus, the Town Tything of Ramsbury was surrounded by common fields with Ramsbury Manor and its associated land a little distance away. The other Ramsbury tythings surrounded the centre except to the south which bordered Savernake Forest. This royal forest prevented expansion of the village and access was strictly forbidden to all the villagers.[11] The tythings, namely Ramsbury Town, Axford, Park Town, Eastridge, Preston and Whittonditch, contained variously common arable fields, common pastures, water-meadows and woods. Sheep were the most important animals in the area but there were also some pigs and cattle. To supplement their meagre diet the villagers poached rabbits, pheasants, pigeons and fish from the manor grounds and the forest.

There were some diversions to the daily grind for the medieval villagers of Ramsbury. Successive kings visited and presumably stayed in the bishop's house, and there were fairs. In 1227, Henry III granted Ramsbury the right to hold a weekly fair but this was disputed by the merchants of Marlborough who jealously guarded their own market, with the result that after nearly a hundred years of argument the King ordered that Ramsbury could hold only two fairs as authorised in 1240. So, from 1319, Ramsbury held a cattle fair in May and a hiring fair in October. These events continued until 1939 and the 1950s respectively although the hiring fair eventually became a carnival to raise money for local charities.[12]

The Black Death of 1349, which swept across England killing a third or maybe half the population, must have affected Ramsbury but the details are not known. Certainly by the time of the 1377 Poll Tax, which assessed everyone over the age of 14 years, Ramsbury parish had a total of 372 tax payers. Of these 161 were in the Town Tything with 133 in the tythings of Axford, Park Town and Eastridge and 78 in Whittonditch and Preshute, which was possibly Preston. The adjacent parish of Aldbourne had 312 on the tax roll.[13]

For the villagers of Ramsbury, life for the next 200 years progressed steadily; the population increased slowly but living conditions did not improve. Some harvests were good while others were bad. Poverty, disease and famine were familiar to all and steadily the manorial system of farming was changing. Progressively fewer people rented more farming land leaving many as labourers with the use only of the ever-decreasing common land. Wars took place mainly overseas and sometimes men were sent from the village to participate. The Wars of the Roses do not seem to have affected Ramsbury but the arrival of the Tudor era did have an impact on the village.

At this time, the bishop's household was large and numbered over a hundred. When, in 1538, the distinguished antiquary, Leland, visited Ramsbury, he described the parish

> as fruitful of wood and corn and the normal sheep and corn husbandry of the Wiltshire chalklands has predominated in the usual pattern of meadows on the alluvium, arable on the gravel and chalk, and permanent pasture on the steepest slopes of the chalk. The highest land, covered by clay-with-flints, has been wooded, arable, and pasture.[14]

A few years later, in 1545, there occurred an event of the greatest importance to the village: the bishop's manor passing out of Church hands. By an Act of Exchange the manor was given to the Lord Protector of the Realm, Edward Seymour, Earl of Hertford. However, after Seymour's execution for treason in 1552, the manor of Ramsbury, Baydon and Axford, the hundred of Ramsbury and the Ramsbury parks, Old park and Great park were granted by Edward VI to William Herbert, Earl of Pembroke. In addition Pembroke was granted considerably more land, which included Rodbourne, Bedwyn, Froxfield, Pewsey and Hungerford.[15]

The Earl of Pembroke was well known in court circles and had married Anne, sister of Catherine Parr, Henry VIII's sixth wife. In 1542, the immensely wealthy Wilton Abbey estates were dissolved and granted to him. He built the great mansion, Wilton House, and followed this a few years later by building a new house at Ramsbury. In addition, Pembroke was granted Baynard's Castle on the banks of the river Thames which provided him with a London residence and extensive lands in Wales. He was an executor of Henry VIII's will and one of the 12 Privy Counsellors who guided the young Edward VI. His eldest son married Lady Catherine Grey, sister of Lady Jane Grey whose claim to the throne he supported. On the accession of Mary Tudor, he rapidly changed sides and was appointed to command the army against Wyatt's Protestant rebellion in 1554. He endeared himself to the Protestant Elizabeth I on her accession in 1558, and became one of her Privy Counsellors. He risked royal wrath again in 1569 by supporting the marriage of the Duke of Norfolk to Mary, Queen of Scots. He was arrested but managed to persuade Queen Elizabeth of his loyalty. He died at Hampton Court shortly afterwards.[16] Fortunately his political activities do not seem to have had an impact on the village at Ramsbury.

Shortly after his grant of the Ramsbury lands, Pembroke ordered a survey to be conducted of all his new properties. A further very detailed study of all his estates was undertaken a few years later and published in April 1567, two years before his death. This survey was a slightly surprising enterprise because Pembroke, allegedly, could neither read nor write.[17] Nevertheless, the record provides a most valuable insight into life in Ramsbury along with many details about all the tenants on the estate. An ancestor of Matthias Alexander, Stephen Appleford from a long established family at Axford, was the steward or beadle of the estate. He was fortunate and unlike most of the population of Ramsbury had considerable assets which he steadily increased throughout his life. He was given a house near the new manor, a watermill with three acres of water-meadows, an unspecified Regarder's charge for the custody of the park and, together with an allotment in the park, he had permission to graze his cattle and pigs at the Earl's pleasure. In Axford, he had considerable holdings including 122 acres of arable land, 31½ acres of meadow, 12 acres of woodland, common for 184 sheep, 12 cows and 10 horses, plus three messuages, two tenements, a barn and a watermill.[18] The survey showed that in the Ramsbury area there were about half a dozen large farms, some thirty-five yeoman farmers, about twenty cottagers mainly in the village and an unknown number of labourers who had no holdings or common rights. In addition the survey showed that 23 households in Ramsbury were paying rent to the Earl and a further 42 households in the surrounding hamlets.[19] The Lay Subsidy of 1576 listed 32 taxpayers in Ramsbury of which Stephen Appleford was one.[20]

While the Applefords were succeeding in Ramsbury other ancestors of Matthias Alexander were living in the adjacent village of Lambourn. The parish comprised a large acreage of downland which today is famous for training race horses. In the 16th century the area was a rather secluded and isolated place as no major highways met in Lambourn. However, there were regular markets and fairs.[21] It was here that John Selwood and his wife Margaret lived and where the family remained for the next hundred years. Their children Mary, John and Alice were baptised in Lambourn between 1617 and 1624. John junior married and he and his wife, Sarah, had a daughter Sarah who was baptised in 1661. In 1687, Sarah married a local man Richard Flower, son of Austin and Hester, and they had three children, namely Hester and Sarah who were baptised in 1689 and a son, Richard, who was baptised two years later. Although Sarah died in infancy, Hester survived and in 1715 she married Richard Brackstone from Ramsbury in the church at nearby Hungerford. Richard came from a well established Ramsbury family. His great grandparents Giles, described as a husbandman, and Elizabeth had married there in 1638 and their third son, Richard, also a husbandman, had married Averin Bryant at the Ramsbury church in 1667. This Richard was buried in May 1690 a year after the marriage of his son, another Richard, to Elizabeth Martyn.[22] The couple had a number of children, the oldest of which was yet another Richard who was baptised in 1690 and at the age of 25 years married Hester. They were Matthias Alexander's great great grandparents.

The major event for all the population in England during the 17th century was the Civil War. Although the Earl of Pembroke and the Pophams of Littlecote along with the majority of Members of Parliament for the area were on the side of Cromwell, it is likely that the villagers were more circumspect in their outlook. Throughout the war small garrisons, both Royalist and Parliamentarian, set up in Wiltshire and nearby Berkshire. In particular Wiltshire became a routeway through which the rival armies continually passed to other battle grounds and one can imagine the Ramsbury villagers coming out of their little hovels to welcome the King and then a few days later re-appearing to cheer Cromwell and his followers. They must have heard the explosions of the ammunition wagons and seen men wandering back through the village with news of the fighting. Certainly, the King with 9,000 troops stayed a couple of miles from Ramsbury, then later the Earl of Essex as Commander in Chief of the Parliamentary forces also stayed in the village. A skirmish between the rival armies took place on nearby Albourne Chase and several of the wounded soldiers were taken to the town of Hungerford, a few miles from Ramsbury, where some of them died. But, other than some possible damage to the church, the Civil War, the aftermath and the Restoration had little direct effect on the villagers although local trade and industry had suffered.[23] The villagers paid their rent and tried to provide enough food for their families. Some of them had to pay taxes but there was considerable hardship in the area as the Hearth Tax listings proved. This tax was paid by the occupier of every dwelling at the rate of 2s. a hearth but people in houses worth less than 20s. and not paying parish rates and those people who were receiving poor relief were exempt. In 1670, the Ramsbury parish lists produced by the vicar, John Wilson, showed 44 households in receipt of poor relief and a further 79 occupiers who were exempt.[24] Meanwhile the fortunes of the Pembroke family had declined and, in 1676, the 5th Earl was forced to sell the manor to pay his debts. The manor was bought by a syndicate who began a programme of selling the leasehold and copyhold tenancies mostly to the tenants and by 1681 all that remained of the once great estate was the manor house, the parks and the woods.[25]

It is probable that some Alexander ancestors gained by the sales. On 31 October 1708 John Alexander married the 16-year-old Elizabeth Brackstone, the sixth of Moses and Elizabeth Brackstone's nine children. Although Moses Brackstone may have been related to the previously mentioned Richard Brackstone the link was certainly distant. Moses was described in his will as a labourer, but as he voted in the elections held at Wilton on 22 May 1705 he must have owned a freehold property yielding at least 40s. a year.[26] John and Elizabeth, great great grand parents of Matthias, had 15 children, one every two years from November 1709 to 1735. Of these three children died in infancy and one, the oldest son, John, who probably did not marry, predeceased his father. A lease dated March 1732 between Richard Jones Esq. and John Alexander was for the lives of John and two of his sons, William and Edward. The lease was for 'a cottage or tenement with the barnside and garden thereunto'. An initial rent of 5s. was paid and thereafter 1s. a year.[27] Life in the tiny Alexander cottage was congested but, as was common in the reign of George I, children were apprenticed at an early age. John and Elizabeth's second child, Jane, was apprenticed for seven years as a mantua maker, a modern-day dress maker. So in 1724, just before her ninth birthday, she went to live with her master, John Adam, and his wife Elizabeth in the nearby village of Froxfield.[28] Therefore, Jane had left home before the birth of the ninth child.

Eleven of the Alexander children definitely survived to adulthood and all married. Some of them had very large families but this was not the case with their tenth child and fifth son, Edward, who in 1757 married Elizabeth Brackstone, a daughter of Richard and Hester. Hester had died in 1724, probably during the birth of her fourth child, leaving Richard to bring up the four small children. They appear to have survived and the three daughters including Elizabeth married in Ramsbury church. Less than four months after the wedding of Edward and Elizabeth, Edward's father, John, died. John was described in his will as a yeoman and he left all his ten surviving children one shilling. In addition, he left to Edward a plot of land of 24 poles that he had bought from Roger Langford together with the dwelling house, out houses and other buildings on the land. His wife was scheduled to receive the house they lived in and all the contents together with another house which was occupied by a widow, Margaret Bunce. In the event Elizabeth predeceased her husband so these assets passed to their youngest daughter, Rebecca, by now married to Ben Hobbs.[29] John had prospered and despite the expense of so many children had significant assets by the end of his life.

During this period the village of Ramsbury steadily changed and provided a number of other people with opportunities. The sale of the majority of the manor lands in the 1680s loosened the ties between the manor and the villagers with the result that Ramsbury became an open village. Now people could move in and out of the area freely and Ramsbury became a centre for craftsmen of all types, tradesmen and shop keepers. The area was well served with water from the Kennet and both brewing and tanning became important industries. Beer was accepted as the safest drink of the day as both milk and water were often infected. Ramsbury had the water supply and the area produced the right quality of barley with the result that the beer had a good reputation. There were many village inns and the travellers who passed through the village ensured that the reputation of Ramsbury beer was known over a wide area. It is recorded that the beer was consumed regularly in London.[30] This industry was hazardous and the cause of a number of fires in the village. But while these events produced hardship and suffering, the industry employed many people including coopers who made the barrels. Similarly the tanning industry developed. There were numerous trees near Ramsbury and the hides from cattle and the skins from the sheep and goats were all needed for this commercial enterprise. Some of Matthias Alexander's ancestors were involved in this trade. His great grandmother, Hannah, daughter of Robert Talmage and Anne Hine, had several brothers one of whom, William, was a breechmaker and another, James, who was a cordwainer. Fashionable footwear as well as working boots were produced along with high quality gloves and bags.

Meanwhile Edward Alexander continued life as a yeoman and he and Elizabeth had two children, Edward who was baptised in 1758 and John who was baptised three years later. Edward senior appreciated that life would be different for his sons and that the days of the small farmer were limited. The Ramsbury Enclosure Act of 1778 allocated Edward, along

1   Blind Lane.

with most of the other smallholders, very few acres of land but as the amount was less than fifteen acres it was not quantified.[31] This was not sufficient for his sons and so Edward arranged for them to be apprenticed, Edward the younger as a carpenter and his brother as a wheelwright. When Edward senior made his will, which he signed with some difficulty shortly before his death in 1807, he detailed five freehold dwellings that he owned. One he occupied as a widower as his wife Elizabeth had died in 1802, and the others were rented by his nephew William Hobbs, Thomas Pike, Thomas Dobson and Edward, his son, whose house was known as The Braxtons. At least two of these cottages were in Blind Lane and these were purchased by Edward in 1775. In addition, he had two leasehold properties that were occupied by Mary Williams and Mary Merchant.[32] Edward bequeathed his properties to his two sons but he did not identify which of them should inherit the specific dwellings. This caused some difficulty in later years, particularly as both his sons had sons called John and Edward!

On 22 January 1782, Edward's younger son, John, married Hannah Smith the daughter of John Smith and his wife Hannah Talmage whose brother, William, was now a prosperous and respected breechmaker in the village. John and Hannah had 12 children over the next 19 years but six of them died in infancy and the oldest daughter, Ann, died unmarried at the age of 31 years. Of the remaining five, four of them, Edward, James, John and Hannah, all married in Ramsbury and had children. Both Edward and John were carpenters but James appears to have been a labourer. Little is known of the youngest son, Joseph, although he

2   Oxford Street, c.1914.

was a labourer in Chipping Lambourn in the mid-1840s.[33] John's wife Hannah died in 1814 and shortly after this John, by now a grocer as well as a wheelwright, remarried. He and his new wife Mary Ann Day had five, maybe six children.

John and Hannah's oldest son Edward, a carpenter, was Matthias' father. He married on 27 September 1803 a local girl Jane Pike. Jane came from a long established Ramsbury family. Her father was David Pike who was baptised in Ramsbury in 1757 and was the son of David Pike and Elizabeth Appleford. David Pike was probably the son of James who had been the baker in Ramsbury in the early part of the century. Elizabeth was one of two daughters of Stephen Appleford, a yeoman from the well-known Axford family. When he died, in his will, dated 1762, he left his leasehold estate at Coombe Hill, Axford, a dwelling and five acres of arable land to Thomas Griffin, husband of his youngest daughter, Mary.[34] The Applefords had farmed in Axford for many years, and in 1678 Simon Appleford and Thomas, son of another Stephen Appleford, had bought a holding called Coombe farm.[35] Later, various members of the Appleford family gained significant land as a result of the 1727 Axford Enclosure Agreement.[36] The leasehold ground called Latimers, a house, water-meadow and land with a barn along with all his household goods and chattels Stephen Appleford bequeathed to David Pike. David and Elizabeth produced six children, one of whom died as a youngster. They both died within a few days of each other in 1784 but by now their fifth child, David, had married Elizabeth Dowling. She was born in Ramsbury, the sixth child of Edward Dowling and Catherine Harris. They had married in the nearby village of Shalbourn in 1738 but it would appear had spent all their married life in Ramsbury. The Dowlings were also an established Ramsbury family, Edward was baptised there in 1708 and his father, Richard, had married there the previous year. Richard's wife was Anne Vivash who came from Great Bedwyn, a village in the local area.

David and Elizabeth Pike had six children, the third of which was Jane. She was 14 years old when her mother died in 1799. Two years later, her father remarried and a further four children resulted from that marriage. When Jane and Edward Alexander married they were both 18 years of age and Edward was working as a carpenter. Both of them had had difficult childhoods. Although Edward's older sister, Ann, had survived, the four children born after him had all died within a few months of their birth. When he was 11 years old and again when he was 15 years, two other children had died within six months of birth. Jane had coped with the death of her mother and of her next younger brother, who had died when he was eight years old. Her father had remarried and their first child, Harriet, was born just before Jane's marriage. Where Edward and Jane lived directly after their marriage is not known but it is assumed that at some stage Edward was given some of his grandfather's Blind Lane estate by his father. By the 1830s there were some thirty cottages in this lane and nine of them, with small gardens amounting to 23 perches of land, were owned by Edward and he and Jane lived in one. A further nine cottages were owned by his father and these were all rented.[37]

Shortly after their marriage, Edward and Jane started a family and in July 1804 their first child, Maria, was baptised. She was followed by Joseph baptised in 1806 and Jane who was born in 1808 but whose baptism was not recorded in Ramsbury or any of the nearby parishes. Next was Matthias, Frederick Matthias' grandfather, baptised in 1810, John baptised in 1812, Edward baptised in 1815, and Henry who was baptised at Avington Church on 21 September 1817. This village was only a few miles from Ramsbury near Hungerford in Berkshire. In 1800, Sir Francis Burdett, 5th Baronet, inherited from his aunt the Ramsbury Manor and a number of other local manors including Avington. Already a wealthy man with a principal seat in Derbyshire along with a house in London, Sir Francis was a Member of Parliament for a 'Rotten Borough' bought for him by his father-in-law, Thomas Coutts the banker.[38] This connection between Ramsbury and Avington probably explains why Edward, Jane and their family moved for a short time from Ramsbury to Avington. Their next son, George, was born in 1819 but his baptism was not recorded in Ramsbury or Avington. In some records he declared that he was born in Ramsbury, in others he stated that his place of birth was Avington. After a short interval Edward and Jane had three more children all of whom were baptised in Ramsbury, Susannah in 1824, Charles in 1826 and William in 1828. A total of ten children over 24 years ensured that the Alexander cottage was very crowded for many years but this was a common problem for all but the gentry throughout history. As throughout the rest of England, the population of Ramsbury was also increasing steadily. In 1801 there were 1,963 inhabitants in the parish accommodated in 379 dwellings, and by 1831 the parish population had increased to 2,290, of whom some 1,538 were in the Ramsbury town tything.[39]

3 High Street, pre-1917.

Life in Ramsbury during the time of the Napoleonic Wars is difficult to assess and little is known about the upbringing of Matthias. In fact whether or not he went to school is a matter of conjecture. There were schools in the village and in 1818 the select committee on Education of the Poor recorded that approximately 120 children were taught to read in the village schools on payment of 4d. a week.[40] Whether they were taught to write is, of course, another question. Matthias, like his father, became a tradesman and was described as a hurdle maker. His older brother, Joseph, became a wheelwright. During Matthias' time in Ramsbury the village began to change at a faster rate than before and with this came a change in attitudes. No longer was the Church of England the only religion. The Rev. John Wesley had visited the village during the 1770s and, although he did not get a good reception, over the next few years groups of dissenters formed a number of different sects in Ramsbury including Wesleyan Methodists, Congregationalists and by 1829 Primitive Methodists. This latter group used as their meeting house a carpenter's shop loaned to them by a John Alexander.[41] This Alexander was possibly Matthias' uncle, his father Edward's brother. This John had married Jane Pike's sister, Phoebe, in 1812 and they had four children. Phoebe died in 1822 and six months later John married her half sister, Harriet, and they produced more children. In March 1823, Matthias' older sister, Maria, married Ambrose Woolford, a local man, and a year later Joseph married Elizabeth Brown. Both these weddings took place in Ramsbury church. Joseph and Elizabeth had three children, Elisha baptised in 1827, Josiah baptised in 1828 and Mary Ann baptised in 1830.

At this stage, Matthias had not married and there is nothing to indicate that he had ever travelled far from the village. His ancestry was deeply rooted in Ramsbury. All his great grandparents had lived their adult lives in the parish and many of their ancestors had lived for generations in this area of Wiltshire. Over the years, the family had adapted to change but, with the exception of the Applefords, few had any significant assets. Moses Brackstone and possibly Edward Hine, although the name was shown as Hinde on the list of freeholders, had voted in the 1705 elections which showed property ownership, but the Appleford family were the only ancestors with sufficient wealth to own a pew seat in the church in 1710.[42] However, the situation had changed by the church renovation in 1779 partly owing to the significant increase in the number of pews available. The list of pew owners now included yeomen and some of the more influential craftsmen of the village and so the names of Alexander and Talmage featured.[43] The number of freeholders who voted in the 1772 elections had increased slightly since 1705 and the Alexanders and Talmages were listed along with the Applefords and the Brackstones. In both these elections everyone from Ramsbury voted for the same individuals.[44] This was not the case in the 1818 elections when three brave souls declared for a different person, but none of these were Alexander ancestors.[45] A year later the names of Dowling and Smith were added to the voting lists, though whether the Smiths were connected with Matthias' grandmother is open to question, but grandfather John Alexander was shown as a grocer rather than a wheelwright.[46] The family was continuing to adapt and accept new challenges as times changed. The Alexander family was typical of many in rural England. Their background was one of mainly minor yeoman and agricultural labouring stock that became village craftsmen and tradesmen.

2
CAPTAIN SWING RIOTS

Do ye hear the children weeping, O my brothers,
Ere the sorrow comes with years?
They are leaning their young heads against their mothers,
And that cannot stop their tears.
The young lambs are bleating in the meadows,
The young birds are chirping in the nest,
The young fawns are playing with the shadows,
The young flowers are blowing toward the west-
But the young, young children, O my brothers,
They are weeping bitterly!
They are weeping in the playtime of the others,
In the country of the free.

E.B. Browning: *The Cry of the Children*

Rural England changed dramatically between the middle of the 18th and 19th centuries. The population increased significantly. Wrigley and Schofield calculate that in 1791 the population in England was 7.74 million; by 1831 it had increased to 13.2 million.[1] During this period profound changes took place. As a result of the Enclosure Acts, between 1750 and 1850 well over 6 million acres, or something like one quarter of the cultivated acreage, changed from open field, common land, meadow or waste into private fields. Three-quarters of the 4,000 private Acts of Parliament which revolutionised English farming were concentrated in the 1760s and 1770s and again during the French Revolution and Napoleonic War period (1793-1815). The increase in grain production was dramatic. In the 1830s, it is estimated that production covered 98 per cent of British consumption; this shows that cereal output kept pace with the population increase and nearly doubled in 40 years. This increase was not the result of mechanisation but the change from small family enterprises to larger commercially-based farming units employing labour.[2]

The effects of the Enclosure Act in Ramsbury in 1778 on the Alexander family have been identified. However, the same effects were felt by thousands of people throughout the country. Prior to the enclosures even the lowest labourer did not depend on his wages alone. He took his wood for fuel from the waste land, he had a cow or a pig that could wander and feed on the common pasture and he probably raised some crops on a strip of the common land. Suddenly, these sources of income were denied to him and he was dependent on his wages; thus, he was reliant on his farmer boss who, over the years, became a more and more remote figure. The enclosures had a dire effect and were described by some as fatal to three classes of people: the small farmer, the cottager and the squatter.[3] However, it is probably more realistic to say that these people were a special case in a more general situation, the growing inability of tiny marginal cultivators to survive in a system of industrialised manufactures and capitalist agriculture.[4] What is clear is that the rural poor had emerged as a significant and now more obvious group of people.

The Poor Law, an institution dating from the Tudors, cared for people who came upon hard and difficult times. The system was village based and the local overseer of the poor provided either 'out-payment' to people who remained in their own dwellings or 'in relief' to people housed in the village poor houses. The system could cope only if the poor, who could not maintain themselves, remained relatively small in numbers. For centuries, the system worked well providing a welfare structure for village life and a financial safety net for all. However, by 1795, the numbers of poor in many areas exceeded the resources available. Thus, on 6 May 1795 the Berkshire Justices of the Peace met at the *Pelican Inn* at Speenhamland. This gathering was to evolve a policy, which would be adopted gradually in almost every part of England, that was to give a fatal impetus to the reduction in wages. This was not the objective; the aim was to raise wages, make the labourer independent of parish relief and provide relief, where required, with as little expense as possible to the landowners who supplied the money by means of their taxes and tithes. The meeting agreed that the present state of the poor must be improved. They resolved that relief to all poor and industrious men and their families should be related to the price of a loaf of bread. Therefore, when the gallon loaf of second flour, weighing 8lb. 11oz. cost one shilling, then every poor and industrious man should have for his own support 3s. a week, either produced by his own or his family's labour or an allowance from the poor rates and for the support of his wife and every other member of his family 1s. 6d. If the price of the loaf increased to 1s. 4d., then, the rate should be 4s. a week plus 1s. 10d. for every family member.[5]

The Speenhamland policy was in theory ideal, but in practice the system was most effective in keeping wages low. As an example, in 1824, Lord John Russell chaired a committee to discuss agricultural wages. It was noted that in the north of England, where the Speenhamland system did not operate, wages were 12s. to 15s. a week, while in the south, where the system did operate, wages varied from 8s. to 9s. a week to 3s. for a single man and 4s. 6d. for a married man.[6]

For the dispossessed rural labourer life was harsh. Without doubt, the rural poor became poorer and, as a result, more lawless. There were food riots; these took place in periods of harvest failure and high prices, in 1795/6, 1800/1, 1810-13 and 1816-18. The Game Laws were enhanced making poaching to supplement the meagre diet more hazardous; these laws created an even greater divide between the landowners and the villagers. In 1803, resistance to arrest was made punishable by death and, in 1817, a punishment of seven years transportation was introduced for armed poachers caught at night. There was some relaxation in 1828, when transportation was awarded only for the third poaching offence. The first and second offences were punishable by three and six months imprisonment respectively.[7] It is estimated that, before Peel's reforms in the 1820s, there were some 225 capital crimes on the Statute Book. However, Peel's reforms of 1827 are frequently given as the reason for the doubling of the transportation numbers from that year.[8]

The poverty and the desperation of the rural poor increased as the 19th century progressed. By 1815/16 many of the men had returned from the Napoleonic wars unemployed, underfed and itinerant. It is estimated that approximately 250,000 men appeared over a short period and totally swamped the rural labour market.[9] The situation continued to deteriorate and the bad harvests of 1828 and 1829 together with outbreaks of disease among the livestock were almost the final straw.[10] However, it was the invention and introduction of the threshing machine that was the catalyst to the extensive rioting which took place in the latter part of 1830. Traditionally, labourers had worked in the fields for much of the year and threshed the corn through the winter months. The machine replaced most of the men and left them out of work for almost six months a year. People's patience became exhausted and on 1 June 1830, with the destruction of farmer Mosyer's ricks and barn at Orpington in Kent, began the Swing Riots. They were named after a probably fictitious 'Captain Swing' who, if he did exist, was never identified. These riots were to spread across the country but, within six months, would produce savage retribution from a frightened government and a more terrified landowning community.

During the summer, there were further fires in the Bromley, Sevenoaks and Orpington areas of Kent and by the end of September there had been reports of some twenty such incidents in these areas. However, it was the night of 28/9 August 1830 that brought the first attack on a threshing machine. The event took place in Lower Hardres, Kent; the machine was ruined. The following day the gang, mainly the same men, broke a threshing machine at Newington near Hythe. On 18 September two machines were sabotaged at Upper Hardres and nine more machines in the Canterbury, Folkestone, Hythe area were vandalised over the next few days. By the third week in October, approximately a hundred machines were reported destroyed mainly in East Kent. Meanwhile, in early September, the first threatening letters appeared. These 'Swing' letters were to become a common feature of the labour movement in Kent and other counties.[11]

On 22 October 1830 the first machine breakers were tried before Sir Edward Knatchbull, who discharged the seven prisoners with a caution and a three day prison sentence. He hoped 'that the kindness and moderation evinced this day by the magistrates would be met by a corresponding feeling among the people'.[12] This was not the case. Further riots took place almost immediately and machines were demolished in the Canterbury, Sittingbourne, Sandwich area. Rapidly, the situation deteriorated, labourers started to meet in large numbers, making demands for a minimum wage of 2s. 3d. in winter and 2s. 6d. in summer. By early November the restlessness had spread across Kent and into Sussex. There was considerable tension across the area with reports of the disorders appearing in the national and local newspapers. The landowners attempted to re-establish the Yeomanry to quell the riots but found resistance from the farmers. The government was asked to send troops. On 15 November 1830 Sir Robert Peel, Home Secretary, announced that he had made arrangements to send every disposable cavalry soldier into Kent and eastern Sussex under the command of General Dalbiac. The 7th Dragoon Guards at Canterbury were to cover East Kent; the 2nd Dragoon Guards at Maidstone were to cover Mid Kent and the 5th Dragoon Guards at Tunbridge Wells were to cover East Sussex.[13]

However, the turmoil spread; there were riotous assemblies, numerous fires and many threshing machines were wrecked. By 19 November the labourer's uprising had reached Berkshire, Buckinghamshire, Hampshire, Lincolnshire, Norfolk, Surrey and Wiltshire. Two days later, lawlessness was recorded in Cambridgeshire, Huntingdonshire and Oxfordshire. On 22 November, Hobsbawn and Rudé list 79 disturbances in counties throughout southern England which now included Cornwall, Dorset, Essex and Northamptonshire. Towards the end of November, Bedfordshire, Derbyshire, Gloucestershire, Herefordshire, Hertfordshire, Somerset, Staffordshire and Worcestershire were all involved.[14] The rioting was widespread with many incidents of arson and extorting money. This caused great fear among the population at large and considerable disquiet in government circles.

In the 'open' village of Ramsbury, the social structure and control were loose in contrast to 'closed' villages where the local squire or gentry had effective control over many aspects of village life and often supervised the settlement and building of cottages. Ramsbury was an area of large, mainly absentee, owners that contained a number of plots owned by shopkeepers and artisans. On these plots the owners built cheap cottages to rent to labourers; this attracted otherwise homeless people. Additionally, Ramsbury was a major sheep farming area. The conditions in 1828 were extremely bad for sheep and sheep rot was prevalent. The following year was bad for crops and that winter brought heavy snow with high mortality among the sheep and cattle. The summer of 1830 produced a less than average harvest and sheep rot was again a major problem.[15]

In such a place, where lack of ownership of anything was coupled with extreme poverty, it was not surprising that unrest abounded. On the day that Lord Grey's Whig Government took office, 22 November 1830, the Ramsbury and Aldbourne mob went on the rampage. The reports of the events over the next few days show that this mob committed 'dreadful excesses', damaging machines, extorting money from owners, breaking windows and stealing food and drink.

The rioters visited John Sheppard's mill and smashed a threshing machine; they wrecked a chaff cutting machine in Ramsbury and threshing machines belonging to James Jones, farmer Thomas Osmond and farmer David George at Axford, a nearby village. The *Devizes and Wiltshire Gazette* records:

> On Tuesday afternoon they broke the doors and windows of houses, taking all the eatables and helping themselves to as much drink as they wanted. A mob proceeded from Ogbourn in the morning to Rockly, where they were remonstrated with, by Mr. Baskerville, a magistrate, and Mr. Oliver Codrington, both of whom they began to beat with sticks; the latter was so dreadfully injured, that at one time his life was despaired of; he is this morning, I am glad to say, better. The mob then proceeded to break the machines in the village, and went on to Temple Farm, where they also committed violence. The Marlborough Troop of Yeomanry overtook them on the Downs, where they all surrendered. This (Wednesday) has been a decisive day. A meeting at the Town Hall, Marlborough, took place last evening by adjournment, when it was agreed by the tenantry then present, they would assemble at Aldbourne this morning, and with the assistance of the Cavalry, attack the mob there. Upward of 200 of the tenantry on horseback, with the magistrates at their head, assisted by the Cavalry,

succeeded in securing about 20 ringleaders. The Marlborough Troop also yesterday dispersed a mob of 300 or 400 near Milton, and took the leaders to Marlborough. In this part of the county, I consider the rioting is over. The tenantry and others, assemble again at Rockly tomorrow, at 9 o'clock, to go to any part of the county they may be wanted; a force equal to put down any mob that may dare to assemble. An insignificant mob was dispersed or taken into custody at Chisledon, where they broke a machine of Mr. Dyke's this afternoon, after the party returned from Ramsbury.[16]

In Ramsbury and the immediate vicinity during 22 and 23 November some 17 threshing machines were smashed, together with two other agricultural machines; there were eight recorded riots and four cases of robbery with menaces. In Wiltshire alone, in those two days, 64 machines were demolished; a further 26 were broken over the next two days. It shows perhaps how quickly the insurrection was quelled in Wiltshire that the total number of machines of all kinds destroyed throughout the Swing Riot period was 101.[17]

On 29 November, the *Salisbury and Winchester Journal* reproduced on the front page of the paper 'A Proclamation by King William III'. The Proclamation was dated Tuesday 23 November 1830 and 'commanded all Justices of the Peace, Sheriffs, Under-Sheriffs and all other Civil Officers within the counties of Wilts, Kent, Surrey, Sussex, Hants and Berks to use their utmost endeavours to discover, apprehend and bring to justice persons concerned in riotous proceedings'. It offered rewards of £50 to any person who discovered or apprehended anybody who was subsequently convicted and £500 if the individual reported was proved to be the perpetrator of a fire.[18]

Joseph and Matthias Alexander were members of the Ramsbury mob that visited John Sheppard's mill. They were seen there by Thomas Channon, William Watkins and William Woodley allegedly breaking a threshing machine. Subsequently, they were arrested and, with Joseph Liddiard, were charged with destroying machinery, the property of John Sheppard, at Ramsbury. They were held initially at the Bridewell in Marlborough. With them was their father, Edward, who was charged with aiding and abetting in destroying machinery at Ramsbury. Also in the gaol was their distant cousin, Ambrose Alexander, who was charged with destroying machinery, the property of James Jones at Ramsbury, and Richard Church at Aldbourne.[19]

By early December 1830 most of the riots were over, although, there were some sporadic outbreaks of trouble during the rest of the month and throughout 1831. However, for the authorities, the major problem was the large number of people held in gaols up and down the land. Justice needed to be dispensed rapidly and the perpetrators punished as an example to other would be rioters. Therefore, it was decided to form a Special Commission to hear the charges particularly in Berkshire, Buckinghamshire, Dorset, Hampshire and Wiltshire.[20] The first Special Commission arrived at Winchester on 18 December but the hearings did not begin until Monday 20 December. The Commission sat for eight days, 20 to 24 December and 27 to 29 December. An interesting feature of the trials was the number of men just above the condition of the agricultural labourers who joined in the disturbances; village mechanics, wheelwrights, carpenters, joiners, smiths, bricklayers, shoemakers, shepherds and smallholders often played a prominent part.[21] The court scenes were distressing and the sentences harsh. The *Salisbury and Winchester Journal* records that 'after passing a sentence of death on 3 men, Mr. Baron Vaughan told them that all hope of mercy was excluded', and concluded thus:

4 Joseph Alexander.
With permission of the Pioneer Village Museum, Burnie, Tasmania.

'I have now only to pass the dreadful sentence of the law upon you, and I hope you will earnestly repent you of your sins, and make full confession of them. The sentence of the Court upon you is, that you, Robert Holdaway- you, James Annetts- and you, Henry Cooke, be taken to the place from whence you came, and from thence to a place of execution, and that you be severally hanged by the neck till you are dead and may the Almighty have mercy on your souls!' The prisoners were then removed. Every one in court appeared much affected, and as we sat, we could, during the Learned Judge's address, hear the heavy sigh, the suppressed sob, and see the quivering lip of the prisoners. Altogether, a more dreadful sight we have never witnessed: for it must be remembered that the prisoners tried during this Commission have not been persons usually met with at the Assizes- hardened thieves, but men who have been deluded into the commission of outrages, and who had before- most of them- been men of good character, and respectable in their class of life. [22]

On 31 December, the Special Commission, Mr. Baron Vaughan, Mr. Justice J. Parke and Mr. Justice Alderson, arrived in Salisbury for the Wiltshire Special Assizes which opened the following day. The trials lasted eight days from 1 to 10 January 1831 excluding Sundays. During that time, upward of 330 people appeared before the court. Amongst them the four Alexanders who had been transferred to Fisherton Anger Gaol in December prior to the hearings.

Joseph and Matthias Alexander together with Joseph Liddiard appeared before the court on 4 January 1831. They were found guilty of destroying a threshing machine. The next day they were brought before the court again for sentencing. This event was eloquently described by *The Times* correspondent:

> Matthias Alexander, Joseph Alexander, and Joseph Liddiard, were put to the bar, having been convicted of a like offence. Mr. Justice Alderson said the case of these prisoners was very different. They belonged to a class of persons who had not even the vain pretence that these machines could affect them in any manner. One was a carpenter, the other a blacksmith, and the third a woodman. Such outrages by any party must be put down; but the law would visit with the strictest severity, such persons as the prisoners, when proved to have taken the part in them which they were proved to have done. The sentence of the Court on each of the prisoners was that they should be transported to such place beyond the seas as His Majesty should direct for the term of seven years.[23]

And so ended the short hearings of Joseph, aged 24, his brother, Matthias, aged 20, and Joseph Liddiard, aged 24, the results of which would change completely their ways of life. Ambrose Alexander appeared before the court on 8 January but the Jury decided that the evidence was not sufficiently clear, and so acquitted him on both charges. Joseph and Matthias' father, Edward, was not prosecuted and he also returned to Ramsbury a free man.[24]

Of the 334 Wiltshire men tried over the 8 days, 50 were sentenced to death, 105 were transported, 53 were imprisoned and 126 were discharged. The press reports of the day make sad reading and the following example illustrates the atmosphere of the occasion:

> On leaving the court, we mixed amongst the crowd who were waiting to see the prisoners leave. The scene here was heart-breaking beyond everything: a mass of women were standing bathed in tears, supported by men who looked as having hearts which nothing could daunt, but which had given way to feelings of their better nature, and, in endeavouring to support the weaker sex, they themselves could not but betray their grief, and were actually shedding the tears of pity and affliction. At length the cell door was opened, and the unfortunate criminals appeared chained together. We thought that in the court, and before the door was opened, we had seen distress of mind in almost every form. We had witnessed it (in those who had given way to it, and had let the bursting tear escape),- we had also watched those who, having more command of themselves, had prevented the outward show of grief, but in whose countenances what they felt inwardly could easily be discovered; but we had a sight to witness even more distressing than all this. As the men came out, their wives, their mothers, their sisters, and their children, clasped them in their arms with an agonising grip. The convicts, whose hearts had not been hardened by having been before incarcerated in a gaol, gave way. They wept like children. They no longer attempted to settle their feelings; or brave their children; nature had begun to play with every force, and the heart was broken. It required every effort on the part of their attendants to get them into the cart and at last the door was closed. Then we could hear the exclamations of regret and of farewell, and many a female hand was forced through the bars to take a last grasp of him who was about to leave those who were dear to him, and to whom he was as dear for ever. The cart drove off

and some wretches from within gave a cheer. Nothing was now heard but the deepest lamentation, or the kind words of sobbing men, endeavouring to console their more afflicted friends. We left the scene with a hope that it would have the effect desired, accompanied with a prayer that we might be spared from again being witnesses of such dreadful distress.[25]

When the Special Commission had finished its work in Salisbury, it moved to Dorchester and then to Reading, completing the task at Aylesbury some four weeks after the first case was heard at Winchester. In total, as a result of the Swing Riots, 1,976 criminal cases were brought; 252 people were sentenced to death, of whom 19 were in fact executed; 505 were transported; 644 received jail sentences; one was whipped; seven were fined and 800 were acquitted. In all 390 threshing machines were destroyed along with 53 other machines but, probably more serious were the 316 incidents of arson.[26] This destruction of property, ricks and barns full of corn could only increase the plight of the village labourer.

The final number eventually transported from Wiltshire was 152. Nearly half these men described themselves as ploughmen and a quarter were listed as agricultural labourers but the remaining quarter comprised village craftsmen. This latter group included carpenters, joiners, wheelwrights, smiths, bricklayers, tailors, clockmakers, shoemakers, cordwainers, tanners, maltsters and shepherds. Among them were Joseph Alexander, the wheelwright, and Matthias Alexander, the hurdle maker.[27] They and the other men from Ramsbury left behind their families, their friends and their way of life. For Edward and Jane, their parents, it must have been a terrible time; for Joseph's wife, Elizabeth, perhaps worse, as she had three young children, the youngest only 3 months old. Now she had to fend for herself and her family. A number of other families in Ramsbury village were left in the same difficult position, one of whom was the Taylors. William Taylor was transported on the *Proteus* to Van Diemen's Land and he left behind his wife, Elizabeth, and his children, six of them living at home. The oldest of these six boys was 16 years. The situation was as bad throughout the rest of southern England as it is calculated that just over half the men transported were married.[28] In addition, the loss to the villages of so many skilled men had a major effect on rural communities. Hobsbawn and Rudé sum up the situation by declaring, 'In the south of England, there were whole communities that, for a generation, were stricken by the blow. From no other protest movement of the kind—from neither Luddites nor Chartists, nor trade unionists—was such a bitter price exacted.'[29] Against this, it is pertinent to note that the Swing Riots were at a time when parliamentary reform was at a critical stage and in Cobbett's view had more effect than the urban disturbances. Mingay considers that the riots also had:

some influence in bringing in the New Poor Law of 1834 and the Tithe Commutation in 1836 both concerned matters that had incensed the labourers. And, in the long run, the movement for state-supported education drew strength from those who believed it to offer an answer to the labourers' poverty and naïvety.[30]

After the riots, the general situation in Ramsbury deteriorated. By January 1835, the position was so bad that Rev. Dr. Meyrick wrote to the Poor Law Board in London. He advised them that 'the poor were numerous, upwards of 50 men were employed on the road and a full 30 young, single men had no apparent means of livelihood. The overseer paid

1s. 4½d. for a full week's work'. The cottages for the poor in Ramsbury had been sold, and so the final refuge for some was the workhouse in Hungerford.[31]

Blind Lane in Ramsbury was an area where agricultural labourers congregated. Although, not as cramped as the nearby Tankard Lane, in 1841 there were some 172 people in Blind Lane living in 30 tiny cottages.[32] Nine of these dwellings, together with gardens totalling 23 perches, were owned by Edward Alexander.[33] He worked as a labourer and floater in the Ramsbury water meadows where he probably made the hatches which controlled the water flow from the river across the meadows. This practice of 'floating' the water started in Ramsbury in the middle of the 17th century and continued until about the outbreak of the Second World War. The system provided early grass for the ewes and their lambs and then, when the sheep had moved to other pastures, more 'floating' encouraged the hay crop. Up to three crops of hay were produced from this land.[34] Edward, together with his wife, Jane, and their youngest children Susannah, Charles and William lived in one of his Blind Lane cottages. Another he rented to his daughter-in-law Elizabeth and her three children, all of whom including 10-year-old Mary, were described as agricultural labourers. In a third cottage was Edward's brother James with his wife and three of their children. Their other two children lived next door with William and Charlotte Pearce. Elizabeth Taylor, wife of the transported William, was also in Blind Lane with three of her sons. She and the two younger boys were classed as agricultural labourers but the oldest son was a tanner.[35]

Life was very difficult and many residents in Ramsbury decided that there was a better life elsewhere. Some were recruited by the Van Diemen's Land Company and went to Van Diemen's Land as indentured employees. Amongst them was Matthias Alexander's friend John Dowling. Many emigrated, some to New Zealand and others like Matthias' uncle, John, his father's brother, to America. Uncle John's son, Hezekiah, went to America in 1831 and he was followed, in about 1840, by two other sons, Cornelius and John junior. The reports from America were encouraging because, in 1845, John senior decided to follow his sons and leave Ramsbury. He took with him his wife Harriet and their seven other children, one of whom, Joseph, was married and came with his wife, Hannah, and their baby, Jabez, and a nephew, Charles. This party of 12 Alexanders took six weeks to cross the Atlantic on the St James, which arrived in New York in July 1845. They joined Cornelius, his wife and Hezekiah in Albany, New York where they were assisted by the Methodist Church. John Alexander, senior, who was a carpenter, having served his apprenticeship under Robert Newman of Ramsbury, was 54 years of age.[36] His youngest child was two years old. Despite the difficulties of a new country and so many dependent children, the family prospered.

Two sons and a daughter lived out their lives in Albany. Two other sons went to Osceola in Iowa. One daughter went to Chicago and then, eventually, to Iowa. Joseph decided that he did not want to remain in Albany so he took his family to Watertown in Wisconsin Territory. Soon afterwards, his parents, John senior and Harriet, together with their other children joined him in Watertown. John senior became the proprietor of the Watertown general store. His daily book of sales show that he sold a wide variety of items including butter, tobacco and plants. On 25 October 1846, one month after the birth of their second child, Joseph and Hannah suffered the loss of their first child Jabez. Interestingly,

5 Joseph Alexander's log cabin.

Hannah made the trip back to England for the birth of her third child, another Jabez. The next three children were born in Watertown but, by the birth of the next one, on 29 April 1857, the family had moved to Rochester, Minnesota. This child was one of the first white children born in Olmsted County. In all the couple had 13 children. In October 1854, Joseph had walked the 150 or so miles from Watertown to Rochester. He liked what he saw and brought his family to join him. He established a saw mill in Rochester, then a furniture factory, two grist mills and a woollen mill. His wife, despite her child bearing, had a millinery store. The family lived in a log cabin near the woollen mill on Bear Creek, but later Joseph built a 12-roomed house. Joseph wrote regularly to George Rosier, who from 1851 was the Primitive Methodist steward in Ramsbury. George Rosier, in his letter dated 17 August 1853, assured Joseph that 'his uncle and aunt, Edward and Jane Alexander, are about the same'. He went on to say that many people in Ramsbury wished to go to America and join the Alexanders, adding that he was thinking about it himself. He asked for a message to be passed to George Woolford from Ramsbury who had recently arrived in Watertown. George Rosier gave a further interesting insight into life in Ramsbury by recording that at the Temperance Society meeting about 700 had sat down to tea and that some 1,000 people had attended the Sunday Camp meeting.[37]

6 Joseph Alexander's mill.

Joseph was a deeply religious man and an enthusiastic preacher. Apparently, he spent hours reading the Bible and when he thought the Bible was in error he would note corrections in the margins. He conducted marriage and funeral services and travelled with his herbal remedies. He was the first white man to treat patients in Olmsted County. By the 1890s, it must be assumed that he had ceased this practice as Dr. W.W. Mayo had moved to Rochester, Minnesota and owned a farm adjacent to the Alexander land. Mrs. Mayo was a regular customer at Hannah Alexander's millinery store. Joseph's son Henry was the carpenter foreman and superintendent for the building contractor of the first Mayo clinic.[38]

To return to Ramsbury, Edward and Jane had a hard life as did their daughter-in-law Elizabeth with her three young children. Her son Josiah married Hannah Ward on 25 July 1846 and he and his wife had two sons, John and Thomas. Josiah died of typhus on 15 March 1849 leaving his wife and children destitute. For the next few years they lived with Hannah's parents in a cottage in Mill Lane.[39] Her other son, Elisha, a woodman, married Fanny Brown on 12 October 1846 in Ramsbury. They lived in Oxford Street for a while

1890

GROVE MEETINGS!

There will be a series of meetings held in the
Grove near the Woolen Mill. East
Rochester. for

Free Thought and Free Speech.

The meetings will be held at.3 o'clock each
Sunday afternoon.

Joseph Alexander

will lead the meeting next Sunday, July 27.
Subject: "Life Everlasting and the Immortality
of the Soul." He will also give Bible proof of
what was said last Sunday

Subject for Sunday,

All are invited to attend, and any one will be
given the privilege of speaking. COME ALL.

7 Joseph's church meetings.

and produced four children, Jane, Britannia, Joseph and Elizabeth, but Fanny died in the Newtown area of Ramsbury on 12 November 1866.[40] On 11 August 1878, Elisha remarried in the Primitive Methodist Chapel in Ramsbury. His new wife, Ann Lewis, was a middle-aged woman born in nearby Axford. They lived in Ramsbury High Street for a long time and on 11 February 1897 Ann died there.[41] Elisha continued to work as a woodman for a few more years but died in the Hungerford Workhouse on 14 March 1909. Joseph and Elizabeth's only daughter, Mary Ann, survived childhood; later, she travelled to Van Diemen's Land as a free immigrant and joined her father. Elizabeth remained in the cottage in Blind Lane for some years and then, after her sons had married, she obtained employment as a nurse at Rudge, a substantial house in the nearby village of Froxfield.[42] She died on 8 December 1855 aged 50 years in Oxford Street in Ramsbury. Jane Alexander died in Blind Lane aged 75 on 10 February 1859 with her daughter Jane Woodley in attendance. Edward, now a widower, went to live with his son, Edward, and his family at Anniss Cross, near Bradfield, Berkshire. He remained with Edward for the next ten years moving with the family the short distance to Stanford Dingley where he died on 16 February 1869.[43]

3
LONDON AND THE OLD BAILEY

Any man's death diminishes me, because I am involved in Mankind;
And therefore never send to know for whom the bell tolls; It tolls for thee.

John Donne: *Devotions*

Conditions in the 18th and early 19th centuries were harsh in rural England but did not compare with the severity of those in London for all but the wealthy. So what was life like in this bustling capital city for Frederick Matthias Alexander's grandmothers, Mary Reading and Maria Davis? Mary lived in the St Pancras area and Maria Davis lived in the Minories in the City and later in the Whitechapel area.

In 1831 the population of the City of London within and without the walls was 123,683; in the Hundred of Ossulstone, Holborn Division, which included St Andrews, Holborn, Paddington, St Pancras and St Clement Danes, it was 346,255, and in Ossulstone, Tower Division, which covered the East End including Bethnal Green Hackney, Poplar, Shadwell, Shoreditch, Stratford le Bow, Wapping and Whitechapel, it was 359,864.[1] Many of these people were housed in overcrowded conditions; those who had the money moved out to the surrounding areas, whilst the poor gravitated to the centre. Some of the 'Rookeries' of London were still in evidence. These Dorothy George described as 'an object lesson in horror that had once been far more general'. She went on to declare, 'on reading descriptions of the state of London in the 1840s it is hard to realize that things could ever have been worse'.[2] Certainly, the bad sanitary conditions were the major cause of ill health. There are numerous accounts of narrow London courts and lanes where dirt and filth accumulated in heaps that were seldom removed.

In 1838, the medical officers of the London parishes, in the Fourth Report of the Commissioners under the Poor Law Amendment Act 1834, reported on the dire living conditions which caused ill health under two headings. The first covered causes for which the sufferers could not be considered responsible: these included 'imperfection or want of sewers and drains; uncovered and stagnant drains or ditches; open stagnant pools; undrained marsh land; accumulation of refuse in streets, courts etc; exhalations of cess-pools and slaughter-houses; and burial-grounds'. The second class concerned causes which arose from social conditions and included 'The state of the lodging-housing of mendicants and vagrants and of a certain class of Irish poor; overcrowding; gross want of cleanliness; intemperance; the habit of lodging in previously deserted houses, cellars, etc; keeping hogs in dwelling houses; indisposition to be removed to the hospitals when infected; and neglect of vaccination'.[3] Clearly, the large number of animals kept in London, particularly horses each producing upward of 20 lbs. of manure a day, added to the unhygienic conditions.

The descriptions of the areas inhabited by the Irish are particularly dreadful. In 1816 it was recorded that they often shared rooms with pigs and other animals. The conditions were aggravated by the Irish custom of sub-letting accommodation. Thus, it was said in 1837 that there were instances of single rooms, sublet in portions to three or four different families and even these portions were sublet. A further custom of the Irish which caused hygiene problems was the wake. The corpse, regardless of the cause of death, was laid out often on the only bed and remained there until sufficient money had been collected from the neighbours for the funeral. This could take some time! There is a record of a particularly gruesome case in 1817 where a mother raised three successive subscriptions for her daughter's burial but each time spent the money on drink. Eventually fever broke out in the house and six were buried and eighteen or twenty taken ill. The parish had to bury the girl![4]

The living conditions, poverty and hardship in the centre of London caused many people both young and old to turn to crime. Henry Mayhew decided that there were two kinds of London criminal, one group who were professionals and who objected to working for a living, the second category being people who committed 'accidental' crimes through force of circumstances.[5] In his extensive wanderings around London during the 1840s he interviewed many people involved in criminal activities. His description of female pickpockets whom he recorded dressed in 'fashionable attire' is interesting. 'They were often superior in intellect to the men and more orderly in their habits. They seldom married but cohabited with pickpockets, burglars and other infamous characters.'[6] The crowded conditions and the difficulties of sheer survival made the City of London and the adjacent areas a centre for beggars, thieves and destitute people.

There was discontent; throughout the 18th century disturbances abounded. This social upheaval was often caused by parliamentary action, for example the Black Act of 1723, the Turnpike Acts and the Enclosure Acts. By the early 19th century there were the Corn Law Riots, the Luddite uprisings and, as discussed in the last chapter, the Swing Riots of 1830. This lawlessness affected people throughout the country but particularly those in London, many of whom had migrated from different parts of England. There were also numerous riots in London, from those at Tyburn against the Surgeons in the middle of the 1700s to the Millbank prisoners Bread Riots in 1818. M. Halévy was of the opinion that from 1810 to 1815 there was 'a perpetual ferment both in London and the country'.[7] The crime rate rose: in 1805 there were 4,605 recorded committals' by 1834 this had risen to 22,451.[8]

In London, the law for many people was synonymous with the Old Bailey. In this street a Sessions Hall had stood for many years where trials were heard for both the City of London and the Shire of Middlesex. A new court house was erected in 1773 but this was destroyed in the Gordon Riots in 1780. It was rebuilt and enlarged in 1809 by using the land of the old Surgeon's Hall.[9] This Justice Hall adjoining Newgate prison was known by its popular name the Old Bailey and it was here that commissions for that gaol delivery were executed. As Newgate was the principal gaol for both Middlesex and London, so the commissions gave jurisdiction in both areas. This complicated the judicial situation in London and the Metropolis. There were no Assizes in the area, although sessions for Middlesex and the City of London were heard at a number of locations.[10] This meant that people from both Middlesex and the City of London appeared at the Old Bailey Sessions on criminal charges. In 1824, a second Sessions House was built so by 1832 trials were heard in both the Old and New Sessions Houses.[11] The majority of these cases were for stealing and associated crimes, although there were some for rape, bigamy, forgery and coining.

The adjacent Newgate prison, which had existed for hundreds of years, came under the jurisdiction of the City of London civil authorities. Over the years many thousands of men and women were incarcerated within its walls. The old gate and the prison suffered severe damage during the Great Fire in 1666 and had to be rebuilt.[12] During the early 1700s there were a number of outbreaks of gaol fever which culminated in a particularly serious problem in 1750 when the disease spread from Newgate to the Old Bailey. This resulted in many deaths including those of the Lord Mayor, two Judges and an Alderman.[13] This spurred the Corporation of London into action and they began to investigate the costs of rebuilding Newgate gaol. The matter became urgent when the press-yard of the gaol was destroyed by fire in 1762. The new prison building was begun in May 1770 but within a few years the entire prison was destroyed by the Gordon Riots of 1780.[14]

Newgate prison was rebuilt, but within a few years suffered from severe overcrowding. In the main gaol, apart from the debtors of both sexes, there were male and female criminals. The females were in four different categories: those awaiting trial; those under sentence of imprisonment; those awaiting transportation, and those awaiting execution. All these women were herded together and by 1813 some 300 women and their children were contained in two wards and two cells, a total area of 192 square yards.[15] The conditions were appalling, most of the prisoners were clad in rags, they had to sleep on the floor, they were desperate for food and drink and the whole area was filthy beyond description. The Quaker, Stephen Grellet, visited the women in January 1813 and was so disturbed that he inspired Elizabeth Fry to visit the prison.[16] By 1817, Elizabeth Fry had formed a school at Newgate for the children and with 11 members of the Society of Friends had formed an association for the improvement of female prisoners at Newgate. This Committee existed until 1878.[17] At least one of the Committee visited the prison daily, a matron was employed, clothes were provided for the women and they were given work materials. In addition, the women were introduced to the Holy Scriptures which the Committee believed produced 'habits of order, sobriety and industry'. Rules of behaviour were established within the female prison and the female workshop produced clothes for the convict settlement in Australia. The Lord Mayor of London visited the prison in 1817 and could hardly believe that 'this hell on earth where only a few months before abandoned and shameless women affronted his eyes now appeared more like a well-regulated family'.[18] A careful system of supervision was established; over every 12 or 13 women, a matron was placed who was answerable for their work and kept an account of their conduct. A yard woman maintained good order in the yard and the sickroom was ruled by a nurse and an assistant. These managers were all prisoners.[19]

By 1818, Mrs. Fry was an established prison reformer and in that year she gave evidence before a House of Commons Committee on London Prisons.[20] It is interesting to note that in 1818 there were 518 prisons throughout the country and upward of 100,000 prisoners were committed in the year. There was no attempt whatever to separate the men and women in 59 of the gaols.[21] Mrs. Fry's opinions were sought throughout England and from many places in Europe. However, in 1818 she faced a potential riot at Newgate with a group of prisoners about to be transported. Normally, the night before their departure they broke up the furniture, smashed the windows and generally caused chaos within the prison. The following morning, they were put in irons, loaded onto open wagons and driven to the river for embarkation through jeering crowds. Mrs. Fry persuaded Governor Newman to permit the women to travel in closed hackney-coaches with the turnkeys escorting them, She joined the end of the procession in her own carriage. When the party arrived at Deptford the women were herded on to the *Maria*. The women from other gaols who arrived in irons, with hoops around their waists, clambered awkwardly aboard. Mrs. Fry was deeply distressed by the cramped conditions and immediately she divided the 128 convicts into classes of 12 based on the Newgate system. A small space in the stern of the ship was set aside for the schoolroom for the 14 prisoners' children who were old enough to read and sew. A school mistress was appointed and if she worked well the Captain would pay her at the end of the trip. The Ladies Association bought material from which the women could make patchwork quilts during the journey for sale on arrival in Australia. Before the ship sailed, Mrs. Fry went on board to read the Bible to the assembled gathering of convicts. For the next 20 years, whenever she could, she personally inspected female convict ships before they left London. She tried to ensure that the women would live decently and piously throughout the voyage.[22] During her long involvement with prison reform Mrs. Fry never accepted the concept that prisoners should be separated. She believed that isolation produced 'vacant minded people devoid of stimulus'.[23]

Other people involved in prison reform did not agree with Mrs. Fry. John Howard (1726-90), one-time High Sheriff of Bedfordshire, toured many of Britain's prisons during 1774 and in 1777 his book *The State of Prisons* was published.[24] This book changed the whole basis of debate and discussion on prisons. Howard was a researcher and a realist; he laid down principals of humane separate containment but his ideas of separation were distorted by others who adopted his philosophy rigidly.[25] Another prison reformer, the theorist and philosopher Jeremy Bentham (1748-1832), believed that there should be a general plan of punishment adopted by which solitary confinement would be combined with labour.[26] He produced an elaborate scheme for a national penitentiary. His proposal was to build an enormous circular structure so that all prisoners could be under the constant observation of the supervisors. As he thought that imprisonment was awarded to few outside the poorest class, he considered that prison life should be just a little less bearable than the life of the honest poor, with a strict regime and isolation.[27] He expressed the view that reformative influence could be brought to bear on the delinquent so that positive good could be attained by the offender and society as a whole.[28] Undoubtedly, the prolific writings of Bentham found favour with many influential people. For, although his proposed prison was never built, by 1840 the Government had succumbed to pressure for prison reform and commissioned the building of Pentonville prison. This prison, which opened in 1842, contained 520 individual cells and was to be the model for many subsequent prisons.[29] The redevelopment of Newgate prison was considered as early as 1830 but the proposals were costly and the land available too small. However, with the introduction of the Pentonville system, the City Corporation decided to build a new prison along these lines at Holloway where the authority owned some 20 acres of land. Work commenced in 1849 at an estimated cost of £79,000. The prison was designed to contain 404 convicted prisoners who were sentenced to short terms of penal servitude. After the completion of Holloway prison, Newgate was used almost entirely as a prison of detention.[30]

Before the development and provision of the large penitentiaries, people awaiting trial were kept in the county gaols similar to Newgate. With the number of people brought before the courts, these institutions were totally inadequate for holding the convicted as well. The solution, as early as the reign of Elizabeth I, was a form of transportation. In the 1600s undesirables were sent to the Galleys, but, by the Transport Act of 1718, courts were empowered to transport individuals for seven years for robbery, forgery and burglary. In the early days, people were transported to America and the West Indies. This form of punishment had a number of benefits. Firstly, it banished apparently undesirable people from England and, secondly, such a drastic punishment deterred offenders, or so it was hoped. The war in America and her subsequent independence posed significant problems for the British authorities. The immediate solution, adopted as a temporary measure in 1776, was to authorise the use of hulks. These hulks were moored on the Thames and the convicts were accommodated on board.[31] Over the next few years hulks were used in other parts of the country, and at Portsmouth the convict labour was used in the dockyards. In the meantime, many different places in the British Empire were investigated in an attempt to find a suitable location for the convicts. The problem became more urgent in 1785 when there was a great danger of 'infectious distemper' in the hulks.[32] Therefore, it was decided to found a penal settlement at Botany Bay in New South Wales, Australia. This decision met a number of the government's aims. It solved the problem of what to do with the convicts, it removed from England some of her undesirable citizens, and it provided the labour force to found a new British Colony. So, in 1787, the First Fleet set sail for Australia to begin an era of transportation of convicts from the United Kingdom that was to last until 1867 when the last convict ship sailed for the antipodes.

It was against this background that Mary Reading and Maria Davis lived their young lives. Mary Reading lived in the parish of St Pancras. This was a large parish which in 1831 covered some 2,600 acres, with a population of 103,548, stretching from St Giles in the Fields and Bloomsbury in the south to Finchley and Hornsey in the north. However, this population was not evenly distributed.[33] The area near Ossulton Street where Mary lived was densely populated while the northerly part was more rural. The Reading family were Roman Catholics from Ireland. Originally, they probably came from County Limerick where Mary was born, but lived for a while in Fermoy, County Cork, where her younger sister Julia was born.[34] When they came to England is uncertain, but by 1832 the family consisted of Mary, her parents, at least one brother, Martin, and at least one sister, Julia.

It was in that year, nearly two years after Matthias Alexander's trial, that his future wife, Mary Reading, was tried at the Old Bailey. On 29 November 1832, aged 16 years, she appeared before the court charged with stealing a dress worth 5s. The offence took place on 22 October 1832 in Ossulton Street St Pancras. The Indictment reads as follows:

Mary Reading late of the Parish of St Pancras.

The Jurors of our Lord the King upon their Oath present, that Mary Reading late of the Parish of St Pancras in the County of Middlesex, Spinster, on twenty second day of October in the third year of the Reign of our Sovereign Lord, William the Fourth, by the Grace of God of the United Kingdom of Great Britain and Ireland King Defender of the faith, with Force and Arms at the Parish aforesaid in the County aforesaid, One gown of the value of five shillings of the Goods and Chattels of Francis Healing then and there being found feloniously did steal take and carry away against the Peace of our said Lord the King, his Crown and Dignity.

Thursday 29 November 1832 Case no. 29. Mary Reading was indicted for stealing, on the 22nd of October, 1 gown, value 5s., the goods of Francis Healing.

Ann Healing. I am the wife of Francis Healing—we live in Ossulton Street, St Pancras. On 22nd of October I heard a person come in and go upstairs, who I thought was my son—I called him twice, but he did not answer—I then heard my bed-room door open; I went up, and saw the prisoner in my yard—I said, 'what do you want?' she said, 'I came to see a lodger of yours;' I said 'I had no lodger'— she then went round my yard; I went to her and said, 'It is curious you should come into my house without asking me,' and I saw my gown in a basket in her hand, and there were some plates and knives and forks in it; the gown had been in my bed-room, where I had wrapped it up about ten minutes before—she ran away, but in about half an hour she came opposite my house; my son and another lad ran after her—this is the gown.

David Barry: I went in pursuit of the prisoner—she ran down several streets, got into a stable, and hid herself, but the dog smelt her; I went in, and found her—when I got her out, she fought and scratched my face very much, but I got her to my mistress, who took her to the station; the dog was poisoned on the Saturday afterwards.

John Walker (police-constable S40). I received the prisoner, and the property.

Prisoner's defence. I was going with my brother's dinner, and on passing the prosecutor's I saw the gown rolled up—I took it, and put it in my basket; the prosecutrix snatched the basket from my hand, and said it was hers—I ran back to tell my mother, then went to her house, and went with her to the Watch-house.

Verdict: Guilty. Aged 16 years. To be transported beyond the Seas for the term of Seven years.[35]

Young Mary Reading was taken back to Newgate prison where she remained until she was transported to Van Diemen's Land.[36]

To assess the severity of this sentence on a young girl, it is perhaps relevant to review other cases heard at the Old Bailey during this period. The Sessions were recorded by Mayoralty years, which commenced in November. In the 1832-3 session some 1,400 men and 340 women were brought before the court. Of these 102 men were found guilty of capital offences and sentenced to death; 605 were sentenced to transportation; 320 were imprisoned; seven were fined; 33 had their judgements respited; 292 were found not guilty; and 14 were shown as guilty but no sentenced was recorded. In addition, 28 boys were sentenced to be whipped. By comparison, among the women, four were guilty of capital offences, of whom three were sentenced to death and one was awarded 14 years' transportation; in addition, a further 124 were sentenced to transportation: 97 were imprisoned; five were fined; 5 had their judgements respited; 100 were found not guilty; and seven were found guilty but no sentence was recorded.

There are some cases of particular interest because of the age of the individuals involved and the sentences awarded to them for the offences that they had committed. The first was a case against two youngsters, John Smith aged 17 years and James Smith, a cripple, aged 12 years. They were charged with breaking and entering the house of Alexander Thompson at St Leonards, Shoreditch on 4 March 1833 and stealing three vices valued at 12s. The boys were found guilty and sentenced to death; this was remitted to transportation for life.[37] The second case involved two boys aged 13 years. The boys, Daniel Clark and Edward Pickard, were found guilty of breaking and entering the house of John Place Hebden at St James, Westminster on 14 August 1833 and stealing seven handkerchiefs valued at 22s. They were sentenced to death but this was remitted to transportation for seven years; however, the records showed that eventually the boys went to the Penitentiary.[38] The third case involved a 10-year-old boy, Michael Shaw, who was found guilty of stealing two hats valued at 18s., the goods of John Dando, Holborn, on 26 February 1833. His sentence was seven years' transportation.[39]

Judgements made against women showed that nearly one third were found not guilty or had judgements respited, nearly one third were imprisoned, often for only a few weeks although there was one case of 18 months, and just over a third were sentenced to transportation. In comparison with the men, very few women were tried for capital offences; during that year there was a total of seven women, three of whom were found not guilty. Of those found guilty, the first, Mary Brown, a 40-year-old married woman, and Charlotte Smith, a 26-year-old spinster, were tried together for feloniously assaulting James Charles Gates and stealing 6s. at St Pancras on 16 February 1833.[40] They were found guilty and sentenced to death; this sentence was remitted to transportation for life.[41] The next was Mary Jones, an 18-year-old spinster, who was tried for feloniously breaking into the house of a Mr. Price of Stepney and stealing goods worth 9s. She was found guilty and although she was sentenced to death, the Jury recommended mercy.[42] Her sentence was remitted to transportation for life.[43] The last woman, Sarah James *alias* Willis, was a 19-year-old spinster who appeared before the Old Bailey Sessions on a number of occasions during the year. As a result of her various misdemeanours, she was sentenced to 14 years' transportation.[44]

The great majority, 116 of the 124 women found guilty of non capital offences, were charged with stealing, although four were charged with making and counterfeiting coins and four were charged with receiving. Nearly half these women, 59, were aged between 20 and 29 years but 32 were under the age of 20, including one, Mary Robert, who was 11 years old. She was charged with stealing various goods from Charles Terry of Aldergate Street on 6 March 1833. She was found guilty and sentenced to seven years' transportation. The Old Bailey Session Papers record that judgement was respited but this was not recorded in the prison records and, certainly, she travelled as a convict aboard the *William Bryan*.[45] The oldest woman was aged 60, a widow, Mary Hewett. She was charged with receiving stolen goods valued at 3s., and sentenced to 14 years' transportation, but she was removed from Newgate to the Penitentiary on 16 January 1833 and so did not travel to Australia.[46] A further 11 women were also sent to the Penitentiary. One of these, Sarah Gear, was sentenced to life transportation, but this was reduced to seven years on 23 February 1833. Five days later on 28 February 1833 she was transferred to the Penitentiary.[47] In addition, two women, Elizabeth Copping and Elizabeth Wratten, were sent to the House of Correction.[48] A further four women were pardoned.[49] The interesting feature of all these cases was how quickly the charges were heard at the Old Bailey Sessions after the offence was committed. In most instances the cases were heard at the next available Session which was often a few days later. Furthermore, the majority of women sentenced to transportation were dispatched on the next available ship. There were only six women who spent more than six months in Newgate prior to embarkation.

Nearly nine years later, on 14 June 1841, Mary Reading's younger sister Julia, aged 22, appeared before the Old Bailey. This was the second such incident; the first occurred in 1837, when she was charged with stealing. On that occasion she was sentenced to be confined for six months. This time she was charged, with Michael Ragan, of stealing 216 handkerchiefs, valued at £17, and 7½ yards of cambric, valued at £3, the goods of John Horatio Canning. Both Julia Reading (Redding) and Michael Ragan were found guilty and sentenced to seven years' transportation. Like her sister before her, Julia was taken back to Newgate gaol to await transportation.[50]

Maria Davis lived her early life in the Minories. This road, of approximately a quarter of a mile, runs from The Tower to Aldgate abutting the outside of the City wall on the east side and is within Portsoken Ward. In the Middle Ages there stood here an abbey of the nuns of the order of St Clare, called the Minories, founded in 1293 by Edmund, Earl of Lancaster, Leicester, and Derby and brother to Edward I, to receive nuns who were brought from Spain by his wife Blanche, Queen of Navarre. The nunnery was surrendered by Dame Elizabeth Salvage, the last abbess, to Henry VIII in 1539. After the dissolution, the nunnery became the residence of many great people.[51]

Stow, in 1603, recalled that

in place of this house of nuns is now built divers fair and large storehouses for armour and habiliments of war, with divers workhouses, serving to the same purpose. Near adjoining to the abbey, on the south side thereof, was sometime a farm belonging to the said nunnery; at which farm I myself in my youth have fetched many a halfpenny worth of milk, and never had less than three ale pints for a halfpenny in the summer, nor less than one ale quart for a halfpenny in the winter, always hot from the kiln, as the same was milked and strained. On the other side of that street lieth the ditch without the walls of the city, which of old time was used to be open, always from time to time cleansed from filth and mud, as need required; of great breadth, and so deep, that divers, watering horses where they thought it shallowest, were drowned, both horse and man. But now of later time the same ditch is enclosed, and the banks thereof let out for garden-plots, carpenters' yards, bowling allies, and divers houses thereon built, whereby the city wall is hidden, the ditch filled up, a small channel left, and that very shallow. From Aldgate, east, lieth a large street and highway, sometime replenished with few, but fair and comely buildings; on the north side whereof, the first was the parish church of St Botolph, in a large cemetery or churchyard. This church hath been lately new built at the special charges of the priors of the Holy Trinity.[52]

By 1831, the parish of St Botolph without Aldgate, inside the City boundaries, had
a population of 9,615, with slightly more
women than men. The adjacent parishes of
Christchurch, Spitalfields and St Mary,
Whitechapel were densely populated.
Christchurch, which covered about 70 acres,
had 17,949 people and St Mary, which
covered some 160 acres, had 30,733 people.[53]
Without allowing for shops, offices,
uninhabited buildings (given as 510) and
industrial premises, this shows that there
were nearly 28 dwellings and approximately
212 people per acre as an average for the
two parishes. They were congested places,
particularly as this was before the days of
high rise flats. Today 14 houses per acre is
considered very cramped with 10-12 being
the more acceptable figure for urban
development. Conditions west of London
were rather better. In the Ossulstone
hundred, Kensington Division, approximately
88,000 people occupied 19,220 acres; 2,351
adults were employed as agricultural
labourers. By 1841, the situation in both
Christchurch and St Mary was even worse;
the population figures had increased giving
a total of some 54,489 souls occupying the

8   Maria Davis.

same 230 acres. This represents nearly 237 people per acre. The situation in St Botolph
without Aldgate had improved slightly with a decrease of 90 people.[54]

This was the world of Maria Davis. Her parents James Davi(e)s and Maria Ord married
by banns on 6 April 1823 at Christchurch, Spitalfields. The witness to the marriage was
Henry Ord, who was probably Maria's father.[55] Certainly, a Henry Ord aged 54 died in
Little George Street, where James and Maria Davis lived, on 21 February 1830.[56] Although
James signed the register it would appear that the Rector, West Wheldale, signed for Maria.
The banns were read on 22 December 1822, 29 December 1822 and 5 January 1823. It was
stated that both James and Maria were of the parish.[57] Maria Elizabeth Davis and her brother
James Evan were baptised on 28 August 1825 at St Botolph without Aldgate. James was born
on 7 December 1823 and Maria on 7 July 1825. The address was given as Little George
Street, The Minories. Another brother, Henry, was baptised there on 6 January 1828. He
was born on 7 June 1827 and the address given was 8 Little George Street. A fourth child,
Martha, was born on 31 January 1829 and baptised at St Botolph without Aldgate on
15 March 1829. On this register it was noted that James and Maria Davis were from St Mary,

Whitechapel.[58] The registers show that James was a silk dyer. This was quite a popular trade at that time. The 1831 records show 65 in the City both within and without the walls and 738 in Ossulstone, Tower Division. The grand total for the City, the Ossulstone divisions and Middlesex was 2,428 which by 1841 had increased to 2,701. The Census listed some 280 different trades but none could match the figure of over 45,000 shoe and boot menders although there were over 41,000 tailors.[59] Clearly, shoes had a very hard life on the foul, unkempt streets of the day. Perhaps another illuminating sign of the times was the numbers of people listed in the 1831 returns as 'Capitalists, Bankers, Professional and other Educated men'. Christchurch parish boasted 68 such persons while Whitechapel had 531, representing 0.37 per cent and 1.72 per cent of their populations. In the City of London the figure was nearly 5.5 per cent.[60]

Life for the Davis household in 1831 must have been difficult in the new surroundings of Whitechapel. The area was congested, housing cramped and money in short supply. On 8 April 1842 the 17-year-old Maria Davis appeared before the Old Bailey court charged, with John Pearce, with feloniously receiving stolen goods acquired by William Hawes. William, aged 12, was indicted for breaking and entering the house of Frederick Edwards, on 3 March, at St Mary, Whitechapel and stealing various silver items belonging to Frederick Edwards. William Hawes pleaded guilty and was recommended to mercy by the Prosecutor, believing him to have been seduced. He was sentenced to be confined for one year. However, Maria Davis and John Pearce were not so fortunate. Maria admitted pawning pieces of silver, given to her by John Pearce, on two occasions but she stated that she did not know that the items were stolen. The court did not believe her and she, together with John Pearce, was sentenced to seven years' transportation. She was returned to Newgate to await transportation to her new life at the other end of the world.[61]

4

SHIPS

As one reads history, ... one is absolutely sickened not by the crimes
the wicked have committed, but the punishments the good have inflicted.
Oscar Wilde: *Soul of Man under Socialism*

Green fields of England! whereso'er
Across this watery waste we fare,
Your image at our hearts we bear,
Green fields of England, everywhere.

Sweet eyes in England, I must flee
Past where the waves' last confines be,
Ere your loved smile I cease to see,
Sweet eyes in England, dear to me.
A. H. Clough: *Green Fields of England*

It is hard to imagine the feelings of Joseph and Matthias Alexander, Mary and Julia Reading and Maria Davis as they awaited transportation. Perhaps it was beneficial that, with the exception of Julia, they were sent on their journeys with considerable speed.

Joseph and Matthias were the most fortunate as they had each other for company. After their trial they were returned to Fisherton Anger Gaol, Salisbury, and some three weeks later they were taken to Portsmouth and transferred to the prison hulk *York*.[1] The hulks both at Portsmouth and on the Thames were infamous; usually they were decommissioned naval ships, in a poor state of repair, anchored in rows providing a fearsome sight. The conditions on board were cramped, unhygienic and extremely unpleasant. These old ships were decrepit, very damp and lurched about in the water providing a most uncomfortable, wet and unhealthy abode for the prisoners. The *York* was built as a 74 gun ship of the line at Rotherhithe and launched in July 1807. She had a tonnage of 1743 and was converted to a prison ship in 1819. Fortunately for the Alexander brothers they were only on board her for about two weeks. Then they were transferred with 222 other Swing rioters to the *Eliza* for their journey to Van Diemen's Land, renamed Tasmania in 1855.[2] The *Eliza* was 538 tons built in India in 1806. She sailed from Portsmouth on 6 February 1831 under John S. Groves, the ship's master. William Anderson was the surgeon. She took 112 days to reach Van Diemen's Land where all 224 convicts arrived on 29 May 1831.[3]

The ships used throughout the period of transportation varied considerably because no vessel was specifically designed or built as a convict ship. The crew usually consisted of a

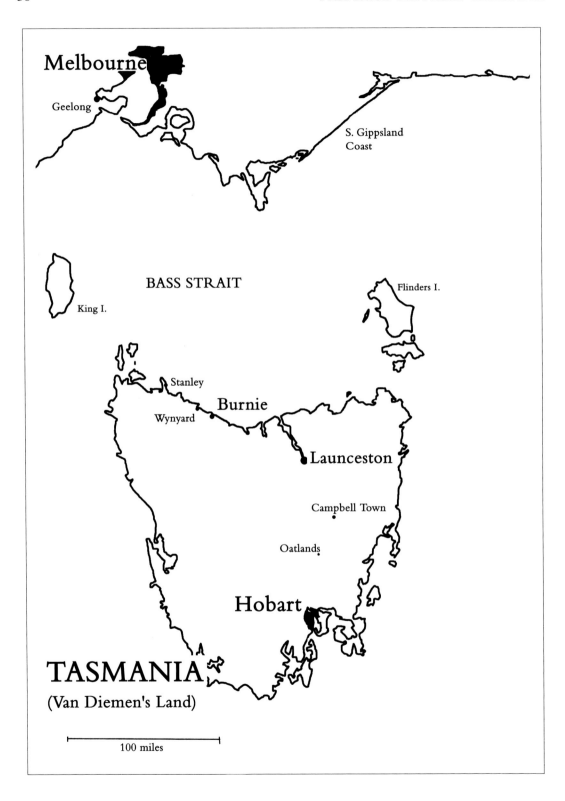

9 The *York* hulk.

master and three officers and a crew of between 25 and 30 men. Although the naval authorities could do little to ensure high standards amongst the officers and men, they could and did make sure that only the better class of vessel was hired for convict service. Their examinations were thorough and they insisted on a reasonable standard of seaworthiness. A few convict ships were wrecked on the trip to Australia but no transporter foundered on the passage although losses in other trades were heavy.[4]

Travelling in the 1830s on any ship for such a long time would have been tedious and unpleasant. On a small convict transporter it must have been terrible. It defies the imagination to contemplate the conditions below deck in temperatures of 90 to 100°F. Many of the surgeons reported that the stench of the prison, crowded with perspiring humanity, was indescribable. The sleeping berths were double bunked, each berth was six feet square and accommodated four convicts, thus providing each individual with 18 inches of sleeping space.[5] Although these conditions sound appalling by today's standards, they were little different from those endured by an ordinary seaman in the Royal Navy at that time. On the other hand, they were significantly better than the conditions suffered on the slave traders of the latter part of the previous century. The convicts were not normally shackled and the surgeons insisted that everybody was allowed on deck for a period each day. Only very severe weather conditions prevented this fresh air and exercise routine. It says much for the surgeons that there were so few deaths on the voyages. These gentlemen kept extensive logs in which they recorded details of all the convicts and, where appropriate, the children under their care. They noted the level of education of the convicts and whether or not they could read and write. Sometimes details about the convicts' place of origin were given. In these journals the surgeons recorded the state of health of each convict when the individual embarked on the ship and all treatment given throughout the long journey to Australia. At times the surgeon decided that a particular convict was too ill to be transported and refused to allow the person on the ship. Most of the doctors paid unremitting attention to the enforcement of measures to reduce disease on the crowded ships. They ensured that fresh meat and vegetables were brought on board whenever this was possible and carefully distributed lemon or lime juice to reduce the risk of scurvy. Even then, if the journey time was extended because of severe weather, scurvy could develop towards the end of the journey.[6] Between 1831 and 1850, nearly 84,000 convicts were transported. Of this total of 69,300 men and 14,600 women only 1,355 died between leaving the British gaols and arriving in Australia and this included a number who died before embarkation. Also included in the total were some 530 who drowned when four transporters were wrecked at sea.[7]

The *Eliza* had an uneventful and one could say successful trip. She arrived with all her convict cargo alive and many in good condition. Without doubt they were an unusual group of men, quite unlike the normal convicts. Indeed, the Lieutenant Governor, Colonel Arthur thought so and he went on board the *Eliza* when she arrived in Hobart. He was confronted by many rural Englishmen like the 5 foot 4 inches, brown haired, blue eyed, stout Matthias Alexander.[8] Colonel Arthur addressed the convicts telling them that he needed men with trades, possessing strength, shrewdness and simplicity to help build the Colony.[9] The skills of the Alexander brothers were much in demand.

The following year, after her trial on 29 November 1832, the 16-year-old Mary Reading returned to the unpleasant conditions of Newgate. Fortunately, she did not remain there long. On 14 January 1833, she was taken down to Woolwich to board the *Jane*, a small 272-ton ship built in Calcutta in 1825.[10] Her master was Mr. F. Tupper and the surgeon was Robert Dunn. She appears to have taken a long time to load her cargo of 115 women convicts but she eventually set out from Torbay on 22 February. She was to take 128 days on the voyage and two women died on the way; she arrived in Hobart on 30 June 1833.[11] On arrival, Mary described herself as a cook/housemaid. She was 5 feet 2 inches tall with a fresh complexion, reddish brown hair and grey eyes and by religion a Roman Catholic which would be appropriate as she declared in London that she came originally from Limerick in Ireland.[12]

Mary Reading was more fortunate than she probably realised as the third ship after hers to take female convicts from London was the ill-fated *Amphitrite*. The *Amphitrite*, under the Master John Hunter, sailed from Woolwich on 13 August 1833 carrying 101 convicts, one of whom was tried only six weeks after Mary, and 12 of their children. She was bound for New South Wales.[13] As the *Amphitrite* sailed passed Dungeness she met a violent storm; on the morning of 30 August she hove to and by noon she was lying about three miles east of Boulogne Harbour. During the afternoon there were strong winds and mountainous seas and despite the master's efforts she continued to drift towards the coast. Apparently her plight was observed by thousands of people who rushed on to the beach to watch the stricken vessel. A French pilot boat went to assist the *Amphitrite*, but the master refused all offers of help and the surgeon insisted that the women prisoners should not be landed as they might escape! Another attempt was made to assist the *Amphitrite* a little later but again the master refused; this time with a pistol in each hand. It is impossible to imagine the fear and chaos below decks in the convict areas. Suffice to say, the women broke down the hatches and rushed frantically on deck. According to reports 'their piteous cries carried clearly on the rising wind to the shore'. When the flood tide began, the *Amphitrite* was pounded heavily against the sand and about 11p.m. she broke in two amidships. She went to pieces in a few minutes. Only three sailors survived. An eye-witness recorded that the 'French and English wept together as body after body was brought in and transferred to rooms near the shore'.[14]

There was outrage at this disaster. The *Amphitrite* had undergone repairs at Deptford some five months earlier under naval supervision. The naval examination had certified her seaworthy and well-found. The subsequent inquiry established that if the master had accepted either of the offers of assistance, passengers and crew might have been saved. The inquiry concluded that it was this error of judgement that was the real cause of the tragedy.[15] So ended the lives of 101 women convicts and their 12 children.

A little less than nine years after Mary, her sister Julia set forth for Australia on the *Emma Eugenia*. She was a 383 ton barque built at Whitby in 1833; her master was George Kettlewell and the surgeon was John Kidd. She set out from Woolwich on 24 November 1841 some four months after Julia's trial. The probable reason for the delay was that Julia was pregnant. She had been living with James Simpson for a year before her conviction and her daughter Mary was born just prior to her transportation. Unfortunately, the trip was a long one of 136 days stopping at the Cape of Good Hope. The only advantage of this for the convicts, who were not released from the ship, was that fresh food was undoubtedly brought on board. She eventually arrived in Hobart on 9 April 1842 with 190 of her 191 women convicts, one unfortunate soul having died *en route*.[16] Julia and her 4½-month-old baby survived the ordeal apparently none the worse for the experience. She described herself as a needlewoman; she was 5 feet 1¾ inches tall, with brown hair, hazel eyes, a freckled face and a sallow complexion.[17] It is somewhat amazing that the Australian authorities, unlike the Newgate officials, did not see fit to mention that she had lost her right leg.[18]

The last to travel was Maria Davis. She boarded the *Royal Admiral*, after only 2½ weeks in Newgate, at Woolwich on 25 April 1842.[19] The *Royal Admiral* was a 414 ton barque built at Lynn in 1828; her master was William Fell and the surgeon was John Roberts. She was to have the longest trip of them all. The *Royal Admiral* left Woolwich on 5 May 1842 and went via the Cape of Good Hope to arrive in Australia 142 days later on 24 September 1842.[20] A total of 206 women embarked on this ship but, as the surgeon recorded, there was a tremendous amount of illness prior to sailing. The women suffered on the journey from the prisons to the ship at Woolwich. The weather was bad and many were dressed in poor, flimsy clothing. The women came from many different parts of England, Scotland and Wales; they often arrived on board in a distressed and filthy state very late at night. Some had no additional clothing or possessions. Apparently, the women had been told that if they took any more, these possessions and clothes would be removed from them and destroyed. The surgeon was distressed by this state of affairs and recorded that nearly all the women needed medical treatment before the ship left Woolwich.

At the start of the voyage the weather was good but soon it became sultry, with oppressive calms and heavy seas; the temperature on deck was 85°F. By the time that the *Royal Admiral* arrived at the Cape of Good Hope on 29 July, two of the women had died of dysentery. Fortunately, at the Cape the water casks were resupplied and fresh meat and vegetables were brought on board. This was of great benefit to the women. However, the remainder of the trip was difficult, and a further five women died between 22 and 28 September of diarrhoea and associated conditions. In addition, five babies died during August and early September; the youngest was six days old and the oldest 18 months. During the voyage seven babies were born. The surgeon commented that, with a few exceptions, 'the women convicts were well behaved, clean, industrious and willingly disposed to improve themselves'. Moreover, he considered that the Newgate and Edinburgh women were 'decidedly the best behaved and orderly and the impressions made there on their minds with very few exceptions appeared favourable and beneficial and their grateful recollections of much kindness and care was deeply implanted and cherished by them'. There were four matrons, from amongst the women, appointed to supervise them. Furthermore, the convicts were allowed on deck when the weather permitted; in the hot weather they were under awnings. They took their meals on deck whenever possible.

On this journey, illness was a major problem amongst not only the convicts but also the crew and their families. In all, including those who were ill before sailing, the surgeon treated 226 patients, of whom 214 were returned to duty, five were sent to hospital on arrival in Hobart, and seven adults died. As Maria Davis was not recorded as a patient either before or during the journey, she must have been an extremely tough, fit, resilient young woman. On 3 October, all but 80 of the convicts were disembarked in Hobart. The remainder, escorted by the surgeon, went on the government barque *Lady Franklin* to Launceston where they landed in good condition on 14 October.[21] When she arrived, Maria described herself as a nursemaid. She was 4 feet 8¼ inches tall, of fresh complexion with brown hair, brown eyes, a broad face with dimples and a scald mark on her left wrist.[22] The ship's record, which described her as a housemaid, stated that she could read, how well is not defined, but as there was no comment about her writing, it must be assumed that she could not write.[23]

When FM's ancestors arrived in Van Diemen's Land, they faced a totally new way of life in a strange land. Probably their first thoughts were to get ashore on to dry land away from the unpleasant conditions on board ship. So what awaited them? Did they ever think that they might return to the land of their birth? Normally, in the 1830s, when convicts arrived they were put to work on government projects or assigned. The assignment system involved companies, free settlers and emancipists, who were in fact free convicts. Some wealthy individuals had a large number of assigned convicts, other people had only one or two. As convicts became, in some respects, the slaves of the people to whom they were assigned the system was open to considerable abuse but the convicts were not the chattels or property of their masters. All were able to earn some money on the free market. They could appear in court as witnesses, bring civil law suits and petition the Governor. A convict could, in theory anyway, bring a master to court for ill treatment.

The system was beneficial to the government: firstly, the convicts were dispersed around the Colony; secondly, they were removed from government prisons and their living expenses were paid for by the masters; and, thirdly, they were free labour for the settlers. If the convicts behaved satisfactorily the Governor granted 'Tickets of Leave'. These certificates freed the prisoners from their assigned masters or government labour and enabled them to work as they wished within the Colony. The ticket was issued for a year and then had to be renewed but it could be revoked at any time. The next stage in the freedom from bondage was a Conditional Pardon. This gave the convict citizenship within the Colony but no right to return to England. The last stage was the Certificate of Freedom, which was issued usually at the end of the sentence. Occasionally some people obtained Absolute Pardons quite early in their sentence. This restored all rights including that of returning home.[24]

Life in Van Diemen's Land in the early days was undoubtedly harsh. However, Governor Arthur (May 1824–October 1836) had had a great impact on the island. He adopted measures which controlled the convict population, subdued the aborigines, repressed lawlessness, and established comparative tranquillity. He achieved major improvements in the assignment system and the administration of the convicts improved immeasurably. Furthermore, he assisted the free settlers, many of whom arrived with slender resources. He was a capable and dedicated administrator who brought discipline both to the settlers and the convicts. He divided the island into police districts, each subject to a Stipendiary Magistrate, which brought the prison population under the more direct control of the government.[25] His police constables were mostly ex-prisoners; this policy of 'setting a thief to catch a thief' was most successful. In addition, Governor Arthur introduced a system of preparatory servitude of four, six or eight years for those sentenced for seven years, 14 years or life, following which the Ticket of Leave was awarded.[26]

So it was into this distant country, approximately the size of Ireland, on the other side of the world that the Alexander brothers arrived to start their new lives. Not surprisingly, of the convicts on board the *Eliza*, Governor Arthur retained 30 of the craftsmen to work in government departments, among whom was Joseph. He sent 25 to Launceston to work for the Van Diemen's Land Company and three, one of whom was Matthias, to Norfolk Plains to work for the Van Diemen's Land Establishment, more commonly known as the Cressy Company. The rest were assigned to farmers, landowners and other private employers.[27] At this time, 1831, there were 23,678 people in the Colony of which some 10,000 were convicts. The majority of those categorised as free were emancipists, a title given to convicts who had served their time or received pardons, or descendants of such individuals. The ratio of men to women was approximately three to one. In Norfolk Plains, which covered a substantial area in the central part of the island and included the little townships of Longford, Carrick, Bishopsbourne and Cressy, there was a population of 1,332. Almost half this number were convicts.[28] By the end of the following year Joseph was still working for the government but the records show that Matthias had been moved to work for the Van Diemen's Land Company. This may be an error as it is probable that he remained in his previous employment in the same area.[29] Certainly, when he became free he lived for a number of years south of Longford in the Norfolk Plains district.

Matthias was granted his Ticket of Leave on 1 June 1835 and his brother his a few weeks later on 26 August.[30] This was in accordance with normal procedure. However, the severity of the sentences awarded, particularly by the Special Commissions, to the Swing rioters was criticised in certain quarters in England. Even before the *Eliza* sailed from England, a campaign to obtain an amnesty for the convicts had begun. Over the next three years support for the cause grew and in August 1835 Lord John Russell, as Home Secretary, announced that 264 machine breakers were to be pardoned.[31] This good news was announced to some 220 of the Swing rioters, who had travelled to Van Diemen's Land on the *Eliza* or the *Porteus*, by means of the *Hobart Town Gazette* dated 5 February 1836. The list included the Alexander brothers. The government notice stated that the

> Lieutenant Governor has been pleased to direct the names of the following individuals who have received absolute remissions of their sentences and of which His Majesty's allowance has been signified, shall be published for general information. The individuals in whose favour the pardons have been granted, will therefore apply at the Muster Master's office, Hobart Town or to that of a Police Magistrate in the interior, in order that the instruments of Pardon may be forthwith issued, as each person until possessed of such document, is liable to be treated as a prisoner of the Crown.[32]

One can only hope that both Matthias and Joseph heard of the amnesty reasonably quickly. At this point they could have returned to England if they had the money for the fare. Some of the rioters, who had clean records within the Colonies, had to wait a remarkably long time for their pardons. As qualified tradesmen, Matthias and Joseph would probably have had no difficulty in obtaining employment settling as they did in the Norfolk Plains area of Van Diemen's Land.

In 1827, Governor Arthur commissioned the building of a female factory, or House of Correction as it was officially called, at the Cascades, three miles from Hobart, with provision for solitary confinement and hard labour at the wash tub. The women were divided into three categories: the first were women recently arrived from Britain who had behaved well during the voyage and were awaiting assignment; the second group were women who had committed minor offences; and the third category were women who had committed offences during the voyage or more serious crimes within the Colony, and this category was colloquially known as the 'crime class'. Women could earn progression from one group to another by good behaviour.[33] Women who misbehaved had their heads shaved and were put in irons. Unfortunately, soon this prison became overcrowded and life for the inmates became more and more intolerable. By 1838, a reporter stated the 'one room, used as a nursery, contained 70 people, there was no ventilation and the room received no sunlight'.[34] As early as 1827, plans were produced for a new female factory at Launceston but construction did not begin until 1833. The building reflected the ideas of Bentham. It was octagonal in shape to ensure easy supervision of the convicts and the yards and corridors could be readily surveyed but, unlike Bentham's plans, the women were not kept isolated except as a punishment. This institution was to replace the old building at George Town, some miles from Launceston, which at best was cold and damp and, by 1829, was reported to be without windows. Situated between the gaol, on the corner of Bathurst and Paterson Streets, and Margaret Street, on the site of the present Launceston College, the Launceston factory was eventually completed at the end of 1834. The first women convicts were admitted in November of that year.[35]

Soon after Mary Reading arrived, she was assigned to Captain Crear. All seemed to go well for the first year but then trouble started for this young Irish girl and for the rest of her time as a convict she was in almost continuous trouble. On 13 June 1834, Captain Crear reported her for insolence and neglecting her duty. She was sentenced to seven days on bread and water. By December, her conduct had deteriorated and Captain Crear reported her again for misconduct and 'quitting' his house on 11 November. She was sentenced to four months in the female House of Correction, Hobart, and was not to be released to the service of her master. Governor Arthur signed orders on 18 December 1834 for her to be moved to the factory at Launceston, where she was one of the early occupants of this establishment. Her next offence of fighting and disorderly conduct took place in the factory and she was sentenced to 10 days solitary confinement on bread and water. She was released from the factory and assigned to Mr. Findley, but in March 1836 he reported her for abusive behaviour and absenting herself. Some six weeks later Mr. Smith reported her for idleness. She was awarded 14 days in the House of Correction in Launceston and removed from her service. On 19 July, she was found drinking in a public house and sentenced to seven days solitary confinement on bread and water. During August 1836, Mr. Capon reported her a further three times for stealing, drunkenness and disobedience. Her term of transportation was extended by three years, and she was reprimanded and sentenced to six weeks 'crime class'. During early 1837 she had at least three different masters and was reported by each of them for various misdemeanours including misconduct, being out after hours and being in Launceston without a pass. For the last offence, in late June, she was sentenced to one month's 'crime class'. On 3 August she was out all night and awarded a further three months 'crime class'. A day later, she went absent without leave and was given a further three months in the House of Correction. At this point she behaved herself; however, when she was released into service, she absconded and was reported by Mr. Bell. Her existing term of transportation was extended again by a further six months. This decision was confirmed by the Lieutenant Governor on 7 April 1838.[36] It was perhaps fortunate for both Mary and the authorities that, on 3 October 1838, Matthias Alexander applied for permission to marry her. The wedding took place on 14 November 1838 at the Chapel for the Convict Party, Campbell Town and her one-time master William Capon acted as a witness.[37]

Transportation to New South Wales ceased in 1840 and all convicts were now sent to Van Diemen's Land, placing great strain on the resources. The increase in the numbers of convicts presented severe problems. As the Lieutenant Governor John Franklin advised Lord Stanley, the Home Secretary, in his letter dated 22 July 1842, '6 convict ships have arrived in rapid succession since my last dispatch and this had increased anxieties about numbers'.[38] On these ships came 1,206 men and 190 women. What Franklin did not appreciate was that five more ships would arrive within the next four weeks bringing a further 968 men and 137 women.[39] He also commented that since the introduction of the probation system in

1840 numbers had 'greatly exceeded that which I was led to expect'.[40] The new system of probation ordered by the government in London dispensed with convict assignment and required convicts to pass through five stages on their way to reformation and liberty. Stage one was detention; stage two, which was for men only, involved working in probation gangs; stage three was the granting of a probation pass which enabled the holder to work for wages for an approved settler or for the government; stage four was the granting of a Ticket of Leave; and the last stage was the award of a conditional or absolute pardon.[41] This system replaced assignment in all but a few areas and placed considerable strain on prison facilities that were already overcrowded. Moreover, there were significant difficulties in the way of stage 3 (or Class 3, as it was more usually known) convicts obtaining employment. Under the assignment system, the masters did not pay wages but with the new system the convicts had to be paid. Very quickly there was a surplus of untrained labour looking for work.

Into this new system in April 1842 came Julia Redding (Reading). She appears to have been a very well-behaved prisoner at first, as nothing is contained on her record for the first two years. However, on 1 April 1844 she was awarded three days solitary confinement for misconduct. This was presumably a minor transgression, as she gained Class 3 status on 12 April 1844. By August she had offended again and was sentenced to four months hard labour in the House of Correction in Hobart. She was transferred to Launceston on 9 August. She obtained her Ticket of Leave on 11 November 1845.[42] Obviously, at Launceston she was much closer to her sister, Mary, and after her spell in the factory, probably in early 1845, she went to or was near her sister. On 2 April 1846, she married James Gadsbury, a 35-year-old, single, free man, albeit an ex-convict, at Christ Church, Longford, relatively near the home of Matthias and Mary Alexander.[43]

Meanwhile, Maria Davis had arrived in September 1842. Her conduct sheet was brief and contained only one entry which stated that on 28 February 1843 she was found guilty of misconduct 'being found concealed for improper purposes'. She was sentenced to three months hard labour in the 'crime class'. On 12 April 1844, she gained Class 3 status in the probation system which meant that she could find her own employment and work for wages. By 11 November 1845 she was granted a Ticket of Leave and her Certificate of Leave on 16 April 1849.[44] A few days before she gained her Class 3 status, she married Thomas Brown at St John's Church, Launceston on 8 April 1844. By then Maria was 19 years old and still officially listed as a prisoner. On the other hand Thomas Brown, with a declared age of 31 years, was single and free and unlike Maria he could write his name.[45] He was a constable at Launceston and, as such, was undoubtedly a former convict.

5

LONGFORD TO TABLE CAPE

There is a pleasure in the pathless woods,
There is a rapture on the lonely shore,
There is society, where none intrudes,
By the deep sea, and music in its roar.
Lord Byron: *Childe Harold*

In February 1833, John Alexander, younger brother of Joseph and Matthias, arrived in Hobart. He was baptised in Ramsbury on 20 December 1812 but, unlike his brothers, does not appear to have been involved in the Swing Riots. However, on 16 July 1832, together with James Shuttle also of Ramsbury, he was charged at the Berkshire Assizes, held at Abingdon, with stealing 10 pigs valued at £10 from William Atherton of Ramsbury on 1 June 1832. He was described as a labourer who could read but not write.[1] He was found guilty and sentenced to seven years transportation. Like his brothers before him, he was transferred to the prison hulk *York* at Portsmouth.[2] From there he and James Shuttle travelled with 182 other men on the *Georgiana*, a 406 ton barque built in Calcutta in 1820; she left Portsmouth on 16 October 1832 and arrived, 108 days later, in Hobart on 1 February 1833, having journeyed via Tristan De Cunha. All the convicts safely disembarked.[3] Initially, John was assigned to Mr. A. Tolney; thereafter he was transferred a number of times before he became a free citizen.[4]

On 14 August 1837, while still an assigned servant at Lake River, now called Cressy, John married Margaret Bourke, who was free, at Christ Church, Longford. They remained in the same area of Van Diemen's Land at a place called Snake Banks, now known as Powranna, south of Perth, and had two children: Edward, who died in November 1838 aged five months, was buried at Perth, as was the other son, Richard (Ambrose), who died aged three months in March 1840. A week later, on 8 March, the unfortunate Margaret was also buried at Perth. On 11 November 1841, as a free man, John remarried, again at Christ Church, Longford, Martha Coleman. In the meantime, Matthias and Mary were also producing children. Their first two sons were also born at Snake Banks. Edward Redding, the first son of Matthias, was born in May 1839 and a year later Reading James was born but he only survived for eight days. Shortly after this all the Alexanders moved to Illawarra where they joined their kinsman, John Dowling, who was an overseer on the Wickford estate then owned by Henry Clayton. John Dowling was born in Ramsbury and baptised there in October 1807. He lived through the difficult times of the Swing Riots but was not charged with any offences connected with them. The traumatic events of that period had

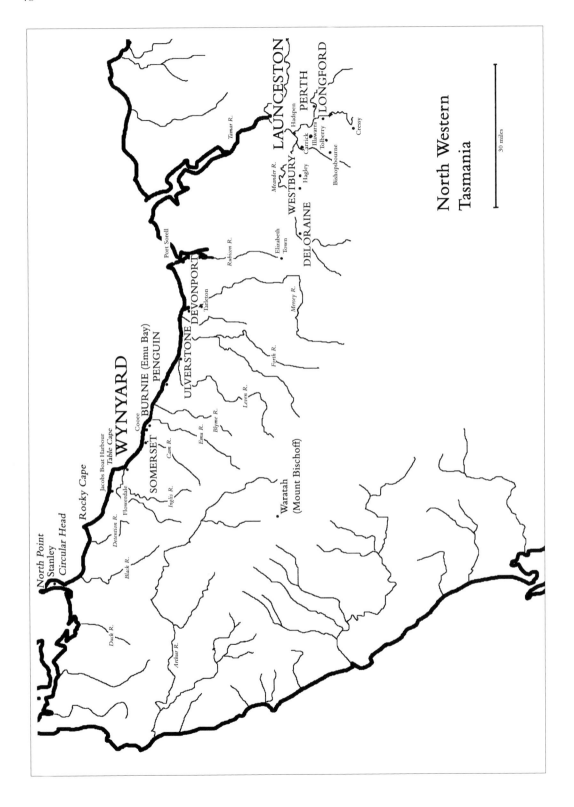

North Western
Tasmania

30 miles

10   Perth Church.

an effect on the young Dowling and he decided to become an indentured shepherd with the Van Diemen's Land Company. At that time this company was recruiting young men to work on their vast lands at Circular Head, where subsequently the town of Stanley developed, on the north west coast of the then Van Diemen's Land. John Dowling left England some ten months after Joseph and Matthias Alexander in November 1831. In 1839, he married Maria Turner in Longford and was working as a shepherd, presumably at Wickford because a year later he was an overseer at that estate.[5]

The Alexanders and the Dowlings lived at Wickford for a number of years. They worked hard and prospered, making money that was to provide independence for all of them in the future, but life was far from easy. Fortunately, the Alexander brothers were resilient; they accepted life as it came. Perhaps more importantly, they were enterprising men. Matthias and Joseph lived in adjacent wooden houses. Although Matthias and his wife, Mary, and their sons lived as a family unit in their dwelling, in Joseph's house there were a number of other people; namely his brother John, his second wife Martha and their child, Jane, who was born on 26 November 1841 at Wickford, and four single men of whom two were Ticket of Leave men.[6] Later, at Wickford, John and Martha had two more children; Martha was born on 27 January 1844 and John Charles (Hezekiah) on 15 February 1845, but on 22 October 1846, Martha, aged 25 died of consumption. This left John a widower for a second time but now he had three small children. Meanwhile, Matthias and Mary produced a further five children, one every two years; Joseph Redding was born at Wickford on 16 June 1841, Frederick Matthias' father John on 16 June 1843, Matthias on 22 April 1845, Mary Ann on

11   Wooden house at Wickford.

1 March 1847 and Martin Reding on 6 March 1849. During this time John Dowling and his wife, Maria, produced five children, the last of which died within a month of her birth in August 1848. Following this misfortune, John and Maria Dowling decided to move to Launceston where they took over the *Brisbane* hotel.

At about this time, during the latter part of 1849, Matthias and John decided to embark on a more independent lifestyle. Matthias acquired some 500 acres of land at Redlands in the Deloraine area and John about five acres at nearby Red Gate.[7] This district became a strongly Roman Catholic one and was soon inhabited by many freed convicts. It is likely that Matthias and John went to their new properties to build houses for themselves and to begin to farm the land. John Alexander was not satisfied with this and decided to try to improve the family fortunes by visiting the goldfields in America. He embarked on this adventure with Mary Ann Crowther, née Thewlis, who travelled as his wife. They departed from Launceston on the *Spartan* on 12 May 1850 bound for California. As there is no record of the children on board, it must be assumed that John left his three children with Matthias and Mary.[8]

In the meantime Matthias was probably at Redlands working the land and preparing for his family to join him. Tragically for all concerned, on 16 September 1850, at the approximate age of 34 years, the lively, Irish lass Mary died of consumption. She was still living in the Longford area at the time of her death. This left Matthias with nine children aged

12   Convict accommodation at
Wickford.

between 18 months and 11 years, his own six and John's three. As his brother Joseph did
not have a wife in the Colony, Matthias had a major problem. Undoubtedly he turned to
the only female member of the family available, his sister-in-law, Julia Redding. In 1846,
she had married James Gadsbury in Longford and was now the mother of three children
under 4 years but what had happened to baby Mary who had travelled with Julia to the
Colony in 1841 is uncertain. History does not relate how the one-legged Julia managed to
cope with this situation. At least 12 children under 12 years of age would be a challenge
to any woman, in her predicament one can only marvel at her endurance, particularly as she
continued to produce a child every two years. It is highly likely that Matthias moved his
family together with all the Gadsbury family and possibly Joseph to Redlands. Joseph Aloysius
Alexander, a great grandchild of Matthias born in 1892, recorded that Matthias and Joseph
lived in Red Hills (Redlands) near Deloraine for a few years.[9] Certainly the Gadsbury family
lived in John Alexander's house at Red Gate for a period of time. By 1859 James and Julia
had had at least seven children although one died in infancy. James Gadsbury, who was
apparently lavishly decorated with tattoos, died of dysentery on 25 February 1864; six
months later the indomitable Julia married John Williams of Red Hill, Deloraine, at which
time she moved from Red Gate.[10]

John Alexander and Mary Crowther returned to Van Diemen's Land sometime during
the latter part of 1851. How successful John was in California is uncertain but it must be

assumed that the adventure was profitable because soon after his return he began to buy significant acres of land at Table Cape on the north west coast of Van Diemen's Land. On 22 November 1851, the land abutting the River Inglis at Table Cape was surveyed and shortly afterwards John was permitted to purchase 94 acres of Crown land on the banks of the river. In April 1852, the *Hobart Gazette* recorded that John had not paid the first year's rent on Lot 12, some 2,000 acres on the river. It seems that this matter was resolved because in July 1852 John bought an additional 200 acres of land near the River Inglis. This land was described as 'adjoining Lot 431', the original 94 acres already purchased by John, and 'Lots 718 and 719 purchased by John King but now occupied by or belonging to the said John Alexander'. The land previously owned by John King, who had died some years before, was a huge area of some 2,000 acres covering a very large part of Table Cape.[11]

On their return from California in late 1851, it is assumed that John and Mary returned to the Deloraine area; Mary to help Julia look after all the children and John to help on the farm, although it would appear that he was more interested in land at Table Cape than Deloraine. It seems that the brothers agreed it was Matthias' turn to have an adventure because he, along with many men from Van Diemen's Land, decided to go to the newly discovered goldfields in Victoria. He travelled with a friend, Gregory, and another man, George Ramskill, but they agreed to separate and meet up again in Melbourne for the trip home. By all accounts Matthias was successful on the goldfields and at the due date prepared for the trip home across the Bass Strait. The trio departed from Melbourne on 5 August 1852 on the *City of Melbourne*. She was described as a fine new auxiliary screw steamer under the command of William Saunders. She left Melbourne Bay on Friday 6 August and encountered what was described in the newspapers as a typhoon. The trip to Launceston should have been a short one but by Saturday afternoon she was overdue. The *Cornwall Chronicle* announced a fortnight later that there was still no news of her but that the brig *Fantome* was to depart that day, Saturday 21 August, to seek 'some tidings of her'. It was reported that there were upward of 300 people on board. In the event, it transpired that the ship met a heavy gale off the notoriously dangerous coast of King Island and the captain was forced, for the safety of all on board, to run her ashore. This news was transmitted to the world by the *Cornwall Chronicle* based in Launceston. They received their intelligence from an overland messenger from Circular Head, some 125 miles up the coast, who had been dispatched when the mate from the *City of Melbourne* had arrived at that town. He had come in an open boat through very heavy seas from King Island. In the letter Mr. Saunders sent with the mate, he gave the ship's exact location, explained that she would be difficult to refloat, and stated there were about 250 people on board with six days provisions. As a postscript he stated, 'I forgot to mention that no lives were lost.' Mr. Fenwick, J.P., a passenger, gave a much more graphic account and said that they only had three days provisions. Moreover, he requested prompt measures 'to have us immediately relieved from our perilous circumstances'. In addition, he asked that 'two constables be sent as most of the passengers were on shore clamouring for provisions'. Fortunately for all concerned, the good Mr. Emmett at Circular Head was a level-headed man. Within two hours of the arrival of the mate on Thursday 12 August, he dispatched two schooners, each with a good supply of provisions, with the unfortunate mate. He sent his letter overland to Launceston and asked

13 Table Cape from Nurses retreat.

that the good news that all were safe be published. It was some days before the rescue ships arrived, by which time food was in very short supply. Eventually, Matthias and his friends returned to Launceston apparently none the worse for the experience.[12]

After his trip to the Victorian goldfields, Matthias and his brother John went to Table Cape where they set about clearing the huge trees from the land. Both brothers appreciated the value of the wood as palings were in short supply in Melbourne and on the Victorian goldfields. Clearly, if they could send this wood across the Bass Strait it would prove a most profitable venture. Therefore, they needed a ship. In their usual enterprising fashion, they found a man, William Pringle, and contracted him to design and supervise the building of a suitable vessel for produce and timber trading.[13] In addition, they established the little township of Alexandria, opened an Inn and grew crops to feed themselves.[14] At this stage, Matthias was undoubtedly joined by his children, namely Edward aged 13, Joseph aged 11, John aged nine, Matthias aged seven, Mary Ann aged five and Martin aged three years. As John, the elder, was now accompanied by Mary, the lady who went to California with him, she presumably looked after everybody including John's three children by his previous marriage. Joseph may have come to Table Cape for a short time but very soon he left to go to Stanley near Circular Head. This left only James and Julia Gadsbury and their ever increasing family in Deloraine. All Matthias' land at Redlands was rented out to other farmers.

Life at Table Cape was not without its excitements. On 15 September 1853, the little settlement received rather unwelcome guests in the form of bushrangers. These men, Bradley and Connor, came from Circular Head, a settlement further up the coast, where they had terrified the district. The bushrangers were armed and arrived at Alexandria with a posse of police and aggrieved private citizens in hot pursuit. They entered Matthias' small, brick Inn and demanded food and drink. Soon they were disturbed by the arrival of the group from Circular Head so they rushed to the landing stage where the schooner *Sophia* was anchored. They hijacked the ship and shots were fired between the ship and shore. Apparently, Matthias Alexander's red cap made him an obvious target. Fortunately, nobody seems to have been hurt, but the ship departed to Victoria under her new commanders much to the chagrin of the ship's captain. It reached the South Gippsland coast 24 hours later and the bushrangers headed for Melbourne, murdering a young ploughman along the way in order to acquire his horses. Shortly afterwards, they were apprehended by mounted troops. They were taken to Melbourne where they were tried, convicted of murder and duly hanged on 24 October 1853.[15]

Life at Table Cape quickly returned to normal. Matthias and John continued to clear their land, prepare wood for shipment and grow crops. By late 1853, their ship the *Alexander* was launched under the captaincy of George Ramskill, Matthias' friend from the goldfields. A few months later, in March 1854, the 40 ton schooner, in an apparently very unfinished state, brought the Mackenzie family from Launceston to Table Cape. The journey took three days and proved a most uncomfortable trip for the passengers. The Mackenzies spent their first night at the home of John Alexander and Mary. Thereafter, until their new dwelling was constructed, they lived in the Carpenters' House, so called because it was here that the men who had built the *Alexander* had lived during her construction. Charles Ross Mackenzie had left Rosshire in Scotland to serve the East India Company as an officer in the 26 Madras Native Infantry. After a little over 20 years service, he retired as a Captain on the grounds of ill health and rejoined his family at Perth in Van Diemen's Land, where he had settled them some five years earlier. In 1853, he purchased 1,500 acres at Table Cape. His son, Charles John, became a prominent figure in Van Diemen's Land serving as a Justice of the Peace for over 50 years, a member of the House of Assembly for 25 years, and a member of a variety of public boards. In addition, he was a dedicated churchman serving for many years as a church warden, Lay reader and Synod representative.[16] Although young Charles John Mackenzie was to remember all his life his unpleasant trip in the *Alexander*, the little ship traded in timber and produce up and down the coast and to Victoria for many years. After all, she was built as a cargo vessel not a passenger liner. Conditions in Van Diemen's Land at that time were very much ones of compromise!

Perhaps the general state of northern Van Diemen's Land and the difficulties of travelling around are best described by Captain Butler Stoney, who toured extensively around the Island in 1854, the year after it ceased to be a penal colony. Captain Stoney was entranced by Tasmania, as the Island became known in December 1855: he enthused 'there is no land in the world that appears more lovely than this Island'.[17] His description covers flora, fauna, forests, minerals and pastures. Of particular interest is his journey from Launceston to what he described as the 'unexplored regions of the north-west coast, which abound in riches still unknown, with goodly ports as yet seen but by a few, with lordly rivers hitherto untraversed, and with mineral wealth still hidden and unsought for'.[18] First, he travelled from Launceston to Deloraine, passing through Hadspen, then the impressive estate of Entally; from there his route went through woods until he reached the Vale of Carrick and a fine race course. After passing the Quamby and Hagley estates he reached Westbury, which he considered to have some 'fine land and several pretty places'.[19] The road from Westbury to Deloraine was partly through forest with some farms and cultivated land which Stoney described as the 'last town ere we enter the wilds of the north-west'.[20] On leaving Deloraine the party entered the Black Forest but, as Stoney observed,

> a considerable change has taken place in this part of the country within the last year: a good open road has replaced the old bridle track, which was often difficult to find; good bridges have been erected over the rivers, and planked causeways over the dangerous swamps; a township called Elizabeth Town has also been laid out.[21]

From here the existence and quality of the road was variable; the party had to ford a river and a little later had a 'charming' six-mile canter across the Native Plain. Eventually they reached the township of Tarleton near the coast.[22]

After a number of diversionary trips to Port Sorell and the surrounding area, Stoney undertook alone the trip up the coast. It proved to be hazardous with a number of difficult rivers to cross. He gave a graphic account of crossing the Forth river. It would appear that although he did not think the river safe to cross, as it was late he preferred a swim to a night in the bush on his own. Thus, he and his horse 'plunged into the boiling surf'. His mare lost her footing, he was unseated and the tide was pulling them strongly out to sea. 'Hope nearly deserted' him, he recalled, but as the mare swam freely by him, he grabbed her flowing tail and in this way both animal and man made it safely to the river bank.[23] The intrepid traveller continued up the coast to Ulverstone, from where he entered the 'wild forest to some 10 miles of hardly discoverable track' until he reached Blythe. Having crossed a 'most dangerous' ford he continued to Emu Bay, where the land, mainly owned by the Van Diemen's Land Company, was more open and the town of Burnie was laid out. Stoney was impressed by the town which he described as a 'very pretty spot, and well calculated for a fashionable and healthy watering-place'.[24] He also noted that the steamer from Launceston visited twice a week. The route from Emu Bay was on a 'devious track along the sea coast and over precipitous densely forest-clad hills, having several dangerous fords to cross'.[25] Some four miles from Burnie is the Cam, a small river which, nevertheless, 'at high water can be used by vessels of 40-50 tons, with good anchorage for several miles'. From the Cam, Stoney proceeded to the Inglis; 'passing over the extreme end of a long chain of hills which run inland, you meet heathy land, poor and ferny'.[26]

Stoney considered the Inglis not as large as the Cam and fordable at low water. However, he noted, there was some good land and several clearings beyond the river. This was the area of Alexandria. He enthused about the area as follows:

> The promontory of Table Bay runs out to seawards; it is high level land, with a bold bluff cliff, but affording good shelter from westerly gales. Five hundred acres of this level promontory, now densely covered with forest, is reserved for a township. Within the last year several settlers have come to this very beautiful spot, and the land proving of the best description, more will soon follow. The township of Wynyard, on the Inglis, has lately been surveyed and sold, and the Messrs. Alexanders, large and enterprising landholders up the Inglis, cut up a part of their property and sold it to great advantage.[27]

14   The Nut, Stanley.

John and Matthias were doing well. Stoney concluded his account with this hopeful view of the future:

> Each year, changes of considerable magnitude will, beyond all doubt, take place in Tasmania; and what we see to-day will assume a different description tomorrow. The forest-clad township of this year may become a well-inhabited town the next; steamers will glide on waters not now even known; and roads—perchance railroads—will, ere many years, traverse the now impervious bush or the mountain steep.[28]

It was in this beautiful but isolated outpost that Matthias and John tried to carve out a life for themselves and their families. Joseph was at Stanley, the little township near Circular Head, the home of the Van Diemen's Land Company. Both places were very different from the Wiltshire village of Ramsbury they had left behind. However, it is unlikely that this thought was uppermost in any of their minds. The task now was to make a success of life on the North West coast. In 1854, all three brothers remarried.

First Matthias, on 26 January, married Ann Eden Thewlis; she was 20 years old and had come out to the Colony, from Leeds in England, with her parents, John and Alice Thewlis, on the *Royal Sovereign* in 1843 as free settlers.[29] The marriage ceremony was conducted by the Reverend John West who was born on 17 January 1809, the son of a Wesleyan clergyman. He was admitted to the Congregational Ministry at Thetford, Norfolk. In 1829 he married, and in September 1838, with his wife and five young children, he set out for Van

Diemen's Land to be a minister for the Colonial Missionary Society. Initially he went to Hobart, but very soon he moved to Launceston. He did not think of himself as an itinerant missionary, and so conducted his ministry mainly from Launceston. He became a leading protagonist against transportation and his work with the newspaper, the *Launceston Examiner*, enabled him to express himself strongly in public. He regarded the campaign to end the system as 'a moral crusade'. On 26 April 1853, news reached the Colony of the success of the campaign. The last convict ship reached Hobart on 16 May and, on 29 December, the Order in Council making Van Diemen's Land a penal colony was revoked. In 1854, West accepted Fairfax's offer of editorship of the *Sydney Morning Herald* and he remained in that position until he died in 1873.[30] He conducted the marriage service for Matthias and Ann in his own home in Launceston rather than in his Congregational Church; perhaps he did this in cognisance of the strong Wesleyan/Methodist background of Matthias.

One of the witnesses at the ceremony in Launceston was John Dowling. Life was proving difficult for him because in September the previous year his wife Maria had died, leaving him with seven children, the oldest of whom was 14 years old. He had written to Matthias saying that he wanted to join him at Table Cape and asking his advice. The matter was presumably discussed when the two met for the wedding because a short time later John Dowling and his family moved to the North West coast. First they went to Circular Head where, in November 1854, his youngest son John was scalded to death. A few months later, he purchased 100 acres of land on Table Cape and moved there with his young family; the property became known as Inglis Park Farm.[31] In 1856, at a ceremony conducted at the house of Matthias and Ann at Table Cape, he married Ann Tapley and had a further 12 children, of which one died in infancy. Ann died during childbirth in 1875, leaving John with 11 children aged from 19 years to a new-born baby. Again fate struck John a double blow, his 19-year-old son, John, dying of typhoid within three months of his mother's death.

The next Alexander wedding was on 26 May 1854, when Joseph married Mary Dyer aged 40 years in a civil ceremony at Stanley, Circular Head. And last, on 10 October, John married Mary Ann Crowther, née Thewlis, the lady who had accompanied him for the past four years, in a civil ceremony witnessed by Matthias and Ann Eden Alexander, the latter being Mary Ann's niece. Mary Ann had travelled with her family and husband on the *Royal Sovereign*; she married Joseph Crowther in Leeds in 1835. Soon after their arrival in about 1844, Joseph disappeared, probably to Melbourne, thus enabling Mary Ann to remarry in a civil ceremony under the requisite '7 years of separation by water' rule that applied in Australia at that time.

Matthias and John with their wives and families settled into life at Alexandria. Joseph with his new wife lived at Stanley, Circular Head, where he owned and had the licence of the *Emily Hotel*. Now known as the *Union Hotel*, this is still in operation today; in addition he had a substantial number of other small properties which he rented to a variety of people.[32] Sadly, some 17 months after their marriage, in October 1855, Mary died.

John had the licence of the *Table Cape Inn* but both John and Matthias concentrated their efforts on clearing the land, selling wood palings and producing crops; according to reports they were making 'great headway clearing and improving their land'.[33] In 1855, Matthias' young wife, Ann, started a production line of six children. The first, Alice Jane,

15   Belinda and Emma Jane, daughters of Joseph senior.

was born on 24 July at Stanley, Circular Head, where there was a doctor, a luxury that did not exist at Table Cape which did not even have a midwife. The following year Ann returned to Stanley for the birth of her next child, William, on 10 October 1856 but he survived for only a short time. The remainder of the children were born at Table Cape: Emma Maria on 31 January 1858, who died three months later; Harriet in 1859; George

Ambrose on 7 June 1861; Sarah Ann on 13 June 1863, and Martha Matilda on 4 September 1865.

In 1856, Joseph remarried; the ceremony took place at Table Cape on 12 January, but he and his young wife, Harriet Gee, returned to Stanley shortly afterwards. Their first daughter, Emma Jane, was born on 11 December 1856; the next, Belinda, on 10 October 1858, by which stage Joseph had handed over the management of the *Emily Hotel* to Michael Lyons.[34] Joseph was now a shop keeper. Their last daughter, Henrietta (Harriet), was born on 7 March 1862 after the family had moved to Table Cape. In December 1856, the ship *Donald McKay*, arrived in Australia bringing two brothers, Thomas and William Watts, together with Ann (Mary Ann Alexander) Watts, Joseph's only daughter by his first marriage.[35] This trio from Ramsbury soon found Joseph because, on 10 July 1857, a son, Thomas William, was born at Stanley to Thomas and Ann Watts. A few days before the birth of their next child, Elizabeth Ann, on 17 February 1859, Thomas Watts, aged 40 years, a shop keeper at Circular Head, died of a brain disease. The following year Ann married William Watts. They lived and farmed near Stinking Creek, Table Cape, and had nine children. Later they moved to Flowerdale, where William died on 9 March 1896 and Ann on 11 May 1908 aged 77 years.

On Table Cape, Matthias and John and their respective families continued to prosper. In 1858, Matthias grew 3,000 bushels of wheat on part of his land which he sold at 12s. a bushel.[36] In addition he still owned his land at Deloraine which he had rented to various farmers. The most notorious episode of that year was a murder on Table Cape. The trial took place on 5 July 1858 of William Bannon who was charged with the wilful murder of Samuel Oakes on 5 May. The murder occurred either on or very close to Matthias' land. The evidence showed that John's wife, Mary Ann, amongst other things, made and sold clothes, that there was an Alexander blacksmith shop at Alexandria, that Matthias' son, Joseph, was running the Inn and that another son, Edward, was farming some 25 acres of John Alexander's land on Table Cape. Additionally, John Gadsbury, Julia's oldest boy, aged about 12 years, gave evidence. He stated that he lived with his uncle Matthias. The defence objected to John Gadsbury as a witness on the grounds that he did not understand the meaning of the oath. John Gadsbury enlightened 'His Honour' and proclaimed, 'I can't tell my age, never went to Church or Chapel in my life; never was taught catechism, the Lord's Prayer or anything of the kind.' The Judge was unimpressed with John Gadsbury, and Matthias said in his evidence that:

> the boy Gadsbury has been living with me for the last three or four months. I go to Church myself at Table Cape; the boy would not go as he says he is a Catholic. I am aware of the disgraceful state of ignorance the boy is in and I can do no good with him, I wish to return him to his father.

The lengthy case concluded with William Bannon being found not guilty.[37]

There were some light-hearted moments in the harsh life of Table Cape. Christmas Day and Boxing Day as well as New Year's Day were recognised as sporting times. There were cricket matches between Table Cape and Circular Head (Stanley) and Emu Bay (Burnie). Sometimes there were picnics on the 'Middle Paddock' of the Alexander estate; everybody came to these rare social gatherings. Another attraction was the race course. Here there were regular meetings with John Dowling as clerk of the course. The Alexanders frequently

16 First Burnie Wharf, 1880.

participated in the sport and one of the leading lights was Matthias' son, John, who trained and raced horses most successfully.[38]

Obviously, one of the main problems at Alexandria was crossing the River Inglis, to say nothing of the numerous other creeks and ravines in the area. By 1860, the Table Cape Road Trust had organised the construction of a number of bridges including one across a long and deep ravine on the Alexanders' farm. The following year the first substantial bridge was built across the Inglis.[39]

In 1860, Joseph, the elder, moved with his wife and family to Wynyard and took over the *Wynyard Arms Inn* on the Esplanade, although he retained ownership of his numerous properties in Stanley. In addition, he owned 11 acres of land near the River Inglis. In 1867, he was in charge of the *Court House Hotel* in Wynyard, which was probably a new name for the *Wynyard Arms Inn*.[40] However, when he died on 20 May 1878 from 'the decay of nature' at the age of 72 years he was described as a farmer. At the time of his death only one of his daughters, Belinda, was married. She married, in 1876, Richard Brown, the fourth child of Thomas and Maria Brown (née Davis). Over the next five years, they had three children but then it would appear that Richard died. As a keen sailor, he probably drowned at sea and this would explain why there was no death registration. In 1891, Belinda remarried; she and her new husband, Thomas Ellis, a Methodist minister, had five children and remained at Wynyard for about ten years. Then they moved to Launceston. Joseph's other two daughters, Emma Jane and Harriet, married in the next few years. Emma Jane married

Henry James White in 1881; they had six children and remained in Wynyard. Harriet married James King Percy in 1886; they had four children and after some years in Wynyard moved to Launceston. Joseph's widow remained living on the Esplanade in Wynyard for many years but moved to Launceston to be near her daughter shortly before her death on 25 May 1912. She is buried in a grave adjacent to Harriet and James Percy.

Towards the end of the 1850s, John turned his attention from farming to shipping and became very involved with marine board matters. For many years there had been serious problems with the lack of port facilities at Burnie. Ships' masters found the area treacherous and so diverted to other ports nearby causing considerable difficulties and expense to the farmers who were trying to export their produce to other parts of Tasmania and Victoria. Discussion continued over the years, but no progress was made and major problems remained with unloading both passengers and cargo even from those vessels prepared to tackle the treacherous waters. Then, in 1859, John leased a small section of the foreshore at Burnie from the Van Diemen's Land Company. In 1860, he built a framework for a 'pig-sty' wharf but a storm swept this away. By now he had moved to Burnie. In early 1862, he applied for permission to build a jetty and obtained agreement from the Van Diemen's Land Company who owned the land abutting the shore. He built a timber jetty which proved most useful, but the only way that John could obtain reimbursement for his efforts was to charge wharfage tolls. This caused considerable disquiet, and in some cases outrage, amongst the local farming population. However, no alternative was built until 1872, when the wooden jetty had almost rotted away.[41]

The new small iron pier that was erected was known locally as the 'Birdcage' but boarding or landing from a steamer was still an exciting and hazardous affair.

> Vessels anchored about half a mile out and sent passengers off in the ship's boats. If it were fine the boat generally made close to the rocks where the men passengers could get ashore on foot and ladies and children could be carried ashore by the sailors. If this could not be done, the boat lay off the end of the birdcage and the jetty crane lowered down a large cargo or coal basket into which the passengers were tumbled as gently as the pitching of the boat would allow. The signal to hoist away was not always correctly timed, with the result that the basketful of suffering humanity sometimes failed to escape the cold embrace of the next surge of the sea.[42]

John Alexander diverted his energies to ship owning. He and his son-in-law, John Jones, who had married his daughter Martha Ann in 1860, commissioned the building of a 120-ton schooner which they named the *Martha and Jane*; John Jones was her captain. Tragically, in 1870, some 10 years after their wedding, while on this ship, Captain Jones was accidentally knocked overboard and drowned.[43] He was buried in the Alexander Cemetery on Table Cape, which is a couple of miles from the lighthouse. His grave is one of the few where the headstone has survived. It reads, 'Captain Jones Aged 34 years drowned 10 July 1870, "The Lord gave and the Lord hath taken away blessed be the name of the Lord." Farewell thou loved one so good and kind, so deeply mourned by those you leave behind. Though now thou movest in realms beyond the sky Thy memory here below shall never die.' Two years later Martha Ann married Alexander Shekleton of Table Cape and they had seven children. With the loss of his son-in-law, John Alexander returned to farming on Table Cape. His son, John Charles (Hezekiah),

17   Burnie, 1883.

unmarried, described as an idiot and living in an institution, died of consumption in 1877 aged 31 years. His wife Mary died the following year, and his other daughter, Jane, who did not marry, was admitted to the institution where her brother had died, in August 1889. Although described as an idiot, the records noted that she was an epileptic.[44] She died a few months later of acute bronchitis at the age of 48 years and was buried on 24 May 1890. John lived in Wynyard for a time but he died at his property at Detention River a few miles from Table Cape on 9 June 1898 aged 85 years and was buried on Table Cape in the Alexander Cemetery.[45]

Meanwhile, Matthias, his wife and their young children, as well as his six children by his previous marriage, lived in Alexandria on Table Cape. He continued to farm his land, and from 1860 he took over the licence for the Inn.[46] He rented some 530 acres of his land in Deloraine to 15 other farmers.[47] He was apparently fit and healthy but, one day in 1865 whilst at work, he caught a chill which soon developed into pneumonia. Dr. Wilson, the local doctor, was called in but he could do nothing. Dr. Smith came on the mail track from Stanley, but, although he diagnosed the trouble, it was unfortunately too late. Thus, eight weeks after the birth of his seventh child by his second wife, on 31 October 1865, Matthias Alexander died. The event was graphically recorded by a Wynyard resident: 'The death of Matthias appeared to give the district a staggering blow. Things never appeared the same. His death was deeply regretted for all knew they had lost a sincere friend.'[48] He was the first of the three brothers to be buried in the Alexander Cemetery on Table Cape. Of all of them he was the only one to beget sons in Australia to carry on the Alexander name, and even he had six daughters. Therefore, not surprisingly, most of the Alexander descendants now spread around the world do not bear the name Alexander.

PART TWO

FREDERICK MATTHIAS ALEXANDER 1869-1904
TASMANIA AND MAINLAND AUSTRALIA

Somerset River Cam

Our dwellings stand by the riverside,
And flowers in the gardens grow,
And the good ships lie on the gleaming tide
At their moorings down below;
And the breezes dance in the quivering leaves
Where the gay birds flutter and sing,
And surely there is not a heart that grieves
This joyous and happy spring.

Down by the shore where the ocean shines
The broad white sands are seen,
Where pebbles lie, and the seaweed twines,
And the waves roll cool and green.
There is sunlight flashing on all around,
And the deepest blue above;
Of labour I hear the cheerful sound
From the beings that round me move.

There's work at the mill, where the sharp harsh saw
Whirls in its dangerous round,
And work for the men who the timber draw
Away from the saw mill ground.
There's work in the forest, the homes, the fields,
And few would their duties shirk,
For here nought greater enjoyment yields
Than happy and useful work.

And though not often there's news to tell,
And things seem heavy and slow,
And though our troubles will sometimes swell
As troubles will do, we know,
Our homes are here, and our work is here;
We've butter, we've bread, we've jam,
And those places are few that are held more dear
Than Somerset on the Cam.

Somerset correspondent *Launceston Examiner* 25 December 1885

6
EARLY LIFE

The death of Matthias was a severe blow not only for his widow, Ann, but also for his 12 children. Ann was left with six children aged 10 years to two months. Fortunately for her, John's son-in-law John Jones came to the rescue to sort out Matthias' complicated financial affairs. He had left considerable land and money, although over 500 acres of land at Deloraine was rented to tenants as was some of Table Cape land. Matthias left his house and its contents to his wife and his estate to his second son, Joseph, but each child of both marriages received the significant sum of £417.[1] Obviously, life was difficult for Ann, although she continued to run the *Table Cape Inn* for a short time, but by 1870 Thomas Wiseman was the proprietor.[2] In that year Ann married John Reid, a carpenter, and the couple moved to Burnie; they had three children. John Reid died on 9 April 1904 and Ann on 30 September 1912.

When Matthias died a number of his children were already married. His oldest son, Edward, married Elizabeth Chambers née Bartleman, a Scottish widow with two children, at Port Sorell on 30 June 1860. He returned to farm at Table Cape and the couple had three children. However, a year or so after Matthias' death they had moved to Flowerdale, where Edward died in 1912. His wife lived to be 100 years old and died in 1935 still living in the old farmstead with its earth floors. Until about two years before her death she drove her horse-drawn buggy into Wynyard on a regular basis.[3]

In the same year, 1860, Matthias' next son, Joseph, married the second daughter of John Dowling, Sarah. The couple remained at Table Cape for a few years; Joseph continued to farm, was the local shoemaker, and in 1867 he became the innkeeper of the *Table Cape Hotel*.[4] In 1869 he and his wife moved to Jacob's Boat Harbour, Rocky Cape, a few miles from Table Cape towards Stanley.[5] However, when it was decided to re-route the track and make a road from Wynyard to Stanley, Joseph found himself isolated. So, in 1875, he moved to Burnie, first as a store-keeper and then as a hotel keeper; he took over the licence of the *Ship Hotel* in Burnie in 1880 on the retirement of licensee W.H. Oldaker.[6] By the end of 1885, Joseph declared his main occupation as farming. He lived on his farm in Upper Burnie on the New Country Road (View Road) in his house Kia Ora. It was here that he remained with his wife, Sarah, until his death in January 1917. Sarah died on 26 January 1929.[7] The couple had 14 children, some of whom maintained an interest in the hotel trade for many years, particularly their oldest son, known as JT, who built the *Club Hotel* at Burnie in 1912.

The year before his death, Matthias' oldest daughter Mary Ann married a master mariner John Stark at the Table Cape Church on 19 July 1864. The couple had one child, Janet. Shortly after this John drowned, and on 10 December 1868 Mary Ann married John Wells,

18 Mrs. Claire Alexander's house
given to her as a wedding present
by Joseph Alexander the younger.

a farmer in the Somerset area near the Cam. They farmed there for many years and had 11 children. John died on 31 March 1892 and Mary Ann went to Wynyard where, on 27 July 1907, she married Thomas Albert Senior. In the late 1920s she went to Melbourne, where she died on 14 January 1940 just before her 93rd birthday. By this time three of her 12 children had predeceased her.

Shortly after his father's death, in 1866, Matthias the younger married Elizabeth Law at the Chapel in Wynyard and they had five children. He became a carter and lived with his wife for a number of years on the Law's farm near Burnie. The highlight of 1871 was the building of the *Mary Bannatyne*, the largest ship ever constructed on the nearby River Cam. She was a brigantine of 115 tons. On the day of the launching people gathered from all parts of the Coast to watch the spectacle. Not surprisingly, given the weight, the wooden slipway sank into the sand and the ship refused to move. The launch was postponed. Matthias had a solution and departed for his draught horse Peter. A little while later a 40 foot long pole was secured as a lever and attached to a treble purchase block and tackle, Peter exerted all his strength and, to the delight of the crowd, the ship glided into the river.[8] It is interesting to note that Frederick Matthias' much loved horse, some 60 years later, was also called Peter. Obviously Peter was a favourite name for the Alexanders.

The next recorded incident to involve Matthias junior occurred in 1873. A Mr. Keoppler, The Don Company manager at Mount Bischoff, fell ill and, although he was treated by a doctor who struggled up the mountain to see him, he died, much to the distress of his workforce. The doctor had returned to Burnie before the death but he had assumed that nothing could save the manager; therefore, he had arranged for Matthias to take his best bullocks and an empty dray up the mountain to recover the body. Well aware of the dangers involved, Matthias had insisted on a payment of £10 before he was prepared to undertake

19 Martin Alexander and his family.

the commission. He obtained the guarantee and set forth for Waratah near Mount Bischoff. When he arrived the coffin was loaded into the dray but, before he could depart, he was addressed by a spokesman for the workers. This man praised Matthias for his humanitarian action in attempting such a difficult journey to recover a body and assured him that they could not let him depart without offering him some recompense for his actions. As they were poor working men they could not contribute large sums of money but they had collected £10. Matthias, it appears, was softened almost to tears at this unexpected generosity and without more ado pocketed the £10 and set out with his cargo for Burnie. The trip down the mountain was most hazardous and it took Matthias three days.[9] Perhaps he did earn his double payment! Sadly, in 1877, his wife aged 30 years died from consumption. Their youngest son, Albert, who later fathered 11 children, was brought up by Edward and Elizabeth Alexander at Flowerdale. The next youngest child, Belinda, may also have lived in that household as she married a son of Edward and Elizabeth. In 1878 Matthias married Catherine Atkinson, née Saunders, at the Primitive Methodist Church in Penguin. They had two children which, when added to the ten that Catherine already had by her previous marriage and Matthias' three, possibly four, made it quite a busy household. After only a few years, Catherine left home to live with Henry Charles and, as a result, Matthias obtained a

20 Jim Alexander, grandson of Martin Alexander, at work 1987.

divorce on the grounds of adultery in 1892.[10] The following year he married Mary Hartlett and they went to Waratah where Mary died in 1907. Matthias then departed to Melbourne where he died on 20 April 1912.

Matthias senior's other two sons, John and Martin, both remained in the Table Cape area after their father's death, although the youngest Martin was the only one to remain for the rest of his life farming on Table Cape. On 14 April 1880 he married Maria Grace Bramich; they had ten sons and two daughters, one of whom died in childhood. Martin died on 24 June 1906 leaving his wife with six of the children under 16 years old. Maria lived another 45 years and died in Wynyard on 28 August 1951, when by all accounts she had become a rather difficult old lady.

Initially, John continued to live at Alexandria where he worked as blacksmith. Although he had received little formal education, he was a man endowed with considerable common sense, innate practical ability and expertise with horses. As a young man he learnt his trade from an experienced blacksmith and wheelwright who also made light carriages and iron and steel implements for farming and domestic use. John became a highly skilled craftsman who took a great pride in his work and he was equally successful in fashioning a set of fire tongs, poker, shovel, plough share and farm tools as he was in shoeing a horse with his own home-made horseshoes. He could mend all types of machinery and was particularly adept at repairing wheels. He would cut the tyre and remove it and then weld the separated points

21 Jim Alexander's house at Alexandria.

so that the tyre would fit back on the wheel easily. In addition, he could temper steel implements of all kinds and his help was frequently sought by those working on the farms.[11]

On 6 February 1866 he married 18-year-old Betsy Brown in the schoolroom at Somerset on the Cam. Betsy was the second daughter of constable Thomas Brown and Maria Davis, who had married in Launceston in April 1844. The Browns had six children, all of whom were born at various addresses in Launceston: Jane Maria on 13 January 1845; Betsy on 24 September 1847; Thomas James on 28 September 1849; Richard on 28 June 1851; Mary Ann on 23 September 1853 who died of whooping cough some 14 weeks later, and Agnes Tasmania on 28 February 1855. At the end of that year Thomas Brown, then a district constable in Launceston, went to Circular Head on board the *Titania*, a new iron steamboat that traded up and down the coast between Launceston and Circular Head calling at many of the intermediate ports. Commanded by Captain Brown, she sailed from Launceston every Tuesday and returned from Circular Head on Thursdays. On Thursday 20 December, Thomas Brown, Captain Brown and the second mate left the *Titania* in one of the small boats and went out cray fishing. The little boat had three oars and a sail. Apparently Captain Brown and the second mate were pulling and Thomas Brown was steering. By the evening the little ship had not returned to the *Titania* so a search was mounted but nothing was found. It was presumed that all three were drowned.[12]

This unhappy event left poor Maria in a very difficult situation with six children under 11 years old. So it was perhaps fortunate that, a little less than a year later, in October 1856, she married Captain Thomas Lewis. The marriage took place at St Mark's Church, Collingwood, near Melbourne. Thomas Lewis was a sailor from Haverfordwest in Wales where he was born the son of a blacksmith. He went to Tasmania as a young man and was

22 Betsy.   23 John as a young man.

most successful, although some of his activities gave the authorities cause for concern. He bought land in the Somerset district near the River Cam and it was here that Maria brought her young family.[13] Initially, he had the licence of the *Ship Inn*, then in 1858 he built a house and obtained a liquor licence for this property which he called the *Ferry House Inn*; from here he ran a ferry service across the Cam.[14] He was a major timber trader for the area but his principal occupation and interest was shipping. He had joined the Merchant Navy as an apprentice in 1845 and became a master in 1851; between then and 1874, when he applied for master mariner status, he was master of the *Ariel*, the *John Bull*, the *Ida*, the *Helen Ann* and the *Maldon Lewis*. Both the latter ships he owned. In 1875, he had built, on the Cam river, the 53-ton schooner, the *John Lewis*, and she traded from the Cam to Melbourne until 1892 when she was sold.[15] Meanwhile, the indefatigable Maria was producing more children. Between 1857 and 1870 she had a further eight: Ann Victoria, Margaret Maldon, Rachel, Maria, Amelia Frances, John Reynolds, Maud Mary and Rhoda. In fact, Maria was still producing children when her daughter Betsy, having married gave birth to her first son,

24 John, *c*.1900.

With permission of the Pioneer Village Museum, Burnie, Tasmania.

25 *Ferry House Inn* on the Cam.

26 The house today.

Frederick Matthias (FM), on 20 January 1869 at Table Cape. His baptism is registered at St George's Church, Burnie on 27 February 1869.

The following year, 1870, another bridge was completed across the River Inglis for the Wynyard to Stanley road.[16] This bridge was upstream and effectively diverted all the traffic from Alexandria and Table Cape. John and Betsy appreciating that this would have a serious effect on John's blacksmith business decided to move the short distance, some two miles, to Wynyard. They occupied a cottage with an adjoining smithy and just under an acre of land, the property of John's uncle Joseph, who with his wife and three daughters lived almost next door.[17] It was in this cottage that their second son, Arthur John, was born on 16 August 1870. Following the normal pattern for that time, Betsy produced a child nearly every two years for over 20 years. Her next child, Agnes Mary, was born on 4 November 1872, followed by Albert Redden (AR) on 15 June 1874; Richard Thomas (Dick) arrived on 21 September 1876 and Amy Maria followed a little over two years later on 23 January 1879. Her youngest daughter, May, was born on 25 May 1881, followed by Horace on 28 April 1883, then Beaumont on 28 February 1886, and finally Stanley Gordon on 18 July 1892, a total of ten children.

Wynyard in the 1870s was a small township of about 150 people situated near the mouth of the River Inglis close to where Camp Creek enters the river on what was then a marshy, sandy rather barren area. The land immediately adjoining Camp Creek became the commercial centre. By the river there was a wharf and along the river bank and the creek there were various jetties. Across the Inglis was the magnificent headland of Table Cape, a rich and

27   Wynyard from the ruins of King's Farm, 1879.

28   Camp Creek, Wynyard.

fertile farming area, though at this time some of the Cape was still thick forest as was the area surrounding Wynyard. To clear these huge trees was a formidable undertaking, particularly with the tools available. Local Tasmanian folklore maintains that the trees were so enormous they could not be cut with an eight foot saw. At Camp Creek there was a prosperous saw mill, the owners of which, Quiggin and Moore, built a wooden tramway for horse-drawn trucks which ran from the nearby forest, where they owned 4,000 acres of land, to their mill. They shipped much of the timber across the Bass Strait to other parts of Australia and New Zealand.

The township was a centre for the surrounding agricultural districts but the roads, which were little more than tracks, were very poor and frequently became quagmires in wet weather, making the journey along the coast to Somerset, some seven miles distance, or to Burnie, an additional five miles, very hazardous in bad weather. The principal means of communication were the electric telegraph and the overland mail.[18] When rich tin deposits were discovered in December 1871 at Mount Bischoff some 42 miles away, access was a major problem; even the Hellyer gold diggings with a Chinese work force about 26 miles away were very remote. In the middle of 1878, 100 people from the Wynyard area signed a petition to Parliament which stated that the community was 'praying for a metalled road from Wynyard to Bischoff'.[19] In June of the same year, a little bridge between Table Cape and Wynyard was washed away in severe storms and it was some months before a new one was erected. In the meantime, people had to wait until low tide before attempting to cross

29 Low tide, River Inglis.

the creek.[20] By the end of the following year, the bridge across the Cam river at Somerset was completed. This benefited everyone except possibly Betsy's mother and step-father, Captain Lewis, who amongst other things had operated the Cam ferry. They moved to Melbourne shortly afterwards.

The most satisfactory way to travel to Launceston, approximately 100 miles away, or Hobart was by sea. The Inglis river with adjoining Camp Creek were busy waterways with a great variety of ships, from the large commercial vessels taking passengers and freight to other places in Australia and beyond to little boats ferrying people from Wynyard to Table Cape.[21] It was considered a much more pleasant trip than the walk along the muddy track to the bridge. The only problem was that the Inglis was tidal and the current flowed very fast as it still does today. In a small rowing boat in a strong ebbing tide the journey was difficult if not dangerous, and a number of people were drowned including several small children; other children drowned when they fell into the river while playing by the river bank. For the young Alexander children the river was a wonderful place and Richard and Amy in particular enjoyed rowing about in their flat bottomed boat with their friend Arnold Alpheus Peart.

Arnold Peart, who was three months younger than Amy, was the youngest son of William and Emma who had married at Table Cape in 1857 when Alexandria and not Wynyard was the centre. Emma was the daughter of John Thewlis, who farmed on the Cape, and the younger sister of Ann, who had married Matthias Alexander senior in 1854.

30   Alexander family with Arnold Peart, *c*.1889.

William was by trade a carpenter and during the 1860s he undertook many building works including the provision of a school, improvements to the little port jetty and the erection of a bridge across the River Inglis which was known for years as Peart's bridge, and in 1870 he was appointed harbour master. He and his wife lived on Table Cape at their property of some 40 acres near the Inglis and their family steadily grew in size. Although one child died at the age of three months, by 1870 Emma and he had four children. Then disaster struck and there was an outbreak of diphtheria and within a week all the children were dead. For Emma this was particularly sad as less than four months before, her mother, at the age of 66 years, had been crushed to death by a falling tree. Undoubtedly the small community was devastated by the tragedy and young couples like John and Betsy must have been relieved that the disease did not spread and kill their baby, Frederick Matthias. The Pearts continued to live on the banks of the Inglis and had four more children all of whom survived to adulthood. William became an accomplished boatman and took part in a number of sea rescue operations so undoubtedly he ensured that the boat he produced for his son Arnold and the Alexander children was as safe as it was possible to be.[22] Clearly he taught them boating skills to help them enjoy the river.

Despite the remote and largely inaccessible location, the little township of Wynyard had developed during the 20 years since the first Alexanders had arrived at this inhospitable, heavily forested place. Travelling around the area had become progressively easier with the provision of bridges over many of the numerous rivers; some of the tracks had been gravelled, which made life a little less arduous for the stage coaches, horse carts and bullock drays, although frequently around Wynyard carts were stuck up to their axles in thick red mud. Transport remained a major problem for Wynyard for years to come as the railway line to the town was not opened until 1913. Before this, most people rode horses or travelled in horse-drawn carts or coaches. By the 1870s Wynyard had a few streets, with 14 wooden houses, two hotels, the *Court House* and the *Commercial*, and some shops including the post office. One of these streets became the main central road and was called Goldie Street although it was, and still is, known as The Street. It was here that the shopping area slowly developed. Some of these shops, such as Stutterd's general store, were most impressive wooden buildings with verandahs, which in winter kept people dry and prevented the footpaths becoming too muddy, and in summer provided a cool area out of the strong sun and protected the shop frontage and thus the shop's contents from the bright light. One of the main problems was that all the buildings were made of wood and were a major fire hazard, particularly in summer.

A small school was established on Table Cape in 1856 with 17 pupils. In 1871, the first public government school was opened in Wynyard, a shingle-roofed, single-room timber structure in Hogg Street opposite the Alexander home, which was very convenient for the children of John and Betsy who attended this all-ages, all-abilities establishment. By this stage, the township had a reading room which soon developed into a library. It also had an Episcopalian Church and a Roman Catholic Church and, in 1878, an Independent Church was built at Table Cape. The church was opened in November with Rev. L.H. Palfreyman as the Minister.[23] This little wooden building was physically moved to Wynyard in the early 1890s and not replaced with a brick church until 1921. When the church came to Wynyard, John and Betsy had their youngest child, Stanley Gordon, baptised into the Methodist faith, the baptisms of all the other children being registered at the parish church of St George in Burnie. A number of the Alexanders were married in accordance with the Methodist Rites during the 1880s, as was John and Betsy's second son, Arthur, in 1898. A Gospel Hall was built very near the Alexander home and, in November 1879, it was decided to form a Temperance Society there to be called the Emu Bay and Table Cape Band of Hope.[24] On 16 December, a public meeting was held to 'advocate the principles of total abstinence'. The Rev. Palfreyman was elected chairman of the meeting and it opened with singing and prayers. Thereafter, various people contributed to the proceedings, including Joseph Alexander senior's widow, Harriet, with her daughter, Emma; they sang 'The mother and her dying child' and 'Touch not the cup'. Harriet's youngest daughter, Henrietta, sang 'Dare to be a Daniel,' and John Alexander read 'The Teetotal Mill' and then gave his comments, which were described by the local reporter 'as good common sense'.[25] By the following

September, some 60 people in Wynyard had signed the pledge; the Band of Hope was
proving most successful and was energetically supported by Harriet whose piano was used
for meetings. There were well-patronised tea parties. The main loser from this turn of events
was Betsy's older sister Jane and her husband, James Pearce, who was the licensee of the
Court House Hotel.[26] Soon they accepted defeat and, in November 1880, moved to Waratah
where they opened another hotel.[27]

So it was in this isolated place that the young Frederick Matthias Alexander and his
brothers and sisters spent their childhood: a wonderful natural area by the sea with one of
the most scenic headlands in the world; a place with few people but large areas of unspoilt
countryside providing unlimited opportunities for children. Living as they did in a small
cottage next to the smithy, life indoors must have been cramped, so all of them learnt to
enjoy outdoor pursuits. The most essential thing in life was to learn to ride, otherwise at
Wynyard one could not travel very far. Both John and Betsy were expert riders. John was
an excellent judge of horses and his opinion was often sought by people in Wynyard and
the surrounding district. He could handle a horse in any situation and he became the self-
taught veterinary expert of Wynyard. He learnt some of his skills from his friend, the local
doctor Thomas Wilson, who lived on the east side of Camp Creek at a place known to this
day as Doctors' Rocks. His ability to help horses and cattle in difficulties was recognised
throughout the district. As a horseman he was extremely capable, often winning races at the
local meetings. Betsy was similarly a most accomplished horsewoman and was known locally
as the lady with the magic hands by the way she held the reins. For the local horse shows
and race meetings she always had a choice of four or five horses and the one she chose to
ride usually won.[28] She rode everywhere and after the birth of her first child she would strap
the baby Frederick Matthias (FM) on to her back and gallop off across the bush jumping
any hurdle that came in her way. All the Alexander children learnt to ride from a very early
age and FM and his brothers were to become particularly accomplished horsemen maintaining a life-long love of horses.

There were a number of other sporting activities including regular cricket matches
against local teams. Usually the Table Cape team, as the Wynyard side was called, won and
sometimes there were about 200 spectators.[29] Betsy's brother Richard was a regular member
of the team. He was also an impressive sailor and usually won races at the annual New Year's
Day Regatta held on the Inglis.[30] From late 1879, there were regular wood chopping
matches and John Alexander was in great demand because the wood choppers were always
confident if he had tempered their axes.[31] More cultural activities included concerts, when
Betsy's step sisters, the Misses Lewis, came over from Somerset and played the piano and
sang. There were lectures and magic lantern shows in the Reading Room and sometimes
there were dances; on one occasion the first dance was a quadrille.[32] There were regular
entertainments in the Assembly Rooms given by touring groups, including the Wheeler
Comedy Troupe and the Walker Family of Bellringers.[33]

As a small child, FM was delicate and had difficulty digesting food and so Dr. Wilson
was a regular visitor to the cottage, becoming a great friend of the family. Betsy learnt a
number of medical skills from him and would frequently go and help the sick. Sometimes
she delivered babies when Dr. Wilson was unable to attend. She partially solved FM's

problem when she discovered at an early stage that he could digest goat's milk, a love of which was to remain with him for the rest of his life. Although he continued to have medical problems, a healthy outdoor life was the prescribed cure. At home, Dr. Wilson and Father O'Callaghan, the Roman Catholic priest, were regular visitors and they had a standing invitation to look in at meal times. Later, after his arrival in Wynyard in 1879, Mr. Robertson, the school master, had a similar invitation and frequently came to eat with the family. There was always a side of bacon and a cooked ham ready for emergencies, carved by father John. He would not allow anyone else to do it as he believed that it was a special task requiring great skill and practise. He took the view that the ham needed as much care as a baby. Certainly, the smell of the bacon being cooked was remembered forever by the Alexander children and FM maintained that it gave everyone a hearty appetite. He also believed that the fact the pigs had plenty of peas in their diet was the reason the fat survived the cooking and did not melt away, which was his experience later in life. Father O'Callaghan was particularly fond of bacon and regularly came to breakfast. The butter, in a basket containing several pounds, came from the Alexander farm up on Table Cape, there was plenty of fruit and vegetables that grew well in the virgin soil, a ready supply of fresh fish and good quality meat and an ample supply of crystal clear spring water. Betsy was an excellent cook and produced memorable meals on her very rudimentary cooking range. She gave all her children, and in particular FM, a love of good basic food. She was always busy and during this period was surrounded by small children, her first eight youngsters being born in a little over 14 years. Her hands were never idle and even when she was sitting in her upright chair beside the fire she always had some sewing. She was a most creative and artistic woman who designed and made all the clothes required by her family and everything else that was needed in the home.[34]

Betsy was determined that all her children should learn to read and write well and she ensured they attended the Sunday School which, by January 1881, had 90 youngsters with twelve teachers.[35] The local school opposite the Alexander cottage in Hogg Street provided a basic form of education under difficult circumstances as there was only one room and one master. It was fortunate for FM that 1879 saw the arrival of Mr. Robertson as school master. FM proved a most disruptive influence on the little class and his ever-questioning habit had caused severe difficulties. Very quickly the new young master realised that every one of his pupils was suffering, including FM, so he decided that the only solution was to expel the disruptive pupil and allow the rest of the children some peace during school time in order to learn. This wise teacher recognised that the young FM had considerable innate ability and after school he instructed the boy individually, which amongst other things introduced FM to poetry and Shakespeare and gave him a life-long love of drama. This private tuition was invaluable; FM obtained a sound basic education and was able to progress at his own speed, but perhaps more importantly it enabled him to spend his days exploring the countryside. Here he began to develop his powers of observation. His father, John, was very fond of saying 'we rarely see what is at our feet'. Later in life FM was to explain this as 'few people see what is obvious either as something observed by the use of the eyes or something understood by the use of the thinking or reasoning process'.[36] Clearly his father's words made a deep impression on the young boy and he spent much of his time when everyone else was at school observing animals and their behaviour. Thus, these few years were to prove vital to FM's work later in his life and it was at Wynyard that he started to learn the art of watching and observing. He thoroughly enjoyed the outdoor life as he rode his pony, swam in the sea and the river, rowed his boat, walked through the forest and across the lovely headland of Table Cape and learnt to hunt, shoot and fish. Fishing became very popular in the area, particularly with the Chinese who were often seen dragging their nets on a calm evening.[37] He spent many happy days on the Alexander farm at Table Cape now run by his uncle Martin. He had an ideal childhood, possible largely because of the wise, understanding and capable Mr. Robertson.

The little township of Wynyard remained small throughout the 1870s and by the Census of 1881 contained 168 people with 900 in the district.[38] John Alexander and his family prospered and, in June 1881, John together with Joseph Alderson stood surety of £100 each for Patrick Linnane when he was charged with perjury.[39] At that time, a 4lb. loaf of bread cost 7d., a pound of sugar was 4½d. and a pound of peas, barley or rice cost 2d.[40] The highlight of the year was the visit to Wynyard by the Governor and Lady Lefroy, accompanied by the Premier, Mr. Gilblin, and the Colonial Secretary, Mr. Moore. Sir John Lefroy spent an afternoon at the school talking to all the children while the Premier addressed a large assembly of the adult community.[41] This visit came at a time of hardship for the farmers of the area as most of the crops had failed, the oats were blighted, the wheat was rusty, the potatoes had died from lack of rain, and the fruit crops were poor. In addition there was a serious outbreak of measles which began in October 1880 and continued for some four months. Dr. Wilson's remedy for the condition was gin! Plenty of gin appears to have been successful as only one person in the area died, Joseph Alexander's 15-year-old son Walter.[42] Despite the difficulties, the population of the little township continued to have entertainments in the Assembly Rooms, sometimes given by travelling groups and on occasions by members of the community, to raise funds for a variety of projects including the provision of a piano for the Assembly Rooms.[43] When the new Governor made his Vice-Regal visit in 1882, some 50 horsemen rode five miles out of Wynyard to escort him to the town where about 130 children sang 'God Save The Queen' in greeting. The Governor began his formal visit to the public school at 8.30 the following day.[44] At the end of the school year various prizes were awarded, Agnes receiving one for regular attendance and Richard one for winning the 30 yards' race for under seven-year-olds.[45]

Early in the new year of 1883, Captain Lewis with his wife, Betsy's mother Maria, departed from Somerset and went to live in Melbourne, although Captain Lewis continued to trade his vessel, the *John Lewis*, between Somerset and Melbourne for the next few years.[46] In April, Betsy gave birth to her eighth child, Horace, and four months later her husband John had a riding accident. Such events were common but this particular fall was serious and merited comment in a Launceston newspaper which stated that 'Dr. Wilson attended him and he was progressing as well as could be expected.'[47] At this difficult time, with eight children under 15 years old, none of whom were working, and no state sickness provision, Horace contracted meningitis. The baby cried and screamed endlessly but, despite the best efforts of Betsy with her 'healing hands' and Dr. Wilson, the baby died on 11 October at the age of 5 months. The trauma of this event was to remain an abiding memory for the older Alexander children. During this unhappy time, Father O'Callaghan's parish was divided and he was moved from Wynyard to Burnie to cover Burnie and Waratah; Wynyard and Stanley now formed a separate parish.[48]

While the death of Horace and John's accident had a significant effect on the Alexander family, in Wynyard life continued in much the same way. A new bridge was built across Camp Creek; the Assembly Rooms received a new roof and the long-awaited piano; and to the delight of the townspeople a brass band was formed.[49] The culmination of a bad year for the Alexanders occurred a few days before Christmas 1883 when Betsy's step father, Captain Lewis, was badly injured while the *John Lewis* was being loaded with logs. One log fell crushing the Captain beneath it, and men rushed to extricate him from his predicament but he bled severely and they did not expect him to live. Although he survived he had to remain in Somerset for many weeks recovering.[50]

During 1884, the main project in Wynyard was to organise an agricultural show. A committee was formed and many events were held to raise funds for an exhibition building and prizes for the show. In addition, there were entertainments, concerts, athletic events and bazaars organised to raise funds to pay for more instruments for the Brass Band.[51] The town continued to expand albeit slowly, and by the end of 1884 the Assembly Rooms were extended, new houses were built, a new bridge replaced the old and dangerous one across the River Inglis to Table Cape and the roads were improved. Particularly significant was the work carried out to Goldie Street and residents hoped that the following winter they would not have to walk 'up to their knees in mud' as they tried to go down the main Wynyard street.[52] During the last few weeks of the year, Mr. Burnett gave lectures throughout the area proclaiming the virtues of abstinence and during the tour some 450 people in Burnie, Wynyard, Stanley and the district areas signed the pledge.[53] On Boxing Day the Pastoral and Agricultural Society organised a number of events including horse races, athletics, a tug of war and, in the evening, a concert and a trapeze artist display. People came from far and near for the event. Wynyard had never seen such an array of vehicles: from a modest spring dray to buggy and pair and a coach and four. Two days later there was a chopping match with 12 contestants and many enthusiastic supporters who managed completely to 'block' the Esplanade.[54]

In 1885, the new exhibition building (a construction some 120 feet long and 24 feet wide built on the banks of the Inglis) was opened and a fancy dress ball was held to commemorate the occasion.[55] In May, the first Table Cape Agricultural Show was held and about 1,000 people attended, some of whom travelled from Burnie aboard the *Wellington*. The day was glorious and Wynyard was crowded with people from far and near. The new exhibition building proved a most suitable venue for all the vegetable and floral displays and the standard of the displays of stock animals was high. Apparently the Brass Band played to the enjoyment of all; certainly, the whole event was declared a resounding success. In October another show was held, and although the weather was gloomy and overcast there were about 150 entries and a large attendance of spectators. The event was highly successful and enjoyed by everyone who attended.[56] Throughout the year, there were numerous visits by performing tour companies such as Hall and Hamilton's Electric Sparks, Messrs. Dean and Standfield Company, Miss Georgie Smithson, Miss Marian Medway's Dramatic Company,

the Australian Dwarfs and Magnetic Lady Company and Matthew's Circus, whose performance was attended by some 400 people. There were a number of entertainments performed
by local people to raise funds for various projects and all these ventures were well attended.[57]
There were sporting fixtures and meetings of clubs such as the Rifle Club, and on Boxing
Day about 1,000 people attended a most successful sports day where the events included
horse jumping, chopping matches and a tug of war.[58] The Bishop of Tasmania visited to
conduct a confirmation service.

The River Inglis was a focal point for the township. In May, the SS. *Australia* visited,
and at 260 tons she was the largest steamer ever to have come alongside the wharf. She was
successfully loaded with 35 tons of potatoes and other produce and a day later sailed to
Burnie.[59] The river continued to provide entertainment and drama. One day the resident
engineer, Mr. Bell, was going across the river in a boat when the sea was rough and the
tide was ebbing. Suddenly there was a gust of wind from the shore and Mr. Bell, unable
to row against the tide and wind, was fast disappearing out to sea. Desperately, he grabbed
a marker beacon as he was being swept by, his boat disappeared from under him and
careered out to sea while he was left clutching the beacon with, according to an onlooker,
a degree of affection seldom, if ever, seen even in a ballroom, his lower half embraced by
the surging tide. Fortunately help was at hand, and a local fisherman experienced with the
ways of the river rescued Mr. Bell.[60]

By the latter half of 1885, the time was drawing near when the oldest Alexander would
need to find regular employment and earn money. The problem had been solved temporarily
by Mr. Robertson, the headmaster, who had employed FM to assist at the school, which
meant that his education could continue. But now he was nearly 17 years old and the oldest
of the family and, money being short, he had to obtain full-time paid employment and help
with the family finances. Therefore it was not possible for him to try to qualify as a teacher.
Moreover, Mr. Robertson was returning to England early in 1886 for a visit and a new
teacher would be appointed. FM was not physically strong and was not suited to manual
work; therefore, there was little available to him in Wynyard and so, late in 1885, he made
the journey to the booming town of Waratah to try and find clerical work.

7

WARATAH, WYNYARD AND MELBOURNE

He sent the flint stones flying, but the pony kept his feet,
He cleared the fallen timber in his stride,
And the man from Snowy River never shifted in his seat–
It was grand to see that mountain horseman ride.
Through the stringy barks and saplings, on the rough and broken ground,
Down the hillside at a racing pace he went;
And he never drew the bridle till he landed safe and sound,
At the bottom of that terrible descent.

Andrew Barton (Banjo) Paterson: *The Man from Snowy River*

The discovery of tin in December 1871 at Mount Bischoff had transformed the area, once a most inaccessible place just over 40 miles, as the crow flies, from Wynyard and about the same distance from Burnie. Mount Bischoff was surrounded by thick forest and to cut a track from the coast up to the mountain was a formidable task. Initially some ore was excavated and taken to Burnie from where it was shipped to Melbourne; the ore proved to be extremely rich. In 1873, the Mount Bischoff Tin Mining Company took over the mine and a small centre formed at Waratah near the Waratah river about a mile from the mountain, with a tramway built to the mining area.[1] Climatically the area was difficult, with regular rainfall and heavy winter snow, but access to Waratah also proved a major problem. Moving men, machinery and supplies through the dense forest and thick undergrowth a climb of some 2,000 feet from the coast to Waratah proved almost impossible. Eventually a track was cut which was difficult for pack horses and a major challenge for bullock drays as for months at a time it was a morass. In the early days it was alleged that the trip from Burnie to Waratah was about 50 miles up the tracks and a return trip took about 10 days. With constant use and the felling of thousands and thousands of trees the track improved, and by 1878 a horse-drawn tram on wooden rails was in operation to within three miles of Waratah.[2] The wooden tracks deteriorated rapidly in the wet conditions and the ride was very uncomfortable, taxing the horses almost beyond endurance.[3] This system was superseded in 1884 by a steam train on conventional iron rails.[4] A regular, if not always reliable, train service commenced in March 1885 and took three and a half hours.

The tiny outpost of a few people in 1873 developed rapidly in the true tradition of mining towns. By the early 1880s there were three hotels, one of which, *Pearce's Hotel*, was owned and run by Betsy's sister Jane and her husband James, two boarding houses, a number of shops, including one run by the Stutterds of Wynyard, and tradesmen of every description.

31   Mount Bischoff train at Burnie, 1884.

32   Waratah, *c.*1920.

33   Old Railway Bridge.

There was a hospital, a large meeting hall where the Mechanics Institute held regular functions, a well-stocked library, a games room, a bank, a post office, a police post and a school but only two metalled roads; the other roads were often knee-deep in chocolate-coloured sticky mud.[5] There was plenty of entertainment and visiting groups and individual artists were a regular feature; in addition, there was a local brass band.[6] Frequently, there were sports events and teams from Burnie and Wynyard and sometimes further away came to play cricket and football. Bazaars were held to raise money for a variety of projects. The Anglican and Roman Catholic churches held regular services and the Salvation Army was active. Perhaps one of the most memorable years was 1884 when, in March, the electric lights were switched on in the dressing sheds, a notable achievement.[7] A little later other mining workshops and offices were also lighted. In July, the new railway from Burnie to Waratah was completed and a banquet was held to celebrate the event.[8] The weather was bad and the gaily decorated train arrived from Burnie in heavy rain which by evening had become snow.[9] There were approximately 1,000 men working at the mine and another 1,000 people living at Waratah. The Mechanics Institute organised nightly social events and the four hotels with their bars were popular places, although one of these establishments, the *Waratah Hotel*, the first hotel in the town, was destroyed by fire in August 1885.[10]

It is perhaps not surprising that FM decided this booming town was the place to seek employment. Many of his friends and some of his relations were already at Waratah, where his uncle and aunt, James and Jane Pearce, ran the now well-established *Pearce's Hotel*. The town was part of Father O'Callaghan's parish and he was a regular visitor, frequently conducting services and marriages, and FM's old school teacher, Mr. Robertson's predecessor

Mr. James Seagrave, was the bank manager. FM went to his uncle's hotel which was about 100 yards from where the ore was crushed, the continuous noise of this procedure causing him some sleepless nights when he first arrived. Later, he had a greater difficulty on Saturday night when at midnight the battery was shut down for 24 hours and peace reigned.[11] Mr. Frank Horne, the company accountant of the Mount Bischoff Tin Mining Company, also lived at *Pearce's Hotel* and he offered FM a job as a clerk in his office. Both he and the mine manager, Mr. Kayser, were very kind and helpful to FM during his time at Waratah. The young Alexander progressed well and soon obtained an increase in salary. After a few months he also became the collector of rates, a charge levied to maintain the roads, and subsequently he acted as the agent for the Life Insurance Company recommended by the officials to their miners and other workers. With three sources of income, FM's quality of life began to improve and he was able to save some money.

Life in Waratah was busy, for in this isolated place people worked hard but also enjoyed their leisure time. The facilities were steadily improving, and by the time FM arrived there were proposals to build a new railway station. The Mechanics Institute intended to build a substantial new hall at a cost of over £1,000 and the Recreation Committee had plans to extend and improve the sports ground and the adjoining facilities. Football and cricket matches against local teams and athletics meetings were regular features.[12] A racing club was formed and a race course built near the railway line, and an amateur dramatic club was established.[13] Every month a travelling entertainment company or circus made the trip to Waratah and provided a wide range of productions. There were numerous locally produced entertainments, dances and other fund raising activities for a diverse number of requirements such as the Waratah hospital, the cemetery and a new Mechanics hall. Shortly after FM's arrival, Mr. Horne as Vice President and Captain of the Waratah Gymnastics Club persuaded FM to become Secretary of the Club.[14] They both joined the newly formed drama club which gave regular entertainments. Of particular note was the production of *Ticket of Leave Man* in September 1886 which was heralded an outstanding success. Both Mr. Horne as Mr. Gibeon and FM as Sam Willoughby took part; the performance, which was greeted by round after round of applause, was considered to be the best ever given at Waratah by either professional or amateur performers.[15] Additionally, FM tried to teach himself to play the violin, performed recitals and spent considerable time training his horse, Estelle, on which he won the Consolation race at the end of year meeting, beating the favourite by a length and a half. His prize was £7 10s.[16] The family came up from Wynyard to watch the event and stayed a few days in the township and, not to be outdone by her older brother, Amy participated in the New Year's Day sports and came third in the girl scholars' race.[17]

The most important event of 1886 for the residents of Waratah was the laying of the foundation stone for the new Mechanics Institute hall to be called the Athenaeum. Fortunately the day was fine for the splendid parade that was led by the Bischoff Brass Band followed by the members of the two Oddfellows Lodges and the temperance societies with their banners. This parade, which was watched by a large number of people, was followed by speeches before Mrs. Kayser laid the stone and used a suitably inscribed silver trowel from Melbourne to spread the mortar. In a cavity in the stones were placed a few coins and newspapers of the day. In the evening, the drama club gave a most successful performance in aid of the building funds.[18]

Although life at Waratah was exciting and vibrant, conditions were very basic and many of the buildings had earth floors. According to one contemporary traveller, after a three hour trip through picturesque wild country, the sight as the train rounded the curve leading to Waratah station 'excited feelings of wonder and expressions of amazement'. Here in the middle of the Australian bush thousands of feet above sea level were 'streets bristling with activity and business excitement'.[19] Delightful as it may have appeared to a visitor, life was made more difficult by the climate in the winter. There was snow, frequent rains and severe storms which caused damage which was followed only weeks later by bush fires. The smoke from these fires was hazardous. On one occasion the train driver, who could not see through the smoke, was not aware until too late that a tree had fallen across the track. Fortunately in this incident nobody was badly hurt. Fires were a constant danger, and in the middle of the year one broke out during the night at *Pearce's Hotel*; it was discovered just in time to save the building and the flames were extinguished without much damage.[20] The Mechanics Institute was not so fortunate. A fire was discovered in one of the committee rooms and the alarm was raised, the Mount Bischoff Company bell was sounded and a large number of people assembled very quickly to assist but the building, comprising a hall, stage, dressing rooms, library, committee room, reading room and recreation room, was totally destroyed. The new hall, which was still under construction, was saved as were the nearby cottages. However, the loss was significant because although the building was insured, contents were either not insured or (like the library) considerably underinsured.[21] To add to the difficulties of life at Waratah the terrain was most inhospitable and when gold was discovered at Mount Lyell it proved almost impossible to get there. A track was eventually built but it was a formidable task.[22] There were many dangers in the area around the immediate town and one of James Pearce's young sons had a very narrow escape when he fell into a water-race. Fortunately a man was passing the spot when the accident occurred and he was able to rescue the boy.[23]

Meanwhile the township of Wynyard prospered. During 1886 new buildings were erected and some old ones, particularly one of the hotels, underwent major renovation.[24] A general store, Flemings, opened in a splendid new building, Wynyard House, in Goldie Street. Opposite, another impressive two-storey building was erected for Mr. King of Somerset, the largest to be built in Wynyard to date. Also in Goldie Street, a chemist and a saddler had both opened for business.[25] A drama club was formed, a singing class was started and the brass band prospered, and many local people took part in a wide variety of entertainments to raise money for local projects. The township continued to be on the itinerary for visiting entertainers and sometimes a circus.[26] A Rifle Corps was formed to the delight of many of the young men.[27] The football and cricket matches against local teams were enthusiastically supported, as were the chopping matches and sports days.

The highlight of 1886 for most of the inhabitants was the Agricultural Show and Bazaar. The weather was marvellous and people came from all along the North West Coast. The day was a general holiday in Wynyard and Burnie and coaches and wagonettes were travelling between the two townships all day; the *Wellington* made a special trip from Stanley at Circular Head bringing about 90 passengers. Everyone had a most enjoyable time. The Show Committee had worked extremely hard and had improved the grounds and buildings.

Of particular importance was the refreshment bar and the publican's booth which were appreciated by the large crowd of visitors and locals alike. The atmosphere was enhanced by the performances of the Wynyard Brass Band. The standard of the horses, cattle and pigs was high and the vegetables from Waratah were especially commended. The Bazaar organized by the ladies of Wynyard was popular and significantly helped to increase the profits for the occasion by £138.[28]

For all the progress, life in the little township was still difficult. The ever present snakes continued to cause major incidents. Early in the year young Matthias Alexander, John's nephew, was bitten in the finger by a carpet snake. His friends tied tight bands round his wrist and arm and escorted him on the 10-mile ride from Flowerdale to Dr. Wilson's, where Matthias fell unconscious from his horse on the doctor's verandah. The doctor, well used to snake bites, revived him and administered a tot of brandy and an injection of ammonia. Then Matthias, supported by his two friends, was kept walking for the next two hours while the doctor gave him brandy and ammonia at regular intervals. A further two hours and reputedly two bottles of brandy later, the young man had recovered sufficiently to ride home.[29]

The sea, always dangerous, continued to bring sadness to Wynyard. Early in the year two local fishermen went out in a small boat but, despite an extensive search for them, they were never seen again and presumed drowned.[30] Travel by sea was convenient, however, and used by many people, and boats, particularly small passenger ones, were regularly built at Wynyard.[31]

In the following year, 1887, the major celebration throughout Tasmania and probably throughout the Empire was Queen Victoria's Jubilee on 21 June. In Wynyard great plans were made for this national holiday and the Oddfellows decided to organise a sports day. There was to be a torchlight procession and some manoeuvres by the Table Cape Riflemen at night.[32] In the event the loyal citizens of Wynyard had extended festivities. The houses were decorated with Chinese lanterns, bunting and flags ready for 21 June but on the day the weather was dreadful and the rain poured down throughout, so the Oddfellows arranged to hold their events on the following Wednesday, 29 June. A procession of the Wynyard Oddfellows, the Riflemen of Table Cape, and the Cam and Emu Bay schoolchildren were led by the Table Cape Brass Band through Wynyard to the cricket ground, where a good crowd gathered to participate in the day's events. The weather was still poor but the sports were enjoyed by the assembled gathering and Richard Alexander upheld the family honour by coming second in the 100 yards race for boys under 12 years. Unfortunately the conditions deteriorated and the evening torchlight parade had to be cancelled as did the concert.[33] The festivities at Burnie were also badly affected by the weather but they had decided to hold their parade on 22 June so that the Table Cape Brass Band could participate. Although not quite as wet as the previous day, it was not conducive to enjoyable outdoor activities. A concert was held that evening in Burnie and the takings were donated to the band funds.[34] In Waratah the celebrations began on Monday 20 June with the Oddfellows' ball held in the Mechanics Athenaeum. The following day amidst the rain and the mud there was a football match against a team from Burnie and in the evening the drama club presented a play, *The Lancashire Lass*, which was highly acclaimed by the audience.[35] The general sentiment across the North West Coast was that the pitiless rain that fell during the Jubilee celebrations could not dampen the loyalty of the population.

With permission of the Queen Victoria Museum and Art Gallery, Launceston, Tasmania.

34 Main Road to Waratah.

There were other events during the year that also caused great excitement. Firstly, there was the annual Table Cape Agricultural Show which took place in April. Wynyard was bedecked with bunting for the occasion, the weather was magnificent and about 1,500 came to the event, which was declared an outstanding success. Many improvements had been made during the year to the grounds and the display buildings and the standard of most of the exhibits was high. There were a number of splendid horses and the cattle were of a good calibre. The root vegetables were judged to be first class as were the vegetable displays from Waratah, the dairy items were of a good standard and the Chinese gardeners won many prizes with their produce. The Table Cape Brass Band entertained people throughout the day and the ladies produced an excellent lunch and fine articles for the Bazaar. This memorable day was concluded with a fireworks display.[36] Secondly, in July, there was the appearance of a large whale close in shore at Emu Bay. Immediately the Burnie Rifle Brigade manned a boat and set forth for the whale. They fired a volley and then returned swiftly to shore. A telegram was dispatched to the Cam, Table Cape and Circular Head: 'Whale with two bullets in it travelling towards your port'. This missive caused some concern up the coast. At the Cam a ship's captain manned his vessel with a contingent of the Somerset

Rifles and set off in pursuit. As he approached the whale the captain turned his ship and ordered the brigade to open fire. This they did, apparently with coolness and precision, but the whale escaped so a telegram was sent to Table Cape: 'Whale still travelling with six bullets in it'.[37] By now it was getting dark and history does not relate what the Table Cape Rifle Brigade were able to do under such conditions or in fact whether the whale went on to Circular Head or perhaps it decided to return to the safety of the open sea.

One major achievement for Wynyard and Waratah in 1887 was the commencement of the construction of a road between the two places which clearly it would take a long time to complete, but after years of argument, the project was finally under way. For Wynyard the population was increasing, causing many changes, developments and improvements. The school, now run by Mr. Cole, had between 70 and 80 pupils, there was a police sub-inspector and a constable, although an arrest at Wynyard was still a rarity, and there were two banks and three hotels. The main street was improved and widened but to the dismay of the residents no pavement was provided.[38] A new covered wharf was built, a firing range was created, a much needed lighthouse was under construction on Table Cape and significant improvements were made to the Town Hall. The Tasmanian House of Assembly agreed to spend £1,500 on a new Wynyard harbour. On the social side a football club was formed and played matches regularly; a racing club was started and a 73-acre site selected for the race course; the Band of Hope was reconstituted, the members met monthly and soon began to give entertainments; there were frequent visits by travelling entertainers and local people gave lectures and magic lantern shows.[39]

In Waratah there was also significant progress, with the Mechanics Athenaeum finished. This splendid hard wood and pine building with an impressive verandah could seat nearly 500 people in the main hall, and was complete with stage and a number of other rooms for the various activities sponsored by the Mechanics Institute. There was a new hospital, numerous new dwelling houses were built, the roads were repaired and the drainage was improved.[40] The main event that affected the young Alexander in Waratah was the decision of his uncle and aunt to leave the township and move to Melbourne. In October, they sold the hotel they had owned for seven years and left for Burnie on the first stage of their journey to the main land, much to the regret of the local population, many of whom came to the station to see the family depart.[41] At this stage FM decided to stay at Waratah; he was enjoying life and earning good money. The township remained lively, with many visitors including numerous entertainers and sports teams, one of which was the Melbourne cricket eleven. There were many locally produced entertainments and during the year the latest Tasmanian craze of roller skating arrived at Waratah. A rink was built and skating events were held frequently.[42] More gold and silver deposits were found in the area but all were in isolated places that were extremely difficult to get to, even from Waratah; however, it was decided to open the relatively nearby Heazelwood silver mine and many people from Waratah, Wynyard and Burnie invested in the company.[43] The weather continued to cause difficulties and at one stage during 1888 the snow was 15 inches deep.

In Wynyard, 1888 started with serious bush fires that caused considerable damage near to the township and a number of farmers lost their crops.[44] For the Alexanders the fire did not pose a problem. However, Bertha Victoria, the daughter of John's younger brother,

35 Table Cape Lighthouse, looking across original Alexander land, 1995.

Martin, who farmed on Table Cape, choked on a nut and died at the age of nearly four years.[45] The township continued to develop and more buildings were erected. Of particular importance was the building of the lighthouse on the Cape. The area was very dangerous for shipping and Charles Fenton was the prime mover in achieving a lighthouse for the area. Fenton was a son of the pioneer North West Coast settler and historian, James Fenton, who had come to Tasmania in the 1840s. He bought a farm of 2,000 acres on Table Cape and a further 1,000 acres at nearby Flowerdale in 1880 and thereafter became a great advocate of the township. He was elected as the local member of the House of Assembly in 1886 and devoted his not inconsiderable energies to furthering the development of the area. Before the lighthouse was built, Charles Fenton kept a kerosene lantern burning after dark in a window of his home, Norwood, which was situated on the summit of the Cape. The lighthouse building was completed in April and the event was celebrated by a great picnic on the Cape.[46] The biggest problem encountered during construction was the wallaby. It was alleged that over 2,000 were slaughtered by the builders.

The light was turned on at the beginning of August when there was an official ceremony performed by members of various local Marine Boards. These personages arrived by sea and landed near the base of the cliff where they were faced with the not insubstantial climb to the lighthouse. Not surprisingly, two of the gathering were unable to cope with this task and very quickly turned back; they found their way to Wynyard where the more energetic

36 Bullock Dray on Table Cape,
2 April 1988.

of the two acquired a horse and rode the four miles to the lighthouse by crossing the Inglis bridge and then proceeding over the Cape to the end of the peninsula. Meanwhile his comrades tackled the almost vertical climb up the cliff. There was no track and it took over an hour and a half for the party to complete the 550 foot ascent. Undaunted by their experiences, the party waited until it was dark and then with due ceremony switched on the light. By now they were unable to face the descent and so set forth to trudge through the mud and sludge back to the river. Fortunately, Martin Alexander was on hand with Beauty and Blossom harnessed in tandem to a farm cart. The journey was not the most comfortable as the only seating was bags of chaff and the horses lurched from side to side often up to their flanks in mud. But the task was accomplished and on their arrival in Wynyard the party was given a meal before they embarked on their sea journey home.[47]

March 1888 was a busy month for horse racing. In the middle of the month Stanley held their annual gathering and people made the journey by boat from Wynyard and Burnie to join the festivities.[48] On 22 March the Table Cape Racing Club held their first meeting and the day was declared a general holiday in Wynyard. The weather was gloriously fine and it was estimated that about 2,500 people watched the races, visitors coming from all along the North West Coast. The course proved to be most satisfactory and the saddling paddock which occupied some seven acres was more than acceptable, but the road to the grounds was in very poor condition. There were many other activities associated with these events including betting booths and catering facilities and between races the Table Cape Brass Band entertained the crowd. Altogether the day was highly successful and the racing of a good standard.[49] None of the Alexanders entered any horses in the event although Martin Alexander's horse, All Fours, came second in the Maiden Plate two days later at the Burnie meeting.[50] The next major event in the calendar was the Agricultural Show. Again the weather was good and a large number of visitors came to the township for the occasion. The grounds, which had been enlarged, had undergone major improvements and, as usual, there were numerous other activities besides the main show events including displays by the Table Cape Brass Band, the bazaar and a chopping match. The horses were of a high class and the jumping was acclaimed the best ever seen in Wynyard. There was an excellent display of cattle but other stock was of varying quality; as usual the vegetables and dairy produce were very good.[51]

Sporting activities continued and sports days were held and football and cricket matches played against all the local teams.[52] Roller skating came to Wynyard and was greeted by the population with great enthusiasm. A rink was built in Dodgin Street, the next street to the Alexander home, and soon the young Alexanders were keen skaters. Albert Redden (AR) and Amy were particularly enthusiastic about the sport and within a few years were regularly entering dancing competitions together.[53] Entertainers continued to visit the township and local talent produced amateur shows. At Christmas, the opera group entertained the local populace with *HMS Pinafore*. Meanwhile, John Alexander was more occupied with the Christmas races where his horse, Governess, came second by half a head in the Consolation Stakes.[54]

After three years at Waratah, FM had saved a considerable sum of money, and he decided that the time had come to move to the mainland. He followed his uncle and aunt, James and Jane Pearce, and their ever-growing family to Melbourne which at that time, 1889, was a booming town. His maternal grandmother, Maria, and her husband, Captain Thomas Lewis, were also in Melbourne living near the Pearces. The Alexander family remained at Wynyard living in the same cottage. By now John and Betsy's second son Arthur was learning his father's trade and working in the smithy, their oldest daughter Agnes was helping her mother in the home, the next son AR was becoming restless and wanting to travel the world while Dick, Amy and May were still attending school. Young Beaumont, at three years old, was under everybody's feet. All the family rode horses, AR remarkably well, and Agnes learnt to play the piano; she performed to a high standard although she never learned to read music. Amy learnt to sing and young May to recite poems. This was the era of home entertainment and everyone was expected to be able to perform their party piece.

When FM arrived in Melbourne, he lived with his uncle and aunt at Hawthorn, near his grandmother in Burke Road, Camberwell. Meanwhile, the 16-year-old AR departed from Wynyard with his great friend and cousin Will Pearce to Western Australia. They went to seek their fortunes on the goldfields of Kalgoorlie. In this mission they failed, achieving neither fame nor fortune; in fact AR contracted typhoid and became very ill.[55] When he had partially recovered he returned home to Wynyard to the care of his mother.

FM arrived in Melbourne with money in his pocket and was able to buy new clothes suitable for the city. He could afford to visit the theatre and go to concerts as well as travel around the area. However, he did not want to spend all his capital and so he had to obtain a job. He had valuable clerical experience and soon obtained employment with C.W. Gray, a dairy produce auctioning company, in Williams Street where he stayed for about a year. After this, in 1890, he worked as a clerk at George & George, a drapers, in Collins Street where he stayed for the next 18 months. In the evenings, he studied the violin and spent a considerable time at the Amateur Dramatic Club, where he acted in and produced plays,

and he had elocution lessons and practised reciting.[56] By now he was suffering from considerable hoarseness of the throat and he consulted a Melbourne doctor, Charles Bage, who
recommended various remedies over the ensuing months from special diets to resting his
throat, all to no avail. The problem became worse and while he was working at the
department store his condition seriously affected both his work and his acting.

During 1889, Melbourne was coming to the end of a glorious era which had given rise,
some years earlier, to the name 'Marvellous Melbourne', a title attributed to the English
journalist, George Augustus Sala.[57] The town had expanded considerably during the 1880s
but the aftermath of the 'boom' arrived in 1890 when businesses began to collapse and
financial institutions came under increasing pressure. Early in 1890, The Premier Building
Society, the largest such institution of its kind in Australia, ceased payments as a direct result
of reckless land speculation.[58] The following year many banks closed their doors, including
the Imperial Bank, Bank of Van Diemen's Land, which was the second oldest bank in
Australia, the British Bank of Australia, the Standard Bank, the Metropolitan Bank, the Land
Credit Bank of Australasia and the Real Estate Bank. Many building societies including the
Melbourne Permanent Building Society and the County Bourke Building Society collapsed.
In the eight months from July 1891 some 20 major financial institutions with liabilities of
nearly £20 million closed down and about 120 public companies ceased trading.[59] Many
citizens of Melbourne faced financial ruin and there were strikes by the workers. The major
railway expansion begun in the City to support the massive expansion in property development was in severe financial trouble.[60]

Into this scene of ever-increasing financial ruin, in mid-1891, came the world famous
Madame Bernhardt. She and her company gave many performances which FM recalled for
the rest of his life. The ones that particularly attracted his attention were the outstanding
performances as Camille, Adrienne Lecouvreur, La Tosca, Fedora and Theodora. On 3 June,
a Melbourne newspaper proclaimed that 'this evening, His Excellency the Governor has
announced his intention of visiting the theatre, when Madame Bernhardt will repeat her
magnificent impersonation of La Tosca.'[61] Without doubt the whole season was an outstanding success, and Madame Bernhardt received a tremendous reception every time she performed.
However, perhaps it is another report which really sets the scene for that amazing time and
typifies the feelings of those in Melbourne.

> When the words 'C'est Madame' fell from the lips of the waiting maid on the stage of the Princess's
> Theatre on Saturday night, a thrill of rare expectancy ran through the house. A moment later the folding
> doors flew open and the Lady of the Camelias came swiftly down the centre amidst a tempest of
> applause and cheering. She was clad in a robe of light clinging material, and on her right shoulder was
> a knot of white ribbon, the ends of which fell pendant almost to her feet. The uproarious greeting lasted
> for several minutes, during which Madame Bernhardt, 'the divine Sarah', as enthusiasts have named her,
> stood with head inclined and arms extended horizontally. It was a singular attitude, with something in
> it of acknowledgement, something of deprecation, and much of abandonment or surrender.
>
> It was from first to last a memorable evening, the most memorable that has ever yet been recorded in
> the dramatic annals of Australia. But keen as had been the competition for places everything was most
> aptly ordered, so that with an overflowing house there was no tumult, no crushing or struggling inside

or outside the theatre. A goodly crowd assembled at the doors to see the carriages arrive, but the way was kept clear, and there was no more confusion in drafting the audience to their seats than on the slackest night of a dull season.

Nothing, perhaps, demonstrated better the complete hold which the actress established upon her audience than the patience with which the latter endured the lengthy waits between the acts, which as the hour grew late became more noticeable. The feeling in the gallery, however, required no other vent than was provided by a friendly rivalry between two choruses, singing respectively the 'Marseillaise' and 'Rule Britannia', and even this did not last long, as both factions finally joined in a vigorous rendering of 'Home, Sweet Home'. By that time the curtain was raised for the last act, and when the spectators did actually wend homewards they had the gruesome recollection of the Bernhardt death scene to carry with them.[62]

On 16 June, a reporter described Madame Bernhardt's performance as Adrienne Lecouvreur, thus: 'To say that the house was hushed into what may be called a reverential stillness is merely to repeat a platitude. It was awed into breathless watchfulness.' Of the last act he declared, 'It was a magnificent piece of acting, and one which is likely to maintain an enduring place in the memories of all who witnessed it.'[63]

The newspaper reporters followed Madame Bernhardt everywhere she visited and one account highlighted well the conditions of the day:

Madame Bernhardt and a party of 14 arrived at Mrs. Clark's Home Hotel, Launching Place, yesterday morning. The party left Melbourne at 1 o'clock in the morning in two four-horse drays, and drove right through. Relays of horses were supplied at Lilydale by Messrs. Hoyt and Co. and Poyner and Co. Having breakfasted and rested, the company set out for the hills, under the guidance of Mr. Doherty, and had some good sport with the gun. Later, Madame and the party paid a visit to the Don River, and pitched a large marquee close to its banks. The tent was beautifully illuminated with Chinese lanterns, which had a most picturesque effect. The pleasure party was so delighted with the scenery, and the good sport they obtained, that they did not return to the hotel until nearly midnight. Madame expressed herself as being so pleased with the outing generally, and also with the treatment received at the hands of several of the residents, who kindly volunteered to show them the beauties of the place, that she has resolved to revisit this part at some future date. The company returned to town today. The ladies were dressed in Russian costumes, which were picturesque and suitable for tourists.[64]

This visit of Madame Bernhardt made a great impression on everyone in Melbourne and the surrounding area and one wonders how long it was before life returned to normal. The realities of the financial disasters in the city had a major effect. Over the next two years some 50,000 people left Melbourne, there were thousands of empty houses, many individuals went bankrupt and there was a serious typhoid epidemic in the slum area.[65] In 1891 the Yarra flooded and the countryside was plagued with locusts, the next year there were epidemics of measles and influenza, and the following year wool and wheat prices fell causing even more financial disasters.[66] Marvellous Melbourne was fast becoming Miserable Melbourne, but FM stayed. For a short time he continued working at George & George, the drapers, and in his spare time acted in and produced plays at the Amateur Dramatic Club and gave recitals, but the trouble with his vocal cords and his hoarseness became a major problem.

He found that he was frequently gasping for breath. Dr. Bage suggested that he should go to the seaside. He went to Geelong for a few months and obtained clerical employment at a drapers, Miller & Company, in Moorabool Street.

When FM returned to Melbourne he obtained employment with Atcherley & Dawson, tea, coffee and spice merchants in Little Flinders Street in the centre of the city.[67] He had to find new living accommodation as James Pearce and his family had returned to Burnie in Tasmania where James became the proprietor of the *Commercial Hotel*.[68] FM went to live with his elocution teacher Fred Hill and his family in South Yarra; they had a house in River Street overlooking the river. Fred Hill was the son of the respected Australian elocutionist T.P. Hill, who was the author of '*Hill's Oratorical Trainer*.' FM was still determined to become a professional reciter and Fred Hill proved to be a most able teacher, friend and supporter.[69] FM did all he could to prepare himself for this career and gave regular recitations. He wrote a poem entitled 'the Dream of Matthias the Burgomaster' after he had heard Mr. Walter Bentley's outstanding interpretation of the character of Matthias in *The Bells* at the Theatre Royal in Melbourne during September 1892.[70] FM recited his poem to the great acclaim of a number of different audiences and the poem was printed in pamphlet form and retailed at sixpence a copy. He was becoming a well-known and successful reciter in Melbourne and he was delighted when he won first prize in a competition open to all residents in Victoria with a recitation from *Macbeth*.[71] However, throughout this period, his hoarseness continued to be a problem for him and he discussed the matter with Dr. Bage regularly. By now FM was certain that he, himself, must be doing something that was exacerbating his condition. He considered that by study and observation he could find the source of his difficulty, and a detailed appraisal of this early work is given in his third book *The Use of the Self*. After months of self analysis of his own use, he thought he had solved his problem and he decided that he could pursue a career as a reciter.[72] So, in 1894, he returned to Tasmania to test his ability to make a living in this way.

8

FAMILY LIFE IN WYNYARD
AND ALEXANDER THE RECITER

Know then thyself, presume not God to scan;
The proper study of mankind is man.
Alexander Pope: *An Essay on Man*

FM's family were still in Wynyard. The township continued to grow in size and in 1889 there were about 110 houses in the central area of Wynyard and some 739 properties in the district, an increase of approximately 450 in 10 years.[1] By late 1890 there were several large shops, three hotels, a coffee palace and the large multi-purpose skating rink, the Town Hall and a library in Dodgin Street. The latter two facilities were renovated in 1893.[2] There were four blacksmiths, including John Alexander who was now assisted by his son Arthur, and two wheelwright shops.[3] There were Church of England, Roman Catholic and Independent churches, as well as a Gospel Hall, and during the year a Free Methodist Church was built. The state school, which in 1890 had three teachers and 100 children, rising to 130 children the following year, still occupied the single-room building measuring some 40 feet by 20 feet. So in early 1892 an additional classroom was built.[4] A recreation ground was developed and more of the roads were metalled and, to the great delight of the residents, in 1889 Goldie Street was provided with a pavement. However, the state of many of the other roads, the poor, often open, drainage system and the lack of pavements was a source of considerable frustration for years to come.[5] There was an outbreak of typhoid during the very wet weather of June 1890, and the following year a number of the open ditches were converted into covered sewers. Gradually all the ditches and drains were improved, many new by-roads were built and existing roads were maintained on a more regular basis.[6] As early as 1889 there was a suggestion that a company was prepared to build a railway between Wynyard and Burnie but the proposal was rejected by Parliament and although the topic was resurrected and discussed many times the railway did not become a reality for many years to come.[7] Thus, in 1890 and for many years afterwards, to travel the 104 miles from Launceston to Wynyard it was necessary to take the 8a.m. train from Launceston to Ulverstone and then proceed by a horse-drawn coach which arrived in Wynyard at 1a.m. in the morning. The alternative was to travel by sea. The weekly ship that brought heavy freight called at a number of small ports and so this journey took three days.[8]

Despite the difficulties of living in the Wynyard area and the constant threat of bush fires during the hot summer months, new inhabitants continued to arrive at the township and during the early 1890s numerous houses and other buildings were erected. Bush areas around Wynyard were cleared and new farms established. The centre of the township was developed,

37 Road near Burnie, 1906.

38 The Butter Factory, Wynyard, 1892.

and there were new shops including a bakers and two banks, the Bank of Australia and the National Bank. This increase in shopping facilities caused the retailers to review their opening hours and in 1892 they all agreed to close two hours earlier at 6p.m. During 1891 a new small harbour was constructed, although the problem of providing adjacent storage facilities was not addressed for some two years.[9]

Meanwhile, Charles Fenton, the local member of the House of Assembly and famous for cajoling the authorities into providing a lighthouse for Table Cape, turned his attentions to the possibility of a butter factory in the area. At this time of depression, which was affecting Tasmania almost as severely as Melbourne, the difficulty of financing such an operation would have deterred lesser men, but Charles Fenton visited Victoria, inspected butter factories and obtained plans of the building layouts. He discovered from factory managers the problems associated with the designs and returned to Wynyard convinced of the feasibility of the project. He formed a limited company and raised the necessary funds. He believed that the company should issue 2,000 shares and with the milk from about 600 cows the return would be approximately 10 per cent on investment. The land was duly bought and within a few months the factory built, and in September 1892 it was opened for business. It was the first such factory on the coast and with many of the local farmers buying shares the co-operative proved to be a superb enterprise. The butter was of excellent quality and after a few months was commanding a good price in Launceston. The factory made a profit and a year after the formation of the co-operative, in March 1893, it paid a dividend of 10 per cent. A few months later a creamery was built, and the company still functions today. In the same year other enterprises were begun: a factory was opened that made wooden items, particularly axe and pick handles along with wheel spokes, a flour mill was established and a second saw mill was constructed.[10]

The highly successful Wynyard Agricultural Show continued to be held annually and one of the regular prize winners in the fruit and miscellaneous section was Julia Gadsbury. Daughter of the one-legged Julia and James and sister of John who achieved momentary fame at the Murdering Gully trial in the 1850s, she was a very different character from many of her relations. She joined the staff of Wynyard's successful Quiggans family at the age of 20 years. She did not marry and faithfully served the family at their home 'Terra Nova' for over 60 years until her death in 1931.[11] In the appropriate seasons football and cricket were played and matches won and lost; by 1891 tennis had arrived and quickly became a most popular activity, with tennis courts sprouting in the gardens of the more affluent members of the community. Skating remained very popular and there were many special events, on one occasion a fancy dress cricket match on skates. The rifle corps was well supported although the sporting gun men were having problems as the once abundant kangaroos, wallabies and quail were becoming scarce. There were fortnightly dances, the amateur dramatic club and Wynyard band were active and gave public performances and entertainers continued to come to the township. During 1893 the Salvation Army arrived and from then on made an active contribution to life in Wynyard and the surrounding area. Special events were organised for the main public holidays and in addition to these days it was the custom in this area to observe the Queen's and the Prince of Wales' birthdays. Often there were sports days or picnics and sometimes these were held in an area on the Cam road so that people could meet with friends who came from Burnie and Somerset. On other occasions there were boating and fishing parties held on these holidays.[12]

In 1890 a Parliamentary party visited the North West Coast. The party, comprising the Premier, Ministers and Members of Parliament arrived on Monday 6 January and was greeted about a mile from Wynyard by some 50 residents on horseback or in carriages who escorted the visitors to the township. After lunch, the party was escorted by 25 riders the seven miles to Boat Harbour and then they returned to Wynyard via Flowerdale where Mrs. Edward Alexander, John's sister-in-law, had erected an arch of tree fern fronds and flowers across the road. She dispensed fresh milk to the travellers and wished them well on their journey. There was a banquet at the Oddfellows Hall that evening and the following day the visitors went to the site of the Deepwater Harbour for which Parliament had voted £6,500. After further visits around the local area the group returned to Table Cape to join some 400 people who had gathered for a picnic in a paddock near Kings Bluff, which is a few hundred yards from Alexandria, the original Alexander property. Three years later the Premier and some of his Ministers visited the area again and amongst other places they inspected the butter factory which was now producing a ton and a half of butter a week.[13]

The principal interest of John Alexander and the male members of his family was riding and training horses for the local races. The Table Cape races were held twice a year, at Christmas, normally on Boxing Day and in March; similarly, there were two meetings a year at Burnie but only one at Stanley. After John's success with his horse Governess in 1888, the first season of racing on the purpose-built course, he did not have suitable animals for the next two seasons. However, the quality of the Wynyard course quickly became respected and for the March meeting in 1889, there were about 2000 spectators and bookmakers who came from Hobart and Launceston. In the evening the amateur dramatic club performed a play in the Town Hall, while the younger and more energetic members of the community were at the formal opening of the Palace Skating Rink.[14] The March 1890 race meeting was well attended and at the Christmas meeting of that year one of John's sons and George Ambrose Alexander, John's half brother, were sharing the honours. They finished first and second in the Handicap Hack race but these placings were reversed in the Flying Handicap race. In addition, John's son won the Consolation race riding Governess. In the racing results for the North West Coast, the reports listed A. Alexander as the jockey and the only exception was when the article specifically mentioned Abe Alexander. Obviously, the re-ported jockey could have been John's son Arthur or his younger son Albert (AR) but it has been assumed that the jockey was AR for two reasons. Firstly, it is known that AR was an excellent horseman who rode races regularly for his father, and secondly, as a teenager he was remarkably small. His brother, Arthur was four years older and a blacksmith and so it is unlikely that at the age of nearly 22 years, he could have weighed 7st. 12lb. which was the weight listed for jockey A. Alexander in 1892. The Table Cape meeting in March 1891 was successful and various improvements had been made to the course and to the facilities but AR was unplaced in the Maiden Plate race on one of his father's horses.[15]

The end of the year saw a change in fortune for the Alexanders and, at the Christmas meeting at Table Cape, AR riding his father's horse, Bar One, won the six-furlong race for two-year-olds by four lengths. It was a good day for AR, who also won the Handicap Hack race and came second in the Flying Handicap race, riding horses for other local owners. A few days later at Burnie, AR again rode Bar One to victory by six lengths in the race for two-year-olds and came second, by a length, in the Pony race, for horses 14 hands and under. The March races proved most satisfactory for the Alexanders and Bar One, probably the best horse ever owned and trained by John, won easily the races for two-year-olds at Stanley and Table Cape and came second at Burnie only because the young colt was required to carry an additional stone in weight. At Stanley, AR raced Bar One again in the Flying Handicap but this proved too much for the young animal and they had to be satisfied with third place. After the races there was a concert and then the Alexanders repaired to the *Commercial Hotel* for the prize giving. It was nearly midnight when they and a crowd of well wishers made their way to the wharf where it took nearly an hour to tranship Bar One to SS *Herbert*. Eventually, a little after 1a.m., the vessel containing the Alexanders and the now famous Bar One steamed off from Stanley for Burnie. There, in addition to the race on Bar One, AR rode in the Selling race for a local owner and out of a field of 12 came first. A few days later at the Table Cape races, in front of a crowd of 1,500 people, Bar One had his revenge against the filly who beat him at Burnie and proved that he was the best two-year-old on the coast. [16]

Through the winter months John had to stable his horses and he had difficulty in obtaining suitable ground to train them, with the result that they became very out of condition. By the Christmas races only his horse Mountaineer was ready and at Table Cape, after a magnificent gallop, this colt won the race for two-year-olds by a length and a half. AR having gained a little in weight, was considered too heavy for the young animal, so John obtained the services of another jockey. However, AR won the Wynyard Stakes riding a horse for a local friend. John did not enter any horses at Burnie but AR was third in the New Year Handicap and the 16-year-old Dick came third in the Flying Handicap. By the time of the March races, the Alexander horses were in the peak of condition and, at Stanley, Bar One jumped well to come second in the Hurdle race, and out of eight starters Mountaineer was third in the race for two-year-olds. A few days later, at Table Cape, Mountaineer won the two-year-old race, and was equally successful at Burnie, twice beating one of the horses that had defeated him at Stanley. This year a race meeting was held at Burnie in May to commemorate Queen Victoria's birthday and here John Alexander entered his horse, Donaldette, and although she was unplaced in the Birthday Handicap, she was third in the Consolation race. At the end of the year at the Boxing Day meeting at Table Cape, Bar One won the Handicap Hurdles and Mountaineer won the principal event of the day, the Wynyard Stakes, with Bar One second. In the race for two-year-olds AR was third on Fishwife. A few days later, at Burnie, Bar One won both the Handicap Hurdles and the Flying Handicap while Mountaineer won the New Year Handicap and AR rode the winner in the Selling race.[17]

In addition to their great interest in horses, the Alexander family became very committed to the Methodist Church and in time Agnes became a Sunday school teacher. In May 1891, the new Minister, Rev. Carson, reorganised the Band of Hope which was soon giving fortnightly entertainments. Amy was a member of the choir and regularly sang solos and, sometimes, her little sister, May, gave recitations. On one occasion, when the Band of Hope were raising money for Alfred Garner who had been blind for the past two years, Amy sang a solo, May recited 'Happy Little May' and Dick also participated. A few months later the eight-year-old Beaumont was also giving recitations at these entertainments. During the following year the Rev. Carson formed a Mutual Improvement Society, the aim of which was to develop the mental and oratorical abilities of his congregation. The Society met quarterly and both Betsy and Agnes became hard working members. John became a member of one of the committees.[18]

In July 1892, John and Betsy's last child, Stanley Gordon, was born. By now John was 49 years old and Betsy was 44 years. This child was destined to have a short life and died on 7 March 1893. Unusually, his funeral featured in one of Tasmania's main newspapers and was described by the local reporter as the most sadly picturesque he had ever seen. He detailed how the solemn cortége which wended its way from the Alexander home in Hogg Street to the Old Cemetery comprised four little girls, attired in snowy white, carrying in the their hands magnificent wreaths of flowers artistically arranged, walking before the coffin. These, with a similar number of little boys, officiated at intervals as pall bearers. Next to the mourners came a number of state school children with the scholars of the United Methodist Sunday school. The report concluded that 'it was indeed pleasant to have to record that the sympathy of all Wynyard is with Mr. and Mrs. Alexander in their great bereavement'.[19]

The death of Stanley Gordon had a great effect on the Alexander household and when FM returned home to Wynyard in 1894 the little house in Hogg Street was a much sadder place than he had known previously. Times were difficult and the economic depression was affecting everyone in the area. His father had to sell two of his best horses, Bar One and Mountaineer, to James Pearce, and although the Alexanders had other horses none could replace the outstanding Bar One. James Pearce took Bar One and Mountaineer to the Launceston Cup meeting in February but Bar One could only achieve seventh out of a field of 11 in the Tamar Hurdle race.[20]

It was at this stage that FM told his parents that he intended to make a career as a reciter and that he wanted to gauge the reaction to his recitals in Tasmania. He began in Wynyard and, during a very hot spell when bush fires were raging about the district, he organised an entertainment in aid of funds for the Wynyard Brass Band. The programme comprised a large number of recitations by FM interspersed with musical items and one song was sung by his sister, Amy. FM then toured other local towns including Waratah and Burnie. As usual the races took place on the North West Coast in March but there were few successes for the Alexanders although Dick, now 17 years old, rode his horse, Sunshine, at the Wynyard meeting. This horse was the four-year-old daughter of Estella, the horse that FM had trained so successfully at Waratah.[21]

Shortly after the racing season FM moved to Launceston and by May he was ready to give his first recital. His first entertainment, given on 10 May, was at the Mechanics Institute and, although the event had received considerable free advance publicity in the Launceston newspapers, was not very well attended. Despite this the evening was highly successful and FM gave a varied programme of eight recitations which were all very favourably received. He included in his performance, *The Progress of Madness, Keeping His Word, After Marriage, Parhassius, Mark Anthony's speech over the dead body of Caesar, The Country Squire, The Dream*

39 Young Amy.

of Matthias the Burgomaster and *Midnight Charge.* The programme was interspersed with musical pieces. At the end of the evening, Alderman Barrett, an experienced teacher, in his vote of thanks was most flattering and he proclaimed that the recitals were as near perfect as it was possible for them to be. FM's next major performance was given a few days later at the nearby Lefroy. He was supported by the same musicians as in Launceston and again the evening was most successful with FM creating an excellent impression. After this triumph, FM announced that he would give lessons in voice culture during his stay in Launceston. This period proved to be very short because a month later he was in Hobart and gave an entertainment at the Town Hall. The event, under Vice-Regal patronage, had a large and fashionable audience and FM made a good impression. His supporting cast on this occasion included amongst others Robert Young and his wife Edith.[22]

Robert Young was to become one of FM's greatest friends and to remain his most loyal and dedicated supporter for the rest of his life. Robert Francis Young was born in Melbourne on 31 January 1856, son of a Belgian merchant from Antwerp and his wife

40 Young FM in evening dress.

Marie Antoinette who was from the French island of Mauritius. Robert was a talented musician but by profession he was a civil servant. As an amateur performer, he was associated with the Hobart Academy of Music, the Orpheus Club, for many years. During the 1880s, as an accomplished pianist, he toured with the Orpheus Club around Tasmania and had performed in Waratah when FM was living there. By 1891, he had left the Orpheus Club and was operating as a solo act. He took part in major events such as the three-day Chinese Carnival which claimed to be the most magnificent pageant in the history of the Colony. He performed what was described in those days as 'drawing room' entertainment, consisting of cleverly rendered songs and recitations. When his civil service duties permitted he toured Tasmania and in mid–1893 he was enthusiastically received on the North West Coast.[23] In October 1883 he had married Edith Mary Parsons Page at St David's Cathedral, Hobart. Edith was then 18 years old and the second of eight children of John James Page and his wife Eliza Ison.

Edith was born at Lemon Springs, near Oatlands, a substantial estate which still exists today. This rather remote location is almost midway between Hobart and Launceston and suffers from extremes of weather conditions. Originally, when Edith's great grandfather George Page acquired the Lemon Springs land it was situated on the main road, and George built an impressive stone house which in 1832 was licensed as the *Bath Inn*. A few years later a new road was built but this road took a different route, leaving the magnificent Lemon Springs house facing open country with the only access to the new road about a mile to the rear. In the days of horse drawn transport in 1865 when Edith was born this

41   Robert Young, 1899.

42   Lemon Springs House, Oatlands.

43 View from the front of Lemon Springs House, Oatlands.

must have been an isolated establishment and so, not surprisingly, the young Page children were educated by a governess.

The Pages were a well-known and successful family in Tasmania. Having settled all his children in Tasmania, great grandfather George returned to Chelsea, London where he died at the age of 90 years. His son Samuel achieved fame and fortune as the proprietor of Tasmania's main coaching service; in addition, by 1870 he owned well over 20,000 acres of land in the Jericho area which was near Lemon Springs. Another son George was a licensee of various establishments at the termini of Samuel's coach service, and his oldest son John farmed the Lemon Springs estate which had nearly 4,000 acres of grazing and pasture land.[24] John the elder moved to Hobart before 1860 and died there shortly after his grand-daughter Edith was born. The Lemon Springs estate land was divided between his sons with the main house inherited by his oldest son, Edith's father, John James, who farmed his share of the land, some 1,400 acres, and rented a further 1,000 acres of grazing land.[25] He lived with his family in the lovely house with its 17 rooms, whose wooden sitting room fireplace has the initial 'P' carved on either side. There were impressive stone-built stables, stone barn, coach house, carpenter's shop and a variety of other out-buildings. In the late 1870s he sold the property and moved his family to Hobart. Now Edith could enjoy the companionship of other people as well as her family, and it was here that she met Robert Young. She was an outstandingly beautiful woman who loved the stage and, although she supported enthusiastically her husband's amateur career in the world of entertainment, her dream was to become a famous actress.[26]

After the success of the recitals at Hobart Town Hall in June 1894, FM decided to give lessons in voice training. He emphasised that he taught a special system which developed ease and grace in speech and natural elocution.[27] He gave special Shakespearean classes and his charge was one guinea a quarter. His prospectus was available from Messrs. J Walch and Sons, the bookshop and stationers in Elizabeth Street in the centre of Hobart.[28] In early August, FM gave his second recital and musical evening in the Hobart Town Hall. This time he included *Fox's Condemnation of Peel's Corn Law Policy*, *Hood's Eugene Aram*, *Dickens' Death of Poor Joe* and *After Marriage*. There followed a number of short extracts from plays, which included Edith Young as Lady Teazle in *A School for Scandal* and Mrs. Malaprop in *The Rivals*. In this sketch FM played Captain Absolute. Other pieces were from *Richard III*, *The Honeymoon* and *At the Dance*. The evening was described as an 'intellectual treat' by one of the reporters, who was most impressed by the natural way FM delivered his pieces. He considered FM to be clever and talented and was very enthusiastic about his 'dramatic fire and well trained delivery' but what impressed him most was the delivery of the more pathetic and tragic pieces.[29] Spurred by this enthusiastic reception, FM gave more recitals in Hobart and continued to give lessons for the rest of the year. Sometimes he was asked to give special performances; one such occasion was a concert at the Kingston Football Club's Temperance Hall. The Tasmanian Military Band were performing, supported by numerous other artists, but FM headed the bill to give two recitals, *The Dream of Eugene Aram* and *The Kissing Cup*. Towards the end of the year, FM and his pupils gave an entertainment at the Tasmanian Hall. They performed *Fennel* by Jerome Jerome and were supported musically by the Orpheus Club orchestra. After the play, FM recited *The Progress of Madness* and *The Kissing Cup* and with Edith Young performed the humorous sketch *At The Dance*. The final item was contributed by Robert Young who performed his musical sketch *The Silver Wedding*. The evening's entertainment was well reviewed and all the performers were highly praised.[30]

Despite his active and successful life in Hobart, FM remained an enthusiastic racing supporter and he, along with the rest of the Alexander family, was delighted with the results of the Prince of Wales' Birthday races held at Burnie and Wynyard. At Wynyard, young Dick rode his horse, Sunshine, into second place behind Bar One in the Inglis Stakes and won the Selling race but he did not sell his horse. The following day at Burnie, Dick decided that the horse would perform better with a lighter jockey. A man some seven pounds lighter than Dick brought Sunshine home ahead of Bar One in the Flying Handicap, although the race was won by a very high quality animal owned by the famous North West Coast horse-racing family, the McKennas.[31] Dick continued to race Sunshine successfully for the next few years and AR had a number of wins with his horse, Dagma, during the following season.

During his time in Hobart, FM became attracted to the idea of visiting New Zealand. The local doctor in Wynyard who was so enthusiastic about drama and music had departed there in September 1894.[32] Eventually FM decided to write to a contact in New Zealand to enquire about the likely success of a recital tour and he received a most positive and promising response.[33] Suitably encouraged, he set forth for New Zealand and on 2 April 1895 the recently arrived FM gave a recital in the Oddfellows Hall in Christchurch, New Zealand. The *Christchurch Press* declared that 'Mr. Alexander had achieved a complete success'. The report commented on FM's considerable versatility and noted that 'Mr.

Alexander had a very excellent voice, which he used with great judgement and elocutionary power'.[34]

Encouraged by his success in Christchurch, FM decided to go to Wellington. There he was joined by two singers, Miss Rose Blaney, who was advertised as Australia's foremost soprano, and Miss Laura Fisher, a renowned contralto. Together they presented a programme at the Thomas Hall on 6 May. Both the *New Zealand Times* and the *Evening Post* were extravagant with their praises. They considered FM to be an elocutionist of a high calibre. As a result of this success, the trio performed again in Wellington on 8 May at the Skating Rink. As before, the evening was most popular; there were insufficient seats so some of the audience had to stand.[35]

The next performances were at the Theatre Royal in Napier on 13 and 15 May.[36] The events were given good advance publicity by the Napier Press who considered that the entertainers would perform to capacity audiences. In his coverage of the future events, the reporter noted that Mr. Alexander 'had the high honour in the early part of his career of securing the first prize when he appeared in the title role in the murder scene from *Macbeth*, in Melbourne, against all comers of Victoria'. In addition, the article reprinted very favourable comments from the Lyttelton Times on the recital given by FM in Christchurch.[37] The programmes were as successful as had been anticipated; both the *Daily Telegraph* and the *Hawke's Bay Herald* gave extremely favourable reviews but regretted that 'the audience was not commensurate with the merits of the concert'. However, one reporter did suggest that the miserable weather may have accounted for the size of the audience.[38]

The trio decided that before they left Napier they would give a grand sacred concert on Sunday evening. Although the audience did not pay to attend, they placed donations in a suitable box. The result of this event was that FM was charged in the local court for performing on a Sunday. He pleaded guilty to the charge but, in his defence, stated that in Napier such events were not uncommon and only the previous Sunday a concert had taken place; on that occasion nobody was prosecuted. Despite this the Judge fined him 5s., and observed that the considerable publicity given to the case by the New Zealand Press was worth much more than the 5s. fine.[39]

After Napier, the little company moved to Auckland where they performed in the Choral Hall on 29 and 31 May. On 10 June, FM took part in a concert organised by Mr. John Birch at the City Hall, where he played the title role in a one-act play, *Paul Daroon* written by John Birch. The *New Zealand Herald* was most complimentary about FM's acting. Three days later, he performed at the City Hall again, giving his more usual recitals.[40]

On 17 June, FM, Miss Rose Blaney and Miss Laura Fisher gave a most successful concert in the City Hall. FM's recitation of the *Kissing Cup* was described in the *New Zealand Herald* as 'magnificent': it was also noted that the ladies' singing 'fully justified the reputation which had preceded them'.[41] The *Auckland Star*, who were clearly impressed with the performance, recorded that 'the two ladies were returning to Melbourne and gave this concert en route'.[42] FM continued with his recitations and the *Auckland Star* noted on 24 June that he had left his own concert in order to present an item at the YMCA Conversazione.[43]

FM's last major entertainment in New Zealand was his appearance on 26 June at the Opera House in Auckland as Romeo in two scenes from *Romeo and Juliet*. In particular, the

Auckland Star noted that 'the success of the balcony scene was due in a great measure to Mr. F.M. Alexander. His Romeo was a fine piece of character acting and as this was the first time Alexander had appeared in the part he was deserving of the very highest praise.'[44] After this, although he gave some recitals, he concentrated on teaching his method of voice production using rooms in Auckland. He saw pupils from a wide variety of backgrounds including the then famous war correspondent, Frederic Villiers, who amongst other campaigns had witnessed the Japanese war with China, the Serbia-Turkish war and the historic attempt to relieve Khartoum. He lectured on these topics to audiences throughout the Antipodes.[45] He gave FM a reference which was used frequently in the years to come. Although FM's teaching was successful, events at home in Wynyard required his presence. His sister, Amy, had had a serious accident. One day when she was out riding her pony the animal had slipped and she was thrown, but her foot had stuck in the stirrup and she was dragged nearly half a mile. She was badly injured and her leg was so damaged that she could not walk properly. Prior to leaving New Zealand, FM gave a farewell recital in the City Hall, on 20 November 1895. During the interval the Mayor, Mr. Jas. Holland, on behalf of Mr. Alexander's pupils, presented him with a handsome illuminated address, which is preserved to this day, and gave a short speech in praise of Alexander's work. It was a memorable evening.[46]

With the praise of Auckland ringing in his ears, FM returned by boat to Sydney and then by train to Melbourne. His work in Auckland had convinced him of the value of his methods and this encouraged him to continue teaching instead of pursuing a career as a reciter. He visited Wynyard and realised that, Amy would need the very best medical advice available if she was to recover from her accident. This would cost money. He returned to Melbourne and obtained lodgings with Captain William and Mrs. Sinclair at 61 Dundas Place in South Melbourne; he found suitable teaching rooms in Australian Buildings, Elizabeth Street and so began a lifetime of teaching.

In order to attract pupils to his studio, FM concluded that he must give recitals, prepare a printed brief on his teaching methods and advertise his work. As December and January are summer holiday months in Australia, FM had time to prepare his paper on the Work and arrange to have it printed. He gave a recital, which was highly successful, and he was asked to speak. He seized this opportunity and announced that he was prepared to accept pupils. He emphasised that during the previous 18 months he had helped people improve their breathing, vocalisation, health and strength. Two pupils resulted from this recital and FM was launched. In the middle of February he advertised his work in the Melbourne newspapers. He announced that his teaching involved cultivating the voice and ensuring correct breathing using new and approved methods. He advised his readers that his treatise was available free at Messrs. Allen & Co, a well-known musical shop in Collins Street, and that he would interview potential pupils between 11 and 12.30 in the morning and from 1.30 to 3.30 in the afternoons. A month later FM's advertisements also claimed that his methods helped alleviate stuttering, hoarseness and tiring of vocal organs by natural methods.[47] Pupils began to appear at his studio in Elizabeth Street. It was during this time, and against his better judgement, that he was prevailed upon to teach some 19 students at the Theological College. Subsequently FM had reason to be grateful for this experience because, as a result of recommendations from these students, a number of pupils came to him.

FM rewrote his treatise, and this time he produced a 20-page pamphlet outlining his teaching methods which was sold at Messrs. Allen & Co. for sixpence a copy, while the original brief outline of the Work could still be obtained free. It is believed that some 60 copies of the more detailed pamphlet were sold during the first week, probably as a result of the advertising campaign FM launched in July 1896.[48] Many pupils resulted from the advertisements and the new treatise. FM was kept busy and he reduced his promotional activities and concentrated on his teaching. By mid-September he advertised again and during October, November and early December he maintained a steady flow of advertisements in the newspapers always highlighting that he used new methods.[49] This was particularly important because now he could put in his advertisements that medical references were available at his studio.

In Wynyard life was becoming very difficult. The loss of Stanley Gordon, Amy's injury and financial problems largely caused by the depression resulted in considerable stress within the family, and AR decided to join his brother in Melbourne. Now FM was becoming an established teacher with an increasing number of pupils as well as the support of some Melbourne doctors. He was glad that his brother showed an interest in his work and was prepared to assist him. The added advantage was that FM could consider travel outside Melbourne to extend his teaching practice. He invited his sister to come to Melbourne so he could take her to see medical specialists who might be able to help her condition. In fact over the next year or two, FM and Amy travelled Australia and visited all the medical experts available. None could alleviate her condition and so FM started to teach her himself. She improved and slowly her limp disappeared and eventually with better use she no longer had one leg shorter than the other.

For the family in Wynyard things deteriorated steadily during the latter months of 1896, and towards the end of the year Betsy decided she would spend Christmas in Melbourne with her two sons and daughter; she was accompanied by Agnes, May and young Beaumont. They stayed after Christmas to enjoy the summer holidays with FM, AR and Amy, and towards the end of January the Youngs came on holiday to Melbourne. They had travelled from Hobart to Launceston where Robert took part in the Launceston cycling club's annual grand concert. He performed his musical sketches and songs to great acclaim and was described as a clever amateur humorist, with his *The Mother and Her Child* commended as a 'distinct success'.[50] Then they proceeded by sea to Melbourne and joined the Alexanders. In the middle of January FM resumed teaching, and by the end of the month he was advertising that he was forming classes to study natural elocution, singing and breathing-gymnastics based upon his latest methods; by now his more detailed treatise was available free.[51]

While Betsy and her family were away disaster struck in Wynyard. On Thursday 25 February 1897 a fire started in the Alexander house in Hogg Street and the alarm was raised at about 11p.m. The school bell was rung and awoke most of the people in the township, many of whom were quickly on the scene. They attempted to put out the fire with buckets of water but the strong wind made the task impossible, and the smoke and flames meant they were unable to salvage any of the furniture or belongings from the house. The next door property, the house and shop of Mr. F.J. Baker, was in great danger and every effort was made to save the contents and building and to prevent the fire spreading further to Mr. George Peart's house and Mr. Dixon's chemist shop. All the possessions of Mr. Baker were removed across the road to the school but both his and John Alexander's houses were burnt to the ground. John, Arthur and Richard were living in the house but they were all out that evening. John had returned at about 10p.m. but as he was unable to find the key he had departed to find his sons. He did not return until he heard there was a fire and, little realising that it was his own dwelling, went to assist. Although the house was insured the deeds were with the bank as surety for an overdraft.[52] The insurance money did not cover the loan. Without a house and totally without funds, Betsy decided to stay in Melbourne with her children. FM agreed to provide financial support for his family, a task which for a variety of reasons was to last the rest of his life. In Wynyard, John's situation was dire. His house, forge and all the family possessions were destroyed and because the house was underinsured he was severely in debt to the bank. He was facing bankruptcy with little prospect of being able to earn sufficient funds ever to recover the position. FM came to his father's aid and persuaded the authorities that he would underwrite the debt; although it would probably take some years before the loan could be repaid in full, he would ensure it was repaid eventually. The bank was satisfied with this statement of intent and so John and Arthur tried to re-establish the blacksmith business. The following year, in January 1898, Arthur married his first cousin, Margaret Wells, a daughter of John's sister Mary, and soon afterwards Richard decided that the time had come to move away. He went to New Zealand to try and make his way in the world and helped with the family finances whenever he could. He was to remain in New Zealand for the rest of his life. It took John a while to recover from the shock of this complete change in his life but eventually he took solace from his love of horses, racing and his work, and he continued to shoe horses for most of the rest of his long life.

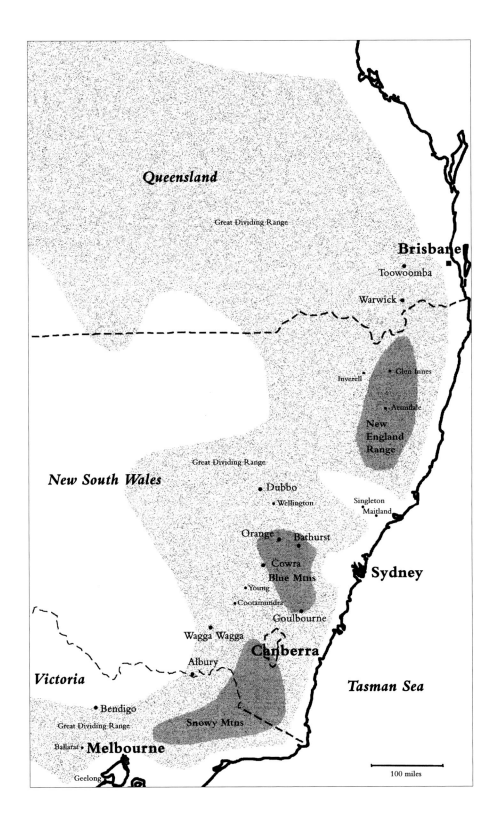

Queensland

Great Dividing Range

Brisbane

Toowoomba

Warwick

Inverell • • Glen Innes

• Armidale

New
England
Range

New South Wales

Great Dividing Range

• Dubbo

• Wellington

Singleton
Maitland

Orange • • Bathurst

• Cowra
Blue Mtns

• Young

• Cootamundra

Sydney

Goulbourne

Wagga Wagga

Canberra

Albury

Victoria

Tasman Sea

• Bendigo

Great Dividing Range

Snowy Mtns

Ballarat •

Melbourne

Geelong

100 miles

9

TEACHING IN MELBOURNE AND SYDNEY

'Tis of a wild Colonial boy, Jim Doolan was his name,
Of poor but honest parents he was born in Castlemaine,
He was his father's only hope, his mother's pride and joy,
And so dearly did his parents love the Wild Colonial Boy.
Anon: An old Australian Bushranger's song

The financial burden and the strain on FM was considerable since he was now responsible for his mother, three sisters and younger brother, and he had the additional worry of a large debt that had to be repaid. Initially Betsy and her children lived in a bungalow in Hawthorn, but the only thing that anybody ever remembered about this establishment was the possums in the roof. After about a year they left Hawthorn and rented another house, before moving to Mathoura Street, Toorak where they remained for a number of years. Meanwhile FM continued to live in his rooms with Captain William and Mrs. Sinclair in South Melbourne and AR remained in a nearby boarding house, although eventually he joined the family at Toorak.

With his new financial responsibilities, FM increased his advertising and placed some large 23-line advertisements in the newspapers.[1] As he was assisted by AR in his studio in Elizabeth Street he was able to expand his teaching practice. His teaching had rapidly become well respected by a number of influential people in the city. His friend and doctor Charles Bage was an established pupil and an enthusiastic admirer of the Work. He was joined by other members of the medical profession including Dr. Donald MacColl and these men recommended FM's methods to some of their patients. As one would expect, there were numerous pupils from the performing arts who were well-known in Melbourne at that time, including Mr. Walter Moore, Mr. H. Newsome, Miss Lily Ballard, Miss Mabel Mattingley and Miss Lillie Bush. In addition, there were many pupils from a wider professional sphere, including teachers, lawyers, churchmen, policemen, businessmen and civil servants. Amongst them were some prominent and important members of Melbourne society. Notably, there was William McCulloch, a Scotsman, who came to Australia in 1852 hoping to make his fortune on the goldfields. Soon he moved to Melbourne and founded one of the largest importer firms in the city; he was a city counsellor for some years and in 1880 was elected to the Legislative Assembly. Later he was to become Minister of Defence, and when the Boer War began he organised and dispatched the first Victorian contingent. This was so well executed that Tasmania, South Australia and Western Australia transferred all the transit arrangements for their contingents to the Victorian government.

44   The Alexander family house at Toorak.

Shortly after this he represented the State of Victoria at the Coronation of Edward VII. McCulloch owned three large properties near Melbourne and invested significant amounts of money in stud cattle, sheep and horses and as he was a great patron of the turf he imported the best strains of English blood stock; some of these animals had most successful Australian racing careers.[2] There was Arthur Robinson, a solicitor, who became a prominent member of Melbourne society. He was elected to the Legislative Assembly in 1900 and became a successful politician. He was knighted in 1923 when he was Attorney General, and during his life he acquired extensive commercial and financial interests.[3] From the academic world came Professor William Harrison-Moore, an English barrister who was the Professor and Dean of the Faculty of Law at Melbourne University.[4]

All the time FM was developing his methods and ideas and by May 1897 his advertisements had changed considerably. Now he announced that cultivating the voice for speaking and singing could be rapidly developed through control and improved breathing. By using his new methods, pernicious habits such as raising shoulders, breathing through the mouth and gasping could be avoided.[5] His advertisements continued to change as he developed his methods although he always emphasised that they were natural ones. In the middle of the year he placed large advertisements which stated that testimonials from leading actors, clergymen, reciters, theological students and members of the medical profession were available

OUR ADDRESS:
"AUSTRALIAN BUILDINGS."

45 Alexander Teaching Rooms, Australian Buildings, *c*.1904.

for inspection. He named two individuals, Mr. Frederic Villers and Professor Liosette, who had supplied references.[6] FM had more confidence in his methods and in his ability to help people now and a few weeks later he inserted an advertisement in which he claimed that he could 'cure stammering and all throat troubles'.[7] This was a claim that would cost him dear in the years to come. However, at this stage the young, inexperienced and in many ways naïve FM did not understand the import of what he was saying. So he continued to advertise widely several times a week in the Melbourne newspapers, placing emphasis on his 'new methods' and his 'cures'. By early 1898, he had added barristers to the list of professional people that had provided him with testimonials and lengthened some of his advertisements to over 50 lines. These large entries were followed for the next four or five days with small notices referring to the large, usually, Saturday column.[8]

In addition to teaching FM continued to give recitals and perform entertainments, and during the early months of 1898 he decided to hire a major venue, the Athenaeum Hall in Collins Street in central Melbourne. He costed the venture most carefully and allowed £30 for expenses. The detailed account listed £13 4s. for 44 advertisements at 6s. each, covering all the important Melbourne newspapers, five guineas for the hall, 6s. for postage, 25s. for programmes, £2 for posters and card tickets, £2 for stage arrangements and £1 for the attendants; in addition he allowed £5 for unforeseen expenses.[9] The entertainment took place on Wednesday, 11 May 1898, when he was assisted by five other performers. The most well-known and respected was the Australian actor James Cathcart who, in his younger days in the 1850s, had acted in various plays including *The Tempest* at Windsor Castle in the presence of Queen Victoria and Prince Albert.[10] Apparently, considerable applause accompanied this veteran actor's arrival on the stage; in Melbourne he was an old favourite. On this occasion he performed a scene from *School for Scandal* with Edith Young who was using the stage name of Tasca-Page.[11] Although the childhood name used by her close family was 'Did', she was known to her friends as Tasca and, of course, her maiden name was Page. Also in the production was Lilian Twycross, an accomplished contralto who, as a member of the Australian Concert Company, had performed in concerts in Hobart during December 1894 when FM and the Youngs were giving entertainments in that city.[12] She performed regularly on the Melbourne stage and taught singing both at her home in the Melbourne suburb of Elsternwick and at Glenns in Collins Street. Very shortly after FM's return to Melbourne from New Zealand at the end of 1895, she had became a pupil and by this stage she was trying to adapt FM's methods into her teaching. In fact her advertisements for cultivating a singing voice were very similar to those of FM and sometimes she advertised that she had a reference from him.[13] The other members of the team were Gertrude Summerhayes, the daughter of the very well-known pianist Cecilia Summerhayes, who performed two violin solos, and Mr. G Bromley, a pianist.

FM gave several recitals, the most successful of which was his rendering of *The Midnight Charge* by Clement Scott. Overall the evening was well received and a few days later FM was able to advertise his teaching by declaring that he had performed with great success at the Athenaeum on the previous Wednesday.[14] Some six weeks later, FM hired the Athenaeum Hall again and this time he increased his part in the entertainment adding two more pieces, *Kissing Cup* and *Napoleon the Great*.[15] A month later FM visited Adelaide and, together with Edith Young, Gertrude Summerhayes and Mr. J Dunn who was the accompanist, put on a show at the Town Hall on two consecutive nights, 21 and 22 July. The performances were very favourably received. The accomplished violinist Gertrude Summerhayes gave four solos which were highly acclaimed by the audience and FM's five recitals were thoroughly enjoyed by everyone. The reporter considered that FM was a master of his art and complimented him on his versatility.[16] Clearly these performances attracted attention, and more pupils arrived at Australian Buildings for lessons but, even so, newspaper advertisements appear to have been essential. FM placed his advertisements on an almost daily basis from July to the middle of December and after the Christmas holidays he continued his campaign to attract pupils with small notices appearing almost daily. His large advertisements appeared weekly under the heading 'The Human Voice cultivated by New Methods' and, perhaps interestingly, appointments now had to be made by letter.

46   Queen's Bridge, Melbourne, *c.*1906.

During 1898 Robert Young's health steadily deteriorated and by early January 1899 he was forced to retire from his job as the Hobart Bench clerk. As he was a highly successful amateur entertainer, he decided that the best way he could earn his living was to become a professional. He undertook a number of engagements in Tasmania and had a reasonably successful short season at Zeehan, then a booming mining town in Western Tasmania.[17] Convinced now that he could earn his living by giving entertainments, he joined his wife, Edith, and her older sister, Maud, in Melbourne. For most of the previous year Edith had been trying to make her name on the Melbourne stage. She had had a number of parts but mainly she had given home entertainments as well as joining FM in his two productions at the Athenaeum and in Adelaide. Robert was an experienced performer and he established himself very quickly on the Melbourne scene. From April 1899 onwards he advertised regularly in the newspapers and almost immediately he was in great demand to provide what were known in those days as 'musical at homes'. In fact, within three months of his arrival he was undertaking several engagements a week with his popularity increasing with every performance.[18] With Robert Young in Melbourne, FM decided to leave the Sinclairs and he joined the Youngs and Maud Page at 55 Leopold Street in South Yarra, a suburb of Melbourne.[19]

During July 1899, the preoccupation in Melbourne was the forthcoming referendum to decide whether or not the Australian States should form a Union. However, both FM and Robert Young were more concerned about their forthcoming show at the Athenaeum Hall. They were acclaimed entertainers in Melbourne and they decided to produce a show comprising a programme of entertainment of the type made popular in London many years before by Mr. and Mrs. German Reed. Maud Page worked for Messrs. Ball and Welch, a clothiers, tailors and outfitters located in Carlton, an area just north of central Melbourne, and she made all the costumes. The show which was directed by George Bryer opened on 26 August 1899 and ran for two weeks; there were nightly performances and in addition a matinee on Saturdays. After the opening night, a Melbourne newspaper, *The Age*, proclaimed 'Messrs. Young and Alexander may fairly claim to have introduced a novelty to the Melbourne public on Saturday night'. The article praised the production and particularly the elocutionist Mr. Alexander.[20] Another paper, the *Melbourne Punch*, reported, 'The novelty, so far as Australia is concerned, of a German Reed Entertainment appears likely to prove a very successful venture if one may judge by the attendance and the enthusiasm at the Athenaeum Hall last Saturday afternoon.' The reporter concluded his article by proclaiming, 'The entertainment throughout is a pleasant and creditable one, and as it fills a distinctly felt want in the world of amusement it should continue long, if not permanently, in Victoria.'[21] The cast included ten people in addition to FM and the Youngs. There was the well-known and respected Australian actor, James Cathcart, who on this occasion performed with Edith Young in the quarrel scene from *School for Scandal*. FM gave recitations which included the death of Joe from Dickens' *Bleak House*, about which one reporter exclaimed, 'No praise could be too great for the simple, unaffected delivery of the extract; the audience listened with breathless eagerness, and when the cart had reached the end of its journey the "right reverends and wrong reverends" present burst into a storm of applause.'[22] Robert Young made a significant and valuable contribution to the show, performing a number of his special musical sketches some of which he had written and composed. According to reports, 'he had the face and manner of a comedian and a neat turn for mimicry'. He was an able pianist and apparently during one item used his teeth most skilfully as castanets. Some reports described Robert Young as 'an artist far above the average' and others as a man who performed most capably and cleverly.[23] The first night was such a success that Fred Hill, FM's friend and former elocution teacher, placed a large advertisement in the Melbourne newspapers proclaiming that Mr. Alexander now appearing at the Athenaeum had been one of his pupils and quoting from a testimonial that FM had sent him.[24]

On other occasions FM mounted entertainments outside Melbourne in order to attract pupils from different areas. In October 1899 he went to Bendigo, a gold mining-town about 75 miles north-west of Melbourne. The performance which received considerable advance publicity was given on 6 October in the Masonic Hall with an admission charge of one shilling. The advertisements announced that FM would give a 'dramatic and humorous recital and exposition on the new methods as applied to the human voice in singing and speaking'.[25] He was assisted in this venture by a number of performers and the programme covered a range of items. FM gave three recitals, *The Midnight Charge*, *The Death of Poor Joe* and *The Amateur Rider*. In addition, he gave 'a chat on the New Principle of Speaking'. These items were interspersed with Josephine Scott's rendering of the overture *Romanza and Study* and her violin solo *Saltarelle*, Mrs. Morgan (Kate Heine) singing *Nevermore* and *The Link Divine*, a male string quartet playing Haydn's *The Emperor*, three soloists, Mr. W. Tinkler, Mr. J. Andrew and Julie Sprenger singing respectively *The Message*, *Hybrias the Cretan* and *The Mission of a Rose*, and St Andrew's choir performing *Moonlight* and closing the show with the song *Evening*. After this performance FM remained in Bendigo a further fortnight while he taught in rooms at the ANA Hall.[26]

47 Mafeking celebrations.

While FM was in Bendigo, the probability of war breaking out in South Africa increased daily. A patriotic fever seized many in Australia and according to reports of the time the emergency had the 'effect of kindling into visible flame the spirit of British loyalty in Australasia'.[27] By the time the war officially began on 10 October 1899, the individual Australian States were assembling their troops to send to South Africa. In London the New South Wales Lancers were assembled for immediate departure. On 10 October they were conveyed by train from their base at Aldershot to Waterloo station from where they marched behind the band of the Grenadier Guards to Fenchurch Street station cheered on by an enthusiastic crowd of some 40,000 people. The contingent went by train to the docks and boarded the liner *Nineveh*.[28]

In Tasmania and Victoria young men were volunteering to join the Army and by 28 October the contingents were assembled in Melbourne prior to embarkation. They came from towns and villages throughout the states and each group had a farewell parade and entertainment before leaving their home bases; many were presented with gifts such as bibles and hip flasks and all were wished a speedy and safe return.[29] The Tasmanian contingent of some 900 men had a special banquet at Launceston and a great farewell parade before they set sail for Melbourne.[30] For the troops, training was intense but at last all was ready for the grand parade and farewell in Melbourne. It was estimated that a quarter of a million people came to bid the troops 'bon voyage' and witness one of the most memorable occasions in the history of Melbourne.[31] In the months ahead the people in Australia would read their newspapers daily for reports of the war, the detailed maps would show them exactly where the fighting was taking place, and the names of Ladysmith, Kimberley, Cronje, Bloemfontein and Mafeking would become household names. Patriotic funds as they were known were launched to raise money for the wives and children of the servicemen, and contributions were sent to the Tommy Atkins Fund organised for the same purpose by the *Daily Mail* newspaper in London. The Tommy Atkins collecting cards all carried Rudyard Kipling's famous poem, *The Absent-Minded Beggar*, written specifically for the fund. Given the poem's stirring opening lines of 'When you've shouted "Rule Britannia" when you've sung "God Save the Queen" ' and the fact that not only were contributors' names listed in the various Melbourne newspapers but also their donations it is perhaps not surprising that the fund was successful.[32]

By now FM was very well-known in Melbourne, his teaching practice was most successful and the public entertainments were helping to publicise his work, so he decided that the time had come to move to Sydney. He left Melbourne in late February 1900 and soon obtained teaching rooms in the Equitable Building, George Street in central Sydney. From March 1900 he advertised his services regularly in the Sydney newspapers, normally stating that he 'cultivated and developed the human voice by new methods for singing and speaking'. He drew extensively on the reputation he had achieved in Melbourne, Tasmania and New Zealand and he named the wide variety of people who had studied his methods and whose testimonials were available for inspection.[33] In addition, FM published a small 32-page pamphlet in which he outlined his teaching methods under the heading *Cultivating the Singing and Speaking Voice by New and Approved Methods, as imparted during 1896-7-8-9 by Mr. F M Alexander*. He included in this booklet press reports about his recitals in Melbourne and New Zealand and numerous testimonials from some of his former pupils. These ranged from Mr. E.W.G Rathbone, a London art critic, and Jas Holland, Mayor of Auckland, to Rev. Prior Kelly of the Carmelite Priory and H. Sumner Martin of the Baptist Theological College. There were a number of others from various churchmen who were all suffering from 'clergyman's sore throat', and several from singers, from the clerk of Petty Sessions at St Kilda and one from a member of the Lands Titles Office in Melbourne.[34] This booklet, which was issued free to interested people, was the only printed guide describing the Work issued for a number of years.[35]

The Youngs and Maud Page along with all the Alexander family had remained in Melbourne. Robert was actively employed with his home entertainments and Edith had received great acclaim from the critics when she performed the lead female role with the Alexandra Dramatic Company in *Vengeance is Mine* at the Alexandra Theatre a few weeks before Christmas 1899. She had great hopes that other important stage roles would appear. However, they did not materialise, and by the middle of the year the Youngs decided to join FM in Sydney. Initially, Robert tried to obtain employment doing home entertainments while his wife attempted to find work on the stage. However, they were unknown in Sydney so it was difficult. Clearly what was required was publicity. At this time, early August, FM was advertising that he was so busy that appointments for his very limited available teaching time must be made by letter. [36] Whether or not this was strictly true or just an advertising gimmick is not known but certainly FM was keen to publicise his work as much as possible. So Robert and FM decided that the best course of action was to put on a public entertainment and Robert joined FM at his studio in Equitable Buildings. Two weeks later they were advertising their show, stating that this was the first appearance in Sydney of 'F.M. Alexander, Robert Young and Edith Tasca Page'.[37]

They staged their first show on 1 September at the Centenary Hall. They were joined by Miss Annie Perry, a soprano, Miss Mary Robinson who was an excellent pianist and Mr. Ernest Truman, an organist and pianist. The whole entertainment was highly successful, and according to the critics, 'future appearances of the principal artists will be awaited with interest.' FM was very well received and presented amongst other items *Shiel's Defence of the Irish People, Kissing Cup, The Clock Mystery* and *Sydney Carton's* pathetic conversation with the seamstress on his way to the guillotine. He was rewarded with extended applause. Robert performed with great versatility a number of humorous musical sketches and was a resounding success, while Edith undertook some recitations. Annie Perry, Mary Robinson and Ernest Truman made useful and enjoyable contributions.[38] Three further such events took place at the Centenary Hall at fortnightly intervals but Mary Robinson did not participate in the second and third performances while Ernest Truman missed the last in the series. All the shows were described by the newspaper critics as exceedingly successful. After the second performance, which was identical in content to the first, one of the newspapers enthused that 'the talents of Mr. FM Alexander, Mr. Robert Young and Miss Tasca Page are such as to entitle them to be classed amongst our most delightful entertainers'.[39] For the third performance, FM changed his repertoire and included selections from Kipling's *Gunga Din, Napoleon the Great*, a scene from *Trilby, The Sea Captain's Story, The Aeronaut's Story* and 'Banjo' Peterson's *The Amateur Rider*. Robert also introduced a completely new programme, as did Edith. They gave a matinee of this performance at Equitable Buildings the week before they presented the programme at the Centenary Hall. Again the programme was thoroughly enjoyed by the audience. For the fourth and last of these shows held on 13 October, both FM and Robert made minor alterations to their respective programmes. All the reports in the various Sydney newspapers were glowing in their praise of all the performers who entertained their audiences for some two and a half hours on each occasion. One critic wrote of 'Mr. Alexander, whose fine voice and excellent elocutionary training, enable him to illustrate admirably the authors whose works he interprets'. Another critic described Mr. Alexander as 'a highly skilled elocutionist, with an agreeable and well trained voice, and a very decided natural gift for impassioned declamation'.[40]

As a result of one particular recital, Dr. William John Stewart McKay, a doctor at Lewisham hospital in Sydney, visited FM and became a pupil. Dr. McKay was born in Sydney in 1866 and after attending Sydney Grammar School, he went to Sydney University where he qualified as a physician. He came to England and then travelled widely in Europe. He studied in Berlin, Leipzig, Heidelberg, Vienna, Paris and Birmingham before returning to Sydney to continue practising medicine where he became a senior surgeon. His main interest outside medicine was horse racing. An expert on blood stock and rearing horses, he wrote articles in the newspapers about forthcoming races for many years. Before the great annual race, the Melbourne Cup, he would publish his selections and explain his reasons.

Apparently, he frequently nominated the winners.[41] He became a staunch supporter of Alexander's work and a personal friend and over the next few years helped FM considerably.

The Alexander teaching practice in Sydney was becoming well-known, and by Christmas 1900 FM's pupils presented him with a gift, and the card which is extant contains the following signatures: J. Dorahy, A. Morris, E.A. Hall, J.O. Fisher, Annie Perry, Blanche McCarron-Maguire, Lily Percival, J.M. Collerson and Gertrude Rosenthal. The *Sydney Daily Telegraph* and the *Sydney Morning Herald* recorded, on 31 December 1900, that the previous Saturday there was an enjoyable evening at Mr. Alexander's studio, arranged by his students. The students presented a programme of singing and elocution and as a token of their appreciation gave FM an address and a solid gold albert.[42]

Although Robert, working in Equitable Buildings, was still advertising that he was giving home entertainments which were popular in the weeks before Christmas, he had decided to teach the Sandow system of harmonious physical development once the festivities were over. When he was in London in 1891 he had met Eugene Sandow on a number of occasions and had become an ardent student of the system which, at that time, was recommended in London for athletes and people employed in physically demanding occupations such as the British Army, the London Police Force and the Fire Brigade. In his younger days, Robert had been athletic and had trained for seven years as a gymnast and therefore understood the importance of exercise that did not strain the human frame. He believed that symmetrical development of the body produced healthy organs and an evenly balanced muscular and nervous system.[43] In the last months of 1900, Robert spent his free time visiting Sydney doctors and showing them the Sandow system in preparation for the launch of his teaching classes early in the following year.

The new year was welcomed with great ceremony because 1 January 1901 was the birth of the Australian Nation. The inauguration of the Commonwealth of Australia was the most important day in the history of that country thus far and was marked by grand processions, parades, banquets and many other celebrations. The festivities continued for several days and the spirit of happiness and joy was only abated by the news that Queen Victoria's health was causing concern. When she died, on 22 January, cities such as Melbourne and Sydney went into deep mourning and the newspapers were edged in black with black vertical lines between the columns. Official parades were held and detailed accounts appeared in all the newspapers of the Queen's funeral, her life was analysed, and pictures of her and other members of the royal family filled page after page for the days between her death and the funeral. During this emotional time, young AR was busy embarking on a potentially dangerous mission.

When his older brother left for Sydney, AR initially intended to continue teaching in Melbourne but very soon he decided that he preferred an outdoor, more adventurous life and that he needed a change from the indoor working environment. The Boer War that everyone had hoped would end quickly was still continuing and during January the Australian authorities, in response to a request from the British Government, called for volunteers to serve in the Fifth Victorian Contingent to go to South Africa. There were thousands of volunteers and amongst them was AR. He went to the recruiting centre where he passed the riding test without a problem and he had no difficulty with the shooting and physical tests. He declared that he was a stockman as, clearly, the tough, manly AR did not think that elocutionist was a suitable occupation for an aspirant in the Mounted Rifles. Thus, on 1 February 1901 he enlisted, becoming No.1442, private, in the Fifth Victorian Mounted Rifles and was paid at the rate of 5s. a day.[44] He went to a nearby training camp at Langwarrin where initially it was expected to train four companies of 120 men each.[45] The first three Victorian Contingents sent to South Africa had been two companies strong but the fourth Contingent had been larger at five companies. In the event the fifth contingent comprised eight companies. The departure from Melbourne was an impressive and emotional event. On 15 February, the personnel were transported by train from Langwarrin to Melbourne. The railway track was lined with people waving farewell and the platforms of each station along the route were filled with people. In Melbourne the Contingent marched thorough the streets and on to Port Melbourne where they embarked on the *Orient*. The horses and sufficient men to care for them travelled aboard the *Argus* and the *City of Lincoln*.[46] The Fifth Contingent consisted of 46 officers, 971 other ranks and 1,099 horses.

The Contingent arrived at Port Elizabeth in South Africa and went from there by train to Pretoria where the Regiment was mobilised between 24 March and 4 April. It was soon in action, undertaking the long treks which were a major feature of this war. The first casualties were suffered in early May but there were considerable successes, over 100 prisoners were captured along with 100 horses, 65 mules and donkeys, thousands of cattle, sheep and oxen and over 30,000 rounds of small arms ammunition. But in June disaster struck. On the night of 12 June some of the Regiment were at Wilmansrust. In the early evening, the Boers crept up on the camp and apparently were not challenged by the guards. They attacked with devastating accuracy. One officer and 18 men were killed and five officers and 36 men were injured. AR maintained that when he heard the first shots he dived out of the back of the tent and ran as fast as he could for cover. Thus he was not taken prisoner nor was he injured. Rumours of this tragedy reached Melbourne some five days later and the information was confirmed in the newspapers two days later when they published a cable from the Secretary of State for War in London which began, 'Deeply regret to inform you heavy loss gallant Victorian contingent …'.[47] At this stage only numbers were printed although lists giving the details of the individuals concerned began to appear on notice boards around the city, particularly at the newspaper offices. Crowds gathered to read the news. The following day the lists were published in the newspapers but the war was a long way away and communications were poor, so the lists required some alterations over the next few days. The newspapers tried desperately to print the names of men that were known to be alive and well but for the families and friends of the Contingent it was a difficult time.[48] Including the Wilmansrust casualty figures, in just two months 25 per cent of the officers and 10 per cent of the men of the Fifth Victorian Mounted Rifles had been killed or wounded.[49]

Throughout the following months, the Regiment trekked hundreds of miles regularly engaging the Boers. By the time they reached Cape Town in March 1902, a total of 54 officers and men had been killed with numerous others wounded. For his courage at Geelhoutboom in November 1901, one officer was awarded the Victoria Cross and a number of others received awards for gallantry. The telegram from General Lord Kitchener, the Commander in Chief, to the Officer Commanding Fifth Victorian Mounted Rifles conveyed his appreciation for the 'gallant and arduous service' the Rifles had given to South Africa. Now all the Australians wanted to do was to go home. Some of the Regiment travelled back on the *St Andrew* while the majority were conveyed by the *Montrose* to Durban and returned from there to Melbourne aboard the *Custodian*. More than fifty of the Contingent missed the boat at Durban and were brought home on a merchant ship, the *Manchester*, which took the troops to Adelaide. The *St Andrew* and the *Custodian* arrived within hours of each other in Melbourne on 25 April and during the early hours of 26 April 1902. The Fifth Victorian Mounted Rifles disembarked and were transported into central Melbourne by train. From there they marched through the main streets of the city lined with cheering crowds to the barracks. After a celebration lunch the men returned home to their families. The Fifth Victorian Mounted Rifles was disbanded shortly afterwards.[50] AR was fit and uninjured but two of his comrades had each lost a leg at Wilmansrust and were awarded an Imperial pension of 18d. a day.[51] AR returned to the family home at 74 Mathoura Road, Toorak, a suburb of Melbourne, where Betsy, her three daughters and Mont had lived throughout this period. Amy had been a regular visitor to Sydney where she had lessons from her brother and learnt about his teaching methods. The Alexanders had watched the progress of the war in the newspapers and read with horror the lists of the Fifth Mounted Rifles' dead and injured. They worried about AR's safety on an almost continuous basis. There had been little good news during the period except perhaps the visit to Melbourne of Their Royal Highnesses the Duke and Duchess of York. The Royal party had arrived at St Kilda pier on 6 May 1901. There was a great parade through the streets of Melbourne and a number of fireworks displays along with some other festive activities.[52]

Now that AR had returned safely to Melbourne, he decided that he was content to return to a more peaceful way of life. Very soon he joined his sister on her regular visits to Sydney and learnt about the developments in his brother's teaching methods, but as FM was away from Sydney for a number of months he worked with Robert and became very interested in the Sandow system. By January 1903, he and his sister Amy were teaching on a full-time basis in Melbourne at Australian Buildings in Elizabeth Street, the same place that FM had used a few years previously. AR was impressed with Robert's ideas and early in his teaching career he concentrated on the Sandow system.[53]

With Robert working on the launch of his teaching project, FM decided to become more involved with Shakespearian works. He wanted to participate with his pupils in a stage production of one of the plays, which he decided would be *The Merchant of Venice*. In order to attract the full cast he advertised in the Sydney newspapers (the *Herald*, the *Star* and the *Daily Telegraph*) and on Saturday 19 January 1901 he announced that the whole of *The Merchant of Venice* would be read on the following Wednesday evening and that he would select people for the various parts. Both the *Herald* and the *Daily Telegraph* stated that it was rare for amateurs to have the opportunity to participate in such a venture and both newspapers considered that there would be plenty of applicants for the parts.[54] In the event various more advertisements were required before sufficient suitable people had responded and then FM decided to form a Shakespeare class to prepare his applicants for the final selection tests.[55] The first production was *The Merchant of Venice* performed at the Theatre

Royal, Sydney on 27, 28 and 29 June 1901. Directed by FM and stage managed by the experienced Mr. D'Orsay Ogden, the production was under the patronage of, and in the presence of, His Excellency, the Lieutenant-Governor, Sir Frederick Darley, GCMG. The newspaper reports stated that the cast was selected from 'Ladies and Gentlemen who were members of Mr. Alexander's Shakespearean Society which he had conducted at his studio in Equitable building.' Many of them were also pupils. FM played the part of Shylock with Edith Young as Portia and the music, which was highly acclaimed, was composed specifically for the production by Mr. E. Stevenson who conducted the orchestra. The performance received favourable reviews and was well received by the audience. The *Herald* made particular mention of the 'rich and picturesque costumes' and the *Evening News* commented on the excellence of FM's elocution while the *Sydney Daily Mail* reporter considered its great virtue was that all the performers were audible.[56]

Later in 1901, FM leased the Criterion Theatre, Sydney for eight nights commencing Tuesday 24 September 1901. The productions were again under the patronage of the Lieutenant-Governor and stage managed by the very capable Mr. D'Orsay Ogden. Again, Mr. E. Stevenson composed music especially for the occasion. The company performed *Hamlet* on each day from Tuesday until Saturday and then *The Merchant of Venice* on the following Monday, Tuesday and Wednesday. FM played the part of the Prince in *Hamlet* and, as before, Shylock in *The Merchant of Venice*, with Edith taking the parts of Ophelia and Portia. In *Hamlet*, the experienced Mr. L. Dunbar from the Holloway Dramatic Company took the part of Claudius. Again the plays received very good reviews in all the Sydney newspapers. In fact *The Merchant of Venice* was so successful that two additional performances were given on the following Saturday and Monday evenings.[57] The Famous Trial Scene from *The Merchant of Venice* was reproduced a few weeks later on 21 November in a performance at Her Majesty's Theatre. This Grand Complimentary Farewell Matinee was for Mr. Bernard Espinasse prior to his departure to London. The programme was extensive and included 10 major items in addition to FM's contribution.[58] During FM's two short seasons at the Criterion Theatre and the Theatre Royal the casts included 44 of his students who were all members of his Shakespearian class. The most famous of the students at that time was Charles Murray, a New South Wales District Judge. Although born in England in 1842 and the son of a London barrister, he attended university in Sydney and was called to the bar in New South Wales in 1867. He married Arabella Maralla O'Connor in 1877. Both he and his wife became supporters of Alexander's methods and their children were pupils of FM.[59]

At Christmas in 1901, the members of the Alexander Shakespearean Society presented FM with a token of their appreciation. The signatures on this document, which is preserved to this day, include W.R. Ellison, Edith E. Ellison, Linda Cooper, Elsie Tait, Myra de Lissa, Wynne Whear Roberts and E. Waldergrave.

Encouraged by the success of his Shakespearian Society and the praise that accompanied the stage productions, FM decided to expand his operations. In November 1901, together with Robert Young he moved to larger premises at Granard, 84 Hunter Street, near Phillip Street.[60] This accommodation offered a number of spacious classrooms which were excellent for his proposed Dramatic and Operatic Conservatorium, of which he was the director; the whole enterprise was under the patronage of the Lieutenant-Governor. FM advertised his

Conservatorium in the Sydney newspapers advising potential pupils that the first term would begin on Monday next, 17 February 1902, at 84 Hunter Street. The aim of the course was to prepare students for a professional career either performing on the dramatic and operatic stage or as teachers. FM undertook to teach the students his methods of voice culture and elocution. This he believed would enable students to attain the really high state of excellence shown by his pupils in the recent productions at the Theatre Royal and the Criterion Theatre. During the course the students were required to participate in Conservatorium productions at a Sydney theatre. A special feature in the course of study was the Delsarte System, as applied to dramatic expression, deportment, gesture and vocalisation, and Herr Slapoffski, a well-known conductor who had recently conducted grand opera performances in Sydney, was engaged to assist with the Operatic Course. Other professional teachers were engaged to assist with this venture. For the full year-long course there were four terms and the cost was five or six guineas depending on whether students wanted to follow the dramatic or operatic course; tuition in the Delsarte System cost extra.[61]

During the second and third terms of the first course, FM decided that his students were ready to give public performances. Instead of hiring a Sydney theatre, his Shakespearean Company, as it was known, toured the area around Sydney by train, performing both *The Merchant of Venice* and *Hamlet*. Moving the company, the stage set and the apparently magnificent costumes over considerable distances in order to perform at a different location almost every night was a major undertaking. For the rest of his life, FM kept a scrapbook containing newspaper cuttings from 29 of these performances although it is possible that the company toured more extensively than the newspaper reports suggest. Certainly, there were occasions when last minute alterations to the venues occurred. In July the group performed at Cootamundra, a town made famous a few years later as the birth place of Don Bradman, but when they tried to arrange another visit in August the authorities requested payment for the hall in advance as well as an extra £2 for possible damage. FM objected to this suggestion and so the tour company went to Albury instead.[62] Many years later, when FM's irritation with the people of Cootamundra was undoubtedly forgotten, his brother, AR, and his niece, Joan, thoroughly enjoyed watching the mighty Bradman play one of his finest innings for Australia at the Oval cricket ground in London.

Generally, the plays were well received and many of the towns were delighted to have such a professional company performing in their area. The local newspapers of all the areas visited featured lengthy articles on the high standard of the performances. However, there were occasions when not all was satisfactory. The first tour began in the old city of Bathurst, some 100 miles west of Sydney. The company gave the first performance on 16 June but the disturbances and shouting from the pit reached such a level that the play was suspended and the police were called. Additionally, the members of the Arts Council present took the law into their own hands and dealt with some of the miscreants.[63] The *National Advocate* headed their article 'A Shameful Exhibition', and the reporter hoped 'for the honour of Bathurst that some further action would be taken against the ringleaders in the miserable exhibition of larrikinism'. Moreover, he 'trusted that during the rest of the tour Mr. Alexander would receive more courtesy than he had at Bathurst'.[64] The *Bathurst Daily Free Press* commented in glowing terms on the play, but 'seriously regretted that steps were not taken to suppress the unseemly conduct of a number of hoodlums who frequent the pit'. The *Bathurst Daily Times* recorded that 'Bathurst is gaining a most unenviable notoriety … as the worst town in the State as far as the behaviour of the audience is concerned'.[65] FM and his pupils took this unfortunate reception in their stride and the following night performed at Orange, a town not far from Bathurst on the slopes of Mount Carobolas. The production was pronounced a success and the audience were well behaved.[66] Then they travelled north-west to Dubbo on the banks of the Macquarie river, a little over 250 miles from Sydney, where for the third successive night they performed *The Merchant of Venice*. At both these locations they received a far better and more appreciative reception than they had at Bathurst.

The next tour took place during the second week in July and the little company went south-west from Sydney visiting first Goulbourn. This was an old colonial town, a centre for the surrounding farming area, and located some 130 miles from Sydney. From here the following day the group moved west to Cootamundra and then the next day they travelled south to Albany on the banks of the Murray river nearly 400 miles from Sydney. For their last performance of *The Merchant of Venice* the company move to Wagga Wagga on the Murrumbridgee river and from here they travelled over 300 miles home.

The company now prepared to perform *Hamlet* as well as *The Merchant of Venice*. The next tour was much longer and more exacting. They began where they had started their first tour at Bathurst and then moved to Dubbo but this time they went to Wellington on their way to Orange. From here they went to Cowra, an old town on the Lachlan river, where the hobnailed boots walking to and fro during the performance had a disturbing and distracting effect. The *Cowra Free Press* hoped that 'they would not have occasion to refer to such a heinous breach of good manners again'.[67] The company survived this experience and gave their next production of *Hamlet* in Young, a gold-mining town on the Western foothills of the Great Dividing Range. Then they moved to the more familiar territory of Albany and on to Wagga Wagga on 7 August.

For the next tour FM decided that his group would stay two nights in each place performing first *Hamlet* and on the next night *The Merchant of Venice*. This time they travelled north first to Maitland, a coal-mining area on the banks of the Hunter river, where they performed on 13 and 14 August. For the next two nights they moved to Singleton, another old mining town, on the Upper Hunter river. From here they continued north to the gold-mining town of Armidale, located midway between Sydney and Brisbane in the New England ranges. Then it was on to the mountains and the scenic town of Glen Innes situated over 3,000 feet above sea level. This lush farming area had until relatively recently in the days of the convicts been the scene of many bush-ranging exploits. The next stop was Warwick, a town on the Darling Downs about 100 miles from Brisbane, and from here on to Toowoomba, a garden town with gracious colonial architecture which 50 years before had been a staging post. Now the company turned south on their homeward journey visiting Inverell, an old pioneer village located a few miles from Glen Innes, where they performed on 1 and 2 September. From here they progressed back to Sydney after a long and very arduous few weeks.[68]

After a suitable period of rest to recover from the strain of the tours, FM resumed teaching and one assumes that his students completed their course. Certainly the tour had not diminished

FM's enthusiasm for the stage and during October and November he performed three times at the Centenary Hall. On each occasion he took part in a show entitled 'Shilling Pop' which was organised by Madam Slapoffski, an accomplished operatic soprano. FM recited his well-known pieces including *Kissing Cup*, *The Christening*, *Midnight Charge* and *The Amateur Rider*. During this period, near the end of October, he and Robert Young moved their offices to the first floor of Tattershall's Chambers, on the corner of Castlereach and Hunter Street.[69]

During the last month of 1902 and the early part of 1903, FM concentrated on teaching and his Dramatic and Operatic Conservatorium, and although Robert Young still taught the Sandow System he became progressively more familiar with and impressed by FM's work. Both of them advertised regularly in the Sydney newspapers. FM's advertisements concentrated on the art of breathing, under headings which included 'Full Chest Breathing', 'Breath is Life', 'Breathing Capacity is the Measure of Life' and 'Mr. Alexander's Breathing Method'. He emphasised that his method prevented 'the heaving of the chest, the raising of the shoulders and enabled the singer or speaker to breath silently'.[70] All the time FM was developing his ideas and his work was steadily undergoing change; this was to continue for the rest of his life. He could discuss his ideas with Robert who now incorporated many aspects of the Work into his own teaching.

During the middle of the year, FM and his Conservatorium went on tour again performing Shakespearean plays. It is interesting to note that about half the company had toured with FM the previous year. They took with them a completely new stage set, and according to reports, beautiful Venetian dresses. In Wagga Wagga in July, the newspaper report commented that *The Merchant of Venice* 'was excellently staged and well played notwithstanding there was a tinge of amateurism in some of the characters'.[71] From the beginning of August onwards FM concentrated on his teaching, which had the support of members of the Sydney medical profession including Drs. Stewart McKay, Bowman, Brady and Hogg, and started to think about producing a book about his work. He helped his brother, AR, and his sister, Amy, who both spent a considerable amount of time in Sydney, to understand his work so that they could teach his methods.

In December 1903, FM announced that his book would be available early in 1904 at a cost of 10s. 6d. He stated that the book would not be on sale in the usual way but should be ordered in advance from him so that sufficient copies would be produced to meet demand.[72] He also produced an article about his teaching but the editor of the *Sydney Daily Telegraph* had some misgivings about publishing the letter. He had discussions with Dr. Stewart McKay and was persuaded and so on, 12 December, he printed the letter entitled 'The Prevention and Cure of Consumption'. In this long epistle FM outlined his theories on the importance of breathing correctly and how proper breathing could cure consumption; however he made the point strongly that the cure would only continue if correct breathing was maintained and that should breathing be altered in any way then a relapse in the health of the individual would result. He argued that the effect that incorrect breathing had on the rest of the human system was such that harmful conditions would arise.[73] During January and February 1904, FM continued to advertise his breathing method together with his new book and advised his readers that unless they ordered the book by the end of February the charge would increase to £1 1s.[74]

WITH Mr. F. M. Alexander's COMPLIMENTS.

❋ ◆ ❋

The Human Voice

CULTIVATED
AND
DEVELOPED
FOR

Speaking and Singing

BY

THE
NEW
METHODS!

THE
NEW
METHODS!

JOHN ANDREW & CO., PRINTERS, SYDNEY.

48 Front cover of FM's booklet about the Work published in Sydney, 1900.

Within a few weeks of AR opening his school of physical culture in January 1903, Lilian Twycross, who had been FM's chief assistant for three years from 1897 to early 1900, moved into Australian Buildings and advertised that she was the only certified teacher in Melbourne of FM Alexander's work.[75] Despite AR's enthusiasm for the Sandow system he also respected his brother's ideas so in his next advertisement, a week after Lilian's one which was published on 7 March 1903, he announced that his students would have the 'advantage of the full chest breathing method introduced into Australia by his brother'. He quoted from a letter sent from Mdlle. Dolores to FM where she said that having read about FM's ideas on the art of breathing that they coincided with her own thoughts on the subject.[76] Throughout most of the year AR continued to emphasise that he was teaching the Sandow system but steadily, through the final months of 1903, he became more influenced by his brother. So by the end of the year, he and Amy were teaching their brother's methods supplemented by the Delsarte system and the Sandow system. A few months later they did not mention either the Delsarte or the Sandow system but advertised only their brother's methods, usually in the form: 'A Perfect Breathing Method' Mr. A.R. and Miss Alexander, Australian Buildings.[77] They used FM's 32-page Sydney booklet to assist their pupils. Amy kept a copy of the document for the rest of her life. The Work developed over the years but to Amy this pamphlet detailed her brother's thoughts when she began teaching and breathing exercises formed such a major part of her life.

During his time in Sydney FM made many contacts and his teaching practice was extensive. However, his career in Sydney and in Australia ended abruptly as a result of one of the greatest pieces of luck in his life. One of AR's friends was Mr. J.N. McArthur, the owner of a horse Marmont, and he advised AR that Marmont should win the Australia Cup and that Mairp, a relative outsider at 25 to 1, should win the Newmarket Handicap in the forthcoming Melbourne races. FM placed a bet of £5 on the double at 150 to 1. Mairp won the Newmarket Handicap on 28 February and two days later Marmont duly obliged on 1 March 1904.[78] Thus, FM had £750 and his dream of going to England became a reality.

PART THREE

FREDERICK MATTHIAS ALEXANDER 1904-1955
FROM AUSTRALIA TO ENGLAND

10

LONDON AND MELBOURNE

Into my heart an air that kills
From yon far country blows:
What are those blue remembered hills
What spires, what farms are those?

That is the land of lost content
I see it shining plain,
The happy highways where I went
And cannot come again.

A.E. Housman: *The Welsh Marches*

The first thing that FM did when he received his money was to pay his father's debt. Now John was free from the threat of bankruptcy and FM was allowed to leave Australia. In the space of just six weeks he organised his trip to London and in April 1904, at the age of 35 years, he sailed for England. The voyage was to last two months and cost him between £19 and £30 for a single journey. Although he had sufficient funds for his first few weeks in England he had none to leave with his family in Melbourne. He travelled on the White Star line ship *Afric*, a substantial twin screw steamer of nearly 12,000 tons. She was built in 1899 and plied the route between England and Australia as a passenger liner for many years. During the First World War she was used as a troop ship and was sunk by enemy action off Eddystone in February 1917. The *Afric* left Sydney at midday on 13 April with approximately 160 passengers and a large consignment of freight including 2,600 bales of wool, 500 tons of coconut oil, 350 tons of tallow, 200 tons of lead, 1,200 hides, 135 tons of flour and 16,000 boxes of butter.[1]

Two days later she arrived at Melbourne where FM, who had been at the new Alexander home in South Yarra seeing his family, boarded. AR was busy on the pier ensuring that his brother's crates were successfully loaded while the rest of the Alexanders started to come to terms with the departure of such an important member of the family. With additional passengers and considerably more freight on board the *Afric* sailed on 19 April for Hobart where she arrived two days later in the early morning.[2] Here FM was able to say farewell to the capital city of the Island of his birth; in addition he dispatched postcards to some of his friends and his family to tell them that he really was on his way to start his great adventure in England. He sailed from Hobart on 23 April carrying with him a number of letters of introduction from Australians, some of whom were members of the medical

49   Port Melbourne, *c.*1911.

profession like Drs. Angel Money, Charles Bage and William Stewart McKay.[3] These letters, which were to prove so valuable, were to the famous surgeon Sir Arbothnot Lane, Sir Herman Weber, Drs. Scanes Spicer (St Mary's Hospital), Percy Jakins (The London Hospital), Mansell Moullin, C. J. Martin (The Lister Institute) and Kelynack. Initially the sea was rough and FM was seasick, but he quickly recovered and became quite used to life on board ship. He had a relatively uneventful trip and made several friends during the voyage. He gave a number of recitals which he thought were very well received. From Hobart the *Afric* sailed to Albany, where again FM dispatched postcards to his family, and then on to the last port of call in Australia, Freemantle. In the middle of May, the *Afric* with her passengers and cargo arrived in Natal and after a short stop proceeded to Cape Town.[4] On 21 May she began the second part of her journey to England.[5] First she sailed to Tenerife and then on 6 June she set forth for Plymouth where she stayed for 24 hours before finally sailing to London where she arrived three days behind schedule at midnight on 13 June.[6] Here FM was met by Edith's sister May and her husband John Charles Piddock. Soon after his arrival he was able to visit the Cooks office and collect the mail from Australia that had come by ships taking the faster route through the Suez Canal. Thereafter there was a constant stream of letters as his mother, AR and Robert Young wrote to him weekly giving all the news of home.

He had left behind at 35 Leopold Street, South Yarra in Melbourne his mother, Betsy, his two brothers, AR and Beaumont (Mont), and his three sisters, Agnes Mary, Amy and

50   35 Leopold Street, Melbourne.

May. His father and his brother Arthur were still in Wynyard and Dick was working in New Zealand. At 89 Surrey Street, Sydney were Robert Young and his wife Edith, Maud Page, and other members of her family. AR and Amy, now the only wage earners for the Alexander household, taught the Work in Australian Buildings, Elizabeth Street where Lilian Twycross also had rooms. In Sydney Robert Young continued to teach at Royal Chambers, taking over many of FM's pupils. FM had left clear instructions with AR, Amy and Robert about teaching methods but the already terminally ill Robert had problems. Fortunately AR was able to assist and he made regular visits to Sydney to help. Instructions flowed from London at weekly intervals and as FM developed his ideas he sent advice to both men. It was vital that they continued to teach and advertise the Work in case FM's mission to London failed and he was forced to return to Australia. Neither men thought this was even a remote possibility and both confidently expected him to be an enormous success in England.

This confidence and enthusiasm was endorsed by Betsy whose belief in her son was touching. To her, his departure for 'home' signalled the beginning of the road to fame which she considered to be an absolute certainty for her beloved and brilliant son. She was so pleased that he no longer had the worry of the debt which she thought was a dreadful thing for him. In her view he had been very brave to stand up to all the strain. Now she

51   Robert Young's house in Sydney.

was content in the knowledge that he would make his fortune and that it would not be long before she and the rest of her family would be joining him in London. She wrote to the family in Tasmania to tell them of the news of her son's adventure and waited expectantly for the reaction. She informed FM, 'I am anxious to get a reply from Aunt Agnes [her youngest sister], what a commotion there will be when she gets my letter. I should like to be at the Pearces [her oldest sister] a little mouse on the wall.' She followed the progress of his ship in the newspaper that AR bought for her. Once she knew that FM had arrived in London she watched the clock and wondered what her son was doing ten hours behind them; apparently she counted the hours back to see if he was up or not. News of their family and friends in Tasmania was transmitted enthusiastically as were details of life at South Yarra. AR had rented a paddock and when this was fenced he purchased some fowls. These particular birds were not a great success; three died almost immediately, a further two became ill and only two laid any eggs, and even they stopped laying after a very short time. Betsy found this most depressing. Amy injured herself at the office and was in great pain with kidney stones but she was able to go into Elizabeth Street to teach and have her music lessons. Her music teacher gave her free lessons in return for breathing lessons. In early July there was an earth tremor and the house shook which gave Betsy 'a nasty turn'.

On the brighter side, she was pleased with May's fiancé, Norman Cleland, who seemed such a pleasant young man. He was learning how to teach the Work which she felt was an excellent idea. AR helped him and he practised on Beaumont who went for some weeks every day to Australian Buildings for his lessons. Agnes undertook dressmaking work and made goods for Sargood, Butler, Nichol and Ewen, a large firm of warehousemen, importers of soft goods and manufactures. They had premises in Sydney, Brisbane, Perth and Ballerat as well as Melbourne. When she was paid, she took Betsy and Amy to the theatre; these outings always proved enjoyable. Lilian Twycross visited Betsy but relations between Lilian and the Alexanders were not very amicable. AR was not impressed that she considered herself the only certified teacher of his brother's work and when she gave singing lessons this really got on his nerves. Relationships between them all deteriorated further when Betsy told Lilian that if her son stayed in London they would all be going over to England. Betsy alleged that Lilian had replied that there was no fear of that, as he would have to come back. Betsy warned her son in strong terms not to pass any information to Lilian about the Work.

These first few weeks after the departure of FM were more difficult for AR than his mother appreciated. He had to pay all the household expenses for the family and, in addition, there were a number of debts that he had to cover for his older brother who had departed rather hastily from Australia. Robert Young had similar problems in Sydney where FM had some outstanding accounts with, amongst others, his advertising agent. Also there were advances that had been paid on the book that he had intended to publish on the Work; he had left before he could achieve this but many people had ordered and paid for their copies. However, both AR and Robert took this in their stride. AR wrote confidently,

> We saw from the paper that you had arrived safely in Cape Town. It is a very monotonous trip, I know how I felt coming back from South Africa and that was only three weeks. Don't worry over us, we will be alright. Business was very good but it has quietened down a bit.

He ended this letter, 'with love and wishing you the very best of luck from your affectionate and ever loving brother'. In his next letter he said, 'I suppose ere this you have a good idea as to whether you are likely to stay in London or not and what the Dr. thinks of your methods.' He went on to confirm that he had been able to pay some of the traders and had paid a years rent for the paddock in advance.

Meanwhile, Robert in Sydney was also busy paying some of FM's debts; moreover, he was very anxious to discover whether FM intended to publish his book in London or if he should repay the Sydney people for their advances. His problems were further exacerbated because, without FM, his wife no longer enjoyed teaching the Work. Initially she wrote a detailed account of the progress of her pupils, but very quickly she declared that she wanted to follow FM to London to fulfil her dream of appearing on the London stage. By the time FM arrived in London she had booked herself a passage on the White Star ship, the *Runic*, and was busy packing. Robert took her to the ship and she sailed firstly for Melbourne where she was met by AR on 17 July. She stayed with the Alexanders for five days and during that time Dr. Bage came to see them to say farewell to her. Edith re-embarked on the Runic on 22 July and arrived in Cape Town on 15 August; she landed in England a month later. When FM heard the news on his arrival in London he wrote to his mother that 'at least she could take the 10/6d. pupils'. Betsy wrote back to disillusion him, suggesting that when Edith was with them prior to her departure she had said that she hated the Work and teaching and that she wanted to go to London to perform on the West End stage.

For FM, London was a very different place from Sydney or Melbourne. London was a huge city at the centre of an enormous empire that spanned the globe, but despite this the heartland of Edwardian London was small and there was an intimacy and cohesion about it. It was a place, and perhaps still is, of many individual villages each with its own unique identity. There were great contrasts between the very rich and the very poor, from magnificent buildings to the squalid slums of the East End. Also it was a time of great change. In the final years of the previous century, many old buildings were demolished and new premises erected and, according to reports of the day, hundreds of familiar landmarks were swept away. A large area east of Drury Lane was destroyed and replaced by Kingsway and the Aldwych. There was a major redevelopment programme in the Victoria area with the provision of countless new dwellings and the new Roman Catholic cathedral. Everywhere there was noise and dirt and a constant bustle of activity, the numerous street vendors shouting about their wares; the organ grinders and the people whistling for cabs added to the general hubbub of the scene. There were only a few cars, although registration plates were introduced in 1903, but there were numerous hackney carriages and a plethora of other horse-drawn modes of transport frequently causing severe traffic jams in London's many narrow streets. The large number of animals and the associated mews areas normally abutting wealthy residential dwellings caused their own problems of smell and litter. Although the streets were constantly swept and watered, dirt, general grime and, in winter, mud were major hazards. This was not helped by the pollution created by the railway steam engines and the huge quantity of open fires which, with the exception of a few gas fires, were the only form of heat. The result was that London buildings were black outside and it has been said that even the grass in the parks was too dirty to sit upon. Thick pea-soup winter fogs were a constant problem and clothes were changed by the majority at frequent intervals. The effort required to undertake the washing was enormous. In fact the work involved in all aspects of day to day living was considerable. Coping with all the open fires and refilling the coal scuttles was hard and dirty work and cleaning was an arduous never-ending task, and even modest homes had servants. The 1901 Census indicates that out of a population of some 32½ million in England and Wales nearly one and a half million people were employed as indoor domestic servants; the vast majority were women, many of whom started work at the age of 12 years.[7]

The Edwardian era was a time of hope and enthusiasm and in many ways was the calm before the storm of 1914. The life style was stable but operated on strict rules and codes of behaviour throughout most levels of society but it was much less restrictive than the Victorian age. It was a world of 'upstairs and downstairs', with a strict hierarchy operating in the servant areas. The nannies in uniform took their charges daily to the London parks almost regardless of the weather because fresh air was a pre-occupation and considered essential for everybody of whatever age. Health was a matter of continual concern, and sickness, particularly consumption, was a regular cause of worry; some milk was infected with tuberculosis and so goat's milk was popular. The water supply in many places was suspect and this caused difficulties. Generally the standards of hygiene were not as meticulous as they might have been, muffins being bought from the wooden tray carried on the head of the muffin man. Despite these sometimes rather lax attitudes, dress was formal and wearing hats was mandatory for all. For many it was a requirement to dress for dinner. Behaviour patterns were vitally important as it was a time when etiquette really mattered and many rituals, such as calling to leave one's card, had to be obeyed. With very few telephones letter writing was an essential and time-consuming part of life.

London was not just a bustling place during the day and at night the gas-lit city had an enchantment all of its own. King Edward VII was a great patron of horse racing and also of the theatre and these establishments along with the music halls flourished. A significant number of new theatres were built at the turn of the century and during Edward's reign including London's largest, the Coliseum, which was technically the most advanced for its time.[8] It was made famous by performances from several renowned artistes including Sarah Bernhardt. It was fortunate for FM that he should arrive in London at this particular moment in history when his interests were very much the flavour of the day.

A few days after his arrival, FM sent a telegram to explain that he had met with Dr. Scanes Spicer. Dr. Spicer was extremely interested in the Work; very quickly he became a pupil, as did his wife and three children, and in addition he sent some of his patients to FM for lessons. Dr. McKay was delighted when he heard the news from Robert. Betsy was to be less impressed a few weeks later when a photograph of Dr. Spicer arrived from FM. She hoped that she was not judging him too harshly but there was something about his face that she did not like although it was undoubtedly a clever one.

Within a few weeks, FM moved into a flat in the Army and Navy Mansions in Victoria Street; it was from here that he was to live and work for the next seven years. Slowly he began to settle into London life and learn the rules about what was and what was not considered acceptable behaviour in Edwardian society. He bought appropriate clothes and learnt how essential it was to wear spats particularly when walking in the streets of London. This lesson he never forgot and he wore spats when outside for the rest of his life and long after the pavements became reasonably clean places to walk. He enjoyed visiting the sights and going to the theatre. He became acquainted with a number of people who supported his work and were either pupils or sent pupils to him, including Drs. Jakins, Harry Campbell, Mansell Moullin and Kelynack, the actor-manager George Alexander, who was knighted in 1911, and the actor Sir Henry Irving, who when he was knighted in 1895 was the first actor to be so honoured. By the end of the year the actress Lily Brayton was a pupil, sent to him by Dr. Spicer. FM was working long hours and having some success on the London scene but his financial situation was far from secure. Image was all-important in London at that time and that cost money. He was getting a variety of pupils with a range of problems but all the time he was learning and developing his ideas. Drs. Bage and McKay were delighted. Dr. McKay, who was particularly pleased that FM had seen Dr. Harry Campbell, physician to the North West London Hospital and Hospital for Diseases of the Nervous System, sent a special message to FM through Robert. He advised him that:

52 Betsy and her daughters, Agnes (top left), May (top right) and Amy (bottom left).   **53** Amy.

on no account was he to pull a long face and frighten the inside out of the pupil by telling him he is terribly bad. You frighten the pupil so they are afraid to come near you. Hope is defeated. You must adopt the following method 'Well your case is pretty severe, but not so bad that we cannot cope with it.' Words need to be soothing.

Mr. Langon of the *Sydney Daily Telegraph* was also delighted with his countryman's success and he strongly recommended that FM should not publish his book at this time as it would expose his methods. He felt that it would be much better to wait a while until FM had established himself.

For those in Australia, life continued with varying degrees of success. Betsy was very upset by May's appendicitis which was a long term problem, and even Dr. Bage was alarmed by her condition; as AR reported, 'she looks awful, she has wasted away so quickly'. Dr. Bage declared that 'only good nursing would save her.' Betsy tended her night and day and Norman brought her a bottle of fresh milk from their cow daily. May survived. Betsy was

54 Collins Street, Melbourne, 1905.

pleased that both Amy and Norman were teaching and helping AR and delighted to have a large number of hens and ducks laying eggs. She was most upset when 'one of the best hens got a pellet in her throat and died in a minute', but practical as ever she cut off its head so the family could have a good meal that night. In November, Robert went to stay with the Alexanders for the Melbourne Cup and Betsy was determined to see that the 'poor old chap' had a good time. He, AR, Agnes and Amy had a most enjoyable day at the races and the girls were dressed in cream silk dresses and cream hats: Agnes made her dress with a little help from Betsy while Betsy made Amy's outfit. AR thought that they were magnificently turned out. May was still too weak to accompany them so Betsy stayed at home with her. She was so grateful that May had survived and very much appreciated the great kindness of Dr. Bage. But Betsy went to the theatre with AR and Amy on Cup night which she thoroughly enjoyed. Amy was causing her some concern because she became so tired, which was not really surprising as Amy, in her long dresses, walked into Elizabeth Street every day a distance of well over three miles and then did her days teaching.

May's wedding, which had been delayed because of her illness, was arranged for 1 February of the following year. Betsy was delighted, firstly, because she liked Norman and thought that he would make a good husband and, secondly, because it would mean that AR had one less mouth to feed. Beaumont had a job and was away travelling around Australia which his mother thought was good for him, particularly as he was making some new friends. Betsy wrote regularly to her relations in Burnie and Wynyard and was well informed about events over there. She was appalled when Peg Sheckleton of Table Cape eloped with Walter Flowers; as she wrote, 'just think of her going off with a married man it is too dreadful for words. I am so sorry for his wife, she is such a good person with two such nice children.' She was saddened by the illness of FM's cousin Molly Lane, who she recounted was 'dying of bleeding cancer. So sad for her husband and four children.' Betsy was delighted at the news she received from her oldest son, which proved to her that she was right and that he would be very successful in London, but she worried about the London fogs and cold English winters; as she remarked, 'you are frozen while we are roasted'.

For AR the months leading up to Christmas were varied. Initially, he and Amy had a good number of pupils and he was delighted to report that Dr. Morrison of Toorak was sending him pupils, 'six of Toorak's elite', he reported proudly to FM. In September, he had an enjoyable visit to Sydney and was able to help Robert with some of FM's pupils. However, as the weather became hotter so the number of pupils reduced, and in November he advertised in the Melbourne newspapers that he and his sister were teaching a special respiratory method. This produced a positive response but AR was still not doing well enough to pay back all the advances paid for FM's book. In fact he was struggling to pay the family expenses but he energetically tried to visit more doctors to engender interest in the Work. When they sent him pupils, he followed their advice carefully when teaching their patients. The rent for his office was increased and that did not help. It was now that he received a message from FM that he might need more money in order that he could remain in London. Stoically, he replied immediately, 'I will understand if you do cable and I hope I will have it to send, if I have you know you will get it.' He was full of praise for his brother and delighted with his success in London. He was greatly heartened by the news that Lily Brayton was coming for lessons and he hoped and prayed that this turn of events would improve his brother's financial prospects.

For Robert, life was difficult. He tried to do his best teaching the Work but he found it hard on his own. He supplemented his income by doing some performances on the stage and taught for a few hours in local schools. Fortunately, Maud Page had a job with Farmers, a large draper and millinery shop in Sydney, and this supplemented the household income. Robert was delighted with FM's success in London and pleased that his wife Edith had settled into a house in Streatham. He begged FM to look after her and told him, 'no matter how angry you may get at times be forbearing always, I know you will as you have promised me. I hope to see you again, but one never knows and so always regard your promises to me as sacred.' A little later he wrote rather forlornly, 'of course she wants to have "her chance" and I suppose she will always have a hankering for stage life.' A few months later Edith did get a small part in a play. Robert was most impressed with AR's knowledge of the Work which helped him considerably and he did begin to attract new pupils. His letters to FM, in whom he had such confidence, were full of encouragement but he advised him to remain in London and not to be attracted to New York at this early stage. He was very pleased in November when FM confirmed that he had decided not to publish the book. Clearly, this gave Robert some problems with the advances paid in Sydney but he still considered that it was the only decision that could be taken under the present circumstances. As he said, 'later on it might be a good move and of course you will have more English prestige to work upon'. He was entranced by the idea of FM 'imparting breathing to the leading lady in the Dressing Room of the Adelphi Theatre', referring to Lily Brayton who starred at that theatre for two years while her husband, Oscar Ashe, managed the Adelphi. He gave FM all the Sydney news including the death of Dr. Angel Money who, Robert reported, 'would have been glad to know you justified his introduction'.

Meanwhile in London, FM was acquiring a reputation as a breathing expert and this was how the letters to him were addressed. In Australia, AR followed his brother's lead and also became a breathing expert rather than an elocutionist. Not only was FM much in demand from members of the acting profession but also he was sent by various doctors pupils who suffered from a wide number of problems. There were many people who heard of his work by word of mouth and he placed advertisements in suitable papers. This success significantly increased FM's income, and in 1905 he was able to improve his status by engaging a servant, William, who was to remain with him for ten years until the First World War intervened and William volunteered for Army service. He sent to Melbourne books, newspapers and magazines that he thought would be of interest to his family, including a book which had pictures of Lily Brayton and Dr. Spicer's medical paper published in the *British Medical Journal* which was relevant to his work.

Family life in the Antipodes continued steadily at Leopold Street. In January 1905 the weather was very hot, and in one town in Victoria the temperature was 125°F in the shade. This caused severe bush fires; in many places homesteads, barns, fences and livestock were completely destroyed and there was some loss of life. Fortunately, these disasters did not reach South Yarra where Betsy continued to nurture her chickens, ducks and turkeys. She reported regularly all the gossip from Melbourne and Tasmania and was particularly amused with the activities surrounding Aunt Joe. Aunt Joe was FM's great aunt as she had married old Matthias' older brother Joseph. She was considered quite wealthy as she was reputed to have £4,000 in the bank and her properties. It appeared that her three daughters quarrelled, and there was a major family row when one of them and her relatively new husband moved into Aunt Joe's house in order, they said, to look after her. Betsy's view was that they were all after her money: 'they all run around making a queen of her, if she were poor they would not trouble about her at all I am sure'. The irony was that old Aunt Joe was to live another seven years.

The major event in 1905 was the wedding of May on 1 February. Brother Arthur, his wife and family came over from Wynyard and by all accounts the marriage was enjoyed by all the family. May was dressed in a gown of white silk, trimmed with white silk lace and chiffon made by Betsy, and she wore an embroidered veil and wreath of orange blossom and carried a shower bouquet. The chief bridesmaid was Agnes, who wore silver grey voile, with cream satin, straw hat and plumes. Amy wore heliotrope voile with cream hat and plumes. The service was conducted by Rev. Bob Carson. After the wedding May and her husband Norman went to Adelaide where Norman hoped to teach. Even this relatively modest occasion was expensive. FM was unable to supply any funds with the result that AR was financially very stretched indeed. He was forced to visit the pawn shop on a number of occasions until he had little of any value left to pawn and still he found himself in serious arrears with some of the household expenses. He and Amy worked as hard as they could trying to recover the financial situation and Agnes did her best to supplement the housekeeping with her dress-making. Brother Dick sent a little money from New Zealand and Beaumont was away a certain amount which helped. Betsy tended her live stock and even put 11 duck eggs under one hen.

Later in the spring AR found another house for them, and although the rent was a little more, AR hoped that, as the house had three acres of land, if they grew the feed for the fowls and all their own vegetables it would be cheaper. This house, Widford, which had a lovely flower garden, was in a beautiful position on the top of a hill in Auburn, a suburb of Melbourne. They moved in April and Betsy was delighted with her new home, which was so much more comfortable than the semi-detached house in Leopold Street, and she was most grateful to AR. At this stage Norman, who was finding life very difficult in Adelaide, decided that he and May should return to Melbourne and they stayed at Widford. By now May was expecting her first child and her son, Horton, was born on 20 November. In the meantime Norman went to Ballerat hoping to find suitable employment. On FM's instructions, AR began to study anatomy and physiology under the guidance of Dr. Bage who found him an appropriate tutor. There was some sad news: the death in May of one of FM's favourite jockeys, Mooney, who was killed while racing, and the death of Edith's father, John Page, in November.

The next six years were to prove highly successful for FM in London. He gained large numbers of pupils, some from the acting profession, including Oscar Ashe, Constance Collier, Sir Henry Irving for a short time before his death in 1905 and his son Harry Irving, Herbert Beerbohm Tree, Viola Tree, James Welch and Matheson Lang, but also a wide range of others referred to him by various doctors.[9] All were of the greatest interest to FM who was progressively developing his ideas. To publicise his work he used his Australian pamphlets for quite a long time. AR working in Melbourne was most anxious that a new pamphlet be written so he could use it in Australia showing how well his brother was doing in England. In February 1905 he wrote hoping that his brother would 'sort one out soon'. In January 1907 FM produced a pamphlet entitled 'The Theory and Practice of a New Method of Respiratory Re-Education'. This booklet was reviewed in the *Morning Post* on 7 March but the critic had some difficulty with the content. At the end of his long article he wondered if the victim of his criticism was,

> (1) a quack with a true method which he wishes to keep secret, (2) a quack with a false method which cannot be explained, (3) a genius with a true method which he had not the literary power to make clear, or (4) a genius with a true method which none but a like genius could understand from the printed page, but which is well understood after actual treatment by actors such as Messrs. Beerbohm Tree, H B Irving, and Oscar Asche, and actresses such as Mesdames Lily Brayton, Constance Collier, and Viola Tree.[10]

In December the following year FM produced another booklet, 'Re-Education of the Kinæsthetic Systems concerned with the Development of Robust Physical Well-Being'. Both these pamphlets were reproduced in FM's first book *Man's Supreme Inheritance* (*MSI*). As well as the latter pamphlet, FM produced two other articles during 1908. The first was a letter published in the *Pall Mall Gazette* on 14 March entitled 'Dangers of Deep Breathing' the main substance of which was reproduced in the preface to Alexander's second book entitled *Conscious Control*. In this article Alexander stated,

> I am prepared to give the time necessary to prove to the authorities (medical or official) connected with the Army, the schools, or the sanatoria, that the 'deep breathing' and physical exercises in vogue are doing far more harm than good, and are laying the foundations of much graver trouble in the future.[11]

In *Conscious Control* he stated, 'I stand by every word of that to-day.'[12] The second article which continued the theme of the first was entitled 'Why 'Deep Breathing' and Physical Culture Exercises do more Harm than Good'.

During the year, Dr. Leeper of Melbourne University visited England from Australia and was requested by the Australian Teachers and Schools Registration Board 'to examine and report on the latest developments of Physical Culture in the United Kingdom and on the Continent of Europe'. He visited Alexander and was most impressed by what he discovered. In his report presented the following year in Australia he commented,

> Training in breathing and voice production has been made an essential part of the curriculum of every Teacher under the Board of Education. In this department, also, just as in the case of gymnastics, there are many competing systems. I have given a good deal of attention to some of the various methods, and have formed a definite opinion as to which is the best of those that came under my observation. I should, without hesitation, give First Place to the system associated with the name of Mr. F Matthias Alexander. He has secured remarkable results.[13]

While Dr. Leeper was in London he had a course of lessons from FM and was fulsome in his praise. Dr. Leeper's report was published in the Australian press and this enhanced the reputation of AR and Amy.

In the summer of 1909, Dr. Scanes Spicer, the eminent London Ear, Nose and Throat consultant surgeon, delivered a paper to the Medical Congress on the 'Mechanics of Respiration', which was published in the *British Medical Journal*.[14] This led FM to write a letter, headed 'Breathing and Cancer', to the *Pall Mall Gazette*[15] to point out that the basis of Dr. Spicer's theories were in fact his own and that he had brought them to Dr. Spicer's attention in 1904; however Dr. Spicer had given a scientific explanation for the Work. This contention was supported in the next edition by Harry Irving. The following month FM produced a pamphlet entitled, 'Why We Breathe Incorrectly'.[16] In this he enlarged on some of the statements made by Dr. Spicer, describing the pamphlet as 'some points in connection with a Scientific Explanation of the Latest Developments in Breathing, Physical Culture, and Voice Production'. In January 1910 Dr. Spicer gave a lecture at the Medical Graduates College, the substance of which was published in the Medical Press. While FM was delighted that Dr. Spicer should choose to lecture on respiration and physical culture and advocate his (Alexander's) principles and methods, he was upset that Dr. Spicer had not acknowledged him. To counter this, in April FM produced a pamphlet which he called 'A Protest against certain assumptions contained in a Lecture delivered by Dr. R H Scanes Spicer'.[17]

At this stage FM was concentrating on producing his first book, *Man's Supreme Inheritance*. In later years he wrote that he was persuaded to write it by doctors, in particular Drs. Spicer and Percy Jakins who were both pupils. He still believed that it was not appropriate to publish his theories and maintained that he would only do so if they were prepared to read and check all the material. He was very busy with all his pupils and the only way that he could produce a book was to work even longer hours, often late into the night. The text was produced with the help of author J.D. Beresford and at last the book was ready to go to the publishers, Methuen & Co. FM expected to pay the cost of publication and asked for the approximate price of the venture. The manuscript was returned with the advice that

55 Young FM in evening dress.

the readers were of the opinion the book should not be published. FM was upset and discussed the matter with the Managing Director of Methuen. The manuscript was returned to them and then sent to Professor Frank Granger of Nottingham University for an opinion. He was impressed and sent a good appreciation to Methuen; a few days later he appeared in London to see FM.[18] The book was published in October. There were numerous reviews in a wide variety of publications. The two that pleased and interested FM most were those in the *Occult* and the *Westminster Gazette*: they were used on the cover of his next book *Conscious Control* as were those from the *Theosophist*, the *Morning Leader*, the *Onlooker*, the *Field*, the *Daily Telegraph*, *Christian World* and the *Birmingham Post*. A criticism by Mr. William Archer was published in the *Morning Leader* on 17 December; the FM response was published on 23 December, when he attempted to counter what he believed was a misconception by Mr. Archer. In March 1911 Methuen published an Addenda to *MSI* which reprinted both letters and covered a number of other points that FM considered important. Most of these aspects arose from correspondence that FM received as a result of the book. The book was successful and had a wide readership, bringing many new pupils, some of whom were to prove valuable adherents and supporters of Alexander for the rest of their lives.

During this period, the Alexanders in the Antipodes continued to enjoy life at Auburn; the teaching was successful and finances were steadily improving. AR and Amy were busy. At the end of 1906 Amy decided to holiday in Tasmania to see various members of the family. She went over just after Christmas and stayed with her cousins Edis and Louie Brown in Bourke Street in Launceston. Edis was the son of Betsy's brother Richard who had died some years previously; Richard had married Belinda Alexander, one of Aunt Joe's daughters. Her cousins in Burnie, particularly Annie Alexander who was one of Joseph's daughters, were most insistent that Amy should go and see them, but on this occasion Amy spent her month's holiday in Launceston. Two years later in 1909 she did go to Burnie to see her friends and relatives although she spent some of her holiday in Launceston with the Browns.

During 1907, Beaumont travelled around Australia. His work took him to Perth and Adelaide as well as the much nearer towns of Ballerat and Bendigo. The next year he spent some time in Newcastle while Amy visited Sydney, a city she knew very well. In the middle of 1908, the Alexander family moved from Widford to 61 Park Street, St Kilda.

56 St Kilda, *c.*1906.

By now Beaumont had married and moved from home. Although the family lost their substantial grounds when they moved, St Kilda was a very pleasant place beside the sea. The house was a short walk from the promenade and the attractive park which abutted the sea front. The following year May's first daughter, Marie, was born in the house at St Kilda on 10 September. Some of the Alexander relations from Tasmania visited the family in their new home and they in return went to Burnie. In September 1910, Robert Young died in hospital in Sydney at the age of 54 years and was described as a 'physical culture teacher'. Now the only teachers of the Work in Australia were in Melbourne. AR was a highly respected teacher and, in 1908, he gave a course of lessons to school teachers at the Melbourne Training College. Dr. Leeper stated that Dr. Smyth of the College was 'most favourably impressed'.[19]

FM was doing extremely well in London. As he wrote that year in the introduction to *Man's Supreme Inheritance*, 'During the past six years I have built up a practice in London which has reached the bounds of my capacity.'[20] His mother Betsy who had always wanted to visit her son in London was delighted when FM invited her to go and see him. He asked her to bring Amy with her as a companion and to arrive in time for the Coronation celebrations of George V in June. It was decided that Betsy and Amy would travel on the same ship, the *Afric*, that had taken FM to England seven years before.

The *Afric* left Sydney for Melbourne on 18 March a few days after the Orient mail liner *Otra* had departed carrying Premier McGow and many other important Australians to

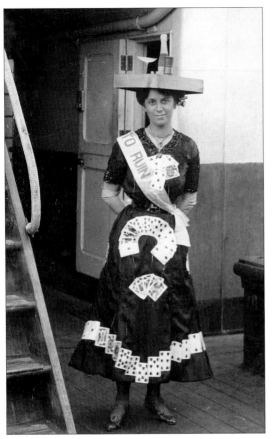

57   Amy on board *Afric.*

London for the Coronation.[21] In addition to the passengers from Sydney was a large quantity of cargo. In the holds were some 8,000 bales of wool, 400 tons of copra, 860 tons of tallow and oil, 100 tons of timber, 2,200 cases of meat, 150 bales of fur, 90 bales of sheepskins, 4,900 hides, 45 casks of pelts, 219 bags of ore, 16,250 carcasses of mutton, 2,000 carcasses of lamb, 162 quarters of beef, 2,500 crates of rabbits, 24,000 boxes of butter, as well as a number of other items.[22] Betsy and Amy along with a large number of other passengers joined the *Afric* in Melbourne on 24 March 1911 on what certainly Amy thought was simply a visit to see FM and a chance to enjoy the Coronation. She expected to be back in Melbourne before the birth of May's next child later in the year.

There were hundreds of people from Australia visiting England at this time. In fact there were so many people travelling on the *Afric* that a special train was organised to leave Flinders Street Station at 10.30 a.m. to convey the passengers alongside the ship at Port Melbourne where a large crowd was expected to witness the departure of the ship later in the day.[23] Amid all the excitement Betsy and Amy said farewell to AR and Agnes and boarded the liner for the long trip to London. Originally it was expected that the Afric would leave Melbourne at midday but, in view of the number of people travelling and the amount of cargo to be loaded, a few days before the date of departure, the time of sailing was amended to 3p.m. In the event she did not sail until 5.30p.m. The weather was exceptionally fine for the crossing to Hobart where the *Afric* arrived at 9a.m. on Sunday 26 March. Here a few more passengers embarked and some 48,000 cases of fruit and 200 tons of copper along with some general cargo was loaded. Unfortunately the weather deteriorated and the frequent heavy rain showers hampered the loading operation. Additionally, it was discovered that the *Afric* was listing and there were fears that she would have difficulty entering port at Durban. So some 100 tons of the cargo loaded in Melbourne had to be moved from one hold to another. Eventually all was made safe and a day later than scheduled the *Afric* set forth for Albany at 11.30a.m. on 29 March. She arrived five days later, some passengers disembarked and were replaced by others and more cargo was loaded. Twenty-four hours later she set sail for South Africa with every berth occupied and a large amount of cargo.[24] She arrived with her 281 passengers at Durban

58   Betsy and Amy in Cape Town, South Africa.

at 7a.m. on 19 April and sailed again the following evening to Cape Town where Betsy and Amy had a most enjoyable time visiting the sights while the ship was in port and were able to dispatch postcards to the family in Australia. The *Afric* left Cape Town at 1p.m. on 23 April and arrived at Plymouth in the early morning on 3 May. She set sail up the English Channel and eventually arrived in London at 3p.m. on Sunday 4 May.[25] Betsy and Amy had survived their long journey and were met by FM with whom they stayed in the Army and Navy Mansions in Victoria.

The two ladies from the Antipodes recovered from their travels and started to find their way around London. They met again Edith Young and a number of other Australian friends who were in London and prepared with all Londoners for the Coronation celebrations which were held in June. To be at the centre of these events was most exciting for Betsy and Amy who had never seen anything like it in their lives. Amy dispatched Coronation souvenirs to her friends and relations in Australia and received letters of thanks which clearly indicated that her friends expected her back in Melbourne soon. FM had other ideas. He had been very busy prior to the publication of *MSI* and now he was inundated with pupils. He needed assistance and so he 'persuaded' his sister, Amy, to help teach, particularly the ladies. Thus neither Betsy nor Amy were at home when May's second daughter, Betty, was born on 30 September. With two of them teaching, FM obtained a flat at 16 Ashley Place for this purpose, although he retained the flat at Army and Navy Mansions as the family home. AR and Agnes continued to live at St Kilda and AR still taught in Elizabeth Street. He was a respected teacher and had some years previously given a course of lessons to the State School Teachers. AR and Agnes expected Betsy and Amy to return, in fact, Betsy and Amy were destined never to return to the land of their birth.[26] Instead when it was clear to FM that there was sufficient work to keep all three of them busy in London he sent the message to AR. Hastily AR and Agnes packed up the family home in St Kilda and set forth for England. On their arrival they moved into Army and Navy Mansions and FM moved his residence to 16 Ashley Place where the three of them taught.

11

THE FIRST WORLD WAR

What passing-bells for these who die as cattle?
Only the monstrous anger of the guns.
Only the stuttering rifles' rapid rattle
Can patter out their hasty orisons.
No mockeries for them from prayers or bells,
Nor any voice of mourning save the choirs,-
The shrill, demented choirs of wailing shells;
And bugles calling for them from sad shires.
Wilfred Owen: *Anthem for Doomed Youth*

The beginning of 1912 found both FM and Amy busy teaching at 16 Ashley Place. Their clientele included many actors and actresses, some members of the aristocracy, clergymen, a Cabinet Minister and the great race horse trainer, Cunliffe Owen. In addition, the arrival of Amy encouraged a number of women to come to Ashley Place, notably Lucy Silcox, Elizabeth Glover and Esther Lawrence.

Lucy Silcox, born in 1862, was the daughter of a Wesleyan minister and educated at Chelsea High School, progressing to Newnham College, Cambridge where she was the College Scholar in 1883 and passed her Classical Tripos in 1885. She was appointed an Associate Member of the College Governing Body 1919-20, and became President of the College Roll 1937-40. After Cambridge, she taught at Liverpool High School before being appointed Headmistress of East Liverpool High School in 1889. She then became Head-mistress of West Dulwich High School and in 1908 moved to Southwold as Headmistress of St Felix School remaining there until her retirement in 1926.[1]

Elizabeth Glover, the daughter of a Baptist minister, was born in 1871. She went to Newnham College, Cambridge in 1892, the same year as Lilian Silcox, Lucy's younger sister. She passed her Medieval and Modern Languages Tripos in 1895 and joined the teaching profession. She taught at Badminton House School, Bristol, and later at Walthamstow Hall, Sevenoaks, becoming Headmistress of Birklands, St Albans in 1910 where she remained for the next 15 years.[2]

Esther Lawrence was born in America in 1862 but as a child returned with her family to England. She attended South Hampstead High School before spending a year at Bedford College. This was followed by study at the Froebel Society Training College from where she obtained a teaching certificate in 1883. For a short time she taught at a private kinder-garten before becoming Head of the Preparatory Department at Chiswick High School in

59   AR, *c.*1912.   **60**   Grace, *c.*1912.

1884. Ten years later she moved to the Froebel Institute, then located in Kensington, and was appointed Principal in 1901, a post she held until her retirement in 1931. She was a pioneer of the Nursery Schools movement in London, founding a Nursery School in Notting Hill in 1908 and two years later another such school in Somers Town. In 1921, she was instrumental in moving the Froebel Institute to Roehampton where the Institute developed into a large residential college in spacious grounds. She was President of the Froebel Society in 1927 and President of the Michaelis Guild from 1905 until her death in 1944.[3]

The interest of these ladies in the Work was to prove most beneficial in later years. One of Amy's pupils was Mrs. William Robinson but whether or not she was the wife of the well-known William Heath Robinson, is debatable. With so many pupils, the Ashley Place team were delighted when AR arrived and could assist them.

AR and Agnes had travelled to England with AR's fiancée, Grace Nixon. Grace was born in Melbourne in 1883 the daughter of Irish parents. Her father, Robert Nixon, came from Fermanagh and her mother, Elizabeth Swanton, from Cork. They married in Melbourne and had six children. Grace was their fifth child and youngest daughter. Only seven years after her birth her father died, leaving her mother with all her six children under the age of 16 years. She was a dressmaker and clearly she worked hard to provide for her family. AR and Grace were married at the Belgrave Presbyterian Church, Halbin Street in the St George's Hanover Square district of London on 20 April 1912, and the event was witnessed by FM and Amy. Now that AR had left home, Betsy, Agnes and Amy moved to 118 Ashley Gardens which was close to Ashley Place.

During the first months of 1912 Methuen published FM's second book, *Conscious Control*. Although not as successful as *Man's Supreme Inheritance*, this publication, developing as it did the ideas in that book, brought to the Alexander teaching rooms at Ashley Place some people who were to play a vital role in the furtherance of the Work. One such person was Andrew Rugg-Gunn, an eminent eye specialist. He had lessons with FM and was a supporter of the Work for the rest of his life. Rugg-Gunn trained at Edinburgh University and St Bartholomew's Hospital in London where he qualified as a doctor in 1907, becoming a consultant ophthalmologist in 1925. From 1915 to 1919 he served as a Captain in the R.A.M.C. and was in the Gallipoli campaign. He worked for many years at the West Ophthalmic Hospital where he became the Senior Surgeon; in addition he was ophthalmic surgeon at the Central Middlesex County Hospital and the Metropolitan Ear, Nose and Throat Hospital, and consultant ophthalmic surgeon at the Cripples Training College, Stanmore. He became a Fellow of the Royal Society of Medicine and participated in numerous activities associated with his specialisation, and had his own medical practice first in Wimpole Street and later in Harley Street.[4] He was a highly respected consultant and in his many articles and academic papers he frequently referred to Alexander's ideas which gave them added credibility.

Another person who was to become a life-long devotee of Alexander's principles was Ethel Webb. Ethel Webb was born in June 1866 into a well-known Unitarian family, the second daughter of George Webb and his wife Ann Theresa Bennett. George came originally from Bristol and his father wanted him to join the family wine importing business but George decided otherwise and became a silversmith. He came to London and went into business with a colleague John Mappin and together they founded the famous silversmith store in London, Mappin and Webb. George and Ann had eight children, three boys and five girls, but two of the sons died early in life at the ages of 12 and 21 years. They were forward-thinking parents who believed their daughters should receive as good an education as their sons. So when, in 1881 at the age of 48 years, George died, his wealthy widow ensured that all the children, then aged between four and 17 years of age, completed their education. One of the girls, Mabel, became a doctor and worked at the Royal Free Hospital but died in 1898 at the age of 31 years. Ethel went to a boarding school where she received a first-class education and her younger sister, Elsie Quendoline, was a founder pupil at Roedean School, where Isabel Fry, from the famous Quaker family, taught. When Ethel had completed her formal education in the mid-1880s, she went to Berlin to study the piano. Here she met and became great friends with a young American, Alice Fowler. Together they enjoyed the European musical scene, but when Alice's father died and her mother was no longer able to afford to pay for Alice to remain in Europe, she returned to New York and taught the piano to private pupils. Ethel, by now an accomplished musician, decided to join her friend and they both taught many pupils from the families of the famous 'Washington Square set'. One of these was the academic Wendell Bush, a millionaire who with his brother owned half of New York docks. His wife and Ethel became life-long friends.

Ethel enjoyed New York, but her mother in England did not approve of her daughter teaching music, even privately and to well-connected families. A telegram was dispatched from England advising Ethel that her mother was ill and wanted her daughter to return immediately. This Ethel did, but when she discovered that her mother was in extremely good health (in fact she lived to the age of 89 years, dying in 1928) she obtained a passage on the next available ship bound for New York. Here she found her friend Alice Fowler very ill and requiring expensive specialised medical treatment. Ethel took over Alice's piano teaching practice and looked after her until she was restored to complete health. This situation was to be reversed many years later when a very tired and ill Ethel arrived in America in 1940. The two friends stayed together for a while and Ethel developed a wide circle of friends amongst the influential citizens of New York. In about 1900 Ethel returned to England and lived with her mother. By now she and two of her sisters had given up their Unitarian life style and become Anglicans. Ethel continued to play the piano daily but her left hand lacked power as a result of an unfortunate smallpox immunisation. She and her sister Elsie decided to tour round Europe visiting the music festivals. They continued this for some years until, in 1907, Elsie married Hans Schumann, a German from Munich.

By now, Ethel had a wide circle of friends in London, particularly amongst the artistic set, which included the poet and novelist John Masefield. As a very able pianist, she entertained her friends and acquaintances regularly but her arm and back were causing her increasing difficulties. She found a copy of Alexander's latest book, *Conscious Control*, and was so impressed that she decided to visit Ashley Place. She began lessons immediately. The improvement in her condition, particularly her back, was profound. Completely fascinated by the Work, she joined the Alexanders at 16 Ashley Place very shortly afterwards, initially helping with the enquiries and organising appointments, in time becoming FM's personal assistant and secretary. She remained working with FM until very shortly before her death in 1952, travelling to America on many occasions. She was instrumental in initiating two other life-long devotees of the Work into the Alexander fold. In the summer of 1912 she went to Rome to study the work of Dr. Maria Montessori; she had read one of the Dottoressa's books and thought there was a connection with the ideas of Alexander. In Rome she met Irene Tasker and Margaret Naumburg. She gave them FM's latest book, *Conscious Control* and the ladies were intrigued by what they read. Both in their different ways were to become important to the Work in the years to come. In 1913, on her way home from Rome to New York, Margaret Naumburg came to London. Ethel Webb introduced her to FM and she had a course of lessons.

Irene Tasker was born in 1887, daughter of Rev. John Greenwood Tasker and his wife Ellen Martha née Sanderson. Rev. Tasker was a Wesleyan minister and one time Principal of the Theological College at Handsworth in Birmingham. Irene attended the King Edward VI High School for Girls, Birmingham and progressed to Girton College, Cambridge in 1907 where in 1910 she passed her Classical Tripos; she gained her MA in 1927. After her time at Cambridge, she taught initially at a little 'home' school for eight- to 14-year-old children.

Her employer was a pioneer of 'New Teaching' and encouraged Irene to study the Montessori method. This she did and she went to Rome in 1912 obtaining a Montessori diploma the following year. On her return to England in 1913, she visited Ethel Webb, who introduced her to FM. He was interested in her short sightedness, which was a serious problem for Irene, but also advised her that she had a bad stoop. He declared confidently that if she decided to have lessons 'we'll make ten women of you'. Irene was horrified by this suggestion as she thought there was too much of her already, but she agreed to have a course of 30 lessons in the summer holidays. During this period she was translating from Italian Dr. Montessori's own handbook; this translation was published by Heinemann in 1913. In 1914 she became a lecturer on the Montessori method at a Training College in Darlington where she remained for two years until wartime constraints forced the college to cease Montessori training. When Margaret Naumburg in New York, heard this she offered Irene a post at her school in New York with the added inducement that in the afternoons she could attend the lectures at Columbia University given by Professor Dewey, a family friend of the Naumburgs. Irene took this opportunity and set forth for New York.[5]

For the Alexanders, 1913 was a successful year. FM, AR and Amy were busy teaching at Ashley Place which was also FM's home. The books were selling well and there were large numbers of pupils with some influential people taking a great interest in the Work. AR was happily married and Betsy and her two daughters were living near FM in comfortable surroundings. Betsy was delighted with this and Agnes was undertaking private dressmaking work. She had her mother's talent and was able to produce the most exquisite clothes which were the envy of every lady who saw them. May and her husband Norman, with their three children, Horton, Marie and Betty who was two years old, were on their way to England to visit the family. Prior to leaving Australia on what was supposed to be a visit, May had taken her children to see her beloved father, John, and her daughter Marie remembered this event for the rest of her life. Betsy was very pleased at the prospect of seeing her youngest daughter again and her three grandchildren. Of her other children, Arthur was still in Wynyard although he, his wife and their children moved to Melbourne a few years later, Dick was still working in New Zealand where he remained for the rest of his life, and Beaumont was also expected in London shortly. For Betsy things could not have been better; perhaps most importantly, FM was succeeding and becoming quite a famous person in certain London circles. She was able to visit the London theatres and write to her relations in Australia about all the exciting events that were taking place around her. To her delight Amy became engaged to be married. Her fiancé was Benjamin George Mechin, a London ivory merchant. George was born in Penzance in 1872, the oldest child of George Mechin who came originally from Gloucester and his wife Marjory Cormack Smith who came from Burray in the Orkney Islands. Betsy considered this an ideal marriage for her daughter as George was a most upright, honest and wealthy man; however, she was slightly concerned about Amy's lack of domestic skills. She was only slightly reassured when George told her firmly that he was looking for a wife not a servant; he felt sure that he could hire suitable staff to meet the requirements of his new household.

The wedding took place on 3 June 1914 at St Augustine Presbyterian Church in New Barnet. FM gave his sister away and George's brother Jack was the best man. Two days later

61   George and Amy Mechin's Wedding.

62   Agnes, *c*.1912.

the newly married couple departed from Liverpool on their honeymoon. They arrived in Quebec on 12 June and spent the next three weeks visiting the Great Lakes, Montreal, Toronto, the Niagara Falls, Albany and New York, where they particularly enjoyed China Town and the enormous Woolworth building before returning home to arrive at Tilbury on 17 July.[6] Little did they appreciate when they went away how fast events would occur that would so change the world. While they were abroad, on 28 June, Archduke Ferdinand, the heir to the Hapsburg Empire was murdered in Sarajevo and a few days after they moved into their new home, Widford, in New Malden, Austria declared war on Serbia on 28 July. The Russians mobilised their troops and Germany declared war on Russia and France and invaded Belgium with the inevitable result that on 4 August Great Britain declared war on Germany; eight days later on 12 August Great Britain declared war on Austria-Hungary.

During the period of Amy's honeymoon, FM and AR continued to teach at Ashley Place with Ethel Webb helping and assisting them, but when Amy returned home a married lady she did not continue teaching at Ashley Place. This might have been a problem had it not been for the war, which caused an immediate reduction in the number of pupils to Ashley Place. Suddenly all London was concentrated on the events in Belgium, the British Expeditionary Force was dispatched to the Continent and the Battle of Mons was less than three weeks away. FM, AR and George were all too old to join the Army although George did try. He volunteered but was firmly rejected as being over age; half a million other volunteers were accepted during the first month of the war. There was a problem for the family with a war under way. George's ivory business suffered but not as much as the Alexanders did through lack of pupils. FM and AR had considerable financial responsibilities in addition to their own households. By now AR had taken responsibility for Betty, May's youngest child, and she was living with AR and Grace. There was also their mother, Betsy, Horton, May's oldest child for whom Betsy had now assumed responsibility, and their unmarried sister Agnes who did earn a little from her dressmaking but not enough to support the household. Additionally, there was Norman with his wife May and their daughter Marie. He had been anxious to return home to Australia with his wife and all his children but now the war made this impossible and they were all stranded in England. Norman was most unhappy about this and found obtaining employment difficult. Lastly there was Edith Young, now a widow, who had not proved

63   Betsy, c.1912.

the success she had hoped on the London stage, living in her London flat. Her sister May and May's husband Charlie Piddock, with their two young children Jeffrey and Bert, were frequently in severe financial difficulties. The future was looking decidedly bleak.

George and FM were very good friends and family matters were now of the utmost importance to them both. George encouraged FM to go to America where he was sure there were large numbers of potential pupils. Margaret Naumburg was in New York; she was most enthusiastic about the Work and had frequently assured FM that she could supply him with as many pupils as he could manage. So the decision was made: FM would go to America and George undertook to pay his fare, while AR would stay in London at least for the moment and teach such pupils as there were available. This meant that Ashley Place could remain open for business for the duration of what they all thought would be a short war. The final decision taken by FM was to marry his great friend Robert's widow, Edith. This wedding took place on 10 August, by licence, at the Registry Office of St George, Hanover Square. Afterwards Edith moved into 16 Ashley Place, where AR and Ethel Webb continued to work. FM made his plans to leave England and on 12 September he sailed on the

Lusitania for New York just as Beaumont appeared in London with some financial difficulties.[7] FM left a message with George that said, 'I have no desire to injure Mont. Let him
have a supply to go on with until the agreement is settled.' This problem was solved by the
ever generous George who later inspected the agreement.[8]

By this time, the war had progressed rapidly. Between 12 and 22 August some 120,000
men of the British Expeditionary Force (BEF), a significant percentage of the total British
Army including Reservists, under the command of the 62-year-old General Sir John French,
had crossed the Channel; they were described by the German Kaiser as 'a Contemptible little
Army'.[9] Just under 36,000 of these men engaged the Germans at Mons with orders to hold
the Mons-Condé Canal on 23 August.[10] Although the British managed to hold the line
against vastly superior numbers, the French were under severe pressure and forced to retreat,
with the result that the British had to retreat with them first to Le Cateau, where on
26 August a stand was made and many British soldiers fought bravely sustaining 8,000
casualties, and then to the River Marne. This great retreat was gruelling; between 24 August
and 5 September, for example the 1st Battalion the Gloucestershire Regiment covered 244
miles with one rest day and on two successive days they marched over 20 miles.[11] The British
survivors of this opening campaign of the war were known ever after as the 'Old
Contemptibles'. The Germans were now almost in Paris; the advance had to be halted. On
5 September the French, supported by the British, mounted a major counter offensive across
the River Marne. Over the next few days approximately a million French troops, of which
about a quarter became casualties, and 125,000 British soldiers forced the Germans to retreat
across the River Aisne.[12]

The *Lusitania* with FM on board arrived in New York on 17 September. This great
Cunarder was sunk by the Germans nine months later with the loss of 1,200 lives. Five days
after the *Lusitania* arrived in America, the British cruisers, *Aboukir*, *Hogue* and *Cressy* were
sunk by German U-boats.[13] The war was proving costly in manpower and hardware. Nearly
half a million men in Britain had volunteered to serve in the Army and the countries of the
Empire were also busy sending troops. By the end of the war, the total number of troops
sent to overseas war theatres from the Empire countries of Australia, Canada, India and New
Zealand was over 300,000, half a million, 850,000, and 100,000 respectively.[14] A significant
number of troops came from another Empire country, South Africa, but many of these
fought in the various battles in Southern Africa.

The first Canadians arrived in England in mid-October.[15] A few days later the First Battle
of Ypres began with the Germans shelling Ypres, severely damaging this ancient city. For
the month following 20 October three main battles ensued, first at Langemark where the
German Army suffered serious losses, secondly at Messines where the young Corporal Adolf
Hitler was awarded an Iron Cross, and a third battle was along the Menin Road. The British,
including many Indian troops, French and Belgium forces combined to provide determined
resistance but in human terms the cost was considerable.[16] By the end of this month-long
campaign, more than half the original 160,000 professional British soldiers of the BEF were
dead or wounded. The total French fatalities in the war so far had reached the horrifying
total of 306,000, those of the Belgians were 30,000 and the German dead numbered
241,000. The German volunteer corps had suffered particularly heavy casualties at Ypres, and

at their cemetery at Langemark beyond the gateway decorated with the insignia of every German university lie the bodies of 25,000 student soldiers in a mass grave.[17] As the year continued the war scene was extended: Turkey entered the war against the Allies; battles took place on the Eastern Front between the Germans and the Russians; the British cruisers *Good Hope* and *Monmouth* were sunk off Coronel, South America, and in a counter offensive a month later a German Naval squadron was destroyed near the Falkland Islands; a British Protectorate over Egypt was proclaimed; the first Zeppelin appeared off the British coast; the first German bombs were dropped in Kent; and German warships bombarded the east coast of England killing 40 civilians and injuring several hundred others. These were the first civilian deaths in Britain caused by enemy action since 1690.[18] The first few months of war had produced thousands of casualties and on the Western Front the Allies and the opposing Germans had 'dug in' to their trenches. The fighting was to be long and bitter.

When FM arrived in New York he knew only two people, one of whom was Margaret Naumburg. Her mother recommended the *Essex Hotel* for teaching rooms and the manager, Mr. Carte, and his wife agreed to accommodate him without the usual advance

64   FM in New York, 1916.

of rent. Margaret was as good as her word and pupils flocked to the *Essex Hotel* for lessons. Two of her most influential friends, the writer Waldo Frank and the businessman Arthur Reis, became pupils within the first few weeks. They were followed by the tobacco magnet J. B. Duke and, later, his brother. Soon FM was working hard all day, barely able to cope with the demand of these important and wealthy people. His future was secure, at least for the moment, as he was earning good money and his work was receiving acclaim from prominent members of New York society, and this was in no small part thanks to Ethel Webb and her most fortunate meeting with Margaret Naumberg in Rome. Without American support at this vital time FM's work would have suffered immeasurably and he would have had to return permanently to England.

One of FM's pupils was a 10-year-old girl, crippled from birth. She was the granddaughter of Carnegie's partner Mr. Schoonmaker. She needed a considerable amount of

65 Lone Pine Cemetery.

work and so FM wrote to Ethel Webb suggesting that she should come to America and become the child's resident teacher. The idea appealed to Ethel and so, early in 1915, she made the journey across the Atlantic and took up residence in New York; she was soon reacquainted with many of her old friends and quickly settled back into New York life. She taught the child and also assisted FM with his increasing work load, caused partly by some of Ethel's friends wanting lessons. Although the American teaching practice was highly successful, in the spring FM felt it was time to go home to see his family and friends.

Thus, in May 1915, FM returned home to England and resumed working at Ashley Place. This was at a particularly poignant time of the war. On 22 April the five week long Second Battle of Ypres began, and on the first afternoon at 5p.m. the Germans released poison gas near Langemark, the French and Algerian troops being the first to suffer from this new form of warfare. Two days later the Germans used gas again and this time it was the Canadians who suffered.[19] On 25 April the first British, Australian and New Zealand troops landed at Gallipoli. This campaign, which was to end nine months later with the withdrawal of all the allied troops, remains one of the greatest tragedies in British military history. Many have said that had it not been for the leadership and heroic actions on the day of the landings of the young Turkish Lieutenant Colonel Mustaf Kemal, later known as Atatürk, the outcome of the campaign might have been different. At Suvla a future Prime Minister, the young Captain Clement Attlee, was in command of a rearguard holding the perimeter around one of the evacuation beaches.

From this beach alone over 83,000 troops, together with nearly 4,700 horses and mules, about 1,700 vehicles and 186 heavy guns were rescued over a 12-day period in December. A few weeks later over 35,000 troops were removed from Cape Helles. The courage and endurance of the British, French, Australian and New Zealand troops was outstanding but the cost was horrific; nearly half a million men took part, over half of them were casualties and of those killed 28,000 were British, 10,000 French, 7,595 Australian, and 2,431 from New Zealand.[20]

Today, near the entrance to the Dardanelles at Cape Helles, on the cliff tops above the British and French landing areas, stand two great memorials, one British and the other Turkish. The smaller French Memorial is nearer the beach. A few miles up the coast are a number of other memorials. Above ANZAC beach stands the Australian Memorial at Lone Pine and on the hill at Chunuk-Bair there is the New Zealand Memorial. Down at ANZAC cove there is a recently erected memorial which carries an inscription written in 1934 by Atatürk, the father of modern Turkey. It reads,

> Those heroes that shed their blood and lost their lives … You are now lying in the soil of a friendly country therefore rest in peace. There is no difference between the Johnnies and the Mehmets to us where they lie side by side here in this country of ours … You, the mothers who sent their sons from far away countries wipe away your tears; your sons are now lying in our bosom and are in peace after having lost their lives on this land they have become our sons as well.

In total there are over thirty Commonwealth war cemeteries marking the heroism of so many gallant men who died in this far off land.[21] One of those who survived was Laurence Frederick Wells from Burnie, one of Betsy's nephews and cousin of FM, AR and Amy; he was a member of the 5th Reinforcement, Third Light Horse Regiment.[22] One of those who was not so fortunate was the poet, Rupert Brooke, who wrote the famous words, 'If I should die, think only this of me, That there's some corner of a foreign field that is for ever England.' He died on the voyage to the Dardanelles on Skyros where he is buried.[23] Meanwhile in Europe, in May the Battle of Aubers Ridge took place, and on 22 May Italy declared war on Austria. In England a Coalition Government was formed on 26 May led by Asquith; he was succeeded at the end of the following year by Lloyd George.

In the middle of this terrible year the Canadian doctor, Colonel John McCrae, serving at Essex Farm near Ypres, wrote what became one of the most famous poems of the war, 'Flanders Field'. The attitudes of the day were reflected so poignantly in the final verse:

> Take up our quarrel with the foe;
> To you from failing hands we throw
> The torch; be yours to hold it high,
> If ye break faith with us who die
> We shall not sleep, though poppies grow
> in Flanders fields.

After this poem was published, an American, Miss Moina Michael, responded with another poem the first verse of which is most pertinent:

Oh! You who sleep in Flanders Fields
Sleep sweet - to rise anew:
We caught the torch you threw.
And holding high we kept
The faith with those who died.[24]

The mood of these poems reflected the opinions of many people in Britain who considered at the end of 1915 that the cost of the war in human terms was so great that for the sake of those who had died the Germans must be defeated. This feeling was increased in October by the court martial and subsequent execution by the Germans of the 49-year-old British nurse, Edith Cavell, who while working in Brussels had helped British and French prisoners-of-war, and Belgians who wanted to serve the allied cause, to escape to Holland. This situation was further inflamed by the wide circulation of a false story that she had fainted on the way to her execution and had been shot by the officer in charge of the firing squad. The publication of a graphic picture depicting this tale in the *New York Tribune* added credibility to this story and increased anti-German attitudes in both Britain and America.[25]

In the Autumn of 1915, FM returned to America, and Ethel Webb, who had remained in New York, assisted him with what was becoming a flourishing teaching practice. Ethel was able to introduce FM to many of her important and influential friends, in particular to the millionaire Professor Wendell Bush, Professor of Fine Arts at Columbia University, and his wife. This association led to introductions to other members of the staff of the university including Professors John Dewey and Wesley Mitchell. Soon these men and their wives were coming for lessons. All of them were to be of great assistance to FM in the years to come. Professor John Dewey, who wrote introductions for three of FM's books, was a famous philosopher of the time. He was born in 1859 in Vermont, New England and graduated from the University of Vermont in 1879. After a short spell teaching, he obtained his doctorate from Johns Hopkins University and in 1884 went to the University of Michigan as Professor of Philosophy. From there he went to the University of Minnesota and then to the University of Chicago after a grand European tour with his wife and five children, during which time one of his sons died of diphtheria. He joined the staff of Columbia University in 1904 as Professor of Philosophy. He was highly regarded in America, publishing books, essays and academic works throughout his long life. [26] He was a great supporter of the allied cause during the 1914-1918 War and believed that America should send troops to Europe to help defeat Germany. He and FM became friends and thereafter the Deweys always entertained FM most generously whenever he was in New York. Pupils from a wide range of backgrounds continued to come for lessons in ever increasing numbers but in the spring FM decided it was time to return home.

When he returned to England, London was preoccupied by the war. The 54-year-old Sir Douglas Haig had replaced Sir John French as the Commander in Chief of the British and Empire Forces and both the British and French Governments were aware that it was essential for the Allies to achieve a major success on mainland Europe; as 1916 progressed this became more important. The Naval Battle of Jutland took place on 31 May, which effectively kept the Germans in home waters for the rest of the war although their submarines continued to inflict considerable damage on allied shipping.[27] On land, the German assault at Verdun in February was proving devastating, and by the late spring the French were getting desperate, the losses that they were suffering almost beyond endurance. The battle lasted nearly ten months, from February to December, and has been described 'as the greatest battle of attrition in history'. On 1 April the Kaiser declared, 'This war will end at Verdun.'[28] The French pledge, given by the Commander at Verdun, General Pétain, was 'Ils ne passeront pas', but the cost was terrible. By the end of June the French and the Germans had each suffered over 200,000 casualties, and on one day it was claimed 7,000 French horses were killed in a bombardment. Among the injured, was Charles de Gaulle, who was taken prisoner by the Germans.[29] Battles continued in the Ypres Salient, and Winston Churchill serving as a Battalion Commander at Ploegsteert, known to the English as Plog Street, was nearly killed on a number of occasions.[30]

In Britain, Kitchener's call for volunteers had met with a great response, 100,000 men a month volunteering throughout 1915, but in January 1916 conscription was introduced.[31] In March the first two Australian Divisions arrived in France, followed a little later by two more Divisions; another Division was subsequently raised in Britain. The Australians had previously fought in the Middle East as well as at Gallipoli. The New Zealanders who had also seen service at Gallipoli arrived on the Western Front in April; their casualty rate by the end of the war was, in proportion to their population, the highest in the Empire.[32] With the addition of these troops it was hoped to secure a victory for the Allies. Therefore, in order to relieve the pressure on the French, it was decided to mount a major offensive on the Western Front. The result was the Battle of the Somme, a battle that, it was said, 'saved Verdun'.[33]

The Battle of the Somme opened with the artillery shelling the German lines for a week before the troops advanced. It was assumed that nobody could survive such a bombardment and that the ground troops would have a relatively easy time. In the event, when the British advanced on 1 July they were mown down, and there were approximately 60,000 casualties on that day, including about 20,000 dead, a fifth of the attacking force. Regiment after regiment was virtually destroyed and some, like the 1st Newfoundland Regiment, ceased to exist.[34] At Delville Wood above the Somme the South Africans made their supreme sacrifice of the war. Today in that bloodiest battle-hell of 1916 there stands a white colonnade of peaceful beauty in commemoration of their heroism and courage and the worst day in British history. The campaign continued until 13 November, by which time 419,654 British and Empire soldiers had been killed or injured together with some 194,451 French soldiers. The total number of allied dead was over 146,000, of which 95,675 were British and 50,729 French.[35] Amongst those killed was the Prime Minister's son, Raymond Asquith, and one of the injured was the young Guards officer, Harold Macmillan, a future Prime Minister. This was the third time that Macmillan had been injured, but on this occasion he did not return to the Front; instead, he remained on crutches until after the end of the war.[36] The Allies had gained a mere 125 square miles. It is said that idealism died on the Somme. Certainly this slaughter of British youth was a tragedy made worse because the volunteers had enlisted with their friends and work colleagues. Thus, the men from one street or factory had all died together. For some mothers this meant that their husbands and all their sons had been killed in a morning. Lists of the dead and wounded were placed on town, village and church notice boards throughout the land; the effect was devastating. The offensive had failed but the war went on. Kitchener, who had been the Secretary of War since 1914, was drowned in June on his way to Russia.[37] The situation was grim.

During the last five months of 1916 a total of nearly a million men had died.[38] It was against this background, during the summer of 1916 in England and winter in America, that FM started to prepare a book for publication in America. His friends and pupils were sure that a book was essential to help promote the Work and in particular John Dewey and Waldo Frank were enthusiastic supporters, offering to help in any way they could. FM decided to combine *Man's Supreme Inheritance*, the addenda to *Man's Supreme Inheritance* and *Conscious Control*, all of which he amended. In Part 1 of the new book he expanded significantly the chapter on 'Race Culture', originally part of *Man's Supreme Inheritance*, and wrote an extra chapter entitled 'Evolutionary Standards' to reflect the intense anti-German views held by many on both sides of the Atlantic. Part of this new chapter was written prior to America entering the war in March 1917 and part after their intervention.[39] In Part 2 of the book, which was based on *Conscious Control*, he expanded the chapter on the 'Process of Conscious Guidance and Control' and added two extra chapters on this topic as well as a chapter entitled 'Individual Errors and Delusions'. While he was in England he was able to visit all his friends and relatives, teach many of his pupils again, and relax at the races. During this time, on 27 July, Captain Charles Fryatt was executed by the Germans in Bruges. Fryatt, commander of the Great Eastern Railway steamer, the *Brussels*, was seized by the Germans when his ship was intercepted during one of its regular crossings from Harwich to the Hook of Holland. He was found guilty at a court martial of trying to ram a German submarine.[40]

When FM was in America during the winter of 1916, he tried to find a publisher prepared to produce his book and arranged with John Dewey that he would write the introduction. He spent all his spare moments making alterations and amendments to the text. Finding a publisher proved more of a problem than had been anticipated. Eventually, FM was taken to dinner by the President of Duttons Publishing Company, John Macrae, who explained that his readers had advised against publication but he had read the text and confirmed that Duttons would publish the book.[41]

FM had a very large number of pupils which he described as a 'real flood'. His pupils included many well-known Americans such as Professor Kallen, Professor Hodge, John F. Waterbury, the banker, the wife and daughter of Mr. Harriman, the railway magnate, Amos Pinchot, brother of the Governor of New Jersey, John J. Chapman and his wife (née Astor), J.B. Duke, and Dr. Jowett, the famous preacher. He enjoyed the hospitality of many influential New Yorkers, visited the theatre regularly and maintained a keen interest in the racing scene in England. He was delighted when the Americans entered the war and was most hopeful that now the war would be soon over. In the spring of 1917 Irene Tasker, who was now teaching at Margaret Naumburg's school in New York, was fascinated by the improvement in one of her young pupils as a result of his Alexander lessons. She wrote to FM to tell him; he asked her to visit him, which Irene duly did, with the result that they agreed she should learn to teach the Work. Irene remained at Margaret Naumburg's school until the end of the summer term, by which time she had completed her studies at Columbia University; she started her apprenticeship in the Work when FM returned to America in the autumn of 1917 after his summer in England.[42]

Meanwhile, 1917 was to prove another dreadful year both on the Western Front and at sea. The German U-boats were inflicting significant damage on allied shipping. During the four years of war more than 2,000 British naval and merchant vessels were sunk, and more than 12,000 sailors and merchant seamen were drowned. In April 1917, 373 allied and neutral ships were lost, a total tonnage of 873,754, which was the highest monthly figure recorded in both the world wars.[43] A success of some sort was essential.

On 9 April the Battle of Arras began. The weather was atrocious, the temperature was low and the rain alternated with snow and sleet. Initially, the attack was successful. Within a few hours the British had penetrated the German front and captured 9,000 prisoners. At Vimy Ridge, just north of Arras, the Canadians triumphed and the Australians captured part of the Hindenburg Line at Bullecourt, but the increasing intensity of the German counter attacks brought this phase of the battle to a close on 14 April. The losses at this stage were twenty thousand. When the battle resumed the Germans had reorganised and a war of attrition began. This went on for a month, by which time a further 130,000 casualties had been sustained with no appreciable gain in ground.[44] Meantime the French attacked at Chemin des Dames. The weather was as bad as at Arras and the Germans, aware of the forthcoming attack, inflicted a massacre on the French troops. There were 130,000 French casualties in five days.[45] The effect on the French Army was considerable and what followed has been described by some as a mutiny. Certainly morale was very low and there were many acts of indiscipline. A significant number of the troops did not wish to participate in further offensive attacks and this general dissatisfaction with the war effort was mirrored by discontent in the civilian population. The French authorities took strong action. There were 3,427 courts martial, 554 soldiers were condemned to death and 49 actually shot. Hundreds of others were reprieved and sentenced to life imprisonment. Order was restored in the French Army but it was not until August that Commanders felt sufficiently sure of their men to order even limited offensive actions.[46] In Russia in 1917, the revolution, abdication of the Tsar and the rise of Lenin brought about, in October, a three-month armistice which effectively ended their participation in the war.[47]

The British hoped that a major breakthrough in Flanders could be achieved and so the assault on the Messines Ridge in the Ypres Salient was launched. British miners had dug for many months previously deep under German lines and in 8,000 yards of tunnelling had planted 20 mines. Nineteen of these mines containing 600 tons of explosives exploded at 3.10a.m. on 7 June causing consternation and complete bewilderment in the German front line and devastation all around. The blast could be felt for miles and, according to Vera Brittain, it seemed as though 'an earthquake had shaken Southern England'.[48] The craters were enormous, and today one of these at Spanbroekmolen, which is 430 feet in diameter, is known as the 'Pool of Peace'. After these explosions, the Royal Artillery commenced a bombardment with 2,266 guns. The resultant chaos enabled the British advance, which included the 20-year-old Anthony Eden, to succeed and Australian and New Zealand troops to secure the ridge.[49] Now the main assault north-east of Ypres could begin. The result was

66 Tyne Cot Cemetery.

a three-and-a-half month campaign known today as Passchendaele which started on 31 July. The conditions were terrible, heavy rain turned the whole area into a quagmire, troop, guns, tanks and vehicles became completely bogged down, and the bombardments created enormous craters that quickly filled with water. Battles took place throughout the Salient including Polygon Wood, Broodseinde, Poelkapelle, Hooge, St Julien, and along the Menin Road. The whole area was soon devastated, filled with the trappings of war and decaying corpses. Eventually, on 6 November, when 70,000 British and Empire soldiers were dead and over 170,000 were wounded, the Canadians took the pile of rubble which had once been Passchendaele.[50] Today, near the rebuilt town, is the largest Commonwealth Cemetery in the world, Tyne Cot, with 11,908 graves and the names of 34,984 missing carved on a curved wall.

Now the Allies transferred their attentions to France and a few weeks later, on 20 November, the first tank battle in history took place at Cambrai. Initially, the attack was successful and on 21 November the bells of London rang out for the first time since the beginning of the war, signalling a famous victory. But this was not to be. The Germans counter attacked and began to engage the tanks which were not supported by infantry. The battle ended many casualties later in stalemate. The 11 days of this battle have been described as the most dramatic of the war, but the most significant point was that the Germans failed to learn from the experience and did not accept the importance of the new weapon.[51] By the end of 1917 almost a complete generation of British youth, as well as Australians,

Canadians and New Zealanders had been subjected to the horrors of trench warfare and a very large number of these men were either dead or seriously and permanently injured. The British had suffered some 400,000 casualties in the offensives in the later part of 1917 alone.[52] The effect on the population as a whole was enormous.

Back in America, FM was finalising the draft of his book, totally devastated by the events in Europe. A number of his friends and relations were serving in France, including one of his wife's nephews. He worked hard teaching a large number of pupils, but his book, that he entitled *Man's Supreme Inheritance*, second edition, was a major priority. He was helped by Ethel and Irene and other friends. Duttons obtained good pre-release advertising in a number of newspapers around America, including the *New York Evening Post*, the *New York Times* and the *Richmond Times-Dispatch*, Virginia.[53] When it was released in late February the book was an immediate success, and very soon Duttons had to produce a reprint. It was reviewed in numerous newspapers, including the *New York Herald*, the *St Louis Globe*, the *New York Times*, the *Indianapolis Star*, the *Boston Evening Transcript*, the *Philadelphia Telegraph*, the *Boston Herald*, the *Brooklyn Daily Eagle*, the *Pittsburgh Dispatch*, the *Chicago Daily News*, the *Springfield Republican*, the *Springfield Union*, Mass.[54] John Dewey wrote a detailed review in the *New York Evening Mail* and a little later he entered into a forthright rebuttal of the opinions of the reviewer in the *New Republic*.[55] In addition, there were a number of reviews in literary and educational magazines as well as religious publications. A few months later, possibly as a result of a reprint, the book was again reviewed extensively in, amongst other newspapers and periodicals, the *Dial*, the *Washington Herald*, the *Baltimore Sun*, the *St Louis Republican*, the *Chicago Evening Post*, the *University of Chicago Press* and the *Indianapolis Times*.[56] In February the following year, Waldo Frank contributed a long and detailed review using his own experience as a pupil, in the *Chicago Tribune*.[57]

At the end of 1918 the book was published in Britain by Methuen and Company, the publishers of the original Alexander books, where again there were many reviews. This edition included appreciations by Professor Granger, who had assisted the publication of the first edition in 1910, and the Reverend J.H. Jowett; additionally, there were three letters recently published in America, two by John Dewey and printed in the *New Republic* and one by Professor H.M. Kallen published in the *Dial*.[58]

With all the publicity, pupils were increasing daily, one of whom, Professor James Harvey Robinson, was to prove an influential devotee in the years to come. With the arrival of spring, there was a dilemma for FM. Earlier in the year, AR had fallen from his horse whilst riding in Rotten Row in London and sustained a serious injury. The lower part of his body was paralysed and some of the specialists that he had consulted were of the opinion he would never walk again. Obviously FM was most concerned, and decided that even though it was a busy time in America he should travel home as usual in April to see his family and friends and give all the help that he could to his younger brother. AR made a remarkable and rapid recovery and by June was well enough to go to the Newmarket races to watch his horse, Firework, run. Ethel and Irene remained in America. Irene went to Chicago and then across to California with the Deweys where FM had arranged for her to teach one of his young pupils in Hollywood. One day at a lunch, she discovered people

67 Amy with her children, Marjory and Joan, 1916.

denigrating the British war effort; immediately she went to the defence of her native countrymen with the result that she was asked to lecture at the Town Hall in Hollywood. She gave the talk not only there but to many other groups in California, raising quite considerable sums of money for the British Red Cross.[59]

The Germans mounted major spring offensives firstly in March 1918 near the Somme and in April in the Ypres Salient. The battles were intense across the Western Front with British casualties over 300,000. Fresh drafts of men totalling 140,000 were sent from England.[60] The Germans continued to advance and by June their troops were within 40 miles of Paris. As in 1914, the French government was preparing to leave the capital and tens of thousands of inhabitants were fleeing the city.[61] During June, 170,000 American troops were put into the line, followed the next month by another 140,000 men. The Allies mounted a counter attack and by the middle of July the threat to Paris was over.[62] During the next few months the Allies were able to maintain the momentum of their advance and many major battles took place. During those months a quarter of the German Army in the field were taken prisoner.[63] Eventually, on 11 November, the Armistice with Germany was signed, by which time fighting in all theatres of war had virtually ceased.

In the four years of war, on the Western Front alone more than six million soldiers had died and a further fourteen million were wounded. The total number who died worldwide was in excess of eight million. On average more than 5,600 soldiers were killed each day of the war. A conservative estimate of the British and Empire dead was a million, with countless more wounded. Of the men aged between 19 and 22 in Britain when the war started a third of them were dead.[64] The bitterness of some of the surviving soldiers was reflected by Siegfried Sassoon, awarded a Military Cross for his gallantry on the Western Front, who wrote, 'Who will remember, passing through this Gate, The unheroic Dead who fed the guns? …'[65] Those 'unheroic dead' are remembered every day of every year at 8p.m. at the Menin Gate in Ypres where buglers of the Ypres Fire Brigade sound the Last Post. This living tribute to the sacrifice made is witnessed by thousands of people a year who stand silently in the early evening to gaze at the list of 54,896 names of officers and men from

Britain, Australia, Canada, India, New Zealand and South Africa who died in the Ypres Salient between 1914 and the middle of August 1917 and who have no known grave. Those who died after 16 August 1917 and have no known grave are listed on the great wall at Tyne Cot on the slopes of Passchendaele. At Arras there is a Memorial to the Missing who died in 1917 and 1918 which contains 35,928 names, and includes all the Royal Flying Corps and Royal Air Force missing on the Western Front. At Loos there is another Memorial with 20,589 names, and at Thiepval near the Somme the Memorial contains 73,412 names for 1916-17.[66] There are many other such memorials in the hundreds of British and Commonwealth cemeteries on the Western Front which are tended today by nearly 500 gardeners.[67] Throughout the rest of world where fighting took place there are numerous other cemeteries and memorials.

68   Amy, 1917.

The relief when the war was over was immense; maroons went off, the church bells rang out, and everyone celebrated. Thousands went into the churches, in London people flocked to St Paul's Cathedral and Westminster Abbey, at the Baltic Exchange they sang the 'Doxology', and at the Stock Exchange they sang 'O God our Help in Ages Past'.[68] People got out their flags and Londoners thronged down the Mall to Buckingham Palace where the King and Queen came out onto the Balcony. Everywhere people cheered and waved, sang and danced and generally made merry.[69] The Alexanders joined in the activities. Amy got out her car and issued her two little daughters, Marjory and Joan, with Union flags. The open top De Dion carrying this trio progressed slowly around the streets of New Malden with Amy hooting the horn and the children waving their flags to the joyous inhabitants. FM's wife Edith, AR and some other members of the family spent two days at the races and various friends and relations were expecting to be demobilised from the Army shortly. Now that the U-boat blockade was lifted, transatlantic ships were readily available and AR made arrangements to go to America at the end of the month to assist FM with the very large number of pupils who wanted lessons. Suddenly the world was a less dangerous if very sad place.

12
THE 1920s

Sow an act, and you reap a habit.
Sow a habit, and you reap a character.
Sow a character, and you reap a destiny.
Charles Reade: *Notes and Queries*

With the war over, life for the Alexanders began to return to normal. AR arrived in America just before Christmas 1918 and was ready to begin work in the new year. Also crossing the Atlantic at this time were many of the American Army returning home from Europe, a very different army from that which had joined the allied cause in April 1917. Then it had been small, inexperienced and poorly equipped and did not, in fact, take an active part in operations until the middle of 1918. After this stage, under their commander General John Pershing they made a significant contribution to the war effort. In total some two million men from America came to the Western Front prior to the cessation of hostilities and in those last few months of the war they suffered some 300,000 casualties.[1] Many of these soldiers had found the conditions in Europe difficult and it is perhaps interesting to note that more died of influenza, 62,000, than died in battle.[2] Without doubt the injection of all these fit, strong, new troops into the front line boosted the morale of the Allies and helped to convince the tired and battle-weary Germans that they could not win the war.

The Alexander brothers were busy at work with all the pupils in their extensive American practice, ably assisted by Ethel and Irene. The success of *Man's Supreme Inheritance* ensured that there was a dedicated following of people interested in the Work. Of particular importance was the support of Professor John Dewey and his friends. In April 1919 an article entitled 'The Philosopher's Stone' by Professor James Harvey Robinson, an Alexander pupil, was published in the *Atlantic Monthly*, a prestigious American magazine. The proof copy of the article was sent by the author to FM with a note, 'These first fruits of a new literature of true freedom are dedicated by the writer to the genius who made the momentous discovery.'[3] Clearly, Professor Robinson was familiar with the Work and his writing showed his enthusiasm and belief in Alexander's teaching. He gave a detailed account of his own experiences and highlighted the difficulties of explaining the Work using the written word, but he considered that in *Man's Supreme Inheritance* the author gave the best description possible of lessons in conscious control. This article was widely read and produced another flurry of pupils to the Alexander teaching rooms. Two of these were from Boston: Carla Atkinson and Mrs. Ernest Amory Codman, the wife of a doctor at the Massachusetts General Hospital. Later both these ladies were to offer rooms in their houses to the Alexanders for teaching; these facilities outside New York were to prove most useful.

Carla Atkinson was the eighth of nine children born to Edward and his wife Mary Caroline Heath. Edward Atkinson was a well-known, highly respected, influential man from an old New England family. He was a descendant of John Atkinson, a native of Bury St Edmunds who went to America in about 1663. Edward, an economist and advocate of free labour was involved during his early life in the cotton industry, and during and after the Civil War he exerted considerable influence on government policy towards that industry. Later he withdrew from cotton manufacturing, and amongst other things became President of the Boston Manufacturers' Mutual Fire Insurance Company.[4] His daughter Carla was handicapped from her early childhood, her heels being about two inches away from the ground so that she walked on the balls of her feet. She was given the best treatment that money could buy, saw numerous medical specialists and underwent many operations. Sometimes she walked with crutches and at other times the advice

69 Carla Atkinson's house at Brimmer, Boston, USA.

was iron boots. As the years passed her condition steadily deteriorated until by the age of 50 she was hobbling badly and was certain that shortly she would be reduced to using a wheel chair.

When she read *The Philosopher's Stone* she was so impressed that she read *Man's Supreme Inheritance* and decided that perhaps the Work might help her, and in the autumn of 1919 she made an appointment to see FM. She began lessons and became a lifelong advocate of the Work. Her improvement was steady and over the next ten years she had regular lessons either in America or in London until a serious car accident prevented her making the journey to England. At this point she did her best to teach herself. She recovered from the accident and continued to make progress until AR returned to Boston in the 1930s and was able to help her.[5] Throughout this period, she lived in a delightful house in a terrace by the Charles River. This prestigious five-storey dwelling in Brimmer, close to Boston Common, had a lovely first-floor living room with a large bay window and a balcony with magnificent views across the river to Cambridge and Harvard University. Between the house and the river was a park and on the river's edge was a landing stage for the Commissioner of the Metropolitan Parks. The advent of the car has spoiled this scene; there is now a major road between Brimmer and the park, but in the early 1920s when FM, Ethel and Irene spent so many weekends working here the area was peaceful and tranquil. Certainly, Carla's generosity and assistance to the Alexanders over a long period was invaluable.

In the spring of 1919 FM returned to England leaving Ethel and Irene in America. AR had returned earlier to teach the many pupils who were now coming to Ashley Place. The post-war era produced a resurgence of interest in the Work and it was vital to ensure that the London practice prospered so that both the Alexander brothers could eventually settle down again in England. However, in the autumn FM decided that he should cross the Atlantic to winter as usual in America. His pupils were delighted to see him and he was very busy, particularly as he decided to begin work on his next book. In England, the Alexanders were all in the London area and met at regular intervals. Betsy was very fit and agile and thoroughly enjoying herself, and Agnes was busy with her dressmaking, but FM's wife Edith was having a difficult time. Her sister May's husband, Charlie Piddock, had died leaving her with her two sons, 14-year-old Jeff and 8-year-old Bert, and her 18-month-old daughter, Peggy, together with arrears of rent and rates and various other debts. Some of May's friends helped her and FM cabled from America offering financial assistance. Amy provided clothes for young Peggy and some toys from her daughters', Marjory and Joan's, collection. Edith started to take a great interest in Peggy's welfare and had her to stay at Ashley Place regularly. Also living at Ashley Place was her nephew, Owen, together with his wife and children. Owen was the oldest son of Lucy, one of Edith's younger sisters, and her husband, Henry Maclean Vicary.

The Vicarys had married in Hobart in 1890 and Owen was born a year later. After his education in Sydney he had come to England and served in the Army during the war. On 4 September 1915 Owen married Gladys Edith Johnson at the Registry Office in Hanover Square in London. Edith found the war very disturbing, and was always most distressed when Owen had to return from leave and go to France. As she said in one of her letters to FM, 'He went into the street as day was breaking and the khaki-clad figure against the grey looked almost like the veldt. You may guess tears were in my eyes and my heart was heavy.' Owen and Gladys, known to everyone as Jack, had their first child, Peter Maclean, in August 1919. Although Peter was born at his maternal grandmother's house in Leytonstone, the family lived at 16 Ashley Place. Discharged from the Army, Owen was without a job but he was very interested in all types of motor vehicles and developed a road haulage business which he started with two lorries funded by FM. By the time his second child, Doreen Maclean, was born in March 1922, he declared himself to be a garage proprietor in Leyton. The name of Doreen did not last long as FM decided that Peter must be accompanied by Wendy and so she became Wendy for the rest of her life.

Two days before Christmas 1919, AR, Grace and their three-year-old son, Max, departed for America. They probably all went on to Australia to visit Grace's family in Melbourne. By the spring of 1920, AR had returned to America and FM came home to England together with Ethel and Irene, all three to work at 16 Ashley Place. Ethel was FM's assistant and Irene helped with the pupils and undertook a variety of other tasks. Ethel had been in America since 1915 and had brought all her possessions with her to her mother's house in Kensington. She was 'helped' with her unpacking by her nine-year-old niece, Erika Schumann, who in return received Alexander lessons from her aunt. So began a long association with the Work which still continues today, with Erika teaching and lecturing in Australia, England and America. Erika had come to England from Germany with her mother Elsie whose intention it was to place her in an English school. This Elsie duly did, selecting a school in Missenden near Wendover run by her former mistress at Roedean, Isabel Fry. Erika stayed a year before returning to Germany. Irene settled back into life in England and during the summer she gave extra help to a young American girl who had been one of FM's pupils in New York. She had a severe curvature of the spine. Irene took the child on a visit to Europe and then accompanied her back to Minnesota in the Autumn.[6]

In Autumn 1920, AR returned to London and FM went to America where he continued to work on his new book as well as teach numerous pupils. He was particularly busy because he had decided that he would not return to America the following year nor would AR replace him in the summer of 1921. They wanted to concentrate on the

70   AR, Grace and Max, *c*.1928.

London teaching practice and FM hoped to complete his new book, which he entitled *Constructive Conscious Control of the Individual*, so that it could be published in America during his next visit in the winter of 1922/3. This 18-month period in London was demanding. By now FM and his wife Edith had adopted young Peggy, Edith's niece, and she was living with them at Ashley Place. Thus, FM wrote much of his new book while subject to the distractions of a young child. He was teaching up to 11 pupils a day, enjoying the London theatres, attending race meetings, riding in Hyde Park and visiting and entertaining his family. He and Edith were regular visitors to the Streatham house of his sister Amy, and her husband George and their children Marjory and Joan. His mother Betsy and sister Agnes were living in Sunderland Avenue in Maida Vale, and AR and his wife Grace were conveniently located in North London, and they visited each other frequently.

At the beginning of 1922 a number of Americans including Carla Atkinson and Mary Olcott, a wealthy and influential lady, came to London for lessons. When these pupils were added to the increasing number of English pupils the teaching task became a challenge for the Alexander brothers. Amongst these English pupils were some long-standing ones such as Lucy Silcox and Elizabeth Glover; others were more recent, including Dr. Peter MacDonald and his sons, Hugh and Patrick, and Dr. Murdoch.[7] Both these doctors were to prove of invaluable assistance over the next few years. Peter MacDonald was a doctor from York, who had obtained an MA from Aberdeen University in 1890 and qualified as a doctor four years later. He became an ophthalmic surgeon and at this time worked as a consultant at the York School for the Blind, the ear nose and throat department of the York County Hospital and the York school clinic. He had served with the Prince of Wales' Own West Yorkshire Regiment during the 1914–18 War as a medical officer and had published a number of medical articles.[8] He was encouraged to have lessons with Alexander by his wife, Agnes, who was a daughter of Joseph Rowntree. The famous Quaker industrialist and social and industrial reformer from York described Alexander's work as 'reasoning from the known to the unknown, the known being the wrong and the unknown being the right'.[9] Rowntree was convinced of the value of the Work, as was his daughter, and soon Peter became a devotee. During 1922 he read the draft manuscript of FM's new book and gave valuable advice and assistance.

The other doctor, Andrew Murdoch, was to become a very great friend and regular racing companion of Alexander. Murdoch qualified in Glasgow in 1884 and became a Fellow of the Royal Society of Medicine. He was the honorary medical officer of the Nazareth Home for the Poor, Admiralty surgeon and was in general practice at Bexhill.[10] He retired from this practice in the late 1920s suffering from angina, and in 1936 he was elected President of the Sussex Branch of the British Medical Association. In future years, both Peter MacDonald and Andrew Murdoch were to write a number of important papers about Alexander's work.

In the autumn of 1922, FM was able to return to America with Ethel Webb and Irene Tasker with the manuscript of his book ready for review by his American friends. Travelling on the same ship as the Alexander party was Emile Coué, a French doctor from Nancy who had developed a system of cures by 'autosuggestion'. On 24 January 1923 the *New Republic* published an article by Professor John Dewey entitled 'A Sick World' in which he detailed the work of Coué in very sceptical terms. Dewey was clearly unimpressed that details of Mr. Coué, his methods, cures and personality, had filled the American papers for weeks; moreover, his journey across the Atlantic had been recorded day by day on the radio and in the newspapers. He compared this with the arrival of Mr. Matthias Alexander, which had gone unheralded, and drew the conclusion that the contrast between the receptions of the two men was a measure of the preference for a seemingly cheap and easy way of dealing with symptoms and the wish to be cured rather than to be well.[11] John Dewey was delighted to welcome FM as were so many of his pupils. He was particularly pleased that the manuscript was ready for review and he gave invaluable help by making suggestions. Additionally he wrote an introduction. This amending and editing was an exacting task, but eventually Ethel and Irene with the help of Carla Atkinson and Edith Lawson had the script ready for Duttons. The proofs were corrected by Mary Olcott and the book was printed in May 1923 after FM, Ethel and Irene had returned to England. Fortunately, AR was able to come to America to cope with the avalanche of pupils produced by the great success of the book which had a second printing in November 1923.

The main reason why FM had to return to England despite the publication of his book was his concern about his family. His mother Betsy had been ill for some time and she went to stay with her daughter Amy and her family in Streatham to recuperate. However, her condition worsened and after a few weeks she was admitted to hospital where, despite an operation, her health deteriorated and on 23 February she died. This was a major shock to all the family but particularly devastating to Agnes who had lived with her mother all her life. She became very thin and the family were most anxious about her. So FM, Ethel and Irene hastened back to England. FM was able to see all the members of his family and to help his sister with accepting her mother's death. While he was in England another problem confronted him. He had had a repair completed on his car but the repair did not meet with his satisfaction and he refused to pay the bill. The matter was still outstanding when, in the autumn, he returned to America and AR came home to England. FM was greeted enthusiastically by his pupils and friends who were absolutely delighted at the success of his book. The first printing had sold out and Duttons were producing another one and it was these copies that FM signed and gave to his family as there were no original ones available. However, the matter of the car repair debt did not go away and in his absence the creditor filed a petition in the High Court of Justice under the Act of Bankruptcy. The first meeting, public examination and adjudication took place while FM was in America and he was declared bankrupt in his absence.[12] This situation was never resolved but FM's assets were not confiscated.

In the spring of 1924 FM returned to England, and as AR did not go out to America to replace him teaching in America ceased. The brothers decided that now conditions were improving in England they would both concentrate all their attention on expanding the teaching base in London. This would give both men the opportunity to settle on a more permanent basis in England. In particular, FM wanted to develop his work further and during the year Methuen spent £425 advertising the Work and the books in numerous newspapers and magazines.[13] Coincidentally that year a young eight-year-old boy was sent back from India for lessons with FM. As he was Irene's nephew, he was under her guardianship and as she explained many years later, she asked FM if she could 'link his lessons in the Work with application to all his school lessons.' This was just the opportunity FM wanted. Soon Irene and her charge were joined by other children having lessons with FM, AR and Ethel.[14] The little school at Ashley Place was established. Irene was able to put to good use her teacher training, her previous teaching experience, her knowledge of Dr. Montessori's work and, of over-riding importance, her understanding of Alexander's principles. FM believed that his work would assist these youngsters who all had individual problems and that in turn he and the other teachers would learn from the experience.

At this time FM, his wife and family were living at Ashley Place, but with FM, AR and Ethel Webb teaching there and the advent of the little school, the building, of which FM had only the ground floor and the basement, was rather crowded. AR with his wife, Grace, their son, Max, and May's daughter, Betty, were living in north London. It was clear that for the next few years Max's education would be very important, and therefore it was most unlikely that AR, Grace and Max would be able to go to America for long periods or visit the family in Australia as they had done a few years previously. The brothers decided that the time had come to move out of London and establish themselves in a more rural location. They chose Sidcup in Kent which was then a country area with a good railway service to central London.

71   Penhill front view.

72   Penhill side view.

FM bought a house at Penhill which, although in the parish of Bexley, was only a mile from Sidcup station. Penhill was originally part of the Lamorbey Estate. This estate comprised a large mansion house with adjoining park land and woodlands, Pen Farm, other properties, arable land and orchards and was in total some 286 acres. After the death of William Steele the estate was divided into six areas and sold at auction in May 1761. Lot 3 contained Pen Farm, barns, stables, yards, dog kennels and a substantial acreage of land.[15] By the time of the national valuation survey conducted between 1910 and 1915, Pen Farm had reduced significantly in size. The property comprised Penhill House, a cottage, stables with adjacent gardens and outbuildings and 19 acres of farm land, and was valued at approximately £3,000. The house was a substantial family home with two drawing rooms, a smoking room, a lobby hall and kitchens downstairs, five bedrooms and a dressing room on the first floor and four servants' bedrooms on the second floor.[16] This property met FM's requirements and he bought it from

73 *(right)*   David Rose, gardener at Penhill.

74 *(below left)*   James Rose, FM's chauffeur.

75 *(below right)*   Hilda Coates née Rose.

76   Arthur Rose with his dog at Penhill.

the Emmets on 25 March 1925. The Rose family comprising Arthur and Fanny and their three children, James, David and Hilda, lived in the cottage. Mr. and Mrs. Rose had worked for the Emmets for many years and had moved with them on two previous occasions. This time they decided to remain where they were and assist the new owners. They proved invaluable for many years. Arthur Rose looked after FM's horses, cows and goats as well as the land and his wife Fanny worked in the house.[17] When the children grew up they also joined the Penhill staff; David did the gardening, James became FM's chauffeur and Hilda assisted in the house, although she did become a nanny for another family in Sidcup for a short time. They remained with FM until the widower Arthur died in 1937. Hilda was engaged to be married and the two men decided that the time had come for a change. Meanwhile, AR bought a substantial house, Ellerslie, in High View Road in Sidcup. This property had a large garden which included a tennis court, was near the Sidcup shopping area and within easy walking distance of schools for Max and Betty. The Alexander houses were less than two miles apart and soon the families were installed in their respective houses with FM and AR commuting daily to Ashley Place.

Before FM and Edith moved into their new house it was apparent that the marriage of Owen and Jack Vicary was in difficulties. Edith was distressed by this as she loved Owen dearly and had become very fond of Jack on whom in many ways she was dependent. Edith was almost 60 years old and found the young Peggy quite exacting, while Jack, with two small children the oldest of whom was only a year younger than Peggy, was much more appropriately aged for the task. The hard-working and competent Jack would not tolerate her husband's affairs any longer so it was agreed that she would move near to Penhill. She found a house called Rose Cottage which had a shop and some land in Upton Road in Bexleyheath, about two miles from Penhill. She moved in early in 1925, before the Penhill purchase was completed, and set about the task of running the shop and providing for her children.[18] Although Peter and Wendy remained on favourable terms with their father, as did FM and Edith, it seems that Owen was not a visitor to the Bexleyheath area.

The Alexander work was attracting considerable attention. This interest was further increased in 1923 by a lecture given by the Yorkshire Medical Association delegate,

77   Ethel Webb and Peggy.

Dr. Peter MacDonald, to the British Medical Association Conference held at Portsmouth, and in 1924 by the publication in England of *Constructive Conscious Control of the Individual*. The lecture and in particular the description of FM's work was reported in most of the main British newspapers including *The Times*, the *Daily Telegraph*, the *Daily Graphic*, the *Daily News* and the *Daily Express*.[19] FM's latest book was most successful and the publishers were able to use the *British Medical Journal*'s comments on Dr. Peter MacDonald's lecture at Portsmouth in their publicity campaign; the book was reprinted numerous times and by 1946 was in its 8th edition. An appreciative review was published in the *British Medical Journal* in May 1924.[20] The reviewer *inter alia* stated, 'the author (Alexander) brings forward evidence that an increasing tendency to physical deterioration is becoming manifest owing to an inadequate appreciation of the means whereby the psycho–physical organization can be used to best advantage'. The review in the *Lancet* was less complimentary and FM responded, suggesting that the reviewer had 'misunderstood and consequently unwittingly misrepresented' his work.[21]

The importance of FM's work to medicine was highlighted by Mr. Mcleod Yearsley, a Fellow of the Royal College of Surgeons, who wrote a number of articles in the *Literary Guide*. In the October 1925 *Guide* he made the suggestion, which subsequently proved controversial, that 'Central Control' as detailed by Alexander 'is advocated by Magnus and referred to recently by Sherrington at the Royal Society'.[22] Professor Rudolf Magnus, an eminent medical scientist, was born in Brunswick in September 1873 and died suddenly in July 1927. He studied medicine at Heidelberg and, after qualifying in 1898, was employed at the Pharmacological Institute in Heidelberg under Professor Gottlieb; here he began his medical research. In 1908 he became the Professor of Pharmacology at the Dutch University of Utrecht. In 1915 he returned to Germany where he served in military hospitals and organised research into methods for protection against chemical warfare. In 1917 he returned to Utrecht where he remained until his death. During his life, an impressive number of his researches were published, over 300 papers issued from the Utrecht Institute alone. Sir Henry Dale considered that the 'greatest contribution made by Professor Magnus and his colleagues was the great series of researches on the factors controlling the changes of animal posture in relation to gravity and on the muscular tone by which such posture is maintained'.[23] Professor Magnus visited England a number of times where he met and worked with, amongst others, Professor Sir Charles Sherrington. Professor Sherrington was an English physiologist who was born in 1857, graduated from Caius College, Cambridge and in 1895 was appointed Professor of Physiology at Liverpool University. In 1913 he moved to Oxford holding a similar appointment. He produced a number of major works of which *The Integrative Action of the Nervous System* published in 1906 constituted a landmark in modern physiology. Also noted for his poetry, from 1920-5 he was President of the Royal Society and awarded an Order of Merit in 1924; in 1932 he received the Nobel Prize for Medicine.[24]

Dr. Peter MacDonald continued his support of FM, and as President of the Yorkshire Branch of the British Medical Association used his address to the Annual Meeting in 1926 to deliver a detailed appraisal of the Work; this was printed in the *British Medical Journal* on 25 December 1926.[25] Earlier that year, FM had felt it necessary to comment in the *British Medical Journal* on a letter written by Dr. Maud Forrester-Brown. He wrote that he found,

> that the instructions given in the series of corrective exercises … not in keeping with principles and procedures involved in the teaching of co-ordination. Take, for instance, the one headed 'Stretching lateral abdominal muscles. First movement: Slowly shrug up one shoulder etc.; second stage: slowly relax, if possible, leaving the rib up, while the shoulder sinks down, etc.' No subconsciously controlled person could carry out such instructions without increasing the malco-ordination and maladjustment already present.[26]

In the following year, the long-standing devotee of Alexander, Lucy Silcox, who had just retired as the Headmistress of St Felix School in Southwold, had an article highlighting the merits of Alexander's teaching entitled 'Swedish Gymnastic Teaching' published in the *Journal of School Hygiene and Physical Education*.[27]

In 1928 the number of published letters and articles about the Work increased. In March the *London Evening Standard* printed one entitled 'The Fearful Foozler' by Sir Ernest Holderness CBE. Sir Ernest was the amateur golf champion in 1922 and 1924 and in his article he explained that he had read *Constructive Conscious Control of the Individual*. He suggested that 'the title should commend itself to all golfers who are aware that they suffer from fear reflexes, and that the more anxious they are to play well the more likely they are to "foozle".'[28] The same month, the *British Medical Journal* printed 'The Reality of Delusions' by Dr. Devine, in which he concluded that a delusion was 'the conscious symbol of a morbid state of functioning of the whole organism'. FM reacted to the article and explained the relevance of his work in this connection.[29] In April *The Times Educational Supplement* published an article entitled 'What does Mental Age Mean'. The article did not mention Alexander and this brought forth considerable correspondence from adherents of his work. The Earl of Lytton, Esther Lawrence, Principal of the Froebel Institute, Miss D.L. Beck, Headmistress, County School for Girls, Ealing and Mr. McDonagh FRCS all had letters published on the subject.[30]

The Earl of Lytton, a highly respected and able man, was of immense value to the Alexander cause which he served with enthusiasm and dedication from the time he first had lessons in 1927 until his death in 1947. Born in 1876 and educated at Eton and then Trinity College, Cambridge, he held many distinguished appointments which included Civil Lord of the Admiralty, British Commissioner for Propaganda in France in 1918, Under Secretary of State for India 1920-22, Governor of Bengal 1922-27, and Viceroy and Acting Governor General of India April to August 1925. He was Chairman of a number of Companies including Palestine Potash Ltd., Central London Electricity Ltd., London Power Company and the Old Vic and President of the Royal Society of Literature, the Garden Cities and Town Planning Association and the Central School of Speech Training and Dramatic Art. He led a number of missions including one for the League of Nations to Manchuria in 1932 and wrote a number of books.[31]

Mr. McDonagh was for many years FM's doctor. He was a distinguished physician in Wimpole Street who became a Fellow of the Royal College of Surgeons in 1909. At one time he was a surgeon at the London Locks Hospital and later he worked at St Bartholomew's. In 1924 he published the first part of his six volume book *The Nature of Disease* and three years later Part II was issued, in which he made reference to Alexander's principles.[32] Part III was published in 1931 and the first chapter contained a review of Alexander's work.[33]

In May 1928 an article was printed in the *Statesman* (Calcutta) entitled 'In Search of Health'. This regretted that Alexander's work appeared to be unknown in India and proceeded to educate its readership.[34] Later in the year Dr. Peter MacDonald reacted to the publication in the *British Medical Journal* of an address by the Australian Dr. W. Colin MacKenzie. He pointed out that Alexander had arrived by independent means at the same conclusions as MacKenzie but had gone much further because he had developed a technique by which he could teach his pupils a better functioning. Dr. Peter MacDonald's letter was supported in subsequent letters from Drs. McGowan, Yearsley and Murdoch.[35] A year later this medical publication printed an article by Mr. McDonagh on 'The Pathogenesis and treatment of Asthma'. In connection with forms of treatment he mentioned re-education as advocated by Alexander.[36] In December the *British Medical Journal* published the first of many letters by Dr. Mungo Douglas, a doctor in general practice in Bolton, on the prevention of scoliosis. Dr. Douglas averred 'that no consideration of scoliosis can be complete which does not take into view the importance of Mr. F Matthias Alexander on the constructive conscious control of the individual'. He suggested that if children were 'trained in the application of Mr. Alexander's principle there would be no need for the treatment of scoliosis'.[37]

Even in America, where there were no teachers, a few people were trying to keep the Alexander message alive. In 1929 Arthur Busch wrote a long article in the *Brooklyn Citizen* highlighting the importance of Alexander's work and directing his readership to *Man's*

Supreme Inheritance and *Constructive Conscious Control of the Individual*, which he considered had 'met with the grossest kind of neglect in a Country (America) which pretends to be on the alert for knowledge that might tend to emancipate man from slavery of his present vast ignorance'. He summarised his views with the following statement:

> Aside from the whole-hearted support of Professor Dewey, Alexander has been almost wholly ignored in America ... The answer probably lies in the fact that he is far ahead of his time ... Certainly it will reflect no credit upon this generation if it does not recognize a man who has made a discovery that eventually will revolutionize many of our present concepts. It is no rash prophecy that Alexander will one day change the whole structure of education and therapeutics and that ultimately the latter will be eliminated altogether.[38]

All this publicity surrounding FM and his work produced a large number of pupils at Ashley Place. Some of these were notable people like Lord Lytton while others were very ordinary souls referred by their doctors or friends. Among this latter group were a number of people with little money. They were unable to pay the normal fees for lessons, but as FM believed most strongly that people did not value things if they were provided free he charged them instead a modest amount. His principle was each according to his means. Many of these pupils were to remain life-long advocates of the Work. They came from all parts of the British Isles and Ireland, several European countries, Australia, New Zealand, Canada, South Africa, South America, Egypt, India and the United States of America.[39] Amongst them was Robert Best who was injured during the War and first came to FM for lessons in 1929. He remained a pupil for many years and his son attended the little school. He was the main instigator behind the commencement of Alexander teaching in Birmingham in the mid-1930s. FM always maintained that he learnt a great deal from teaching this man.

In 1927 Margaret Goldie was a student attending the Froebel Teacher Training College. She had suffered from poor health all her life with spinal curvature, bad digestion, constant tiredness and a great susceptibility to contract any illness or infection that happened to be around. The Principal of the College, Miss Esther Lawrence, decided something must be done about this young woman and so she took her to see FM. She began a course of lessons and steadily, over a three-month period, her health improved. She finished her training and taught in an orthodox school for a year. Then, in 1929, she received a letter from FM asking her to come and help in the little school. This invitation she accepted and so began a lifetime of loyal and dedicated service teaching FM's work.[40] She remained one of his assistants until he died; then she continued to teach until a few weeks before her death in 1997. At the age of 90 years, she still travelled to London three days a week from her home in Richmond and taught seven pupils a day.

The little school prospered and every term they produced a magazine called the 'Alexander Times'. All the pupils contributed and usually there were competitions sponsored by FM and AR and sometimes others. In the Christmas 1929 edition there was a competition entitled 'Mr. FM's Competition-Means Whereby'. There were a number of very interesting entries by the children which showed quite clearly their knowledge and understanding of Alexander's work.[41] This example is written by a teenage girl:

Means Whereby of Grooming a Pony.
Inhibit the desire to groom a pony.

1. Direct the neck to relax, the head to go forward and up, and the shoulders down, to lengthen and widen the back; and continue this. Take the dandy brush in one hand and rest the other firmly (inhibiting stiffness) on the pony's side. All grooming is easier if the feet are apart as the body is then firmer, and it is better to have one, half a pace in front of the other; the weight is then going forwards and upwards into the stroke: lengthen and widen and direct the knee forward to move the feet. Continue lengthening and widening to let the arm go up and bring it down with quick, firm strokes; go all over the horse. this movement is apt to bring the groom's head down, or to make her stiffen her neck: she should watch this. A groom is often told to 'throw her weight' into the stroke, but it is interesting to note that the stroke is stronger when the head goes up to lengthen the back and free the arm. Inhibit brushing the tail, stand to one side of the horse, (not behind the heels) to let the arm go out to brush the tail while keeping on lengthening. Grooming with a dandy is the Means Whereby of loosening the dirt and scurf.

2. Take a Body Brush in one hand and a curry comb in the other. Keep on lengthening and widening to bring the brush down over the horse with long, clean strokes; pass it through the curry comb on its way up, to clean it, between every stroke. Inhibit between every stroke. Grooming with a body brush is the Means Whereby of removing the dust and scurf loosened by the dandy.

3. Go all over the horse with a wisp of damped hay, or with a clout. Keep lengthening all the time. Dust inside the horse's ears with the clout, if the horse is tall you will have to look up for this, inhibit shortening to look up. The hay or clout is the Means Whereby of giving a shine to the coat.

4. Inhibit washing the horse's face. Continue lengthening to let the left hand take hold of the pony just above his nose, with a sponge rinsed in cold water in the right hand remove 'sleepy dust' from the eyes and clean out the nostrils. Many horses object to this and throw their heads up. Do not stiffen the fingers or elbow, the human arm is not strong enough to hold a horse's head. Direct the head forward and up and the back back and the elbow downward from the horse to let the fingers hold the nose; then power will come from the lifter muscles of the back.

5. Inhibit picking out the horse's feet. Take an iron prod or wooden stick and stand in front of the hoof facing the horse. Inhibit stooping. Direct the neck to relax, the head forward and up, the shoulders down, keep this going to lengthen to let the knees go away from one another, and the arm forward and down to the foot. (Ponies generally lift their feet for themselves, steady it with the hand under it.) Clean out the dirt with the prod. Smell the foot carefully, if an unpleasant smell is present scrub out with jeyes as a Means Whereby to prevent thrush. It is wise to do this regularly twice a week.

6. Lengthen and widen to pat the horse and give him sugar or apple, talk to him all the time for he appreciates your friendship. A command such as 'Stand Lad' will often quieten a restive horse, but it is no good to squeak angrily at him and come down on the throttle. Lengthen and widen to smile to let the jaw drop to speak, the horse knows if the voice is firm and controlled. Always inhibit and go slow in the stable. A sudden noise or movement will frighten ponies, for many are nervous. If the rider does the stabling herself the horse is friendlier and both will enjoy the rides better.

'IF YOU CAN'T CONTROL YOURSELF, YOU CAN'T CONTROL YOUR HORSE'

78 Irene Tasker.

At the end of each term the children had a party which was always described as a 'Do' until one of the children pointed out that 'Do' was unsuitable for an Alexander party. Henceforth the occasions were described as a 'No-Do'. As FM recorded in one of the 'Alexander Times' magazines, 'Last Thursday I was present at the No-Do given by the pupils in the little school. I have recollections, pleasing recollections, of the 'Dos' previously given by the pupils, but the 'No-Do' has provided me with even more pleasing recollections. The 'No-Do' afforded a pleasing and exhilarating experience, for instead of the bustle and excitement usually associated with children's performances at end of term, there was a calm and deliberate attitude pervading all that was done … When one little girl forgot her lines she was not in the least disturbed. No shuffling of feet or twitching of mouth and fingers. Just placid 'Non-Doing' until 'Memory became once more faithful to his office', and on she went as if nothing had happened.'[42]

Many of FM's supporters were most anxious that the Work should be available to the general public on the widest possible basis. In order to further this idea a Trust Fund was established in 1930 to relieve him of the financial responsibility of carrying on the school and to provide finances for any future expansion of the educational side of his work. The Trustees were the Lord Lytton, Sir Lynden Macassey, Dr. Peter MacDonald and FM. FM and his small team of assistants at Ashley Place could cope with only a small number of pupils on a one-to-one basis. Therefore, if the Work was to reach more people it was vital that there should be an increased number of teachers. By 1930 FM was convinced, and he set about organising a course. Many of his long-standing and influential pupils were delighted; these included the Trustees and a number of distinguished members of the medical and education professions. They all publicly expressed their belief that training teachers in the Work would be a great service to humanity.[43] The following year Mr. Rugg-Gunn MB FRCS wrote an article, 'A New Profession', in a paper called *Women's Employment* which advanced the professional opportunities of educated women. He highlighted the importance of Alexander's work and promoted the new training course, referring interested students to a number of books which contained appreciations of the Work, now frequently called a Technique, by a variety of authors including Dewey, Ludovici and McDonagh.[44]

This period was for FM a stimulating and exciting time. There were numerous pupils wanting to see him and he was able to develop his ideas and theories assisted by his experiences with this diverse selection of people. The medical profession were becoming aware of the importance of his work; the little school was successful; the Trust Fund was instigated and received some very generous donations, and a training course was about to commence. He was busy, spending considerable time refining and developing his work and preparing his new book. Socially, he was fond of good food and wine, regularly visited Race Meetings, and when time allowed he went shooting. He enjoyed the company of his sister Amy and her husband George, who was often his shooting companion. He invested in a small holiday home at Elmer on the Sussex coast which he visited whenever possible. This delightful place was enjoyed by many members of the family, particularly during the summer months. However, he and AR had significant financial responsibilities. In addition to their own families, they supported their unmarried sister Agnes, who still lived in the family home, as well as their sister May, who was having matrimonial difficulties, and her four children. Their youngest brother, Beaumont returned to London in the early 1920s from

79 May with her children, Marie, Betty and Doreen, *c.*1922.

America, where he had worked for many years for Du Pont, and took over the *New Princes Hotel* which was a most select establishment. Ever the entrepreneur, Beaumont was highly successful and *Princes* became a centre of the social life of London. After a few years, this enterprise encountered financial difficulties and in 1927 Beaumont was declared bankrupt.[45] His wife Sonnie returned to America and he went to live in the family home with Agnes. Beaumont's financial problems were soon resolved and very shortly he was engaged in another productive money-making venture. However, the financial and employment situation in England was deteriorating. The General Strike of 1926, although short lived, had a long-term effect on peoples' attitudes and the Wall Street financial crash in November 1929 was part of a much wider financial depression.

13

THE DEVELOPMENT OF THE WORK

The reasonable man adapts himself to the world; the unreasonable one persists in trying to adapt the world to himself. Therefore, all progress depends on the unreasonable one.

George Bernard Shaw: *Sonnets*

The 1920s had proved successful and the future looked bright for the Work; many influential people were associated with promoting its importance and value. The 1930s were to be even more successful for the Work but for the Alexander family it was a difficult and sad period. From the time that FM purchased Penhill in 1925, he, his wife, Edith and his adopted daughter, Peggy, had all lived there. He and Edith had separate rooms and did not live as man and wife but whether they did before 1925 is a matter of conjecture. However, Edith had never enjoyed the rural life at Penhill as she felt isolated and remote from London. By 1929, she could cope with her existence no longer. She separated from her husband and, with Peggy, moved to an area of London known as Little Venice. Although FM continued to pay all her expenses, they never shared the same house again and she died eight years later in September 1938, five days before her 73rd birthday. Peggy continued to see her adopted father and in the early days joined in the activities of the little school at Ashley Place. After Edith's death, Marjory Mechin, Amy's oldest daughter, moved into the flat with Peggy.

After Edith's departure FM continued to live mainly at Penhill, although during the week he sometimes he stayed overnight at Ashley Place. When he made a short visit to America in 1929 to join his friend John Dewey at his 70th birthday celebrations on 20 October, his sisters Agnes and May with her youngest daughter Doreen, who was born on 2 July 1920, came to Penhill to look after the establishment during his absence. May and her husband Norman had separated recently, although Norman never returned to Australia as he had always maintained he would. FM worked hard; he had numerous pupils and was busy writing his new book, *The Use of the Self*. In this enterprise he was assisted by his teaching assistants, Ethel Webb and Irene Tasker. In addition, he was preparing for the new teacher training course.

The first training course began at Ashley Place in February 1931. There were initially seven students excluding Irene Tasker and Margaret Goldie who attended when their duties with the little school allowed. There was Ethel Webb's niece, Erika, who had been associated with the Work since she was eight years old. Her parents, Hans and Elsie Schumann, were told that she had a curvature of the spine and she had some orthopaedic treatment; at this juncture her aunt Ethel took control and instituted Alexander lessons. In December 1927 her mother died, and in September 1928 she came to England to live with Ethel, and within weeks she had her first lessons with FM. Later she joined in the activities of the little school.[1] There was Gurney McInnes, an asthmatic, who had his first lesson with FM in March 1927, and his sister Jean who had attended the little school.[2] Marjorie Barstow and Lulie Westfeldt came from America. Marjorie graduated from the University of Nebraska in 1921 and taught ballet and ball-room dancing in Lincoln in America.[3] She heard of Alexander's work in the mid-1920s when a friend of hers visited FM in London and returned with his books. These Marjorie read and she was fascinated. In 1927 she came to London with her sister, and for six months she had daily lessons with FM and AR. When FM wrote to her about the course she accepted immediately. Lulie, who contracted polio at the age of seven years, first heard about Alexander's work in 1929, when she was 31 years old, from her friend Kitty Meyrick. She read *Man's Supreme Inheritance*

80 Erika Whittaker née Schumann.

and during that summer a relative died leaving her a small sum of money. She decided to go to England. One of her visits was to her stepmother in Southwold who suggested that Lulie should visit Miss Lucy Silcox; this she did and discussed with her Alexander's work. Lulie was impressed and in September she went to see FM. She had five lessons a week for the next two months and then returned to America.[4] The other two were Irene Stewart, a school colleague of Margaret Goldie who was so impressed with the improvement in Margaret's health that she came to London for lessons prior to joining the course, and George Trevelyan.[5] George was the son of Sir Charles and Lady Trevelyan of Wallington, an estate of nearly 13,000 acres, which was given to the National Trust in 1958 on the death of the donor Sir Charles. George was a student at Trinity College, Cambridge when he first came to FM for lessons in 1928.[6]

Later in the year Lulie's close American friend Kitty Meyrick joined the course. Kitty, who became Countess Catherine Meyrick Wielopolska, had begun lessons in 1926. She had ten lessons a year when she visited London on her annual trip from her home in New York to Italy. In March 1931 she had an attack of schizophrenia and was convinced that FM would not take her on the training course. However, FM honoured the promise he had made previously and she commenced at Ashley Place in September 1931.[7] Two others joined the course later: Peter McDonald's son Patrick, who had first had lessons with FM in 1921 because of his distorted spine, commenced training in late 1932 when he had completed his degree at Cambridge, and FM's niece Marjory on her 18th birthday in May 1933.[8]

As this was the first training course and FM was inexperienced in this field there were, not surprisingly, some problems and from time to time the students had difficulties. In the mornings they were taught by FM, who went round the class giving each person a short lesson, and from this the other students learnt. In the afternoons the students practised on each other, and when they were more advanced they gave lessons to the children in the little school. Frequently the students were helped by AR, whose great sense of humour often defused a tense situation. Additionally, Ethel Webb and Irene Tasker gave advice and assistance; their support and encouragement were particularly valued when students had difficulties understanding certain aspects of the Work. During their time at Ashley Place, these first students were entertained to dinner in the summer at Penhill; they heard numerous stories about life in Australia from both FM and AR, and listened to many recitals by FM, often quotations from Shakespeare.

81   Marjory Mechin and Pat McDonald in *The Merchant of Venice*.

82   Students at Penhill. From left to right. Erika Schumann, George Trevelyan, Margorie Barstow, Peggy Alexander, FM, Margaret Goldie, AR, Ethel Webb, Gurney McInnes, Lulie Westfeldt and Jean McInnes.

FM's passion for Shakespeare involved all his students when he decided that they would perform *The Merchant of Venice* and *Hamlet*. He had adopted this idea successfully many years before with his pupils in Sydney and he believed that the lessons learnt were so vital to the pupils that the exercise should be repeated in London. It did not seem to occur to him that for amateurs to perform in theatres in Sydney and the surrounding areas at the turn of the century was rather different from expecting his students to perform in the 1930s on the West End stage. His plan met with a mixed response from his aspiring teachers but he was not to be deterred. He prevailed upon Reginald Bach, a London producer, to direct the cast and Dame Lilian Bayliss, who was head of the Old Vic and Sadlers Wells Theatre Company, for permission to use the theatres, and so on 5 December 1933 FM and his team performed *The Merchant of Venice* at the Old Vic in London.[9] This great place, so used to the performances of the finest Shakespearian actors in the world, had that evening a slightly more modest production. The reviews were good and so a few days later the play was performed again, this time at Sadlers Well Theatre. The following year, on 13 November 1934, the Alexander team performed *Hamlet* at the Old Vic.[10] The confidence of these unfortunate amateur actors was hardly improved by the appearance at one of their rehearsals of the famous Matheson Lang.[11] One cannot help wondering what this great actor thought of the performance, although he was an enthusiastic Alexander devotee from his days in 1909 when he played *Hamlet* at the Lyceum.[12] Without doubt, FM himself gave outstanding performances and, perhaps more importantly, fulfilled his lifelong ambition to perform on the London stage. The following year, on 3 December, he gave a recital supported by his students at the Rudolf Steiner Hall.[13] This programme was slightly less ambitious and included songs, recitations and scenes from *The Merchant of Venice* and *Hamlet*.

Originally, the course was expected to last three years but in the event the original students stayed for four. During that time a number of other people joined the course and soon training teachers became a permanent feature of life at Ashley Place which was now a very busy place. The little school, the training course and a succession of individual pupils were all crammed into a small number of rooms. The problem became particularly acute each summer when there was an invasion of people from America. In January 1932 the Work received even more publicity with the publication in both the United Kingdom and America of *The Use of the Self*. This book was considered by many to be the most readable of Alexander's books and particularly interesting as he described in great detail the early development and evolution of the Work. Certainly it was popular and the first reprint was produced in May 1932 only five months after the initial issue; it is the only book that has remained permanently available since 1932. Currently published by Gollancz, it is sold by all major book shops in the United Kingdom and translations in various foreign languages are available. The introduction to the book, like Alexander's two previous ones, was written by John Dewey; Peter MacDonald read the manuscript and made important suggestions and criticisms; Ethel Webb and Irene Tasker worked on the text painstakingly for a number of years; Mary Olcott and Edith Lawson revised the proofs, and an index was most carefully devised by two of the trainee teachers, George Trevelyan and Gurney McInnes.[14]

The book aroused considerable interest and was even reviewed in the *Statesman* in Calcutta.[15] The *Student Movement* published an article about the book and Alexander's work

in May entitled 'Using Yourself' by A.G. Pite, Irene Tasker's brother-in-law.[16] Pite was
at the time Headmaster of Weymouth College, the school attended by AR's son, Max,
and Erika Whittaker's brothers. On 4 June the *British Medical Journal* published a letter by
Dr. Cawadias in which he criticised the literary works of non-medical healers. Two weeks
later the magazine printed a response by Peter MacDonald who pointed out that FM was
primarily concerned with education and had never attempted any cure of any disease nor
did he teach treatment. Immediately after this, a letter by FM was printed recommending
that people should read his books and maintaining, 'I have expressly disassociated myself
from any idea of producing a "cure" or "giving treatment"'. A week later the discourse
continued with a letter from Dr. Brock, and again FM responded in the next edition; at
this point the editor closed the correspondence.[17] Other articles about the Work were
published that year including one by Mungo Douglas in *Medical World* and one by Peter
MacDonald in the *Listener*.[18]

Despite the criticisms of the Work many people were staunch supporters of FM, and as
the year drew to a close it was clear that the book was a success and that more and more
people were taking the ideas of Alexander seriously. FM could be well satisfied with events.
The only sadness was the death at George and Amy's home in Streatham of his oldest sister,
Agnes, on 30 July 1932. The following year proved far more difficult. On 24 February 1933
AR's wife Grace died. This left AR with his 16-year-old son, Max, and a large house in
Sidcup. His niece, Betty, who had lived at Ellerslie with the family for so long, was now
grown up and had moved away. Over the next few months family life continued to
deteriorate. Amy's husband George had worked all his life in the ivory business and had a
flourishing factory in Kennington. Until the Wall Street crash of 1929 he had been prosperous and reasonably wealthy, but with the financial difficulties that spread across America
and England the demand for ivory reduced significantly. Life became more and more
difficult and the strain on George increased steadily. His health deteriorated and on 23 April
he died leaving Amy and two daughters, Marjory aged 17 years and Joan aged 16 years. By
now they rented their living accommodation and the factory was suffering severely as a result
of the depression. As Chairman of the company, all George's assets were invested in that
enterprise but the shares no longer paid a dividend. There was no company pension and in
those days no pension from the state. Immediately, FM offered the cottage at Penhill to his
beleaguered sister and her family. Amy and Marjory moved in gratefully and Joan followed
a few weeks later when she had taken her school certificate. Marjory started training at
Ashley Place in May and in September Joan went to a school in Guildford as a pupil teacher.
The ever generous family provider, FM, accepted that he was now financially responsible
for his sister and, to an extent, for her children.

After a few months it was decided that it would be more sensible if Amy moved to
Ellerslie to be with AR and Max and look after the house. So, in January 1934 Amy and
her daughters moved out of the cottage and went to Ellerslie where Amy remained until
AR's death over 13 years later. As had happened so often in the past, the two brothers shared
the extra financial burden. Clearly, both AR and Amy found it difficult without their
respective spouses and AR decided that now he had somebody to look after his home he
wanted to go back to America. Neither he nor FM had taught there since 1924 and there

had been numerous requests for teachers. Many people made the expensive trip to England and spent months in London having lessons but this was not a satisfactory solution. There was an important market in America and the future of the Work depended on a wide understanding and acceptance of the Alexander Technique. AR's son Max left school and started training at Ashley Place after his 18th birthday in 1934 and so AR was able to leave Ashley Place, and by early 1935 he was well established teaching in Boston. He occupied a suite of rooms in the *Braemore Hotel*, a large building in Commonwealth Avenue, a most impressive tree-lined, extremely wide boulevard with trees and statues down the centre. The avenue which runs from Boston Common parallel with the Charles River was designed to be Boston's Champs Elysées; certainly, some of

83   AR's hotel in Boston.

the architecture is reminiscent of Paris, and all the buildings on this incredibly long road are substantial and well designed.

In the meantime the situation at Ashley Place was as cramped as ever, and the prospect of more teachers of the Work when the first course finished made it essential to provide more space. Therefore, it was agreed that the little school should move to Penhill where FM had lived alone for the past five years. This house provided a much better location for the children than central London and its use was made possible by a most generous gift to the Trust Fund which provided much needed finance.[19] Now the children had to board as it was impossible for them to travel each day to Sidcup from their homes spread around the London area. The school, under the control of Irene Tasker assisted by Margaret Goldie, moved in the spring of 1934 together with Mrs. Tiffin, the cook at Ashley Place. Mrs. Tiffin was to prove invaluable at Penhill where the children and most of the staff required full-time catering facilities.

Jack Vicary took on the task of matron. Although she still lived in Upton Road, Bexleyheath the area had changed radically and a new housing estate occupied the fields that had once surrounded her at Rose Cottage. Jack bought one of these new houses in 1930, and together with her two children, Peter and Wendy, she moved into No. 107. FM and Jack, both separated from their spouses, continued to see each other regularly after Edith left Penhill in 1929, and on 12 June 1931 a son, John Graham, was born to this union.

The move of the school to Penhill, now lighted by recently installed electricity, was successful. The children were delighted with the rural surroundings, the animals and the farm activities. FM continued to give lessons to the children but other staff were required for general teaching. So in May, after two terms as a pupil teacher at a school in Guildford, Joan

84 Arthur Rose with John on Peter at Penhill.

85 Peter and John Vicary on Nancy at Penhill.

returned to Ellerslie and joined the staff at Penhill, cycling over there every day. She taught for a year and then undertook a secretarial course in London.

Irene Tasker stayed only one term at Penhill and then decided that the time had come to move elsewhere. FM was often asked if there were teachers in various countries, particularly those of the British Empire, and with AR returning to America along with some new teachers from the course it seemed appropriate for somebody else to go overseas. This idea appealed to Irene and so, in the summer of 1934, she left the school at Penhill and prepared to go abroad. At the end of the year she travelled to South Africa. She lived in Johannesburg

86 FM with John at Penhill.

87 Irene Tasker and Joan Mechin at Penhill with the school children, 1934.

and began teaching in early 1935. Shortly after her arrival she was asked by the Head of the Preparatory School for the South African Roedean, a former pupil of FM, to give a talk on the Work to the Parent/Teacher Association. The event was a success and a number of children were sent to her later for lessons, but the most significant feature of the day was the attendance of Vera Coaker.[20] Subsequently she read *Use of the Self* and convinced her husband, Norman, that he should do the same. He, his wife and children had lessons from Irene and so began an understanding of the Work that was to prove so vital in the years to come when this eminent KC performed such a critical role in FM's libel action in 1948.

Irene gave many other talks to a wide variety of gatherings including the Transvaal Teachers' Association at their Annual Conference.[21] She gave numerous demonstrations generating considerable interest in the Work which resulted in a large number of pupils. Additionally, former pupils of FM who were now in South Africa came to her. Perhaps her most important scheme was her children's class which she ran with the aid of a trained teacher. Irene announced this plan soon after her arrival in South Africa and quickly had a successful class. As time progressed, her little group was joined by children without special difficulties but whose parents wanted them to combine lessons in the Work with its application in class.[22]

In 1936 Irene returned to England for the summer so she was able to visit Ashley Place and have lessons from FM. She went back to Johannesburg in the autumn to the great delight of her pupils. There she continued to teach until Christmas 1938. During the 1930s Irene was remarkably successful; she taught a large number of pupils, helped innumerable children and impressed many members of the teaching profession who learnt to appreciate the value of Alexander's work. People from other walks of life, including doctors, became similarly convinced.[23] Mr. Thomas Hall, when he became President of the South African Chemical Institute, included in his Presidential Address a section on the Work. He ended his speech by declaring, 'Alexander, who is already an old man, will one day be among the immortals along with Pasteur.' This was well reported in the South African press.[24]

Meanwhile at Ashley Place, in 1935 the students from the original course qualified and were considered by FM competent to teach his work, now known as a Technique. Marjorie Barstow returned to America and during the winter months she taught with AR in Boston, and sometimes at the weekends she went with him to New York where they taught. In the summer she returned to her home town of Lincoln, Nebraska. This arrangement continued until about 1942.[25] Lulie Westfeldt also returned to America and taught mainly in New York. Before the 1939-1945 War she returned to London most summers to teach with her colleagues.[26] The other American, Kitty Meyrick, returned home but did not teach on a regular basis like her fellow countrywomen. Of the British teachers, Marjory stayed at Ashley Place as did Erika and Irene Stewart. After a short time with them, Pat MacDonald went to teach in Birmingham, with the encouragement and support of FM and to the delight of Robert Best, a long-time devotee of the Work. Best had tried for a number of years to persuade FM that there should be a teacher in Birmingham. Pat was assisted sometimes by Erika, Irene and George Trevelyan. Later he returned to Ashley Place to teach, and three times a week he and Marjory gave Alexander lessons to the schoolchildren at Penhill. Gurney McInnes went to teach at Weymouth College where Irene Tasker's brother-in-law was Headmaster, and George Trevelyan taught in London for two years mostly on his own in Buckingham Palace Road before becoming a master at Gordonstoun School. During his time in London George took an active part in events at Ashley Place and was very much one of the Alexander team. He assisted when there was a shortage of teachers and helped in Birmingham when required. He was secretary of the Alexander Society and regularly issued bulletins on topics of interest as well as organising meetings of members.[27]

With AR in America, Irene Tasker in South Africa, and Margaret Goldie in charge of the school at Penhill, FM, Ethel Webb and the small, rather inexperienced team were on occasions hard pressed to cope with the demands of the training course and the large number of pupils who wanted lessons. These pupils came from a wide variety of backgrounds and occupations but there were still a significant number from the acting profession, such as Robert Donat, Leslie Howard and, from 1935, Marie Ney. Other well-known people from the artistic world including the poet Robert Nicholls, the artist Paul Nash, the author and philosopher Anthony Ludovici, and the great conductor Sir Adrian Boult, whose step-son, Richard Wilson, attended the school at Penhill. Aldous Huxley began lessons in October 1935 and he publicised the Work in a number of his books, particularly *Eyeless in Gaza* published in 1936 and *Ends and Means* published the following year. In the summer of 1936 George Bernard Shaw and his wife stayed with the Trevelyans at Wallington. Lady Trevelyan persuaded Mrs. Shaw of the benefits of the Alexander Work and she read all FM's books. She held considerable sway over her husband and when they returned to London he was dispatched to Ashley Place for lessons. FM found George Bernard Shaw quite a challenge because, of course, he was a vegetarian and this was quite contrary to FM beliefs in the proper way to eat.[28] However, the men got on very well and enjoyed each other's company, and FM had great respect for his friend's intellect.

FM's Tasmanian background may have stimulated conversation. A paternal uncle of GBS, his father's oldest brother, Edward Carr Shaw, went from Ireland to Tasmania in 1830 where he settled and married Annie Fenton. They had a son, Bernard, born a few years before GBS, who spent most of his life on the North West Coast a few miles from Wynyard.[29] His cousin, Charles Benjamin Monds Fenton, who married Rebecca Ditcham the year FM was born in 1869, lived on Table Cape for many years. As was related earlier, Charles Fenton bought 2,000 acres of land in 1880 and established a farm and homestead, Norwood, on the Table Cape headland near the summit. He was instrumental in having the lighthouse erected in 1888 and was the founder of the Table Cape Butter Factory coopera- tive opened in 1892 which greatly assisted the farmers in the area, including the Alexanders. The Fentons had eight children and in the small outpost of Wynyard must have known the Alexander family.

A further twist to this story was that Edward Carr Shaw had an estate called Redbanks at Swansea. When the Irishman William McKenna, his wife and family arrived in Tasmania in 1857, William obtained employment on this estate. He worked there for nine years and earned sufficient money to buy land near the Blythe river on the North West Coast where eventually the family had a racing stables, a race course and an hotel. McKenna and his sons loved horses and the McKenna stables were famous. The fourth son, Ben, was a remarkably good trainer of race horses and his animals won an enormous number of races.[30] It was here at Blythe and later at Clayton near Ulverston that FM's father, John, now known to everyone as Johnny, spent over 25 years of his life helping Ben with his horses. He and Ben had been friends for many years before he went to live on their land in 1909. Johnny became blacksmith to the stables and Ben and he travelled everywhere together, attending race meetings in many different places in Tasmania and mainland Australia. As Ben's grandson has recalled, 'Johnny Alexander was an icon in his time. He was recognised as the farrier of his era and had a natural aptitude to make shoes for horses with physical disabilities or which had been injured. One of the leading horses that my grandfather trained in the period

88   Johnny Alexander with Mr. and Mrs. McKenna at Ulverstone in 1933.

1909-17 was *Raheney*, a gelding that won races all over Tasmania and on mainland Victoria (32 wins, 31 seconds and 31 thirds between 1908 and 1917). The little horse was only a pony 14.2 hands high and won races on the flat and over fences, carrying 12st. 9lb. when winning a steeplechase at Williamstown, Victoria in 1917. The horse was difficult to train and prone to lameness and Johnny's skills alleviated the lameness by making special shoes. In this era my grandfather, Ben, was recognised as Tasmania's leading thoroughbred trainer he had a horse named *Blue Mountain* that won the Australian Grand National Steeple and a horse named *Baanya* that won several Tasmanian Cups and some races on the Mainland of Australia. He always attributed much of his success to the skills of his farrier.'

When Ben McKenna's hotel at Blythe burnt down, the family moved to Clayton at East Ulverston and Johnny went with them. He lived in a hut very near the main house and looked after the large vegetable garden where he specialised in growing artichokes. Although Ben and Johnny's racing days were over, Johnny was still an excellent horseman and, according to local folklore, rode very well until near the end of his life. He never had any money except what Ben gave him, but for a number of years he would catch the bus to Ulverston once a week and visit a local pub. He was not charged for the transport and his friends and the publican bought him whisky. He would return on the bus and live quietly, tending the garden and awaiting his next weekly adventure to Ulverston. During his time at the McKennas he always ate with the family but in the last years of his life Mrs. Ben McKenna used to cook his meals and take them from her kitchen to his hut. Eventually this became too difficult for the elderly grandmother, and she decided that Johnny should go to a home where he could receive proper care.[31] He died a little while later at the ripe old age of 93 years on 3 September 1936 and was buried in the cemetery at Cornelian Bay in Hobart.

GBS visited Ashley Place regularly and became an advocate of the Work; he said in 1937, 'Alexander has established not only the beginning of a far-reaching science of the apparently involuntary movements we call reflexes, but a technique of correction and self-control which forms a substantial addition to our very slender resources in personal education.'[32]

89 Jan Kelly, great great granddaughter of Matthias Alexander at Johnny Alexander's grave in Hobart.

FM rarely gave talks about his work although he made an exception in August 1934 when he lectured to the Bedford Training College. Perhaps it would be more accurate to say that he outlined his Technique and then demonstrated on one of the students. Supporters of the Work continued to write articles for publication. The *British Journal of Physical Medicine* published one in February 1935 by Mungo Douglas entitled 'Posture', and in June 1936 the *British Medical Journal* printed one by Peter MacDonald's son, Patrick, on physical education.[33] Another article, this time about the relationship and relevance of the Work to children, entitled 'A New Expression of the Self', and written by Oscar Köllerström was published in the *New Era*.[34] A lecture given by John Hilton, Professor of Industrial Relations at Cambridge University, to a conference of the Institute of Labour Management at Buxton was fulsome in its praise of Alexander and his work; this talk addressed a wider and rather different audience from the usual.[35] The most important medical endorsement of the Work came in May of that year, when Dr. Murdoch used his Presidential Address to the Sussex Branch of the British Medical Association to discuss Alexander's work.[36] As a result of this the editor of the *Journal of Massage and Medical Gymnastics* asked Murdoch to write a paper on Posture with special reference to Alexander's theory. And in the following year the substance of Murdoch's address was published as a paper entitled 'The Function of the Sub-occipital Muscle. The Key to Posture, Use and Functioning'. In the same year Mungo Douglas produced a paper on 'Re-orientation of the View point upon the Study of Anatomy'. But the most significant publication of 1937 was a letter printed in the *British Medical Journal* and signed by 19 doctors. The letter referred to the review of Alexander's book *Constructive*

90 FM riding at Penhill.

Conscious Control of the Individual which had appeared in the *Journal* on 24 May 1924. The review had suggested that the book 'had something of value to communicate to the medical profession'. The letter by the doctors some 13 years later suggested, in fact 'begged to urge', that steps should be taken as soon as possible to investigate Alexander's work and technique. These doctors believed that the Work was of vital importance and once properly investigated would be acknowledged and then included in medical training.[37] This did not happen.

All this activity in England was mirrored to an extent in America although there were fewer teachers. When Max completed his training in 1937, he went across the Atlantic to assist his father in Boston where he had a flourishing practice. Many were interested in the Technique and Michael March did his best to stimulate this. In January 1937 he published in the *Brooklyn Citizen* 'The Plight of Educators', in which he reviewed Mr. Kilpatrick's paper on 'A Reconstructed Theory of the Educative Process'. Mr. Kilpatrick, a professor at the Teachers' College at Columbia University, was concerned about 'the growing of the whole child'. March highlighted the importance and relevance of Alexander's work in this area.[38] The following year he wrote another article for the same newspaper publicising the Work and trying to stimulate the Rockefeller Foundation to analyse Alexander's principles and technique.[39] In the same month the long-time devotee and teacher of the Work, Alma Frank, published 'A Study of Infant Development'. This scientific study of the gradual diminishing of well-coordinated movement in young children drew on the work of a variety of specialists and scientists; it discussed Alexander's work and research as detailed in his book *The Use of the Self.*

In London, in 1938, FM, Ethel Webb, Marjory Mechin, Erika Schumann, Irene Stewart and Pat MacDonald were all teaching at Ashley Place. The more senior students on the large training course included Walter Carrington, Wilfred Barlow, Eric de Peyer, Douglass Price-Williams and Dick Walker who taught games at the little school at Penhill to help pay for his training course. One of the new students was Elisabeth Walker. In the summer, Joan Mechin returned to Ashley Place as secretary to FM and Ethel Webb. The school at Penhill prospered and was still run by Margaret Goldie. The books were selling steadily; for the six months up to the end of June 1938, excluding America, 266 copies of *Man's Supreme Inheritance*, 228 copies of *Constructive Conscious Control of the Individual* and 293 copies of *The Use of the Self* were sold.[40] Shortly after this, publication of the books was taken over by FM's friend and great supporter of the Work, Fred Watts.[41] Alexander teachers and people interested in the Work met regularly, and from 1936 this group published regular bulletins which included articles about the Work as it affected people in various professions. In 1937 an Alexander Society was formed and the first society bulletin was issued in June 1937. These bulletins were issued on a regular basis.

Overall the 1930s were successful for FM. He worked hard, had an increasing number of pupils and his ideas were respected by a growing cross-section of the population. *The Use of the Self* was well received and he was busy writing the next book. In addition, he enjoyed his leisure activities. He attended race meetings regularly, bet on horses frequently, and rode his horse, Peter, as often as time permitted. He went to the test matches and was particularly pleased when he was able to watch Don Bradman, whose 'use' FM considered to be 'good'. His other hero was Walter Lindum, the Australian snooker player.[42] Snooker and billiards had interested FM for many years and when he was in America during the First World War he had seen George Gray play billiards. FM considered that the 'mechanical principle of the position adopted by him could be scientifically demonstrated as being as nearly perfect for its particular purpose as any position could be'. He continued, 'Mr. Gray manifests in his play the most remarkable and controlled kinæsthetic development I have yet witnessed. But how many George Grays has the world so far produced?'[43] He continued to enjoy reciting Shakespeare as well as Australian poets Banjo Patterson and Henry Lawson, to name but two. One of the main advantages of London was the plentiful supply of good restaurants where he could indulge himself with first-class food and wine. He was a regular visitor to the Café Royal, a well-known establishment in Regent Street, and to Wheelers, the famous London sea food restaurants, although not all his friends and relations shared his enthusiasm for oysters. Nevertheless, this well-groomed man, who was always immaculately turned out with a carnation in his button hole and wearing his spats, assumed that everyone regarded eating a good meal with equally fine wine as an essential part of life.

SKETCH MAP OF SIDCUP AREA
C. 1939–45

Penhill

The Bungalow
no.26

Black Horse
Hotel

Ellerslie

Queen Mary's
Hospital

14

THE SECOND WORLD WAR

In three weeks England, will have her neck wrung like a chicken.
Some chicken; some neck.
Winston Churchill: Speech to Canadian Senate, 30 December 1941

At the beginning of 1939 FM's main objectives were still the continuing development of his technique, the publication of his next book, and further acceptance of his work by authoritative academics both in England and America. Generally, he lived at Ashley Place during the week and went to Penhill at the weekends. The acquisition of a new gardener at Penhill had had an advantageous effect and FM was delighted. The year started well: 20 January was FM's 70th birthday. A dinner party with dancing afterwards was organised by three Alexander teachers, George Trevelyan, Gurney McInnes and Irene Tasker, at the *Carlton Hotel* in London where his family, teachers and many of his pupils joined in a successful celebration. The evening was chaired by the Lord Lytton, who read birthday messages from many of FM's friends unable to attend the dinner, including John Dewey, Aldous Huxley, James McDonagh, Mary Olcott, Marie Ney and George Bernard Shaw, whose wife wrote, 'we have given up going out in the evening, had it been a luncheon! …' Then the Lord Lytton proposed the toast to FM, who replied. A further toast, to 'The Work and its Future', was proposed by Dr. Peter MacDonald supported by Lucy Silcox, late Headmistress of St Felix School, Southwold, Anthony Ludovici and Irene Tasker.[1] On the same day, AR, Marjorie Barstow and Carla Atkinson, together with other Alexander teachers, friends and supporters, held a similar celebration in Boston, America.[2]

Throughout the early part of the year, the international news particularly concerning events in Germany was disturbing. However, FM, ever the incorrigible optimist, believed most strongly that all the problems would be solved and that nothing serious would happen. He supported Chamberlain and believed passionately in the 'peace in our time' message. When viewed historically, FM's opinions can only be described as naïve and his lack of understanding of military matters is apparent, but, always a man of his time, he reflected the views of a large percentage of the British people. It was perhaps fortunate that not everybody held these opinions, but right up until the end of August 1939, he did not believe there would be a war. Even then he optimistically thought it would soon be over.

On 27 February 1939, AR's son Max returned from America and joined the teaching staff at Ashley Place.[3] Three months later, on 24 May, his father sailed for England on the *Queen Mary*; he arrived at the end of the month and thereafter helped FM. During this period, Drs. Peter MacDonald, Mungo Douglas and Murdoch had letters supporting the Work published in the *British Medical Journal*, the *Lancet* and other medical papers.[4] But the most important development that spring was the publication in April in the *Brooklyn Citizen* of 'The Basic Error of Psychology' by Arthur Busch (alias Michael March) about the work of Professor Coghill in America; Busch asserted that Professor Coghill's findings confirmed the scientific basis of Alexander's practical work.[5] George Ellett Coghill was an American biologist and philosopher. Born in 1872 on a farm in Illinois, he graduated from Brown University in 1896 and gained his MS degree three years later at New Mexico University. He was for four years Professor of Biology at the Pacific University in Oregon, then he taught for a year at Willamette University, Oregon; by 1907 he had moved to Denison University in Ohio where he was Professor of Zoology. Six years later he became Professor in Anatomy at the University of Kansas and in 1925 joined the Wistar Institute in Philadelphia, where he was able to devote himself totally to his research. In 1934 he had a mild heart attack; his medical condition, together with professional disagreements at Wistar, led, in December 1935, to his removal from the Wistar Institute. This severely curtailed his research programme although he did establish a small laboratory at Gainesville, Florida, his retirement home. He had an illustrious career and was honoured by a number of universities and numerous scientific organisations. His study and research into the behaviour and the anatomy of the nervous system of Amblystoma, a small lizard-like salamander, which he began during his time in Oregon, broke new scientific ground and profoundly affected thinking in both biology and psychology. Throughout his life he produced a number of major scientific papers connected with his research. In May 1928 he delivered three highly acclaimed presentations at University College, London entitled 'Anatomy and the Problem of Behaviour' based on his study of Amblystoma.[6]

In 1930 he presented a paper to the National Academy of Sciences in which he referred to reflex and the part played in it by inhibition. He said,

> Postural reactions of the trunk and limbs, also, are established before local reflexes of the legs appear. These reflexes gradually emerge from a total pattern of limb and trunk movements; and this occurs at about the time that antigravity action of the legs can first be observed. Posture and the walking gait as such are therefore primarily total reactions. Also the rotation of the leg in walking occurs first at the extreme phase of extension as a part of a total pattern of leg action ... It is then in a field of total inhibition that the local reflex emerges. The reflex may, therefore, be regarded as a total behaviour pattern which consists of two components, one overt or excitatory, the other covert or inhibitory. The essential anatomical basis for this is (a) in the mechanism of the total pattern of action, or the primary motor system, and (b) in the mechanism of the local reflex, or secondary motor system; the mechanism of the total pattern being inhibited and that of the reflex excited. But since inhibition is not a static condition but a mode of action, the mechanism of the total pattern must be regarded as participating in every local reflex.[7]

In March 1930 Coghill gave a lecture at the University of Minnesota in which he stated, *inter alia*,

> There is nothing immaterial in mind when I use the term pattern. I try to use it consistently to designate configuration or form of action or inhibition. When all overtly mobile parts of the animal appear to

be in action I call the performance a total action pattern. When only a part of the overtly mobile animal is in action I call the performance a partial action pattern. I think of inhibition, also, in the same way. When all of the animal that is capable of action is irresponsive to a stimulus that is ordinarily adequate I call the condition a total inhibition pattern. When only a part of the total action pattern is inhibited I designate the inhibition pattern as partial. At the same time, of course, I recognize that inhibition is not a passive condition. It is a function of the nervous system quite as much as is overt action. It is, so to speak, concealed, a covert action, which is antagonistic to overt action. Some behaviour patterns may, therefore, involve both action pattern and inhibition pattern. The local reflex as an action pattern, for example, is the overt component of a total behaviour pattern, the other component of which is an inhibition pattern. This is shown clearly in Amblystoma in the development of the fore limb …[8]

In a lecture in 1931 at Ohio State University, Coghill continued his theme and stated,

Study of the development of overt behaviour from its beginning in the individual leads inevitably to the conception that the organism is primarily a unit in all its acts, and that normality in behaviour requires that all parts be appropriately subject to this unity, which is the organism as a whole, or, conversely, that the organism as a whole maintains its power of activating the behaviour of its parts. Accordingly, the organism as a whole must be the primary agency of motivity in order to maintain the appropriate integration between itself and the environment.[9]

In his biography of Coghill, Professor Herrick, averred that 'local movement is not an independent event. It is normally a part of a more extensive activity which may or may not be overtly manifest.' He stated that 'it was Coghill's opinion that every such localised movement required not only the activation of the local organs directly involved but also an active inhibition of other related neuromuscular systems.' Moreover, he added that he and Coghill 'had experimental evidence from the Amblystoma programme that this was true, at least in the case of the antagonists of the muscles in active contraction; and Coghill extended this idea to embrace an inhibition of the total pattern as an essential factor in the execution of any local reflex, that is of all components of the total behaviour which would interfere with the local autonomous activity.'[10] Two years later, in 1933, Coghill wrote,

The mechanism of total integration tends to maintain absolute unity and solidarity of the behaviour pattern. The development of localized mechanisms tends to disrupt unity and solidarity and to produce independent partial patterns of behaviour. In the interests of the welfare of the organism as a whole, partial patterns must not attain complete independence of action; they must be held under control by the mechanism of total integration. Parts become integrated with each other because they are integral factors of a primarily integrated whole, and they remain integrated, and behaviour is normal, so long as this wholeness is maintained. But the wholeness may be lost through a decline of the mechanism of total integration or through the hypertrophy of mechanisms of partial patterns. This, I believe, is the biologic basis of that conflict in behaviour which expresses itself widely in the field of psychopathology.[11]

On 1 May the Brooklyn Citizen published a letter by Eric Estorick, Hayden Fellow in Sociology at New York University and subsequently a biographer of Stafford Cripps, in which he criticised the editorial by Arthur Busch. Busch responded in his next editorial that,

Coghill has discovered the actual mechanism of integration and Alexander has perfected the technique of employing it in the improvement of human beings. Coghill, in a word, has proven a principle scientifically, whose import ultimately will revolutionize the whole structure of psychology, medicine and education, and Alexander has perfected the means of putting it into practice.

This dialogue produced a reaction from Coghill, whose letter to the newspaper was published on 12 May. He stated that,

the only reason for public announcement is Estorick's criticism. … Mr. Estorick shows a very superficial knowledge of my research and mentions my name among the names of other scientists in a way that may lead to misunderstanding.

He continued,

The *Brooklyn Citizen* of 7 April shows a more thorough understanding of the fundamental results of my research and a more thorough appreciation of its meaning and implication than one could expect on the part of a layman. Your review (Busch) indicates in fact that you have actually attained a higher plane from which you can view the field of organic behaviour with professional acumen but with freedom from the trammels of the schools of psychology and related sciences.[12]

These editorials and letters led to correspondence between Coghill, Busch and Alexander and a meeting a couple of years later between Coghill and Alexander. Sadly, by then both these able innovators were old men and Coghill was severely debilitated by ill health.

Life was treating FM well in the summer of 1939. He had many pupils, there were 22 students on the training course, his work was receiving publicity in medical journals, Professor Coghill's research appeared to provide scientific evidence to support his teaching, and Penhill was a continual joy to him. Abruptly this happy life came to an end. On 1 September, Max, a volunteer in the Territorial Army, was called up for active service, as was Peter Vicary, and two days later Britain was at war with Germany. Joan Mechin, who was working as his secretary at Ashley Place, was a Red Cross VAD; she was called up for active service with the Royal Navy. Fortunately, at about this time, Dilys Jones, later Carrington, arrived as a pupil. FM offered to give her a daily lesson if she assisted with the office work; she agreed. By 6 September, FM gave up trying to get to Ashley Place as the evacuation of children from London, he considered, made travelling impossible.[13] It was several days before he recommended commuting to London. The school, led by Margaret Goldie, was evacuated to Canock Manor in Devizes, Wiltshire. Fortunately pupils continued to arrive, and one in particular pleased him. This individual, who arrived with his daughter, had been recommended to FM by Dr. Crowley of Sydney, previously of Melbourne. FM was delighted that the daughter, with some of her Australian friends, wanted to attend the training course.[14]

Meanwhile, AR, who had left England before war was declared, arrived in New York on Labour Day, 4 September. His niece, Marjory, who was on holiday in America and staying with Lulie Westfeldt, a colleague of hers from the Alexander course, planned to meet him. Unfortunately, when she and Lulie arrived at the docks AR was nowhere to be found. The following day a rather upset AR rang to advise them that he was on Ellis Island; the neutral Americans did not want to be seen harbouring members of the warring countries, particularly people with apparent medical problems, and AR had a pronounced limp as a result of his riding accident twenty years before. The difficulty was soon resolved and after a medical AR was released and allowed to proceed to Boston where he resumed his teaching. That day Marjory boarded her ship for the return trip to England, where she rejoined FM's teaching staff at Ashley Place.

FM's attitudes to the unfolding events were intensely practical, and as always he accepted things that he could not change. In December he reported factually that, 'if butter rationing really comes about we have a cow just come in and one giving a good deal of milk so we can have our own butter'. His view of the blackout was also down to earth, and typically he noted, 'the blackout was something of a trouble to most people but with my bushman's eyes I don't mind it at all. In some ways, I prefer it to the beastly electric lights at night.'[15]

FM was always loyal to England but his pride and excitement on the arrival of a contingent of Australian airmen towards the end of the year, was touching.[16] The advent of 1940 brought forth a number of happy events: in March his daughter Peggy married, and two months later his niece, Marjory, married Bill Barlow, a medical student and an advocate of the Work. In March the *Literary Guide* published an article by Mungo Douglas on the technique called 'Integrated Conscious Man – A New Creation.'[17] A few weeks later, on 3 April, the *Medical Press and Circular* published an important article by Rugg Gunn, Senior Surgeon, Western Ophthalmic Hospital, Ophthalmic Surgeon, Central Middlesex County Hospital and Metropolitan Ear, Nose and Throat Hospital, London, entitled 'F Matthias Alexander and the Problem of Animal Behaviour'.[18] Rugg Gunn, who had attended Coghill's lectures at University College, London, in 1928, compared Alexander's work with, amongst others, Coghill. And, despite the war, new pupils regularly appeared at the doors of Ashley Place.

By the middle of May 1940 the position of Britain and her Allies was dire and FM described the situation graphically, 'we are in the throes of great stress and danger, such as England and the Empire has never known before in her history.'[19] His anger against Hitler and the Germans was vehement, as was his reaction to Mussolini and the Italians when they entered the war on 10 June. The news that Peter Vicary was missing in France and had not been evacuated at Dunkirk only added to his anxiety. He was relieved that one of his trainee teachers, Dick Walker, who became an officer in the RNVR, had survived. Dick had taken an open boat across the Channel to assist in the Dunkirk evacuation. By this stage a number of FM's friends were urging him to leave England; they feared that as a result of the views he had expressed in *Man's Supreme Inheritance* he could be on a German 'black list'. With an invasion of England by the Germans a distinct possibility time was short, but FM did not want to go. He said he would be terribly distressed if he were forced to leave England, but it was necessary to consider the Work and his friends connected with it. On 19 June the evacuation of the Channel Islands began, and the next day a French delegation commenced armistice negotiations with the Germans. Increasing pressure was applied to FM which resulted in him obtaining a passport and, reluctantly, agreeing to take the school to Toronto, Canada.[20] Plans were set in motion for a possible move in the middle of July. Passage across the Atlantic for a party of adults and children would take some time to arrange. FM's anger at the situation continued unabated, and in his frustration and feeling of helplessness he included the French signing of the armistice with Germany on 22 June in his condemnation of events causing such distress and disaster in England. He was firmly of the belief that with such treachery in France, the French Army and the British Expeditionary Force never had a chance.[21]

Events moved much faster then anybody expected. FM went to the school in Wiltshire for the weekend of 29/30 June, and when he returned to London at midday on Monday he found a message which said that he and the school must be ready to leave London on Wednesday evening. Frantically the party got themselves organised; a farewell dinner was given for FM at Ashley Place on Tuesday 2 July.[22] Unfortunately at least six of the children did not have passports and it was arranged that they would travel on a later ship. And so it was that the 72-year-old FM, accompanied by Ethel Webb, Margaret Goldie, Irene Stewart, Mary McNair Scott, the daughter of Lord Camrose, the famous newspaper tycoon and great friend and supporter of the Prime Minister Winston Churchill, and her four children, together with six other children including Francis Caldwell, Gillian Brakes, John Best and Charmian Dundas, set sail on schedule. The convoy of three passenger liners included the *Monarch Of Bermuda*, a rather flat-bottomed ship more suited to inshore journeys than an Atlantic crossing, and two others carrying German- and Italian-born internees. The *Monarch Of Bermuda*, containing the Alexander party was an 'escape ship' for children and, in addition to millions of pounds of gold bullion and other British valuables she carried mostly babies with their young mothers. The Children's Convoy left the George V dock at Greenock on the Clyde at 0545 hours on 5 July, escorted by the recently commissioned cruiser HMS *Bonventure* and the destroyers HMS *Garth* and HMS *Jason*. As the convoy reached the open sea on that lovely summer morning the escort ships fanned out in front of the three passenger ships. At 1000 hours HMS *Garth* and HMS *Jason* left the convoy and were replaced by the battleship HMS *Revenge* and four destroyers; in addition there was aircraft protection.[23] This impressive armada presented an unforgettable sight for the Alexander party as they sailed through the Western Approaches, where the German U-boats were causing so much damage to allied shipping.

On 5 July Naval intelligence estimated that there were three U-boats in the Western Approaches. HMS *Whirlwind* was badly damaged 120 miles west of Lands End, with 57 personnel killed and seven seriously wounded. Three other ships, previously torpedoed, arrived at Falmouth under tow. The following day there were a number of reported U-boat sightings from aircraft and ships in the Lands End area. The Estonian SS *Vapper* was sunk and HMCS *Restigouche* rescued the survivors. On 7 July it was estimated there were two U-boats in the area. An aircraft reported that a tanker had been torpedoed and the surviving crew were in lifeboats. The Dutch tanker *Lucrecia* was torpedoed with some fatalities near Lands End, and the Swedish ship *Bissen* was sunk some miles south of Cape Clear in southern Ireland, though all the crew were rescued. The Western Approaches were dangerous.[24] Meanwhile on land, the Germans bombers began their daylight raids over Britain and on 6 July dropped high explosive bombs on Aldershot killing a number of soldiers.[25]

Obviously there was no point in dwelling on the hazards of the trip. Now that FM was actually going abroad for what he believed to be the duration his optimism returned. He declared, 'I'm on the wallaby track once more.' He resented having to leave England but was pleased at the prospect of seeing John Dewey again and hoped to meet George Coghill.[26]

At that stage he did not know where he and his party would go but he refused to worry about it. After all, Canada, New York and Philadelphia were all possibilities. He had many American friends, AR was in Boston, and he had been given a number of splendid introductions. Some friends had cabled ahead to advise their contacts across the Atlantic that Alexander and the children were on their way. Now only two things irritated FM, he had been allowed to take only £25 out of the country, and the shortage of ink meant that he was reduced to writing in pencil. He left behind in London his family, his teachers, his pupils, his friends, 16 Ashley Place and his beloved horse, Peter, at Penhill. He was only too aware that they had to face the wrath of Hitler, while he, the head of the family, sought the safety of North America. He was fortunate that Jack Vicary was prepared to assume responsibility for running the estate at Penhill, to take overall charge of 16 Ashley Place and to control all his personal finances in England. Jack with Wendy and John moved into Penhill house and 107 Upton Road was rented out. FM's teaching in London was now in the hands of his niece Marjory, assisted by Walter Carrington.

The position in Britain was now desperate. Only two days after FM left, on 7 July, three Dutch Army officers landed at Yarmouth in a small boat. In their report they stated that German preparations in Holland for the invasion of England were obvious, with large numbers of parachute troops continually practising. They confirmed that the German slogan was 'London on 15 July' and that every craft that was capable of making the crossing was expected to start transporting one and a half million men on 11 July. They advised that the invasion plan was to launch a parachute attack which the Germans hoped would cause the British troops to be withdrawn from the coastal areas and thus facilitate the task of the first landing parties, which would come from all ports from Norway to Belgium. Once the first parties had secured a foothold, the main landing force would arrive in larger ships. The report concluded that the Germans expected the invading force to comprise three and half to four million men. Immediately, the Royal Navy advised all HM ships; the instructions also highlighted the possibility that the enemy would use smoke to cover the landing operations. All HM ships in the North Sea and the Channel were ordered to report any unusual fog or appearance of cloud on the surface. It was calculated that under favourable meteorological conditions smoke could be projected from land a distance of about 100 miles. The masters of merchant ships were advised that any large body of merchant vessels approaching the east or south coast were likely to be enemy transports. These unfortunate masters were instructed to use such armaments as they had available, which in some cases comprised only Bren and Lewis guns, then to manoeuvre their ships to 'ram' the transports, lighters or barges and make full use of all their weaponry. After inflicting all damage possible, the masters were instructed with optimistic Naval humour to leave the invasion area and continue their voyage.[27]

The Alexander party continued their journey. The weather was good and the winds light to moderate. The voyage was uneventful, if such a description is appropriate for an Atlantic crossing of five adults with ten children, some of whom had just left their parents, in the middle of a war. Once clear of the danger zone of the Western Approaches, the convoy escort was reduced to the battleship HMS *Revenge* and the Cruiser HMS *Bonventure*. The convoy made extremely good progress and arrived in Halifax on 11 July.[28] The Alexander party were taken to Toronto where they were greeted by a heat wave and high humidity, but great kindness shown by the Canadians, particularly the people connected with Toronto University. They were expecting some 1,200 children to arrive shortly from England and the great dining hall was stacked with crockery. Soon after their arrival in Toronto, Margaret departed with some of the children to the Canadian lakes, and Irene Stewart and the McNair Scotts went elsewhere in Canada; FM and Ethel Webb remained in Toronto and tried to obtain permission to enter America. This was achieved relatively quickly but not without some suffering on the part of these two elderly, if intrepid, travellers. According to FM's report, they waited for hours in crowded rooms in tremendous heat and humidity. It was an experience, he averred firmly, that 'he did not wish to repeat for many a day'. In early August they crossed the border and went to Alice Fowler, Ethel's long-standing friend, at South West Harbour, Mount Desert in Maine. Ethel stayed in the cottage and gradually recovered from her ordeal, while FM was located in the house with a room overlooking the sea. By 17 August, he declared, he was beginning to 'come back to his normal self'. As the American authorities had directed that nobody could work until October, FM decided to prepare his new book for publication and make arrangements for the school to move to America. He made contact with AR and many of his old friends in America including John Dewey.[29]

In England the Battle of Britain was under way; an invasion was expected at anytime and the country was subjected to air raids. For Amy, without any of the family, at Ellerslie and Jack Vicary at Penhill they were difficult times. The first bomb to land near Ellerslie, which caused damage in adjacent St John's Road, was on 30 August; this was followed three days later by another bomb landing almost midway between Ellerslie and Penhill. On 4, 5 and 6 September bombs landed close to both houses causing significant damage to nearby dwellings. The following day, 7 September, a bomb fell near 16 Ashley Place and a ton of coke, recently delivered to the house, was scattered through all the coal cellars, now converted to air-raid shelters, of Ashley Place.[30] Although FM was grieved by the loss of the coke, he visualised the incident with some wry amusement. In mid September it was decided to close the building officially, although, Walter Carrington, who had married Dilys Jones the previous month, went to the premises daily. He taught a number of pupils and worked on a paper comparing the work of Coghill and Alexander until he joined the Royal Air Force in early March 1941.[31] This proved vital as pupils still kept appearing at Ashley Place. Initially, Marjory went to North Wales and then she was evacuated with Bill to Guildford for a few months. In December she and Bill moved to Oxford where Marjory resumed her teaching.

While in Maine, FM and Ethel continued to work on the manuscript for the new book and FM discussed some of the revisions with John Dewey and Arthur Busch. By late September he was delighted to dispatch a copy of the manuscript to Arthur Busch, who was arranging for publication. The others were still in Canada, Margaret with some of the children in Footes Bay and Irene with Mary McNair Scott and her children at Roaches Point.[32] In mid-October FM, after a short sojourn with AR, and Ethel moved to New York, where Ethel lived with Professor and Mrs. Wendell Bush and FM in the *Hotel Blackstone*. FM's priority was to generate some income, and fortunately Alma Frank was available to

91   The Homestead at Stow.

help him find suitable teaching rooms. He received his permit to work on 22 October.[33] In addition he tried to obtain permission to bring the school into America. A number of people offered premises for the school but these establishments did not meet FM's requirements. FM and AR were now able to meet each other regularly and they discussed the possibility of starting a training course. Time went by and still Margaret and the rest of the party were stranded in Canada although by all accounts they were having a marvellous time. The problem was that the Americans were not prepared to admit one of the severely disabled children.

As the year progressed FM continued to teach, and he was delighted when the publishers for his new book, *The Universal Constant in Living*, and a number of eminent Americans approved of his manuscript. The major difficulty was to find suitable accommodation for the school. Early in January 1941 the Unitarian Association of America offered the Whitney Homestead in Stow, originally known as the Pomposetticut Plantation, Massachusetts, some 20 miles from Boston, free of charge. Set in 129 acres of land, the Homestead comprised two houses, one built in 1760 and the other a much larger and more impressive building erected some 80 years later. The latter house was built using timber from the Whitney estate by Moses Whitney for his daughter, Lucia, after her marriage to her cousin, Edwin Whitney, in 1841. Shortly after the house was completed, Moses and his wife moved from the old homestead to join their daughter in the new dwelling, and another of Moses' daughters, Mary, with her husband James Whitney, another first cousin and their seven children moved into the old house. The new homestead consisted of 16 rooms originally, with four rooms either side of the central hall downstairs and a similar arrangement upstairs. After the deaths of the childless Edwin and Lucia some of their nephews and nieces moved into the home-stead but all of them were childless. The problem of what was to become of their beloved home and estate worried the Whitneys. Eventually, in 1925, Cyrus Whitney on behalf of the family bequeathed the estate to the American Unitarian Association together with a significant sum of money. The Unitarians were reluctant to accept the bequest appreciating how much it would cost to utilise the estate as the Whitneys required: using the land and

buildings to provide for the spiritual and bodily needs of Church members. The old homestead was intended for use by Unitarian women and the newer homestead by ministers and
their wives as well as laymen and women of the church. However, the large sum of money
persuaded the Unitarians they should accept the gift and in 1928, after the death of Adeline
Whitney, they set up a Moses Whitney Memorial Fund with $100,000 of the Whitney
bequest, the income from which was to finance the farming activities. A further $30,000
from the bequest was allocated to modify the houses. To the newer homestead were added
numerous bathrooms, a kitchen, a dining room, a laundry room and a second-floor exten-
sion intended to be a dormitory for use by bachelors.[34]

Despite considerable efforts to publicise this spiritual retreat, the venture was not a
success, and so the Unitarians offered all the Whitney estate facilities to the Alexander Trust.
The newer Homestead provided absolutely ideal accommodation for the school and the
farm, grounds and other house were most useful adjuncts; FM accepted this delightful place
gratefully. One further problem remained, the American immigration authorities still not
agreeing to admit the boy who was severely disabled, so reluctantly it was decided to leave
him in Canada with his mother. But at last, at the end of January in thick snow, all the others
made their way to Stow, John Best clutching his cricket bat; the disabled boy was allowed
into America in late August. The plan was for everyone to live and work in Stow during
the summer and for FM and AR to alternate between New York and the Boston area in
the winter.[35] The arrival of the British party at Stow was heralded by the *Boston Evening
Transcript* newspaper under the heading 'Oh, to Be in Stow, Now That England's There'.[36]

Throughout this period FM was most concerned about everyone in England. In his
letters he constantly referred to how worried he and AR were about events at home. For
the family, bombing raids had become a way of life and for people living in London and
the south-east of England from mid September 1940, the raids took place almost every night.
At Ellerslie and Penhill it seemed that bombs dropped around them on a continuous basis,
houses were destroyed and people evacuated from homes so often that comment was hardly
necessary. A high explosive bomb landed in Penhill Road near the house on 18 September
and on 7 November the house opposite Ellerslie, No.16 Highview Road, was hit. At the
end of the month another two high explosive bombs landed in Penhill Road.[37] On
29 December incendiary bombs fell on the City of London on an unprecedented scale,
creating a swathe of fire on both banks of the Thames. The Guildhall roof and eight Wren
churches were destroyed or severely damaged but heroic efforts by firefighters saved St Paul's
Cathedral. During December civilian deaths as a result of enemy action totalled 3,793.[38] On
12 January 1941 Amy listened, watched and waited as 250 incendiaries landed, most of them
within a quarter of a mile of her, in the space of about twenty minutes. The area was
reported as looking like a 'Brock's benefit', with flares all over the place, in front and back
gardens, on the roads, in open spaces and in houses. Some landed in Highview Road and
adjacent St John's Road, others in the surrounding roads and some fell on the railway station
at Sidcup. Six bombs landed in the goods yard and four more on the booking office, a goods
truck was burnt out, and someone attempted to smother a bomb with coal dust! This entire
raid was over in a remarkably short time and all the available population emerged immediately to assist in putting out the fires. At the height of the excitement one elderly lady

appeared with a shovel in one hand and holding a frying pan over her head with the other to ward off shrapnel! Surprisingly there was only one casualty, at No.12 St John's Road, where three bombs fell in the garden and a 14-year-old boy sustained a leg injury. A significant number of houses were damaged. The bombing continued through the rest of January and February and in the middle of March three bombs from one raid landed almost opposite Penhill.[39]

The accounts of the bombing and the deaths of civilians horrified FM and AR.[40] Despite this, FM insisted upon remaining remarkably optimistic about the war. On 30 October 1940 he was delighted to hear on the radio that the Chinese were inflicting considerable damage on the Japanese. He optimistically expected that the Japanese would be forced to leave China by the end of the year.[41] He was delighted when Roosevelt was re-elected President and pleased that all his teachers and friends in England were keeping the Alexander message alive. However, in February 1941 he noted ruefully that all 'his boys' were or would very shortly be serving in the military services. This included Walter Carrington, Gurney McInnes and Pat MacDonald. FM's main complaint about life in America concerned the food. He disliked the bread and the meat and found the fish 'beyond description', although the oysters met with his approval. He objected to the canned vegetables and yearned for his fresh vegetables from the Penhill gardens. Moreover he hated New York, which he described as 'an ungodly, uncivilized place'. FM's other concern was the letters lost at sea. He wrote regularly to a large number of people and always replied the day he received a letter; he was outraged when anyone suggested that they had not heard from him for some time! In February he also visited George Coghill, who was by now a very sick man. He spent a most interesting weekend with him; they talked almost continuously and FM gave him lessons in order to try to reduce his suffering. To FM's delight, Coghill agreed to write the preface for the new book.[42]

As the war news deteriorated throughout 1941, FM managed to console his correspondents with crumbs of comfort about the enormity of the German losses. He worked on the happy assumption that the Germans always lost four times as many men as the Allies in any battle; therefore, even when the Allies retreated from Crete, Britain and the Empire were still winning. Whether FM seriously believed this is doubtful; it is more probable that he saw it as his responsibility to maintain the morale of all his correspondents. When his niece Joan wrote and told him about clothes being rationed, he replied in typical style, 'Sorry to learn about the thunderbolt on clothing restrictions. Still it is no use to complain about that. As long as one has a suit of clothes what's the difference in war time.' He was much more concerned about Ashley Place which, in the early hours of 17 April 1941, was damaged in an air raid and some furniture destroyed. Jack Vicary was alerted to the problem by Dilys Carrington. Immediately, she abandoned her worries at Penhill and went to London to do what she could to secure FM's remaining possessions, which were now exposed to the elements. He was heartbroken at the plight of the house where he had worked for over thirty years but, in the event, the damage to his furniture was much less than had at first been feared. Worse was to follow. On the night of 19/20 April there was a most extensive raid and the anti-aircraft guns kept up a steady barrage, but for hours the bombers droned overhead and nobody in London and the surrounding area slept for long. There was devastation

92 FM, Ethel, Margaret, Irene and children at Stow.

in Sidcup, with many houses damaged and a number of casualties. At Penhill a number of bombs landed in the roads nearby, including two bombs which fell either side of an elm tree in Penhill fields. These did extensive damage to the house but Jack and John were able to remain in residence.[43] At Ellerslie the occupants were remarkably fortunate as there was no damage to them or the property. During the month 6,065 civilians were killed as a result of the bombing.[44] For poor Jack her troubles were not over. The day after Penhill was bombed she was contacted about FM's holiday home at Elmer Sands. Apparently the property was in the way of Army training, so they had demolished the dwelling and put the contents outside. Jack decided that the situation was so difficult that she abandoned the idea of trying to visit Elmer and recover their possessions.

A further matter of concern for FM was the plight of his nephew, Max, who had contracted meningitis. FM was greatly relieved when his niece, Joan, advised him that she had spent every day for a week at the hospital with him and that now he appeared to be recovering with no ill effects. FM could now concentrate on his teaching, which continued apace with plenty of pupils. He was gratified to receive a splendid appreciation of his work

93   FM and children at Stow.

from Sir Stafford Cripps, which pleased his publisher and the promotion team, and was absolutely delighted with Coghill's foreword for the new book.[45]

In it Coghill gave an insight into how he would apply the principles of integration as manifested in motor and postural control on the physiological plane to human problems at the higher integrated levels of voluntary control. He referred to the work of two other eminent scientists and how it could be related to that of Alexander.[46] One was Sir Charles Sherrington OM, an Englishman who was an authority on the physiology of the nervous system, Regius Professor of Physiology at Oxford University, and awarded a Nobel prize in 1932.[47] The other was Professor Raymond Dart, an Australian who spent most of his working life at the Witwatersrand University in South Africa, where he was Chairman of Anatomy from 1922 to 1958 and Dean of Medicine from 1925 to 1943. He was closely associated with anthropology, and in 1924 discovered the famous Taungs skull.[48]

While FM was at Stow that summer a number of his American teachers visited him, including Lulie Westfeldt. Life there was most enjoyable and everyone was pleased with the arrangements. The south-facing homestead was delightful and the large verandah at the front

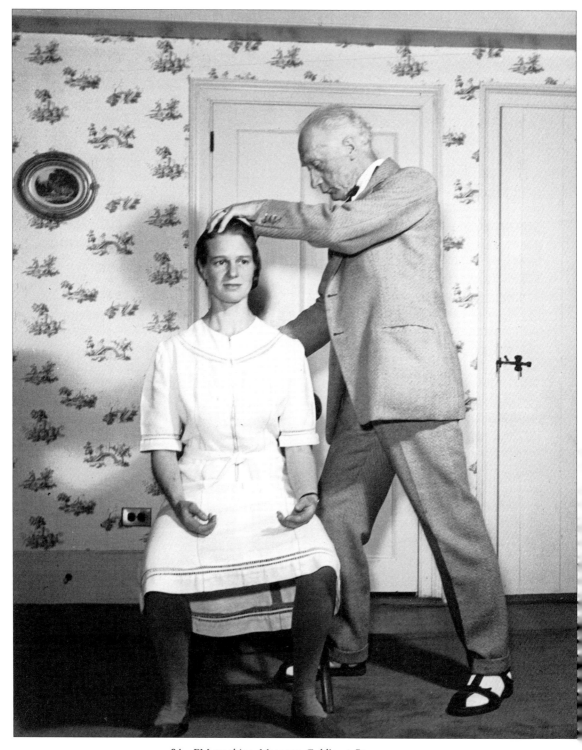

94   FM teaching Margaret Goldie at Stow.

of the house particularly pleasant. FM loved the rural atmosphere and recorded happily, 'I am writing this on the arm of a chair on the lawn under the spreading Chestnut tree.' The only problem with life at Stow was what he described 'as a ghastly growth called Poison Ivy' which, if it touched anything, exuded an oily poison. FM, Alma Frank and a number of the children suffered from this 'Ivy'. After three weeks FM had to consult a doctor, who administered injections; he was not amused. The saddest event of the summer was the death of Coghill on 22 July; FM was upset that he had seen so little of him but lack of money on both their parts had precluded regular visits.[49] However, he was comforted that at least they had been able to write regularly over the past two years and extremely grateful to Coghill for his permission to use his writings, with the exception of one article, in any way FM thought appropriate. In September FM was overjoyed by the publication of an article in the American magazine *WHO*. Written by Arthur Busch, alias Michael March, it gave the American public an understanding of both Alexander and the technique. The author gave an historical synopsis of the early development of the technique and went on, 'By precept and practice, aided by one of the most remarkably sensitive and skilled pair of hands in the world, he taught people structurally, functionally, mentally and physically.' The article highlighted many distinguished people from various walks of life who were or had been his pupils, including a tribute by Sir Stafford Cripps. As a final addition to this captivating account, the author included some enchanting photographs he had taken of FM and the children at Stow.[50] It is little wonder that FM was so pleased and that this publication proved such a marvellous advertisement for the book published in America on 3 October; the British edition was released some months later. As a token of his appreciation of the British people and his unending pride in their courage and determination, he dedicated the book to 'The People of Great Britain'. The book's reputation was enhanced by the very favourable reviews it received, particularly one by Aldous Huxley.[51]

FM returned to New York on 12 October, although he visited Stow every fortnight when he did his regular changeover with AR in Boston. He was greeted with much acclaim by the many readers of his book and acquired numerous new pupils. In November he was persuaded to give a talk about his work to the Dutch Treat Club. He consulted John Dewey beforehand, who assured him that 'the Club members were all professional men, scientists, doctors, lawyers, bankers, editors and literary men, just the kind of people,' he concluded, 'that should know of your work.' FM was surprised and pleased by the reaction of this 300 strong audience, and was overwhelmed with correspondence and new pupils.[52]

On 6 December the Japanese attacked Pearl Harbour, the Americans entered the war and the Japanese advanced successfully on many fronts. By early 1942 FM, like the rest of the world, was stunned by the disasters in the Far East and amazed by the speed of the Japanese successes. The fall of Singapore on 15 February left him particularly bemused. As he said to the Barlows the following day, 'As I write to you we are all suffering the pangs that accompany the fall of Singapore. To think of 60,000 of our people being prisoners of the Japanese is almost more than I can bear.' He would have been even more horrified if he had realised that in fact 130,000 British, Indian, Australian and local volunteer troops were taken prisoner having capitulated to a force half their number in what is described as the 'greatest British military disaster in their history'.[53] The escape of the German ships,

Scharnhorst, Gneisenau and *Prinz Eugen* three days before just added to his frustration; he recorded, 'they sailed boldly through our home waters, as it were under our protection.' But in his typical phlegmatic way he added, 'But it is little use to grumble. We have just to see it through to the bitter end now.' The final straw in this catalogue of disasters was the news that his beloved horse, Peter, had had to be destroyed. All FM wanted to do now was come home.[54]

On the positive side, his book was selling very well in America and the reviews were most satisfactory; in particular, FM was delighted with those written by Professor Frank Jones of Brown University and Walter Millard in America and with the article published in England in the *Lancet*, but less impressed by Dr. Roberts' review in the *New Statesman and Nation*. However, he was comforted by Bill Barlow's rebuttal of Dr. Roberts' criticism which was published in the magazine a few weeks later. He was most grateful to Dr. Mungo Douglas, who at the time was trying to cope with three general practices, for his indefatigable efforts to produce and persuade newspapers to publish reviews of *The Universal Constant in Living*. The summer saw FM back at Stow enjoying himself in the country again. He was very busy with plenty of new pupils, including the Speaker of the State House who was an enormous man of about 6 feet 5 inches. As he related, 'he had ordered a ladder for self and AR'. FM was delighted with the success of the Chinese in the war and declared that 'in his humble opinion Tamoshenta was the General of our time'. He remained confident of the ultimate outcome of the war, an opinion influenced, perhaps, by his great desire to return home. He was not worried by the news from Russia as he was sure 'that the big bear was leading the dingoes up the garden path to their destruction'.[55] Unfortunately, the summer was tarnished with the news that Whitney estate had been sold and that very soon they would have to move. The Unitarians had decided that it was time to break the Will of Cyrus Whitney. The newer house, now known as the Homestead, was resold shortly afterwards to a doctor who turned the place into a nursing home. The Homestead has remained a retirement home and since 1971 has been owned by Mrs. Bonnie Fredette and her daughter, Colbie, who continue to provide a rest home for 25 ladies.

The decision to dispose of the Whitney estate was possibly a blessing in disguise for the teachers and pupils of the school because fuel rationing meant there was a lack of heating oil. The Homestead was large and rambling and difficult to heat with an abundance of oil; with rationing it was impossible. That autumn the school was amalgamated with the Media Friend's school in Pennsylvania where the Work was carried on under AR's supervision. So that winter FM and Ethel were accompanied to New York by Margaret and Irene. Ethel and Irene assisted FM with his teaching while Margaret, who lived with her friend, the wife of the American Consul General, was associated with Wellesley College. She investigated and learnt about their methods of educating children. Throughout the autumn all were very homesick and wanted desperately to return to England regardless of the state of the war. FM was fascinated by the news from Stalingrad and greatly impressed by the Russian resistance; 'what a grand showing of courage and dogged determination,' he declared. He opined that 'the German High Command had made many unsound decisions but the one to attack Russia was the most unsound of them all.' FM was optimistic and, unlike Churchill, considered that the victory at El Alamein and the allied invasion of North Africa was the beginning of the end of the war. He started to make plans to come home. As he wrote to the Barlows, 'the very thought of it makes me walk more briskly than usual.' It was only the memory of his traumatic experiences in Toronto, when he was trying to enter America, that worried him. Then he had lost a stone in weight and Ethel Webb had nearly collapsed on several occasions. He hoped that the formalities required for his departure would be less physically exacting.[56]

AR joined FM in New York for Christmas and they drank a toast to all their friends and relations at home. As FM reflected, the dinner 'was very good for over here' where he thought the food remarkably poor, and wine in hotels and restaurants 'in proper drinking condition practically impossible to procure'. Cocktails he declared were poisonous and

> swallowed so icy cold that the palate is in a state of coma as you drink. Therefore, the sense of taste cannot protect your poor stomach from the disturbing evils which surely must follow the attempt of the digestive organs to deal with the pernicious liquid.

Despite this, FM survived and continued his busy teaching schedule; however, he was becoming more and more restless. He had hoped that his trip home would be organised from Britain but this was proving difficult. By early spring he was actively trying to secure a passage home, making use of every possible influential contact. He was becoming more and more intolerant of the Americans particularly when he listened to the radio about the events in North Africa: 'evidently the British 8th Army and 1st were not there and Alexander, Montgomery and Anderson slept while Eisenhower and Patten covered themselves with glory and in blood and sweat.'[57]

Fortunately for all concerned, FM's time in America was soon to end. By late May 1943 the Battle of the Atlantic had reached a quiet phase. The Allies had lost 2,452 merchant ships in the Atlantic, of nearly 13 million gross-register tons, and 175 warships but the Germans had lost 696 out of a total of 830 U-boats operating in the area. Although the cost in human terms for the Allies, and in particular for the British Merchant Navy, was high, for the Germans the cost was terrible. They had incurred an enormous casualty rate, 63 per cent fatal, 75 per cent overall, which 'far exceeded that suffered by any other arm of service in the navy, army or air force of any combatant country'.[58] Thus, in June FM and his party were awarded 'A priority' and granted a passage almost immediately. They left America and arrived home at Penhill at midnight on Thursday 8 July after a remarkably smooth and enjoyable trip; 16 Ashley Place was under repair.[59] FM put in hand full repairs to Penhill, an action which was later to prove rather premature. AR remained in America to teach the many Alexander pupils and supervise the training course.

> Those who have the will to win
> Cook potatoes in their skin.
> For they know the sight of peelings
> Deeply hurts Lord Woolton's feelings.
> Ministry of Food Slogan, World War II

15

THE SOUTH AFRICAN CASE

God grant me the serenity to accept the things I cannot change, courage to change the things that I can, and the wisdom to know the difference.

Attributed to but never claimed by Reinhold Niebuhr

The London to which FM and his colleagues returned in the middle of 1943 was very different from the place they had left two years before. Then Britain was alone, there was an imminent threat of invasion, and the Battle of Britain was about to begin in the skies above southern England. Now the situation had changed, the war had extended across the world, the Americans had joined the Allies and thousands of their servicemen and women were in Britain, the Allies had defeated the Germans in North Africa and the Russians were on the offensive on the Eastern Front. They had retaken Stalingrad and were determined to avenge the deaths of millions of Russian soldiers and civilians. Every Russian soldier feared being taken prisoner; during the war the Germans captured 5,700,000 Russians of whom 3,300,000 died in captivity, the majority during the first year of the campaign which began in June 1941.[1] The day after FM returned to Penhill the invasion of Sicily began.[2] The tide had turned and now there were victories where before there had been only a catalogue of disasters and defeats.

The scene that greeted FM was a London severely damaged by air raids and filled with military personnel, many of them foreigners, and affected by shortages and rationing, to say nothing of travelling difficulties. Despite this, within a few days of his arrival home he was able to return to 16 Ashley Place to resume teaching. Within three weeks he was reporting that he was extremely busy.[3] He was delighted to see his friends and relations again and to make regular contact with the people who had promoted the Work during his time in America. One of his most vigorous supporters, Dr. Mungo Douglas, had busily written numerous letters to various medical journals refuting criticism of the Work in FM's absence. The good doctor was to continue to do this for many years to come. Unfortunately, the criticism was to take a much more sinister course over the next few years, with far-reaching consequences.

The problem arose in South Africa where Irene Tasker had taught extremely successfully for many years. She had a large group of pupils and over the years had trained a number of teachers. She was highly regarded and respected. Certainly, she had successfully assisted many people during her time in South Africa. In June 1942 a Dr. Ernst Jokl, the physical education officer of the South African Government, had asked Irene to give him a demonstration of her work. This she did and she received a letter of thanks. A few weeks later Jokl asked her to give him a course of lessons and Irene replied that she was not prepared to accept him as a pupil. She wrote a long and detailed letter explaining her reasons, which centred round his lack of understanding of the Alexander principles. She considered that somebody in such an important position as Jokl, affecting the well being of the younger generation of South Africa, should not become a pupil under a misconception. She suggested that should Jokl be convinced of the soundness of Alexander's ideas from reading his books, then he should visit FM and benefit from his long and unique experience of teaching his work.[4]

In July 1942 Irene read a paper entitled 'An Unrecognised Need in Education' to the South African Association for the Advancement of Science. This was subsequently published in the Society Journal. In April 1943 Mr. I Griffith, Headmaster of Rosebank School and President of the Transvaal Teachers' Association, made Alexander's Work the subject of his Presidential Address. [5] Three months later, on 29 June 1943, Dr. Jokl presented a paper, 'The Relationship between Health and Efficiency', to a meeting of the Association for the Advancement of Science in Johannesburg.[6] This was an attack on the Alexander Work; moreover, Jokl stated that not a single medical man of scientific standing supported Alexander's ideas and he ridiculed Dewey, Huxley, Coghill and Sir Stafford Cripps for supporting them.

This article was printed by the Transvaal Teacher's Association in their Journal in July 1943 along with an article defending the Work signed by Dr. T.D. Hall, Mr. I. Griffith, Mr. D.J. de Klerk of St John's College and Mr. N.E. Coaker KC. This showed that men of standing and knowledge commended and supported Alexander's theories and his work. The Association for the Advancement of Science decided not to print Jokl's article in their Journal but unfortunately, damage was done and reputations had been impugned. Irene's position was very difficult and although she had many ardent followers in South Africa, she made plans to come back to England to see FM and discuss the future.

Despite this unfortunate incident in South Africa, throughout the autumn the 74-year-old FM was overwhelmed with pupils; he worked during the week at Ashley Place, frequently travelling daily from Penhill where he always liked to spend the weekend. His books, which were much in demand, were in short supply. This did not stop him sending copies to the library at Burnie in Tasmania, although he did warn his cousin, Annie Alexander, that 'they were not an easy read'.[7] Meanwhile, AR continued in America coping with the increased work load. Fortunately, there were a number of other teachers there, including Marjorie Barstow, Alma Frank and Lulie Westfeldt.

In September the Italian mainland was invaded and Naples was taken on 1 October, the Russians recaptured Kiev and there were various successes against the Japanese in the Far East, and the year ended with the sinking of the German battleship *Scharnhorst*.[8] But conditions in Britain remained very difficult, and in December the government ordered male conscripts into the mines; these young men were more commonly known as the 'Bevin boys' after Ernest Bevin, the Minister of Labour and National Service. In January Irene Tasker arrived in Britain after a six-week voyage from South Africa. She spent a little while in London and then went to join her mother in Cheltenham where she taught the Work.

Walter Carrington, now an RAF pilot, was flying Halifax aircraft with No.462 Squadron in North Africa. FM was delighted to discover this was an Australian squadron. He was less pleased when Ashley Place was burgled on 15/16 January. Although little was taken because the burglars were disturbed, he found three of his suits outside the back door. At this stage he had only a small band of assistants, Margaret and Irene Stewart working full time with Ethel and Irene Tasker coming in one day a week. Despite four bombs landing near 16 Ashley Place in one night, all were very busy.[9] Throughout this period, some of FM's medically qualified supporters struggled to make his ideas more readily comprehensible to the uninitiated reader. For those who understood FM his evolving discoveries were of major significance, but to many less academic souls they remained baffling. His dedicated team of supporters did their utmost to write and get published comprehensive summaries of the Work which many of them now described as a 'Technique'. They attempted to explain the problem to FM. As Dr. Mungo Douglas pointed out to him,

> Coghill's appreciation in *Universal Constant in Living* is a most excellent synopsis of your work in his terms but they are quite incomprehensible to the general reader ... On the other hand the person who has come to that state of understanding of the use of the self through your work where living is total integrated behaviour passing out and into 'individuated patterns' can expand his experience through reading this contribution by Coghill.[10]

FM understood the difficulty as he wrote ruefully, 'A man of the highest education who has occupied the highest positions read Duncan Whittacker's last paper and writes "I am sorry to tell you that I cannot understand one word of it." And this man is one of our supporters. He asks me to explain it to him when he comes again.' Fortunately doctors continued to come to FM, including Dorothy Drew. She came with her two children and subsequently joined the training course.[11]

In March 1944, in a journal called *Manpower*, an official publication of the National Advisory Council for Physical Education in South Africa, Jokl published an editorial entitled 'Quackery Versus Physical Education'. This purported to expose the Alexander Technique, its originator and those who accepted or commended it. It was a scathing and derogatory attack on FM's work. Jokl mentioned FM's Australian origins on numerous occasions and called him an Australian actor or an Australian 'immortal' at least fourteen times, but did not mention that FM had left Australia for London nearly 50 years before and had abandoned his original profession before that. The article inferred that FM was dishonest, untruthful, a charlatan and a quack. Additionally, Jokl suggested that FM gave dangerous and criminally irresponsible advice, concealed the truth and held out false promises for his own (FM's) personal gain. Jokl said that FM gave the impression that the Technique was accepted and approved by members of the medical profession which Jokl maintained was not the case. He also contended that FM's books were full of irresponsible nonsense, amazingly naïve and showed that FM had not the faintest idea about some of the medical matters on which he expounded. Jokl implied that FM was an uninformed lay man of limited mental ability. Moreover, he described FM's followers with considerable disdain, savagely criticising some of them; he mentioned by name Coghill, Cripps, Dewey, Huxley, MacDonald, Murdoch, Mungo Douglas and, from South Africa, Hall, Griffith, de Klerk and Coaker and, by implication, the Lord Lytton.

The matter had gone beyond reasonable bounds. Not only had FM been libelled but also a number of very respected and eminent men, as well as the unfortunate Irene Tasker. The situation was exacerbated when, on 6 July 1944, the *Cape Times* printed an article, supporting

Jokl, entitled 'Physical Quirks'. On publication of this article, a number of South African Alexander supporters including Professor Raymond Dart wrote to the editor of the newspaper. They highlighted the importance of FM's discoveries, the many inaccuracies in the Jokl editorial, and emphasised that Irene Tasker was a highly respected Alexander teacher in South Africa. They pointed out that she was an honours graduate in Classics from Cambridge University and that she had arrived nine years ago in the country with a letter from the Lord Lytton commending her to General Smuts and another from Professor Dewey to the late Professor Alfred Hoernlé. She was a remarkably successful teacher with a large number of supporters, many of them people of education and standing within the community. Mr. Coaker, whom Irene had authorised to act on her behalf when she returned to England, engaged a firm of Johannesburg solicitors to protect her good name and that of the Alexander Technique.[12]

At this stage FM was unaware of the events in South Africa. The general war situation was improving although the loss of life was high. In February 1944 the Americans landed on the Marshall Islands, the Russians advanced to the Estonian border; in May the Allies won the battle of Monte Cassino and by June had advanced into Rome.[13] The D-Day invasion was successful and FM's niece, Joan, now the mother of a 6-month-old daughter, was relieved that her husband, Ivor, a Territorial Officer in the Royal Artillery, had survived his landing on the Normandy beaches in the early hours of the operation. At Dunkirk Ivor and his men had successfully left the beachhead during the final hours of the withdrawal, but his return to France was not so satisfactory, his Battery Sergeant Major was killed by a mine as they went up the beach at Ver Sur Mare. After a few days he was ordered to Arromanches to help defend the 'Mulberry' harbour, and then he and his regiment advanced to participate in the battle for Caen. As he was to say afterwards, he had the misfortune to witness the biggest fireworks display he ever wished to see and when he drove into Caen to view the 'victory' there was nothing left of that once great city. The Allies moved on through France and Paris was liberated on 25 August. On 3 September the Guards Armoured Division entered Brussels and, perhaps more significantly, the following day the 11th Armoured Division advanced into Antwerp. This was the first major deep water port to be retaken and vital for the resupply of the advancing troops. It took two more months and a significant loss of life before the First Canadian Army had secured the Scheldt area in what has been described as the most difficult and unpleasant operation fought by the Allies in the winter of 1944.[14] It was nearly a further month before all the river mines were cleared so that the port could be used. Then the Allies were no longer dependent on the grossly overworked 'Mulberry' harbour at the ever more distant Normandy beach-head. Ivor and his regiment advanced to the flooded island of Walcheren on the Scheldt estuary and spent the winter months of 1944/5 at the island's central town of Middleburg, the main access to which was along the narrow causeway from South Beveland. For the rest of his life he remembered that attractive place with its lovely buildings, huge central square and beautiful Town Hall. In particular he remembered the great kindness of the Town Major and the Dutch people, who had suffered so much in the past few years. He was accommodated in one of the houses, the first time he had known such luxury since he left England five months before.

95 Middleburg Town Hall.

During the year that FM had been in England, the bombing by the German Air Force had been steady but nothing like as devastating as during the Blitz. However, from 13 June 1944 onwards, London and other parts of the country were subjected to attacks by the first of the flying bombs, V1s, more commonly known as 'doodle bugs'.[15] During the second raid on 15 June a flying bomb landed in a park midway between Penhill and Ellerslie and caused extensive damage to the buildings in the surrounding area. This was the start of a major enemy onslaught. The raids were particularly frightening for the population; the bombs had a very piercing whine and just before they landed on their target they went silent. At the end of July FM fell downstairs at Ashley Place when the stair carpet slipped. The resulting fractured ankle caused him to begin his summer holiday a little early and he repaired to Penhill

96 Canadian cemetery, Walcheren.

to nurse his injury.[16] The doodle bugs continued to haunt him; the Bexley and Sidcup areas suffered innumerable devastating raids as many of the doodle bugs landed short of their central London targets. One fell almost midway between Penhill and Ellerslie on 29 July that demolished one house, partly destroyed nine more, structurally damaged 27 and superficially damaged a further 215 dwellings. On 3 August about a mile from Ellerslie one bomb damaged 50 shops and three days later another attack very close to Penhill did a little damage to the house. This bomb destroyed one house, caused four more to be demolished as a result of the damage they had suffered and rendered a further 11 too unsafe to remain occupied.[17] The Penhill pony and trap, driven by Jack Vicary and her son John, was kept busy taking Red Cross workers around the district delivering parcels and essential supplies to the many beleaguered

97   AR.

98   John Vicary taking round Red Cross parcels.

local families. From the time of the first bombing in 1940, Jack had worked tirelessly for the Red Cross. She organised Fêtes and other money raising activities at Penhill and normally undertook other Red Cross duties for two days a week.

In August FM was advised that AR had suffered a stroke. He was devastated and although he wrote to his contacts in America it was difficult to establish the extent of AR's illness. He was told that AR had difficulty talking but that despite this he was determined to start work again. This disturbed FM greatly; he wrote to Frank Jones to ask whether or not he should try to arrange for AR's son, Max, to obtain compassionate leave to come to see his father. Fortunately AR began to recover, and FM was delighted when he learned in early November that he could write again and overjoyed with the news that AR had been able to hold a conversation with Frank. However, FM was frustrated that he could not see his brother and his condition remained a constant source of worry to him until AR returned home in early July 1945.

Towards the middle of August the *Manpower* article which was sent from South Africa to Irene Tasker arrived. She was on holiday but as soon as she had read it she dispatched it to FM. He was stunned and consulted his friends. Sir Stafford Cripps was incensed. As a senior Cabinet Minister, he took great exception to the article which he considered to be a tirade of vulgar abuse.[18] He protested in the strongest possible terms to the South African High Commissioner and asked him to communicate with General Smuts in order to have the article, which had been published by the Union Government, withdrawn as thoroughly scurrilous.[19] Clearly Sir Stafford, along with all the other notable people mentioned by Jokl, could not let the matter rest, regardless of the views of FM. Normally, FM went to considerable lengths to meet and try to teach people who did not understand his theories and concepts but in this case this was not an option. Certainly, the Lord Lytton found it 'regrettable' that an official government magazine had allowed Jokl to make a spiteful personal attack under cover of editorial comment.[20] On Sir Stafford's advice, FM wrote to Sir Walter Monckton, an eminent London barrister who became Solicitor General in the 1945 Caretaker Government, seeking his legal opinion and requesting his assistance on how best the matter should be progressed. On his recommendation, the firm of lawyers Messrs. Theodore Goddard, experts in international law, were appointed. FM wrote to the South African High Commissioner in London, a letter that was delivered personally, asking for the whole article to be withdrawn and for everyone concerned to be advised of the reasons for this action.[21] Sadly this did not happen, and the issue continued to plague FM for the next few years. More importantly, this sorry affair was to have a serious effect on his health.

A further concern during this most unhappy month, was Walter Carrington. His squadron, now renumbered 614, had moved to Italy early in the year and was operating in the highly skilled and exacting 'pathfinder' role. Walter was a Flight Commander and he and his crew undertook missions in support of the Russian military advance over the Balkans. On the night of 22/23 August, five Halifax aircraft were detailed to identify, illuminate and mark marshalling yards at Miskolo, Hungary. The defences consisted of heavy and light anti-aircraft guns, which were scattered and inaccurate, and the weather conditions were fair. Walter took off with his crew of six at 1949 hours to perform the task of Visual Marker, but he and his aircraft failed to return from this mission and were posted missing.[22] His

Halifax had been shot down and unlike the rest of his crew who were uninjured, he sustained a broken jaw, pelvis and collar bone. He was taken to a hospital in southern Hungary from which, a little while later, with the help of the local Jesuit fathers in Szeged, he escaped. When the Russians occupied Szeged Walter reported to the Russian Town Major, who arranged for him to be flown to the British Embassy in Bucharest. From there he was repatriated to England via Italy where he was able to visit his squadron friends. He arrived back in November much earlier than his less fortunate crew, who were prisoners-of-war in Stalag Luft III.[23]

FM returned to work at the beginning of September and was inundated with pupils. His good friend and long-standing pupil, Fred Watts, a publisher who had set up a special company, Chaterson, to take over from Methuen the printing of FM's books, obtained permits for extra paper. But still he could not meet the demand.[24] The war went on; the Allied advance in Europe was temporarily halted in mid September at the tragic battle of Arnhem and the Warsaw uprising was crushed by the Germans in October, but the Allies occupied Athens and the Russians ended the battle for the Baltic States and by the end of that month the Americans had begun the battle for the Philippines. By mid-December the Germans had mounted what was to be their last major offensive of the war, in the Ardennes.[25] In England the winter was harsh, and the lack of fuel created severe problems. At Penhill there were 14 burst pipes and to add to the difficulties the country was under attack from the German long range rockets commonly known as V2s.

At 0820 hours on 20 March a V2 exploded in the Craybrooke Works of Thomas Knight, a builder and decorator. The explosion, which was about two hundred yards from Ellerslie, made a massive noise. Although many windows blew out and there was some internal damage, FM's sister Amy, her daughter Joan, and her grand-daughter Jackie survived unharmed. The explosion completely devastated the builders yard, making a crater 24 feet in diameter and 8 feet deep. Eight houses and a shop were completely destroyed. Additionally, two shops and flats were partially demolished and approximately 1,000 houses, over a radius of about a quarter of a mile were affected. St John's Church and the *Black Horse Hotel* were also damaged. A total of nine people died, seven at the builders' yard, one in the High Street and another in St John's Road. One of these individuals was the air-raid warden. There were 103 casualties of whom 53 were taken to the nearby Queen Mary's hospital and the remaining 50 were tended by the First Aid Post personnel.

The reaction of the emergency services to the incident was immediate. Within six minutes the first mobile team arrived on the scene and set up an incident post. Very quickly the police appeared and diverted the buses and other traffic and the Civil Defence team began to put out the numerous small fires. The rescue teams started to search for survivors and within 13 minutes the first ambulance arrived, followed eight minutes later by two others. The Women's Voluntary Service were quickly on the scene and by 0842 hours had established an incident post. The rehousing department was opened to provided assistance at 0905 hours and five minutes later the Assistance Board was opened for business. One of the local general practitioners, Dr. Barnard, reported for duty a few minutes later and by 0933 hours a mobile canteen was functioning. This canteen, which was required for several days, was reinforced by one from Beckenham on the first afternoon. The search teams with their dogs hunted for survivors all day but at 1620 hours it was decided to abandoned the operation. The clearance of debris and the demolition of dangerous property took several days and repairs considerably longer. During the first day there were a number of visitors to the devastated scene, including the distinguished civil servant Sir Ernest Gowers, who was then the Senior Regional Commissioner. Sir Ernest is probably best remembered for his books *Plain Words* and *ABC of Plain Words* written after the war.[26] This incident typifies the destruction and damage done by one V2.

There were numerous other such incidents in the area around Ellerslie and Penhill, with at least two V2s landing in the houses opposite Penhill. One landed on the nearby golf course, blowing two chimney pots off Penhill's roof and causing significant damage to the house which rather negated FM's earlier repair work. The raids continued throughout the country between 8 September 1944, when these rockets were first fired against London, and 27 March 1945 when the last V2 struck.[27] People in England had to accept the everyday dangers of living but, as FM told his friends in America, 'Whatever trouble you good people have always remember and be thankful that you have been spared the terror of the silent bombs.'[28] The thought of being bombed out during the piercingly cold winter nights in night attire was not something anybody contemplated with enthusiasm. Fortunately for all concerned spring came early that year.

When the bombing of England ceased some 255 properties had been destroyed in the then small borough of Bexley where Penhill was located and a further 635 so extensively damaged they had been demolished; an additional 1,380 premises had to be evacuated.[29] Now at last people could sleep easily in their beds and everyone was greatly relieved that the Doodles and silent bombs had ceased. As FM remarked pertinently, 'to be able to go out of your home without the knowledge that it is possible it may be in pieces when you return and to go to bed without fear of being blown to blazes during the night seems now a strange almost an absurd experience.'[30] It encouraged him to take a holiday and at the beginning of May he went to North Wales for his first proper holiday for five years. It gave him an opportunity to ride again, an activity he loved; as he said, 'I was born riding Gee-gees.'[31] While he was away the Germans surrendered and the war in Europe was finally over. This otherwise happy event was tinged with great sadness. Peter Vicary, who had been captured at Dunkirk, was moved, with other prisoners in his camp, during the allied advance in the spring of 1945, and on this march the inadequately clad Peter died of pneumonia. His mother, Jack, never really recovered from the shock of this news.

In early July AR came home, a rather depressed and exhausted man after a very tiring 11-day crossing sharing a cabin with five other people. However, he quickly improved and on 15 July he went to Lords cricket ground to watch the first day of an unofficial test match between England and Australia. Teaching continued in America both to individual pupils and at the Media Friends' School in Pennsylvania. In April 1945 Frank Pierce Jones had read a paper outlining the Technique to the Parents' Council. When FM read this exposition of his work a little later he wrote and congratulated Jones and 'hoped that it would be helpful to readers'.[32]

The general election in Britain on 26 July 1945 saw the election of a Labour govern-ment and FM was delighted that his friend and supporter, Stafford Cripps, was appointed

99 FM riding in 1947.

President of the Board of Trade. By this stage, he was looking forward to his summer holiday in Eastbourne with his lawyer, Norman Barraclough. Unfortunately the summer weather had been poor and FM remarked that 'we descend to the vale of hope that we may get something very special in August and September.'[33] This did not transpire. However, the good news was that the Japanese surrendered on 14 August and the war was over. On his return, FM started making plans for the future. The training course for teachers was scheduled to begin on 10 September and there were 19 students.[34] Bill Barlow had stressed to FM the importance of an early resumption of the course and he was most anxious to complete his training which had been interrupted when FM went to America in 1940, as were a number of others including Dick and Elisabeth Walker. This large course posed a number of difficulties, such as the lack of teachers and the shortage of accommodation. Marjory Barlow, who had not worked since the birth of her second child, David, in August 1943, was pressed into action. FM did investigate the possibility of

acquiring additional premises but this proved too difficult in London where accommodation of any sort was at a premium.

So the training course remained at Ashley Place in cramped conditions where, in addition to FM, Margaret Goldie, Irene Stewart, Marjory Barlow and Pat MacDonald were
teaching. There was a waiting list for pupils and advertising FM's book had to cease because
the publishers could not meet the demand. As FM pointed out to Frank Jones, now an
established American Alexander teacher, who had written to ask for a copy of the London
Technique prospectus so he could use it in America, 'We do not have a prospectus here
because we do not need it.'[35] However, he did advise him that a new introduction to the
Work would be produced soon and this he could publish in America. In addition FM was
delighted to report that, as a result of Frank's efforts, his personal possessions and those of
his colleagues, that they had had to leave behind during the war, had arrived from America.
AR's health remained a constant source of concern particularly as he was so insistent that
he wanted to return to America. Perhaps fortuitously, the American authorities stated that
it would be at least a year before they would consider his application.

The problem with Jokl's article continued, and in December 1945 Sir Stafford Cripps
and the Lord Lytton visited the South African High Commissioner in an attempt to
resolve the situation.[36] However, this appeared impossible and a court action now seemed
inevitable. FM's friends gathered around him and his medical supporters sent articles
explaining and defending the Technique to medical journals and the newspapers. FM
wrote to Field Marshal Smuts to try to resolve the issue; in addition, he wrote to Jokl
and his colleagues asking them to allow one issue of the *Manpower* magazine to be
devoted to the views of responsible South Africans who supported his ideas. All was to
no avail. In February 1946, Heaton-Nichols, the High Commissioner, advised Cripps that
he had represented Cripps' views to the South African Minister of Education and the
Minister of Justice. The Minister of Justice had responded that he did not think he could
intervene, although he agreed that the language used in the article was 'not altogether
in good taste'.[37] Cripps replied expressing disappointment, and in particular he suggested
that what the Minister described as lacking in taste he would describe as 'mere vulgar
abuse not only of Mr. Alexander but of others like himself and the Lord Lytton'.
Although FM waited until almost the legal deadline for bringing an action, he too
received a totally inadequate response from the High Commissioner. Thus, he had no
alternative but to allow Messrs. Theodore Goddard to issue a summons claiming damages
against Jokl and his associates in the Witwatersrand Local Division Court in South Africa.
And so began a lengthy and expensive court case.

With the die cast, Irene Tasker made plans to return to South Africa. For FM life at
Ashley Place continued to be busy. In March Alma Frank came to England for a six-week
refresher course with him. On 14 April FM's youngest sister, May, died. AR remained in
England throughout the year and this created problems at Media, Philadelphia. There was
little FM could do but he asked Alma and Frank Jones to try and resolve matters. The
highlight of the year was the publication in the autumn of Sir Charles Sherrington's book
The Endeavour of Jean Fernel, in which he had given an appreciation of FM's work. In
particular, he stated,

Mr. Alexander has done a service to the subject by insistently treating each act as involving the whole integrated individual, the whole psycho-physical man. To take a step is an affair, not of this or that limb solely, but of the total neuromuscular activity of the moment-not least of the head and the neck.[38]

FM's letter of thanks to Sherrington produced a most supportive letter from this distinguished man. FM was also in regular contact now with an important South African supporter, Professor Raymond Dart, of the Witwatersrand University in Johannesburg.

By the autumn, FM and his six assistants, Margaret Goldie, Irene Stewart, his nephew Max, Pat MacDonald, Walter Carrington, who was demobilised from the RAF in March, and the recently qualified Dick Walker, were using teaching rooms in Evelyn Mansions in addition to Ashley Place. There were 20 students under training. Amongst them was John Skinner, an Australian who had written to FM earlier in the year from Sydney expressing his wish to enter the training course.[39] FM was delighted at the prospect of an Australian joining him but little did he realise at this stage what a loyal and devoted assistant John would prove to become. At the appropriate time accommodation was organised for this new arrival from the Antipodes. Unfortunately, when John appeared he was bereft of funds. However, with the determination befitting a serviceman who had survived several years as a Japanese prisoner-of-war, he found a cheaper room, hired a cart and rented a garage. Every day he left Ashley Place at 4p.m. and went to his lodgings to make sandwiches. Then this 35-year-old man walked to the garage in a nearby mews and dragged his cart a mile to his pitch at Earls Court station, where he proceeded to sell his tea, coffee and sandwiches. At about midnight he pulled his cart back to the garage and retired to his room for a few hours sleep before his next training session at Ashley Place. Walter Carrington, who in addition to teaching was personal assistant to FM in the absence through ill health of Ethel Webb, watched John's activities with interest and admiration. Eventually he suggested to FM that, as he was helping with the training course and had pupils of his own, it might be appropriate for John to take over as personal assistant before the poor man collapsed in his determined efforts to become an Alexander teacher. FM agreed. John assumed responsibilities which he was to undertake so loyally until FM's death. In October 1946 the *Medical Press* published an exposition of FM's work by Mungo Douglas entitled 'A Unique Example of Operational Verification During Scientific Experimentation'.[40] Mungo had worked on this article for a long time and FM, who had approved the paper before publication, was delighted with the content. In particular, he was pleased that it was produced in a medical journal before the South African trial.[41]

The following year, 1947, was traumatic for FM. The weather in the early part of the year was excessively cold and at Penhill there were some 30 burst pipes.[42] AR's condition deteriorated and he was admitted to a nursing home, but he did not enjoy the experience so he was taken to Penhill where he died on 23 April. The loss of his dearest brother, the man who had supported him so loyally all his life was devastating. FM knew that without his brother's support and his willingness to remain teaching in Australia, providing for their mother and three sisters, he could never have left Australia for London. Furthermore, he was well aware that the development of his work over the past 40 years was the result of his contacts with the wide range of pupils and supporters to be found in England and America. Now it was essential for FM to win the legal case in South Africa and to preserve the Work for future generations.

Clearly, the distance between London and Johannesburg was a problem but, fortunately, Jokl, Cluver and Clerk, the defendants, wished to call a number of eminent British medical men as witnesses. These men could not spare the time to go to South Africa, so it was agreed that evidence from both prosecution and defence witnesses would be taken before a Commission in London. This Commission lasted six weeks and commenced on 2 July 1947 before Mr. A.H. Ormerod. FM was legally represented by Mr. Kenneth Diplock, an outstanding lawyer who became a Lord of Appeal in 1968, and the defendants by Messrs. Beney and Lawson. As FM was required to attend the trial in South Africa he did not give evidence. However, he had seven witnesses all of whom had direct and long experience of his teaching and work. They were two statesmen, both Privy Councillors, the Rt. Hon. Sir Richard Stafford Cripps, a Cabinet Minister, who at the time was President of the Board of Trade, and the Earl of Lytton, a most distinguished diplomat. The other five witnesses were from the medical profession. They were Dr. Duncan Whittaker, a specialist in psychological medicine for the previous 12 years and now married to Erika Schumann, Ethel's niece; Dr. Peter McDonald, for many years an ophthalmic surgeon and recently in general practice; Mr. James Eustace Radcliffe McDonagh, a distinguished physician and a consultant in London for 41 years, and the author of *The Nature of Disease*; Dr. Andrew Rugg-Gunn, an eminent eye specialist, and Dr. Dorothy Stella Radcliffe Drew, a general practitioner.[43]

The array of witnesses for the defence was formidable. There were nine, two of whom were Nobel Prize winners for research in medical subjects: Professor Edgar Douglas Adrian, physiologist and 1932 Nobel Prize winner; Sir Henry Dale, physiologist and 1936 Nobel Prize winner; Brigadier Thomas Harrison Wand-Tetley, physical training instructor and Olympic athlete; Dr. Paul Hamilton Wood, cardiologist and eminent physician; Dr. Freddie Himmelweit, a bacteriologist who worked at St Mary's Hospital as the director of a department of which Sir Alexander Fleming, the Nobel Prize winner was the principal; Sir Alfred Webb-Johnson, President of the Royal College of Surgeons; Professor Samson Wright, since 1930 the John Astor Professor of Physiology in the University of London at the Middlesex Hospital; Lieutenant Colonel Sidney James Parker, physical educationist, Ministry of Education, and Mr. Robert Clark-Turner, Assistant Secretary Ministry of Health.[44] However, none of these eminent men had ever had a lesson from FM and few had read more than one of his books; only Samson Wright declared that he had read them all. Some of the witnesses had only read FM's writings after they had agreed to give evidence.

The following six weeks were terrible for FM as he listened to this intimidating collection of senior medical experts discrediting his work, ideas and philosophies. For people like Marjory Barlow, Walter Carrington and Margaret Goldie, who attended the proceedings, it was devastating. None of them could do anything to help. On 5 August the Commission concluded its work and the 78-year-old FM began planning his trip to South Africa. A passage was booked for him on the *Durban Castle* departing from England on 1 January 1948.[45] In the meantime the Lord Lytton was active on FM's behalf. At the Commission the defence had produced a letter from Lord Horder to Jokl in which he had supported him in his accusations against FM. The Lord Lytton was deeply distressed that one of his friends should express such hostile opinions on another of his friends. He wrote several times to Lord Horder explaining to him that he did not know FM, had never had a lesson from him and, more importantly, had misquoted from one of FM's books which in any event had been written over 35 years before. Lord Horder was unconvinced and remained firmly of the view that FM was a charlatan who was misleading the public, and described him as a menace to society.[46] In October the Lord Lytton died, which was a severe loss for FM who was extremely upset by the departure of such a good friend and forceful supporter. A few weeks later, just before Christmas, FM had a stroke; he had a second stroke a few days later.[47] The strain of the years of worry had finally taken a tragic toll on his health. Although he made a remarkable recovery, he needed complete rest and certainly could not travel to South Africa. He was faced with the dreadful situation where his life's work would be judged by South African lawyers but he was not able to defend himself. Moreover, it was highly unusual for a plaintiff to win a libel action without appearing personally before the court.

Immediately, the loyal Mungo Douglas, Bill Barlow, against the advice and wishes of his medical superiors, thus jeopardising his medical career, and Dorothy Drew volunteered to make the journey to South Africa to give evidence and support Irene Tasker, who had returned the previous year. Dorothy departed by air on 19 January 1948 with Bill, as FM's official representative, and Mungo Douglas following on 7 February. The case was proving to be a very costly affair for FM who by this stage had paid approximately £8,000 in expenses; this included £2,000 required by the South African government in the event that he lost.

The sitting opened on 16 February 1948 before Mr. Justice Clayden in the Supreme Court in Johannesburg. For FM the case was masterminded by the eminent KC Norman Coaker, who had instructed the solicitors, Messrs. Berrangé and Wasserzug. Vernon Berrangé had become a pupil of Irene's in 1942 and was well acquainted with the Work. Before the trial he visited England regularly to have meetings with FM.[48] Coaker decided that it would be more beneficial to the case if he appeared as a witness for FM as he would have more opportunity to attack the defendant's claims than if he legally represented FM. Therefore, he arranged for FM to be represented by Mr. J.H. Hanson KC assisted by Mr. A. Fischer.

Bram Fischer was from a distinguished Afrikaner family, his grandfather having been Prime Minister of the Orange River Colony and his father Judge President of the Orange Free State. Some years later both Bram Fischer and Vernon Berrangé defended Nelson Mandela and his ANC associates in various trials, the last of which, the Rivonia Trial which opened in Pretoria in October 1963, led to Mandela's life prison sentence, the majority of which he served on Robben Island.[49] During this trial, Fischer sought the advice of Mr. Harold Hanson regarding Mandela's statement to the court; additionally, Hanson delivered one of the two pleas of mitigation prior to the sentencing of Mandela and his compatriots.[50] After the Rivonia Trial Bram Fischer went underground but he was captured in 1965 and sentenced to life imprisonment for conspiracy to commit sabotage. In the mid-1970s he was diagnosed as having cancer. As the result of a newspaper campaign calling for him to be released from gaol on humanitarian grounds, he was allowed to leave prison and placed under house arrest at his brother's home, where a few weeks later he died.[51] Mandela described Fischer 'as one of the bravest and staunchest friends of the freedom struggle that I have ever known'.[52]

The defendants were represented by Mr. O. Pirow KC, a formidable advocate, assisted by Mr. M. Van Hulsteyn who had been instructed by the Government Attorney. Oswald Pirow, according to Mandela, 'was a longtime Afrikaner nationalist, and an outspoken supporter of the Nazi cause; he once described Hitler as the 'greatest man of his age'.[53] Pirow was the prosecutor against Mandela and other leading ANC members at their 1959 Treason Trial which opened in Pretoria on 3 August; during that trial, Pirow died of a stroke on 11 October.[54]

Mr. Hanson opened the case with a summary of FM's work, an account of which is published in *More Talk Of Alexander* by Dr. W. Barlow.[55] The evidence from the London Commission was presented to the court; in addition, Bill Barlow, Dorothy Drew, Norman Coaker and Irene Tasker gave evidence for FM. Norman Coaker, who feared the strength of Pirow's attacks on the witnesses, decided that the strain of the case was too much for the elderly Mungo Douglas and that neither he nor Raymond Dart should give evidence. For the defence there was Professor Underwood OBE MA BM ChB (Camb) FRCS, Professor of Surgery at the Witwatersrand Hospital and Senior Surgeon to the Johannesburg Hospital, Dr. E.H. Cluver MA MD DPH FRSI VD and Knight of St John, who studied under Professor Sir Charles Sherrington for three years at Oxford, and Dr. Ernst Jokl. The trial lasted for 12 days, and including the evidence from the London Commission totalled more than 450,000 words.

It aroused considerable interest in South Africa and crowds of people attended the daily hearings. Apparently, the standing room area was always full and there was a queue waiting outside ready to take the place of anybody who left the court.[56] Perhaps the most shocking statements to come from the evidence were those by Jokl. He admitted that he had written to the South African Medical Council requesting that Professor Raymond Dart be struck off because of his support for Alexander. He also agreed that he had told a Mr. Eric Rosenthal that he had heard of a cancer patient who had died because the person was having lessons with Irene Tasker and had not sought medical treatment early enough when, Jokl averred, the person's life could have been saved. The prosecution showed that when Mr. Rosenthal was told this story he advised Irene Tasker and Norman Coaker and they wrote to Professor Craib, who was in a position to know if such a case had occurred; he had replied that he had no knowledge of the case and, certainly, the last thing he wanted to do was besmirch the good work which Miss Tasker was doing in South Africa.[57] It was a very difficult time for the 60-year-old Irene. When she was giving evidence she swayed in the witness box and almost collapsed; Mr. Berrangé rushed forward to support her and after an adjournment a chair was brought for her.[58]

The trial finished on 5 March 1948 but the judgement was deferred until 19 April. For those in South Africa the wait was dreadful; for those in England the strain was perhaps greater. There was nothing anybody could do but wait. The *British Medical Journal* published an account of the trial on 20 March; a further article was printed on 8 May giving the verdict. The judgement when it was delivered comprised a 49-page document by Mr. Justice Clayden. He found in favour of FM and awarded him £1,000 damages with costs. As soon as the verdict was pronounced, Irene sent a cable to England giving FM the good news. His reply was dispatched at 1520 hours on 19 April to Irene in Johannesburg and said, 'Truth

Triumphant we all rejoice in consequence, your cable arrived first, all thanks and our blessings. F Matthias Alexander.' Now the congratulations and praise arrived, particularly for FM and Irene. For FM there were numerous letters from people he did not know. Amongst Irene's was a charming letter from the actress, Marie Ney, a former pupil of FM who was also a pupil and great friend of Irene. One can only conjecture as to the thoughts of FM and Irene at this time. FM was an old man who had devoted over 50 years of his life to his work, which he believed passionately helped mankind. Irene had spent over 10 years working hard in South Africa, building up a highly successful practice and helping many people, particularly children. The relief for them both was undoubtedly immense. FM's family, friends, teachers and pupils rejoiced, as did the many South Africans who had done so much to ensure a satisfactory result in the libel action. At the end of the year, Dick and Elisabeth Walker went from Ashley Place to Johannesburg to teach the many people now so enthusiastic about Alexander and his work. They were joined a few years later by Dr. Drew.

Unfortunately the affair was not over; the defendants decided to appeal against the verdict. This meant another long wait. The appeal was heard in Bloemfontein in March 1949 before the Chief Justice and two other Judges and lasted seven days. Eventually, the judgement was delivered on 3 June in FM's favour. The appeal was dismissed with costs. In addition, the court concluded that the original damages were reasonable even though they were the second highest ever awarded in South Africa. As the defendants were civil servants and the original article was published in a government magazine, the South African government was responsible for paying the damages and costs. It was not until January 1950 that the House of Representatives authorised the Minister to make the payments.[59] As Anthony Ludovici wrote at the time, 'Thus ended an action which, from the standpoint of humanity, its welfare and future, is perhaps among the most momentous in history; an action which as an example of exceptional perspicacity, sound judgement and wisdom on the part of the four learned judges concerned, deserves to stand out for all time as a triumph of Truth and, above all, of South African legal procedure and competence.'[60] The experts testifying against FM, particularly those from England, were formidable, including as they did the President of the Royal College of Surgeons and two Nobel Prize winners, one of whom was Chairman of the Scientific Advisory Committee to the British War Cabinet. With this array of experts, it would have been all too easy for the Judges to have been over-awed and, perhaps, intellectually intimidated. The fact that they were not and found in favour of a medical layman says much for the standards of the South African Law Courts and particularly the Judges of the time. Sadly, life was never to be the same for FM. The case had damaged his health and, despite his success, had cost him a considerable sum of money.

16
FINAL YEARS

All the world's a stage
And all the men and women merely players:
They have their exits and their entrances;
And one man in his time plays many parts.
William Shakespeare: *As You Like It*

The successful outcome of the South African case boosted the morale of all those associated with Alexander and his work. Although there was still uncertainty about the Appeal in 1948, FM was determined to assert the importance of his work, and in the autumn of that year he wrote to the *British Journal of Physical Medicine*. His letter, published in the November-December issue, referred to two previous articles concerning the use of exercises; he highlighted his different approach and referred to his own books and an article by Bill Barlow, 'The Mind-Body Relationship', previously published by the Journal.[1]

FM's health continued to improve and the new year marked his 80th birthday. The event was celebrated by a dinner held at *Brown's Hotel* in London. The toast to FM was proposed by Sir Stafford Cripps, now Chancellor of the Exchequer, and FM replied, Rugg-Gunn proposed the health of the guests and Professor Heath replied. The event was attended by many members of the family, his assistants at Ashley Place, and numerous dedicated supporters such as Anthony Ludovici, the Whittakers, Drs. McDonagh and Mungo Douglas, but there were notable absentees, in particular his brother AR, the Lord Lytton and Dr. Murdoch. The next few years would take an even greater toll on FM's lifelong friends. Those close to FM were concerned about what would happen to the Work when the inevitable occurred and FM died.

After the war a number of attempts were made to form a teachers' society and make arrangements for the future of the Technique but for various reasons these all failed. By now there were a number of teachers in America acting independently of FM. Irene Tasker had taught for many years in South Africa but she had returned regularly for lessons with FM. When she came home she was replaced first by the Walkers and later by others. Some devotees of the Work believed it essential to spread the Alexander gospel widely. While FM approved of his teachers such as Walter Carrington going to Cardiff, Oxford and Guernsey to teach because they returned to Ashley Place, he had more difficulty accepting that people to whom he had issued teaching certificates could teach away from his influence and guidance. He was concerned that his teaching and methods would become diluted and altered. This understandable wish to protect his work did cause difficulties. Inevitably, young

234

teachers wanted to leave Ashley Place. One of the first to do so in England was Charles Neil. He first had lessons from FM in 1932 and qualified as a teacher in 1937; a little while later he left Ashley Place and taught independently. After his Army war service, he bought a house in Holland Park and with another teacher, Eric de Peyer, started to create a flourishing practice. By late 1947 the Cripps transferred their allegiance from FM to Charles Neil, and by the end of December 1948 Lady Cripps had given her name to the Holland Park centre.[2] Charles Neil, other teachers and some Alexander devotees expressed the wish to form a society for Alexander teachers. From the autumn of 1948 until the end of 1949, the Ashley Place team tried again but all the proposals failed. In 1949 Pat MacDonald left Ashley Place and set up a teaching practice in Cardiff. In the same year, Marjory and Bill Barlow moved from Hampstead to Albert Court in Kensington where they taught and shortly afterwards started an Alexander teachers' training course. As a private medical practitioner, Bill could not work for an unqualified person such as FM so the break had to be made.[3] Their practice soon attracted the attention of two senior teachers at the Royal College of Music, Joyce Wodeman and Joyce Warrack. This led to a long association between the Barlows and that Institution and to generations of music students becoming aware of the value of Alexander's work to their profession.[4]

In 1950 the *Daily Telegraph* published an article about Stafford Cripps' state of health and inferred that he was a pupil of FM.[5] Both FM and Mungo Douglas wrote to the editor of the paper and a week later the paper printed an acknowledgement that Cripps had not seen FM for three years prior to his breakdown and that he was now a pupil at the Isobel Cripps Centre. By this stage Eric de Peyer had left the Centre and was teaching in Wellington Square, London. FM was grieved by what he considered a slur on his work but pleased with the newspaper retraction, particularly as it quoted a statement by Stafford Cripps which read, 'I regard it as one of the fortunate experiences of my life that I should have met F. Matthias Alexander at a time when I had been suffering physically for many years, and that I should have had the opportunity of going through a course with him.' FM was less impressed with the editorial comment that the Centre's work was based on 'Mr. Alexander's Technique'.[6] The activities of the Isobel Cripps Centre troubled FM for the rest of his life.

Apart from the problems associated with teachers wishing to secure the future of the Technique, FM's life in 1949 continued steadily: his health improved, he had sufficient pupils, the teaching course prospered, and he was able to attend race meetings regularly. He presented a sprightly image, looking physically younger than his years, still immaculately turned out, albeit nowadays he had difficulty obtaining the spats which were a rather dated form of dress in post-war London. In midsummer, Raymond Dart visited him from South Africa and they discussed the appeal verdict which Dart considered an historic document. There were some difficulties with the teachers at Media in America but FM had no choice but to rely on the good offices of Frank Jones, who taught there weekly, to resolve them. Meanwhile, the small team at Ashley Place headed by Margaret Goldie, Irene Stewart, Max Alexander, Walter Carrington and John Skinner continued to support FM. Ethel Webb was unable to work because of ill health, and although Irene Tasker taught on a full-time basis she worked mainly in her home town of Cheltenham. Later she moved to Cambridge, teaching in London part-time. By the end of the year, FM's youngest brother, Beaumont, with his wife and small children, moved into the basement flat at No.16 where they remained for about two years. In November, unusually for FM, he addressed a group of war disabled at the St Dunstan's Home for the Blind; he gave demonstrations of his work by using various members of the audience as pupils.[7]

Over the next couple of years FM's health continued to improve and his eyesight recovered to the standard it was prior to the stroke. Ethel Webb's health improved but she was not able to work. FM enjoyed attending race meetings and his holidays in Wales. On 1 July 1950 the *Lancet* published an account of the South African libel trial by Bill Barlow which seemed to bring that saga to a close. On 2 November 1950 George Bernard Shaw died at the advanced age of 94 years; he had always said that his lessons from FM had added at least 10 years to his life. Throughout this period FM wrote a number of letters to the medical press as well as newspapers but generally they were not published. In particular the *Lancet* did not print his letter concerning coronary thrombosis and the *British Medical Journal* refused to publish his views on angina. However, the *Journal* did print Mungo Douglas' letter entitled 'Use of the Self' which covered the Alexander Technique and coronary thrombosis.[8]

In the autumn of 1951 John Vicary, who had been training at Ashley Place as an Alexander teacher, was advised to give up for health reasons. He was unable to stand for long periods and this made him unsuited to teaching. He decided to go to Lundy, a small island north of the Devon coast. He departed in October 1951 and remained there for the next few years, although he made regular visits to see his parents.

The following year was to prove a very sad one. Max left Ashley Place and rejoined the Army and, tragically, Ethel Webb, who had suffered another stroke just before Christmas, died in January. FM, who always referred to her as 'our dear Ethel', had lost his longest serving assistant; they had worked together for over 40 years both in America and in England. Two months later, in March, Sir Charles Sherrington died aged 94 and a month later, on 21 April, Stafford Cripps died. In June one of FM's greatest supporters, John Dewey died aged 93. They had known each other since FM's days in America during the First World War. The long established teacher, Alma Frank, who visited England in the early part of the year, was ill in New York. Amidst all this sad news, FM was disturbed by the advertisements in the papers for the Isobel Cripps Centre and incensed by an editorial about the Centre in the *Sunday Chronicle* which suggested that he was dead. Mungo Douglas reacted immediately and advised the paper that FM was very much alive and that the Technique was Alexander's invention and not that of Charles Neil.[9] FM wrote to the *Observer* and the paper printed an article by Alison Settle, who announced 'There is good news for the many readers who ask for information about the Matthias Alexander system of 'constructive conscious control'. Mr. Matthias Alexander himself writes to say that he is still teaching.'[10] Despite all these depressing events, FM enjoyed his visits to Ascot and the Goodwood races and a holiday in North Wales. During the summer he was particularly busy teaching the many Americans who came to London that year. The other good news was that Mungo Douglas had a letter published in the *Lancet* in May entitled 'Joint Strain in Sleep'.[11]

The following year was Coronation year and London was transformed for the occasion. Many months of disruption surrounded the big event, which took place on an unusually wet

2 June. In this month, the American teacher Alma Frank died, and in October FM's great friend and publisher Fred Watts died.[12] A particularly notable feature of the year was the interview FM gave to a reporter from the *News Chronicle*. In the article, which contained a drawing of FM by Ronald Searle, FM made it very clear that he had pupils not patients and that he was an educator not a healer.[13] A few months later the *Lancet* published a letter from Mungo Douglas entitled 'A Philosophy of Medicine', in which he highlighted his belief that the Medical Society in London should formally recognise the Alexander Technique.[14] The following year FM gave two more interviews. The first was with James Dow, who wrote an article for the *Sunday Graphic*. He quoted FM as saying 'special exercises very often do no more than confirm us in the misuse of our bodies'. He continued, 'Diets? Why bother? If one breathed properly expanding the lower ribs and not just taking air into the tops of our lungs, the oxygen would burn up all the excess fat.' James Dow commented that at a recent health conference a doctor had said that 'the average office worker doesn't take in enough air to keep a cat in good condition'.[15] The second article followed the next day in the *Evening News*.[16] The interviewer, David Wainwright, was most impressed by this alert and sprightly 85 year old.

Along with this publicity was the publication of Louise Morgan's book on the Alexander Technique called *Inside Yourself*. The foreword by Aldous Huxley was most supportive of the Work and stated *inter alia* that,

> F.M. Alexander has devoted the greater part of a long and fruitful life to the task of showing his fellows how to maintain and, where necessary, how to restore the proper use of the self. For the precise nature of his discovery and for his methods of applying it in practice, the reader is referred to the following pages and to Alexander's own writings.[17]

In the second chapter of her book, Louise Morgan produced a diary kept by a friend of hers of her lessons with FM; she related how she learnt to use her body so that she could walk again. This amazing story is related in total by Bill Barlow in his book *More Talk of Alexander*.[18] Soon people who had read the book were appearing at the door of Ashley Place for lessons. FM was delighted with the review of the book in the *New Statesman and Nation* and his letter of thanks for 'the excellent appreciation of my technique in your review' was published two weeks later.[19] Mungo Douglas reviewed the book for the *Boston Evening News*.[20] Earlier in the same year, the *Lancet* published one of his letters entitled 'Control of Reaction' in which he highlighted the work of Rudolph Magnus and showed how the Magnus experiments with animals supported and complemented the Alexander Technique.[21] Six months later the *Manchester Guardian* printed another letter called 'De-Tensing', in which Mungo emphasised the importance of Alexander's work. The following year the *Lancet* published yet another letter entitled 'A Visit to Koltush'.[22]

Throughout the post-war period, FM and his widowed sister Amy re-established the very close association they had had so many years before both in London, when they taught together, and in Australia. Amy went to Penhill most Sundays and they spent the day together. Sometimes she accompanied him on holiday. FM used to visit the bungalow in Sidcup where his niece, Joan, her husband Ivor and their daughter Jackie, lived. The visits increased after Amy came to live with her daughter. He always provided the wine which

100   Dick (left) in New Zealand, 1946.

was ceremoniously placed in the sitting room hearth so it could achieve the correct temperature. The food that accompanied this wine, particularly in the early days, was meagre; rationing permitted little else. But there were times when there was a significant improvement in the fare, the result of food parcels from FM's and Amy's brother, Dick, in New Zealand. In the late 1940s there was a volcanic eruption near Wellington where Dick lived. The food parcels stopped and nothing was ever heard of Dick again.

By now it was clear to FM just how much the South African case had cost him in monetary terms. He had never been wealthy but now he was in a difficult financial situation and he decided that he had no option but to sell Penhill and try to buy a smaller property. Unfortunately, this was to prove a long and tedious business. The Kent County Council had imposed a restriction on his land as they wished to use it for educational purposes. This meant he could not sell his property so, early in 1949, he instructed Ivor, now a lawyer in the City of London, to take up the case on his behalf. The fight continued for most of the rest of his life. The Council rejected FM's development proposals and eventually, on 7 July 1953, an Inquiry was held. His Member of Parliament, Miss Pat Hornsby Smith, raised the problem with the Minister of Housing and Local Government but the appeal was rejected. FM believed that the Council had stolen his property as he had had at least two offers for his land, one for £500 an acre and the other for £1,000 an acre provided that the redevelopment was approved; as it was he could do nothing. The correspondence was lengthly and, eventually, FM agreed to accept compensation for his loss

101   Plaque at Table Cape.

102 FM.

of rights. The development embargo did not include the house, the cottage or the 3½ acres of gardens, stables and cow sheds. These, with the exception of the cottage which FM retained, were placed on the market for sale.

Life for FM at Penhill was relaxed and he spent many hours enjoying the view of his garden from the large sitting room where he had his desk in front of the french windows. Sometimes his adopted daughter Peggy visited him with her two young girls, as did Amy, her daughter Joan and her grand-daughter Jackie. In 1950 Amy was admitted to hospital to undergo a hip replacement operation, then in its infancy. She recovered but developed a heart condition. After numerous heart attacks she died at the bungalow on 10 April 1951. FM, once the oldest of a large family, now had only his brother, Arthur, in Melbourne whom he had not seen for 50 years, and his youngest brother, Beaumont, who for the last years of FM's life lived in the cottage at Penhill with his wife and two young sons. In October 1954 FM discovered that Jack Vicary, his friend, companion, mother of his only child and helper for nearly 40 years, had cancer. John came back from Lundy but his mother died at Penhill on 29 January 1955. She had never come to terms with Peter's death and had found it impossible to live in the house in Upton Road so full of memories of her oldest son. After her death FM remained almost permanently in London and Penhill was sold for redevelopment on 18 March 1955. All the Penhill furniture was auctioned and achieved a good price. This money considerably helped FM's beleaguered financial position. Although he continued teaching for the next eight months and was in a generally good state of health, in late September, after a visit to the races, he caught a cold. He died peacefully in London on 10 October 1955.

FREDERICK MATTHIAS ALEXANDER
HIS LEGACY

BY JOHN GRAY

SENIOR LECTURER AND TUTOR OF THE ALEXANDER TECHNIQUE AT THE
ROYAL ACADEMY OF DRAMATIC ART
AND AUTHOR OF

YOUR GUIDE TO THE ALEXANDER TECHNIQUE

WHAT NOW?

At a dinner to celebrate FM's 80th birthday in 1949 Sir Stafford Cripps, the Chancellor of the Exchequer in the post World War 2 Labour government, noted 'there was set up the Society of Teachers of the Alexander Technique, as a central body for the furtherance of the teaching and for the upholding of proper professional standards. To these teachers, Alexander has entrusted the carrying-on of his work in the form in which he has passed it on to them.' Even during his lifetime FM was concerned about certain teachers but after his death those closest to him became more and more aware of odd things being taught in the name of the Alexander Technique; deviation from his strictest principles was already evident in various quarters. Certain pupils, after the most basic course of lessons, would set themselves up as Alexander teachers, little realising that although the principles were simple they were far from easy to apply or teach. They seemed to think it was simply a matter of pulling people about at worst, or skilful manipulation at best. The essential sorting out of a teacher's own misuse, the communication of better sensory experiences through an expert use of the hands, as well as the ability to teach the basic principles of the Technique require major changes to take place over a fairly long period with most people; three years was considered by FM to be the minimum. Even teachers who had undergone this period of training were beginning to develop their own versions and lose some of the essential ideas behind the teaching and consequently some of its effectiveness. This concern for his work led to the setting up of the Society of Teachers of the Alexander Technique in a formal way although in the late 1930s those already trained had banded together, had meetings, produced pamphlets and so on.

In 1958 Dr. Wilfred Barlow and his wife Marjory invited Patrick MacDonald, Peter Scott, Walter Carrington and one or two other teachers trained by FM to found officially a professional body. STAT was finally in being.

Since then the number of training courses and teachers who have undergone an officially recognised training has grown enormously. At first there were just three training courses in London run by the Barlows, Carrington and MacDonald assisted by Scott, but soon second generation teachers were granted STAT recognition for starting courses and they then spread quickly abroad. The training and teaching in the USA had been growing for some time due to FM and his brother, AR, spending much time there. They had trained a number of Americans both in London and in the USA during the Second World War. Marjorie Barstow, Lulie Westfeldt and Alma Frank were trained in London but went on to teach and train with great success in the States. Another hugely influential teacher there, Frank Pierce Jones, who was trained by FM, went on to become a professor at Tufts and Brown

universities and to write a number of papers, a book on the Technique, a compilation of
scientific articles and to carry out research into the subject. Alma Frank's daughter, Deborah
Caplan, founded the first professional society of teachers in the USA, the American Center
for Alexander Teachers in 1964; this in turn gave way to NASTAT, AMSTAT and now
AMSAT. Other founder teachers were Judith Stransky, Barbara Cullen, Frank Ottiwell, who
has long taught at the American Conservatory Theatre in San Francisco, and Judith Leibowitz,
who became the centre's director of training in 1966 until 1981 and taught for 22 years at
the Juilliard School influencing such actors as Kevin Kline and William Hurt.

In Israel there was a strong tradition. Miss Michelson, a piano teacher, had lessons at
Ashley Place after FM's death, the first of a steady flow of students coming to London to
be taught or trained. Likewise from Denmark there was a regular number from the early
days.

Despite a certain resistance from a number of Alexander teachers, who are often highly
individualistic, and despite the formation of one or two other societies at odds with STAT,
the Society flourished. In 1960 it was decided to extend the associate membership of the
Society and within a few months 300 members had joined. There are now around a
thousand teaching members in the UK and almost half as many spread throughout the world
in almost forty other countries. As well as STAT there are affiliated societies in Australia,
Belgium, Brazil, Canada, Denmark, France, Germany, Israel, the Netherlands, Norway,
South Africa, Spain, Switzerland and the USA, and STAT-approved training courses in
Austria and Italy, all continuing to turn out a steady stream of teachers alongside those
trained in the UK. So far there have been half a dozen international congresses of teachers
and students from these societies.

For a long time those doctors who knew about the Technique, many having had lessons
with FM himself, had felt that there was an area of diagnosis which was being ignored in
the profession: how use affects functioning. If you use yourself well you will function more
efficiently, misuse yourself and you function less efficiently. It is therefore a good idea to
know what constitutes good use and to be able to recognise misuse. Many leading medical
and scientific figures had testified to the effectiveness of the Technique during FM's lifetime
and some also after his death. The most eminent was perhaps Professor Niklaas Tinbergen
who devoted his Laureate Oration to the Technique when receiving the Nobel Prize for
Physiology and Medicine in 1974, and delivered the Alexander Annual Memorial Lecture
to STAT in 1976. Some, like those the South African government used against FM in the
libel action, had thought him to be a charlatan and a phoney, to which his reply would be
that they might know all about anatomy or physiology but just look at the mess they're in;
they don't know how to use their knowledge or themselves.

In England the person who did most to legitimate the Technique and make it acceptable
as an approach to many medical problems was Dr. Wilfred Barlow. His lectures, articles,
research and books changed the way many people regarded the Technique. He helped it to
be taken seriously at the time when so many other dubious 'alternative' approaches were
being touted around. It gave him more than a little satisfaction to be called upon to treat
the back problems of some of those former opponents he had had to face when he was a
leading witness in the libel case for FM. The new climate of complementary medicine

spreading rapidly in the 1960s no doubt helped in the wider acceptance of the Technique but the scientific proof of FM's theories was much needed and it still continues today proving that most of FM's ideas were sound.

The usefulness of the Technique in the treatment of psychological problems is perhaps not so well established but it fits in well with the more holistic approach to most problems which is more usual nowadays and those who have had lessons will certainly know the direct connection between mind and body, how the way we feel mentally is reflected in our use, the depressed body indicating the depressed mind, the muscle tension caused by anxiety and so on. The feelings of ease and well-being generated by improved use and a good Alexander teacher often make the mental problems seem irrelevant or at least something which can be dealt with more easily. Links with FM's work and Jung, the significance of posture and movement, and the processes of growth, development and change have all been written about by eminent psychiatrists, psychologists and psychotherapists, many of them testifying to the role the Alexander Technique can play in their fields of expertise.

In areas such as physiotherapy, chiropractic and osteopathy it is now common for the importance of the Technique to be emphasised; most good practitioners will try and sort out the immediate problem and then suggest that the patient goes for Alexander lessons so that it does not recur. There are also a number of other techniques which owe much to Alexander, Rolfing and Feldenkrais being two of the better known.

One of the good things to come out of the reorganisation of the National Health Service in the 1980s, when doctors became managers, was the ability for a group practice or health centre to use some of their resources to fund areas which are beneficial to patients but which in the past were not recognised as conventional or were only available through referral to a hospital or specialist. There are a number of practices around which are organised so that there are funds and space available for patients to receive at least a basic course of lessons in the Technique, but with further changes in the organisation of general practice in 1998 the position has become more complicated, varying from area to area, with the emphasis on cost-effectiveness. Health Promotion Clinics can offer lessons and medical insurance can also cover lessons provided the patient has been referred by a specialist, consultant, or in some cases, simply by a GP. There are, and have been, any number of research projects successfully carried out on Parkinson's disease, cerebral palsy, arthritis, in pain clinics, and so on. The effectiveness of the Technique is becoming well-known to those dealing with sports injuries and is well thought of by the British Association for Performing Arts Medicine.

To sportsmen and women and dancers the Technique is of great value if only to undo the harm caused by these activities. For many it will allow them to find a better, or at least less damaging way of doing what they choose to do. Although it might seem that there are contradictions and conflicting areas in these activities, when compared to the Technique, it must be remembered that 'it ain't what you do but the way that you do it' which matters. The Technique gives them a better way, even in something as unnatural as classical ballet, and modern dance companies often find direct affinities with the Technique and have their own teachers.

In many of these fields the distinction between medicine and education is unclear, which is unsurprising when a process of re-education has so many beneficial effects on functioning and health in general. FM presented it as a re-education technique but encouraged the support of the medical and scientific communities and it took quite some time before the Technique became firmly established in any mainstream area of education.

As early as 1909 the Australian government had had a mind to incorporate Alexander's ideas into the state schools' physical education curriculum but it had been thwarted by a politician, Billy Hughes, who had never heard of Alexander but who twenty or so years later went to FM for lessons after a heart attack, not realising that this was the man who's work he had sabotaged years before. Dewey always maintained that the Technique bears the same relation to education as education does to all other human activities. In his book *Ends and Means* in 1937, Aldous Huxley had set out his views on what constituted good physical re-education and it still holds good today. Since FM's Little School there have been a number of experiments in primary schools which have tried to adopt an 'Alexander' approach but most have been short-lived and folded as the teaching personnel changed or through lack of money to teach in smaller groups. It is in further and higher education where it has flourished.

As so often with the Technique it has been with actors particularly and artists in general where the Work has found greatest favour so that now it is established in most of the leading academies and conservatoires in the English-speaking world and beyond. Dr. Barlow had carried out extensive research and teaching with the students and staff of the Central School of Speech and Drama in the 1950s and from then on it became the accepted best way of approaching all voice work. Joyce Wodeman, formally an actress and at that time teaching acting to the opera students at the Royal College of Music, quickly came to realise that you cannot get opera singers to move and act well without a fundamental change taking place in the way of better co-ordination and improved use, so she asked to be trained as an Alexander teacher by the Barlows, having previously had private lessons with Marjory. A co-founder of STAT, she then became the first professor of the Alexander Technique at the RCM and in the mid-1970s started teaching at the Royal Academy of Dramatic Art where it soon became central to the training of actors and the underlying aspect of all other areas of technique and skill. As I write there are five Alexander teachers on the RADA staff, various visiting teachers, and most of the staff have had lessons in the Technique and are working to its principles. The students there have a hundred scheduled one-to-one lessons during their three-year course. Although it had long been known in the profession at large ever since Henry Irving, Beerbohm Tree (the founder of RADA) and their like had had lessons with FM soon after he arrived in London, it was almost like a secret, being passed on in the profession from generation to generation. Unlike Stanislavsky, who was known to the whole world, Alexander was only known to a small circle, even though those who knew considered him to be of far greater use to an actor. It is perhaps not so surprising that FM himself was an actor and it was in that profession where the Technique first really took hold. Of all artists I suggest that actors best understand its importance and relevance to their art and are most aware of both sides of their make-up, the physical and the mental.

Although the Technique has still not found its place in primary and rarely secondary education, and probably will not until considerably more money and new thinking have been brought to bear on this area, in higher and further education it is most surely established.

Whether or not the full effectiveness and power of the Technique is being properly explored is debatable. To save money many institutions teach it in groups, but since Alexander himself found it impossible to teach properly in groups except in a training situation where students would have usually had many private lessons beforehand, I fear that pupils are being short-changed.

At first not a great deal was written on the Technique after FM's death other than a couple of books of limited interest and the regular supply of scientific papers to appropriate journals from Dr. Barlow and several others. With the publication of Dr. Barlow's *The Alexander Principle* in 1973 a steady flow of books of varying quality and from every possible angle has been forthcoming. FM's books, for some time out-of-print, reappeared and seem to have been somewhat reassessed. If the truth of his work is not to be lost with all the adaptations, deviations and supposed 'developments', they are an essential record.

The list of institutions where the Technique is taught regularly as an essential part of the curriculum is long and will change from time to time but the following will give you an idea of how well established the Technique has become in many of the most prestigious institutions: in the UK at the Royal Academy of Dramatic Art (RADA), the London Academy of Music and Dramatic Art (LAMDA), the Guildhall School of Music and Drama (for both drama and music students), the Central School of Speech and Drama, the Royal National Theatre, the Royal Shakespeare Company, the Royal Scottish Academy of Dramatic Art, the Royal Academy of Music, the Royal College of Music, the Northern College of Music, the Purcell School, the Menuhin School, Eton College, Westminster School and many others; in the USA at the Juilliard School, New York University, the Metropolitan Opera, Mannes College of Music, the Actors' Studio, the American Academy of Dramatic Arts, Northwest University Schools of Music and Speech, Indiana University, Southern Methodist University in Dallas, New England Conservatory of Music, the Eastman School of Music, the Aspen Music Festival and School, the Los Angeles Symphony Orchestra, and one of the oldest established centres for actors learning the Technique has been the American Conservatory Theatre (ACT) in San Francisco where the teacher is also an actor in the company and trains other teachers. The list is far from complete, there being many teachers in educational institutions in several other countries but the tendency for every drama, dance and music department of every university to pay lip-service to the Technique does not mean it is being well taught and it is advisable for potential pupils to check that the teacher is properly trained and that lessons include a large percentage of one-to-one time.

No doubt FM would be amazed by the growth of his work in recent decades but he would be equally saddened by how it is sometimes taught. I hope he would be thrilled to know how central his principles have become to drama training and how important it is to actors, his first love having been the theatre. To many actors the Technique is far more use than Stanislavsky, it answers all those questions Stanislavsky asked but never resolved satisfactorily, and is altogether more effective. Perhaps FM will soon be more revered as he deserves. The wide use of the Technique by musicians would not surprise him since he taught many himself and the benefits were self-evident. He would be more disappointed by the lack of progress in primary and secondary education even though modern educational philosophy is often on his side. In medicine too the climate is right but the resources and time are not yet forthcoming for it to be fully appreciated as a practical approach to many problems, though it is frequently recommended by those who are in the know.

It seems to me that in most admirable philosophies, movements or religions the progress of ideas in the search for truth is frequently from person to person and takes a long time to be fully recognised. The one-to-one aspect of teaching and learning the Alexander Technique is clearly within this great tradition, essential, and FM might not be too keen on some of the variations from this approach. The only real change we can be sure of is in ourselves, so if we are attempting this in a sound manner and applying ourselves to achieving improvement and greater conscious control as individuals, we are doing the best we can with our lives. This is certainly the aim of the Technique but perhaps it still remains to be seen just how far we have gone along this road given the troubling and troubled state of modern civilisation.

JOHN GRAY
December 2000, London

APPENDIX I

MATTHIAS ALEXANDER'S BROTHERS AND SISTERS

Matthias and his brothers, Joseph and John, lived out their lives in Tasmania but their eight brothers and sisters remained in England. These brothers and sisters were Frederick Matthias Alexander's great uncles and aunts. Between them they produced at least 50 children, although some died very early in life. The three sisters and one brother died in Ramsbury but the other four brothers went to Berkshire and lived for many years in the vicinity of Burnt Hill, between Yattendon, Ashamstead Common and Bradfield, and it was here that they died.

The oldest sister, Maria, had married an agricultural labourer, Ambrose Woolford, in 1823 and they lived in Oxford Street in Ramsbury. Over the next twenty years the couple had nine children but three of them died in infancy. On 29 October 1844 Ambrose died, leaving Maria with five children under 14 years of age. Maria continued to live in Oxford Street and worked as a needlewoman. By 1851 her two oldest daughters had left home, her two sons aged 17 years and 10 years were working as woodmen, and her 15 year old daughter was a willow platter, leaving only seven-year-old Jane at home unemployed. The following year, on 29 March 1852, she married a widower, George Brown, a local shepherd, in Ramsbury Church. Later that year, her nephew George Woolford went to America and joined Joseph Alexander in Watertown. Maria and George Brown continued to live in Oxford Street where Maria died of pneumonia on 6 February 1870.

The next sister, Jane, married a labourer, John Woodley, on 22 June 1826 at the adjacent village of Chilton Foliat. She and her husband lived in this village and their first five children were born there. In the early 1840s the family moved to nearby Chaddleworth in Berkshire where another child was born, but by 1851 they were back in Chilton Foliat where four years later John Woodley, described as a shepherd of 52 years, died. On 21 July 1860 Jane remarried at the Congregational Church in Hungerford a widower, George Chivers from Chilton Foliat, who was working as a farm bailiff. They lived in Chilton Foliat for a number of years and then moved to Burnt Hill in Berkshire which is about 11 miles north-west of Reading. Four of Jane's brothers were living in the area, and when her husband George died on 29 January 1881 they were living in a cottage very near brother Henry and his wife. By 1891, Jane had returned to Ramsbury and was living in Blind Lane with her younger sister, Susannah, where she died on 2 April 1893 of senile decay aged 83 years.

The youngest sister, Susannah, married William Ponting, a bricklayer, in Ramsbury on 5 July 1849. The couple remained in the village all their married life, most of the time in a cottage in Blind Lane where William died in 1891 and Susannah a few months after her sister Jane on 19 October 1893. The Pontings had eight children although one died in infancy.

The oldest brother, Edward, married Ann Edwards in Ramsbury Church on 1 February 1838. At that time Edward was working as a groom, but shortly after their wedding the couple moved to Letcomb Regis in the Vale of the White Horse near Wantage in Berkshire where Edward worked as an agricultural labourer. It was here that their first child was born. After a couple of years they moved to Churn Farm in Blewbury, Berkshire, where Edward worked as a farm bailiff. The family stayed at Blewbury for at least fifteen years and during that time their other three children were born. Then the family moved to Anniss Cross near Burnt Hill in Berkshire where Edward farmed some 70 acres of land employing two labourers and a boy. It was to this farm that Edward senior came on the death of his wife, Jane, in 1859. Later the family moved to the adjoining hamlet of Stanford Dingley, which is about 11 miles from Reading and some two miles south of Burnt Hill where Edward farmed 50 acres of land employing two labourers and two boys. Here in 1869, Edward senior died. Edward junior's wife, Ann, also died, and on 30 March 1871 Edward married Ann Jefferies in Newbury. By 1881 the couple had moved a few miles to Herring Farm, which is approximately two miles east of Burnt Hill. This farm was 60 acres and Edward employed 15 labourers and four boys. Ten years later Edward and Ann were at Lucks Hall farm at Anniss Cross, and by now the 77-year-old Edward was a wood dealer and bricklayer. He died on 2 September 1898 from what was described as the 'decay of nature'.

The next brother, Henry, married Esther Matilda Bright who was born in Axford but baptised in Ramsbury on 29 August 1813. The couple were married on 11 January 1840 in the nearby town of Marlborough where Henry was working as a woodman. Soon the couple moved to Swindon, a village in Gloucestershire where Henry worked as a gamekeeper and his wife was a dressmaker. They had four children. About 1860 they moved to Lucks Hall in Berkshire and lived almost next door to brother Edward at Anniss Cross. Here Henry was an agricultural labourer. Ten years later the family moved to Burnt Hill, where Henry worked as a wood dealer and his two sons were woodmen. One of the sons married a local girl and stayed in the area as a woodman for many years. Henry remained in the cottage on Burnt Hill for the next 30 years and died there at the age of 95 years on 27 October 1912.

Brother George, an agricultural labourer, married Priscilla Hiscock in Ramsbury Church on 10 October 1839 and the couple lived in Blind Lane where their first two children were born. In the mid-1840s the family moved to Sandford, a small village in the northern part of Berkshire near Abingdon where George worked as a gamekeeper and their third child was born on 3 April 1845. Their stay in Stanford was a short one and soon they returned to Ramsbury where their next two children were born. A couple of years later George and his family joined brother Edward at Churn Farm in Blewbury. Again they did not stay long and soon returned to Ramsbury where two more children were born. In about 1860 George obtained a job as a woodman, and with his family moved to Barley Park, Ducklington in Oxfordshire, very close to where his youngest brother William and his family were living. Here their eighth child was born but the family were soon back in Blind Lane in Ramsbury living next door to George's sister Susannah and her husband, William Ponting, where their ninth child was born. They appear to have remained in Ramsbury for many years but by 1881, when all the children had left home, they had joined George's younger brother

Charles at Burnt Hill in Berkshire. George worked there for a short time as a general dealer and then George and Priscilla returned to Blind Lane where George died on 9 December 1890. Priscilla continued to live in the cottage, where she died on 1 January 1894. One of their grandchildren, George, went to Queensland, Australia in 1888 and some of his descendants still live there. It is thought that George travelled with another brother who is alleged to have drowned a few years after arrival in Australia in the serious floods in the Mary river area.

The next brother, Charles, married Caroline Dowling, the daughter of a local button maker, in Ramsbury Church on 14 May 1845. Shortly after their marriage the couple went to live in Letcomb Regis near Wantage, where their first two children were born and Charles worked as a greyhound trainer. In the summer of 1851 the family returned to Ramsbury and lived in Blind Lane. Charles worked as a button maker. Two more children were born but both died in infancy and on 21 February 1854 Caroline died. It is not clear what Charles did at this stage with two small children, Edward aged six years and Ann aged four years. He probably stayed in Blind Lane so that his mother Jane and sister-in-law, Priscilla could help look after the children. In the late 1850s George and Priscilla left Ramsbury for Ducklington and his mother died. It is likely that Charles and his children went with his father to join Edward in Anniss Cross where Henry and his wife were also living. Charles worked as a labourer in that area, and on 4 July 1860 he married a local woman Ann Merritt. They went to live in a cottage at Burnt Hill where they remained for the rest of Charles' life. Initially Charles worked as an agricultural labourer, and later as a woodman. In 1881 George and Priscilla were living in the cottage with them and George was working as a general dealer. By 1891 Charles was registered blind but how long he had suffered this affliction is unclear. At that time his wife was working as a laundress. He died on 31 May 1902 from what was described as the 'decay of nature'.

The youngest son, William Adolphus, moved away from Ramsbury as a bachelor and by 1854 was working as a labourer in Taynton in Oxfordshire on the Gloucestershire border. It was here on 17 June 1854 that he married Mary Thornton who was working in the district although she was born in Sherborne about four miles away. The couple stayed in Oxfordshire, firstly in Culham where their first child was born and then at Hardwick in the parish of Ducklington where William obtained work as a gamekeeper. Between 1859 and 1868 William and Mary had their next five children baptised at St Bartholomew's Church in Ducklington. By 1871 William and his family had moved near his other brothers in the Burnt Hill area of Berkshire. They lived at Lucks Hall in the Anniss Cross area very close to Henry and his family. William farmed 20 acres of land. Ten years later William, Mary and their two youngest children were living in a cottage in Burnt Hill, very close to brother Charles. William was farming some 70 acres of land and he and his wife opened a grocery shop. William died in the cottage on 16 February 1889. William's widow, assisted by daughter Emily, continued to run the shop for a number of years.

FAMILY TREES

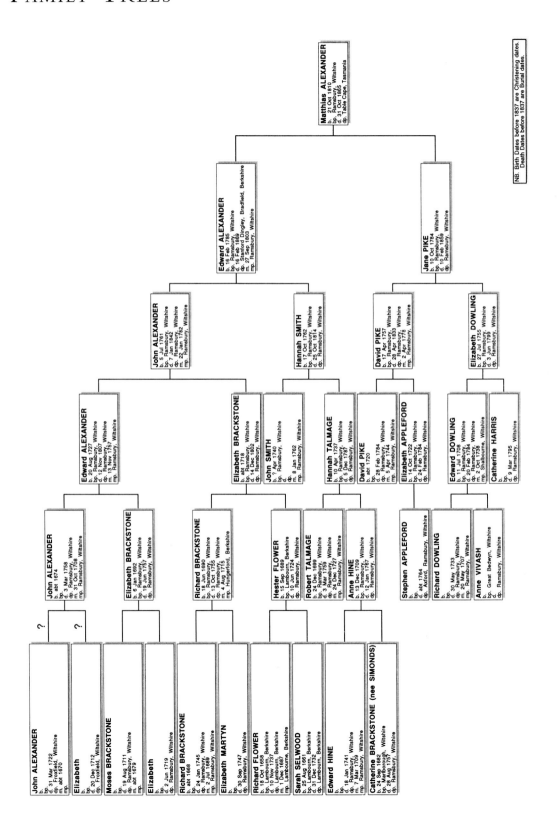

NB. Birth Dates before 1837 are Christening dates.
Death Dates before 1837 are Burial dates.

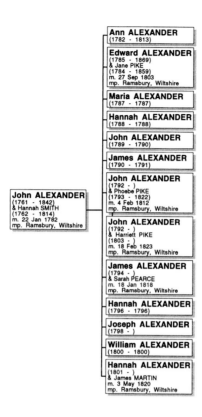

Ann ALEXANDER
(1782 - 1813)

Edward ALEXANDER
(1785 - 1869)
& Jane PIKE
(1784 - 1859)
m. 27 Sep 1803
mp. Ramsbury, Wiltshire

Maria ALEXANDER
(1787 - 1787)

Hannah ALEXANDER
(1788 - 1788)

John ALEXANDER
(1789 - 1790)

James ALEXANDER
(1790 - 1791)

John ALEXANDER
(1792 -)
& Phoebe PIKE
(1793 - 1822)
m. 4 Feb 1812
mp. Ramsbury, Wiltshire

John ALEXANDER
(1792 -)
& Harriett PIKE
(1803 -)
m. 18 Feb 1823
mp. Ramsbury, Wiltshire

James ALEXANDER
(1794 -)
& Sarah PEARCE
m. 18 Jan 1818
mp. Ramsbury, Wiltshire

Hannah ALEXANDER
(1796 - 1796)

Joseph ALEXANDER
(1798 -)

William ALEXANDER
(1800 - 1800)

Hannah ALEXANDER
(1801 -)
& James MARTIN
m. 3 May 1820
mp. Ramsbury, Wiltshire

John ALEXANDER
(1761 - 1842)
& Hannah SMITH
(1762 - 1814)
m. 22 Jan 1782
mp. Ramsbury, Wiltshire

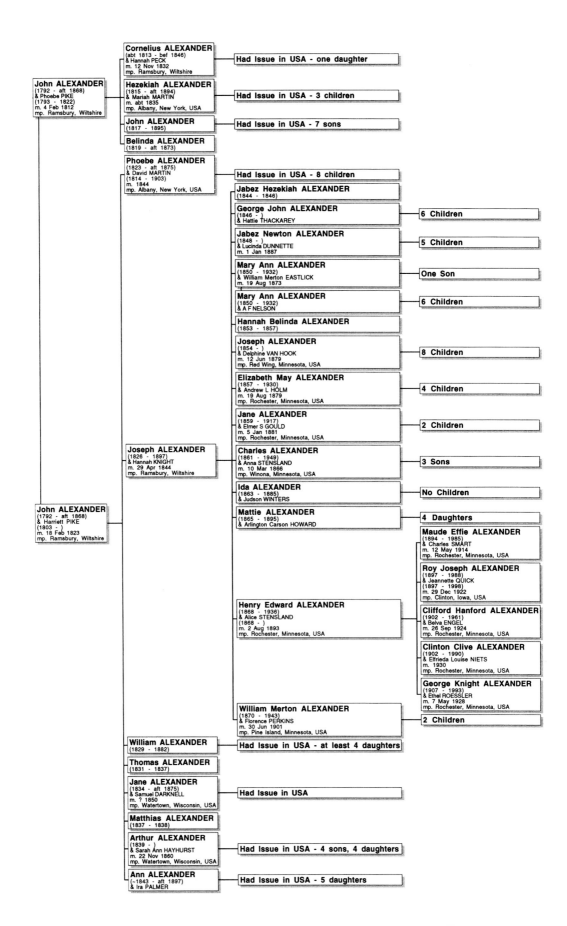

John ALEXANDER
(1792 - aft 1868)
& Phoebe PIKE
(1793 - 1822)
m. 4 Feb 1812
mp. Ramsbury, Wiltshire

Cornelius ALEXANDER
(abt 1813 - bef 1846)
& Hannah PECK
m. 12 Nov 1832
mp. Ramsbury, Wiltshire

Had Issue in USA - one daughter

Hezekiah ALEXANDER
(1815 - aft 1894)
& Mariah MARTIN
m. abt 1835
mp. Albany, New York, USA

Had Issue in USA - 3 children

John ALEXANDER
(1817 - 1895)

Had Issue in USA - 7 sons

Belinda ALEXANDER
(1819 - aft 1873)

Phoebe ALEXANDER
(1823 - aft 1875)
& David MARTIN
(1814 - 1903)
m. 1844
mp. Albany, New York, USA

Had Issue in USA - 8 children

Jabez Hezekiah ALEXANDER
(1844 - 1846)

George John ALEXANDER
(1846 -)
& Hattie THACKAREY

6 Children

Jabez Newton ALEXANDER
(1848 -)
& Lucinda DUNNETTE
m. 1 Jan 1887

5 Children

Mary Ann ALEXANDER
(1850 - 1932)
& William Merton EASTLICK
m. 19 Aug 1873

One Son

Mary Ann ALEXANDER
(1850 - 1932)
& A F NELSON

6 Children

Hannah Belinda ALEXANDER
(1853 - 1857)

Joseph ALEXANDER
(1854 -)
& Delphine VAN HOOK
m. 12 Jun 1879
mp. Red Wing, Minnesota, USA

8 Children

Elizabeth May ALEXANDER
(1857 - 1930)
& Andrew L HOLM
m. 19 Aug 1879
mp. Rochester, Minnesota, USA

4 Children

Jane ALEXANDER
(1859 - 1917)
& Elmer S GOULD
m. 5 Jan 1881
mp. Rochester, Minnesota, USA

2 Children

Joseph ALEXANDER
(1826 - 1897)
& Hannah KNIGHT
m. 29 Apr 1844
mp. Ramsbury, Wiltshire

Charles ALEXANDER
(1861 - 1949)
& Anna STENSLAND
m. 10 Mar 1866
mp. Winona, Minnesota, USA

3 Sons

Ida ALEXANDER
(1863 - 1885)
& Judson WINTERS

No Children

Mattie ALEXANDER
(1865 - 1895)
& Arlington Carson HOWARD

4 Daughters

John ALEXANDER
(1792 - aft 1868)
& Harriett PIKE
(1803 -)
m. 18 Feb 1823
mp. Ramsbury, Wiltshire

Maude Effie ALEXANDER
(1894 - 1985)
& Charles SMART
m. 12 May 1914
mp. Rochester, Minnesota, USA

Roy Joseph ALEXANDER
(1897 - 1988)
& Jeannette QUICK
(1897 - 1998)
m. 29 Dec 1922
mp. Clinton, Iowa, USA

Henry Edward ALEXANDER
(1868 - 1936)
& Alice STENSLAND
(1868 -)
m. 2 Aug 1893
mp. Rochester, Minnesota, USA

Clifford Hanford ALEXANDER
(1902 - 1961)
& Belva ENGEL
m. 26 Sep 1924
mp. Rochester, Minnesota, USA

Clinton Clive ALEXANDER
(1902 - 1990)
& Elfrieda Louise NIETS
m. 1930
mp. Rochester, Minnesota, USA

George Knight ALEXANDER
(1907 - 1993)
& Ethel ROESSLER
m. 7 May 1928
mp. Rochester, Minnesota, USA

William Merton ALEXANDER
(1870 - 1943)
& Florence PERKINS
m. 30 Jun 1901
mp. Pine Island, Minnesota, USA

2 Children

William ALEXANDER
(1829 - 1882)

Had Issue in USA - at least 4 daughters

Thomas ALEXANDER
(1831 - 1837)

Jane ALEXANDER
(1834 - aft 1875)
& Samuel DARKNELL
m. ? 1850
mp. Watertown, Wisconsin, USA

Had Issue in USA

Matthias ALEXANDER
(1837 - 1838)

Arthur ALEXANDER
(1839 -)
& Sarah Ann HAYHURST
m. 22 Nov 1860
mp. Watertown, Wisconsin, USA

Had Issue in USA - 4 sons, 4 daughters

Ann ALEXANDER
(~1843 - aft 1897)
& Ira PALMER

Had Issue in USA - 5 daughters

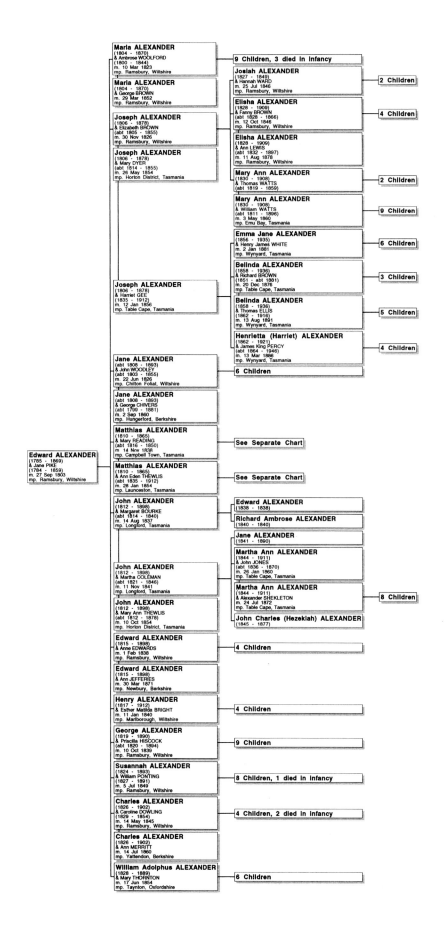

Maria ALEXANDER
(1804 - 1870)
& Ambrose WOODLFORD
(1800 - 1844)
m. 10 Mar 1823
mp. Ramsbury, Wiltshire

9 Children, 3 died in infancy

Maria ALEXANDER
(1804 - 1870)
& George BROWN
m. 29 Mar 1852
mp. Ramsbury, Wiltshire

Josiah ALEXANDER
(1827 - 1849)
& Hannah WARD
m. 25 Jul 1846
mp. Ramsbury, Wiltshire

2 Children

Joseph ALEXANDER
(1806 - 1878)
& Elizabeth BROWN
(abt 1805 - 1855)
m. 30 Nov 1826
mp. Ramsbury, Wiltshire

Elisha ALEXANDER
(1828 - 1909)
& Fanny BROWN
(abt 1828 - 1866)
m. 12 Oct 1846
mp. Ramsbury, Wiltshire

4 Children

Joseph ALEXANDER
(1806 - 1878)
& Mary DYER
(abt 1814 - 1855)
m. 26 May 1854
mp. Horton District, Tasmania

Elisha ALEXANDER
(1828 - 1909)
& Ann LEWIS
(abt 1832 - 1897)
m. 11 Aug 1878
mp. Ramsbury, Wiltshire

Mary Ann ALEXANDER
(1830 - 1908)
& Thomas WATTS
(abt 1819 - 1859)

2 Children

Mary Ann ALEXANDER
(1830 - 1908)
& William WATTS
(abt 1811 - 1896)
m. 3 May 1860
mp. Emu Bay, Tasmania

9 Children

Emma Jane ALEXANDER
(1856 - 1935)
& Henry James WHITE
m. 2 Jan 1881
mp. Wynyard, Tasmania

6 Children

Joseph ALEXANDER
(1806 - 1878)
& Harriet GEE
(1835 - 1912)
m. 12 Jan 1856
mp. Table Cape, Tasmania

Belinda ALEXANDER
(1858 - 1936)
& Richard BROWN
(1851 - abt 1881)
m. 20 Dec 1876
mp. Table Cape, Tasmania

3 Children

Belinda ALEXANDER
(1858 - 1936)
& Thomas ELLIS
(1862 - 1916)
m. 13 Aug 1891
mp. Wynyard, Tasmania

5 Children

Henrietta (Harriet) ALEXANDER
(1862 - 1921)
& James King PERCY
(abt 1864 - 1946)
m. 13 Mar 1886
mp. Wynyard, Tasmania

4 Children

Edward ALEXANDER
(1785 - 1869)
& Jane PIKE
(1784 - 1859)
m. 27 Sep 1803
mp. Ramsbury, Wiltshire

Jane ALEXANDER
(abt 1808 - 1893)
& John WOODLEY
(abt 1803 - 1855)
m. 22 Jun 1826
mp. Chilton Foliat, Wiltshire

6 Children

Jane ALEXANDER
(abt 1808 - 1893)
& George CHIVERS
(abt 1799 - 1881)
m. 2 Sep 1860
mp. Hungerford, Berkshire

Matthias ALEXANDER
(1810 - 1865)
& Mary READING
(abt 1816 - 1850)
m. 14 Nov 1838
mp. Campbell Town, Tasmania

See Separate Chart

Matthias ALEXANDER
(1810 - 1865)
& Ann Eden THEWLIS
(abt 1835 - 1912)
m. 28 Jan 1854
mp. Launceston, Tasmania

See Separate Chart

John ALEXANDER
(1812 - 1898)
& Margaret BOURKE
(abt 1814 - 1840)
m. 14 Aug 1837
mp. Longford, Tasmania

Edward ALEXANDER
(1838 - 1838)

Richard Ambrose ALEXANDER
(1840 - 1840)

Jane ALEXANDER
(1841 - 1890)

John ALEXANDER
(1812 - 1898)
& Martha COLEMAN
(abt 1821 - 1846)
m. 11 Nov 1841
mp. Longford, Tasmania

Martha Ann ALEXANDER
(1844 - 1911)
& John JONES
(abt 1836 - 1870)
m. 26 Jul 1860
mp. Table Cape, Tasmania

Martha Ann ALEXANDER
(1844 - 1911)
& Alexander SHEKLETON
m. 24 Jul 1872
mp. Table Cape, Tasmania

8 Children

John ALEXANDER
(1812 - 1898)
& Mary Ann THEWLIS
(abt 1812 - 1878)
m. 10 Oct 1854
mp. Horton District, Tasmania

John Charles (Hezekiah) ALEXANDER
(1845 - 1877)

Edward ALEXANDER
(1815 - 1898)
& Anne EDWARDS
m. 1 Feb 1838
mp. Ramsbury, Wiltshire

4 Children

Edward ALEXANDER
(1815 - 1898)
& Ann JEFFERIES
m. 30 Mar 1871
mp. Newbury, Berkshire

Henry ALEXANDER
(1817 - 1912)
& Esther Matilda BRIGHT
m. 11 Jan 1840
mp. Marlborough, Wiltshire

4 Children

George ALEXANDER
(1819 - 1890)
& Priscilla HISCOCK
(abt 1820 - 1894)
m. 10 Oct 1839
mp. Ramsbury, Wiltshire

9 Children

Susannah ALEXANDER
(1824 - 1893)
& William PONTING
(1827 - 1891)
m. 5 Jul 1849
mp. Ramsbury, Wiltshire

8 Children, 1 died in infancy

Charles ALEXANDER
(1826 - 1902)
& Caroline DOWLING
(1829 - 1854)
m. 14 May 1845
mp. Ramsbury, Wiltshire

4 Children, 2 died in infancy

Charles ALEXANDER
(1826 - 1902)
& Ann MERRITT
m. 14 Jul 1860
mp. Yattendon, Berkshire

William Adolphus ALEXANDER
(1828 - 1889)
& Mary THORNTON
m. 17 Jun 1854
mp. Taynton, Oxfordshire

6 Children

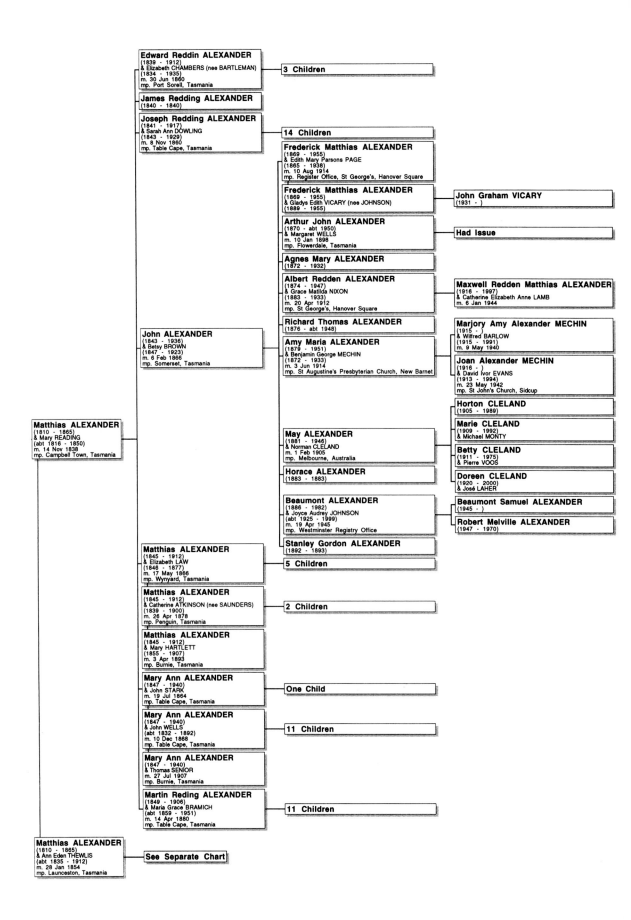

Edward Reddin ALEXANDER
(1839 - 1912)
& Elizabeth CHAMBERS (nee BARTLEMAN)
(1834 - 1935)
m. 30 Jun 1860
mp. Port Sorell, Tasmania

— 3 Children

James Redding ALEXANDER
(1840 - 1840)

Joseph Redding ALEXANDER
(1841 - 1917)
& Sarah Ann DOWLING
(1843 - 1929)
m. 8 Nov 1860
mp. Table Cape, Tasmania

— 14 Children

Frederick Matthias ALEXANDER
(1869 - 1955)
& Edith Mary Parsons PAGE
(1865 - 1938)
m. 10 Aug 1914
mp. Register Office, St George's, Hanover Square

Frederick Matthias ALEXANDER
(1869 - 1955)
& Gladys Edith VICARY (nee JOHNSON)
(1889 - 1955)

John Graham VICARY
(1931 -)

Arthur John ALEXANDER
(1870 - abt 1950)
& Margaret WELLS
m. 10 Jan 1898
mp. Flowerdale, Tasmania

Had Issue

Agnes Mary ALEXANDER
(1872 - 1932)

Albert Redden ALEXANDER
(1874 - 1947)
& Grace Matilda NIXON
(1883 - 1933)
m. 20 Apr 1912
mp. St George's, Hanover Square

Maxwell Redden Matthias ALEXANDER
(1916 - 1997)
& Catherine Elizabeth Anne LAMB
m. 6 Jan 1944

Richard Thomas ALEXANDER
(1876 - abt 1948)

Marjory Amy Alexander MECHIN
(1915 -)
& Wilfred BARLOW
(1915 - 1991)
m. 9 May 1940

Amy Maria ALEXANDER
(1879 - 1951)
& Benjamin George MECHIN
(1872 - 1933)
m. 3 Jun 1914
mp. St Augustine's Presbyterian Church, New Barnet

Joan Alexander MECHIN
(1916 -)
& David Ivor EVANS
(1913 - 1994)
m. 23 May 1942
mp. St John's Church, Sidcup

John ALEXANDER
(1843 - 1936)
& Betsy BROWN
(1847 - 1923)
m. 6 Feb 1866
mp. Somerset, Tasmania

Horton CLELAND
(1905 - 1989)

Marie CLELAND
(1909 - 1992)
& Michael MONTY

May ALEXANDER
(1881 - 1946)
& Norman CLELAND
m. 1 Feb 1905
mp. Melbourne, Australia

Betty CLELAND
(1911 - 1975)
& Pierre VOOS

Doreen CLELAND
(1920 - 2000)
& José LAHER

Horace ALEXANDER
(1883 - 1883)

Beaumont ALEXANDER
(1886 - 1982)
& Joyce Audrey JOHNSON
(abt 1925 - 1999)
m. 19 Apr 1945
mp. Westminster Registry Office

Beaumont Samuel ALEXANDER
(1945 -)

Robert Melville ALEXANDER
(1947 - 1970)

Stanley Gordon ALEXANDER
(1892 - 1893)

Matthias ALEXANDER
(1845 - 1912)
& Elizabeth LAW
(1846 - 1877)
m. 17 May 1866
mp. Wynyard, Tasmania

— 5 Children

Matthias ALEXANDER
(1845 - 1912)
& Catherine ATKINSON (nee SAUNDERS)
(1839 - 1900)
m. 26 Apr 1878
mp. Penguin, Tasmania

— 2 Children

Matthias ALEXANDER
(1845 - 1912)
& Mary HARTLETT
(1855 - 1907)
m. 3 Apr 1893
mp. Burnie, Tasmania

Mary Ann ALEXANDER
(1847 - 1940)
& John STARK
m. 19 Jul 1864
mp. Table Cape, Tasmania

— One Child

Mary Ann ALEXANDER
(1847 - 1940)
& John WELLS
(abt 1832 - 1892)
m. 10 Dec 1868
mp. Table Cape, Tasmania

— 11 Children

Mary Ann ALEXANDER
(1847 - 1940)
& Thomas SENIOR
m. 27 Jul 1907
mp. Burnie, Tasmania

Martin Reding ALEXANDER
(1849 - 1906)
& Maria Grace BRAMICH
(abt 1859 - 1951)
m. 14 Apr 1880
mp. Table Cape, Tasmania

— 11 Children

Matthias ALEXANDER
(1810 - 1865)
& Mary READING
(abt 1816 - 1850)
m. 14 Nov 1838
mp. Campbell Town, Tasmania

Matthias ALEXANDER
(1810 - 1865)
& Ann Eden THEWLIS
(abt 1835 - 1912)
m. 28 Jan 1854
mp. Launceston, Tasmania

— See Separate Chart

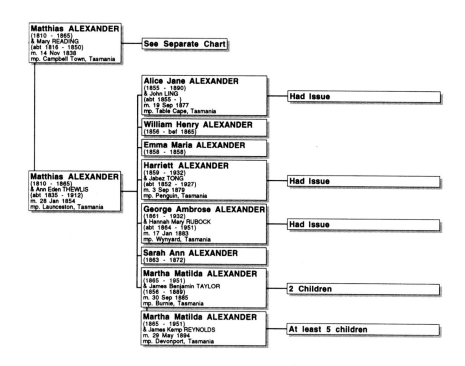

Matthias ALEXANDER
(1810 - 1865)
& Mary READING
(abt 1816 - 1850)
m. 14 Nov 1838
mp. Campbell Town, Tasmania

See Separate Chart

Alice Jane ALEXANDER
(1855 - 1890)
& John LING
(abt 1855 -)
m. 19 Sep 1877
mp. Table Cape, Tasmania

Had Issue

William Henry ALEXANDER
(1856 - bef 1865)

Emma Maria ALEXANDER
(1858 - 1858)

Matthias ALEXANDER
(1810 - 1865)
& Ann Eden THEWLIS
(abt 1835 - 1912)
m. 28 Jan 1854
mp. Launceston, Tasmania

Harriett ALEXANDER
(1859 - 1932)
& Jabez TONG
(abt 1852 - 1927)
m. 3 Sep 1879
mp. Penguin, Tasmania

Had Issue

George Ambrose ALEXANDER
(1861 - 1932)
& Hannah Mary RUBOCK
(abt 1864 - 1951)
m. 17 Jan 1883
mp. Wynyard, Tasmania

Had Issue

Sarah Ann ALEXANDER
(1863 - 1872)

Martha Matilda ALEXANDER
(1865 - 1951)
& James Benjamin TAYLOR
(1856 - 1889)
m. 30 Sep 1885
mp. Burnie, Tasmania

2 Children

Martha Matilda ALEXANDER
(1865 - 1951)
& James Kemp REYNOLDS
m. 29 May 1894
mp. Devonport, Tasmania

At least 5 children

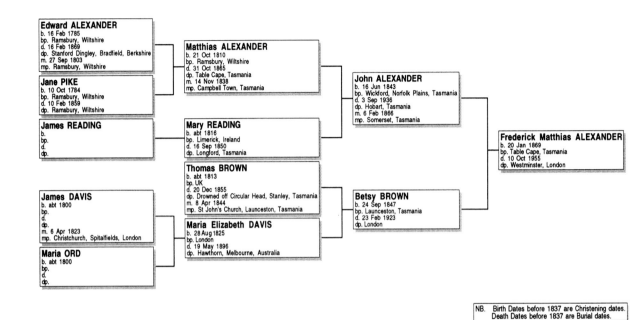

Edward ALEXANDER
b. 16 Feb 1785
bp. Ramsbury, Wiltshire
d. 16 Feb 1869
dp. Stanford Dingley, Bradfield, Berkshire
m. 27 Sep 1803
mp. Ramsbury, Wiltshire

Jane PIKE
b. 10 Oct 1784
bp. Ramsbury, Wiltshire
d. 10 Feb 1859
dp. Ramsbury, Wiltshire

James READING
b.
bp.
d.
dp.

James DAVIS
b. abt 1800
bp.
d.
dp.
m. 6 Apr 1823
mp. Christchurch, Spitalfields, London

Maria ORD
b. abt 1800
bp.
d.
dp.

Matthias ALEXANDER
b. 21 Oct 1810
bp. Ramsbury, Wiltshire
d. 31 Oct 1865
dp. Table Cape, Tasmania
m. 14 Nov 1838
mp. Campbell Town, Tasmania

Mary READING
b. abt 1816
bp. Limerick, Ireland
d. 16 Sep 1850
dp. Longford, Tasmania

Thomas BROWN
b. abt 1813
bp. UK
d. 20 Dec 1855
dp. Drowned off Circular Head, Stanley, Tasmania
m. 8 Apr 1844
mp. St John's Church, Launceston, Tasmania

Maria Elizabeth DAVIS
b. 28 Aug 1825
bp. London
d. 19 May 1896
dp. Hawthorn, Melbourne, Australia

John ALEXANDER
b. 16 Jun 1843
bp. Wickford, Norfolk Plains, Tasmania
d. 3 Sep 1936
dp. Hobart, Tasmania
m. 6 Feb 1866
mp. Somerset, Tasmania

Betsy BROWN
b. 24 Sep 1847
bp. Launceston, Tasmania
d. 23 Feb 1923
dp. London

Frederick Matthias ALEXANDER
b. 20 Jan 1869
bp. Table Cape, Tasmania
d. 10 Oct 1955
dp. Westminster, London

NB.   Birth Dates before 1837 are Christening dates.
        Death Dates before 1837 are Burial dates.

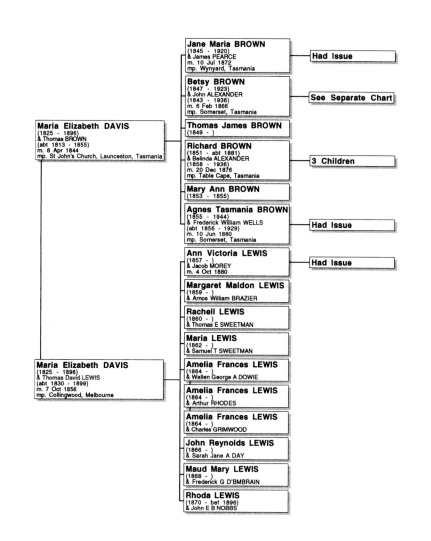

Maria Elizabeth DAVIS
(1825 - 1896)
& Thomas BROWN
(abt 1813 - 1855)
m. 8 Apr 1844
mp. St John's Church, Launceston, Tasmania

Jane Maria BROWN
(1845 - 1920)
& James PEARCE
m. 10 Jul 1872
mp. Wynyard, Tasmania

Had Issue

Betsy BROWN
(1847 - 1923)
& John ALEXANDER
(1843 - 1936)
m. 6 Feb 1866
mp. Somerset, Tasmania

See Separate Chart

Thomas James BROWN
(1849 -)

Richard BROWN
(1851 - abt 1881)
& Belinda ALEXANDER
(1858 - 1936)
m. 20 Dec 1876
mp. Table Cape, Tasmania

3 Children

Mary Ann BROWN
(1853 - 1855)

Agnes Tasmania BROWN
(1855 - 1944)
& Frederick William WELLS
(abt 1856 - 1929)
m. 10 Jun 1880
mp. Somerset, Tasmania

Had Issue

Maria Elizabeth DAVIS
(1825 - 1896)
& Thomas David LEWIS
(abt 1830 - 1899)
m. 7 Oct 1856
mp. Collingwood, Melbourne

Ann Victoria LEWIS
(1857 -)
& Jacob MOREY
m. 4 Oct 1880

Had Issue

Margaret Maldon LEWIS
(1859 -)
& Amos William BRAZIER

Rachell LEWIS
(1860 -)
& Thomas E SWEETMAN

Maria LEWIS
(1862 -)
& Samuel T SWEETMAN

Amelia Frances LEWIS
(1864 -)
& Wallen George A DOWIE

Amelia Frances LEWIS
(1864 -)
& Arthur RHODES

Amelia Frances LEWIS
(1864 -)
& Charles GRIMWOOD

John Reynolds LEWIS
(1866 -)
& Sarah Jane A DAY

Maud Mary LEWIS
(1868 -)
& Frederick G D'BMBRAIN

Rhoda LEWIS
(1870 - bef 1896)
& John E B NOBBS

Notes

1 ALEXANDERS OF ENGLAND, pp.3-14.

1. *The Victoria History of the Counties of England (VCH), A History of Wiltshire (Wilts)*, Vol.4, ed. by R.B. Pugh (The University of London, Institute of Historical Research, Oxford University Press 1959), p.356.
2. *The Victoria History of the Counties of England (VCH), A History of Wiltshire (Wilts)*, Vol.12, ed. by D.A. Crowley (The University of London, Institute of Historical Research, Oxford University Press 1983), pp.13 and 15.
3. Croucher, B., *The Village in the Valley* (Wiltshire: Barbara Croucher, 1986), p.10.
4. Thorn, C. and F. (ed.), *Domesday Book Vol.6 Wiltshire* (Chichester: Phillimore, 1979), p.66a.
5. *The Victoria History of the Counties of England (VCH), A History of Wiltshire (Wilts), Vol.2*, ed. by R.B. Pugh and Elizabeth Crittall (The University of London, Institute of Historical Research, Oxford University Press, 1955), p.49.
6. *Ibid.*, p.32.
7. *The Victoria History of the Counties of England (VCH), A History of Wiltshire (Wilts), Vol.3*, ed. by R.B. Pugh (The University of London, Institute of Historical Research, Oxford University Press, 1956), p.156.
8. Croucher, *The Village in the Valley*, p.29.
9. *Ibid.*, pp.32 and 52.
10. *VCH, Wilts Vol.12*, p.22.
11. Croucher, *The Village in the Valley*, p.43.
12. VCH, Wilts Vol.2, ed. by D.A. Crowley (The University of London, Institute of Historical Research, Oxford University Press, 1983), p.40.
13. *VCH, Wilts Vol.4*, p.310.
14. *VCH, Wilts Vol.12*, pp.12 and 13.
15. Croucher, *The Village in the Valley*, p.62.
16. *Ibid.*, pp.61-4.
17. *Ibid.*, p.64.
18. *Ibid.*, pp.66 and 67.
19. *Ibid.*, p.69.
20. Wiltshire Record Society (WRS). List of Taxpayers for the Subsidy of 1576.
21. *The Victoria History of the Counties of England (VCH), A History of Berkshire, Vol.4*, ed. by William Page (The University of London, Institute of Historical Research, reprinted from the original edition of 1924 by Dawson of London, 1972), p.251.
22. W.S.R.O., Wills, Dean of Sarum and Sarum Consistory Court and Sarum Peculiar and Prebendal Court, Brackstone and Selwood wills various.
23. *The Victoria History of the Counties of England (VCH), A History of Wiltshire (Wilts), Vol.5*, ed. by R.B. Pugh (The University of London, Institute of Historical Research, Oxford University Press, 1957), pp.139-44 and Croucher, *The Village in the Valley*, pp.77-85.
24. P.R.O., E 179/348.
25. *VCH, Wilts Vol.12*, p.19.
26. *A True Copy of the Poll for the Electing of the Knights of the Shire for the County of Wilts* (London, 1705), p.59 and W.S.R.O., Wills, Dean of Sarum and Sarum Consistory Court, R1-307.
27. W.S.R.O., 1883/165-7, Ramsbury leases 1625-1796.
28. P.R.O., IR/17/10/23.
29. W.S.R.O., Wills, Dean of Sarum and Sarum Consistory Court.
30. Croucher, *The Village in the Valley*, p.99.
31. WRS, Ramsbury Enclosure Act 1778.
32. P.R.O., IR 23/96 and IR 38/224 and W.S.R.O., Wills, Dean of Sarum and Sarum Consistory Court and Land Tax Assessments, A1/345/339A, 1783-1804.
33. Declaration by Joseph Alexander, son of John, labourer from Chipping Lambourn dated 21 November 1845 for probate of will of Mary Ann Alexander widow of John.
34. W.S.R.O., Wills, Dean of Sarum and Sarum Consistory Court.
35. *VCH, Wilts Vol.12*, p.48.
36. W.S.R.O., 1883/27, 1727 Axford Enclosure Agreement.
37. W.S.R.O., 1792/38L, 1839 Map of Ramsbury and B. Croucher's listings of owners and occupiers of dwellings.
38. *VCH Berks, Vol. 4*, p.160 and Croucher, *The Village in the Valley*, p.214.
39. *VCH, Wilts Vol.4*, p.356 and Croucher, *The Village in the Valley*, p.156.
40. Croucher, B., *The Village in the Valley* (Wiltshire: Barbara Croucher, 1986), p.185.
41. *VCH, Wilts Vol. 3*, p.49 and WRS, *Wiltshire Dissenters' Meeting House Certificates*, p.126.
42. W.S.R.O., 2027H, Ramsbury Church Pew List circa early 18th century.
43. W.S.R.O., 3035/10, Ramsbury Church Pew List *c*.1780s.
44. *A True Copy of the Poll for the Electing of the Knights of the Shire For the County of Wilts* (London 1705), pp.59 and 60 and *The Poll*

of the Freeholders of Wiltshire for Electing a Knight of the Shire Taken at Wilton on 18, 19, 20 and 21 August 1772 (Salisbury, 1772), pp.66-8.

45. The Poll for the Election of Two Knights for the County of Wilts to Serve in Parliament 1818 (Salisbury, 1818), pp116-7.

46. Wiltshire Poll book 1819, pp.114-5.

2 CAPTAIN SWING RIOTS, pp.15-26.

1.   Wrigley, E.A. and Schofield, R.S., The Population History of England 1541-1871 A Reconstruction (London: Edward Arnold (Publishers) Ltd., 1981), p.529.
2.   Hobsbawm, E.J. and Rudé, George, Captain Swing (London: Lawrence and Wishart (1969), 1970), pp.23-31.
3.   Hammond, J.L. and Barbara, The Village Labourer (London: Longmans, Green and Co. (1911), 1966), pp.93 and 102.
4.   Hobsbawm and Rudé, Captain Swing, p.36.
5.   Hammond, The Village Labourer, pp.158-60.
6.   Ibid., pp.180-1.
7.   Mingay, G.E. (ed.), The Unquiet Countryside, pp.28 and 40.
8.   Rudé, George, Protest and Punishment (Oxford: Clarendon Press, 1978), pp.63-6, by permission of Oxford University Press.
9.   Hobsbawm and Rudé, Captain Swing, p.72.
10. Mingay, The Unquiet Countryside, p.43.
11. Hobsbawm and Rudé, Captain Swing, pp.97-100.
12. Ibid., p.101.
13. Hammond, The Village Labourer, pp.246-55.
14. Hobsbawn and Rudé, Captain Swing, Appendix III, pp.312-58.
15. Croucher, The Village in the Valley, p.145.
16. Devizes and Wiltshire Gazette, 25 November 1830.
17. Hobsbawm and Rudé, Captain Swing, Appendix I, p.305 and Appendix III, pp.329-36.
18. Salisbury and Winchester Journal, 29 November 1830.
19. P.R.O., ASSI 24/18/3 and HO 27/42.
20. Hobsbawm and Rudé, Captain Swing, p.258.
21. Hammond, The Village Labourer, p.283.
22. Salisbury and Winchester Journal, 3 January 1831.
23. The Times, 7 January 1831.
24. P.R.O., HO 27/42, pp.340, 342 and 343 and Salisbury and Winchester Journal, 6 and 10 January 1831.
25. Devizes and Wiltshire Gazette, 13 and 20 January 1831.
26. Hobsbawm and Rudé, Captain Swing, pp.305 and 309.
27. A.O.T. CON 18/6 and Chambers, J., The Wiltshire Machine Breakers, Vol.2, The Rioters (Herts: Jill Chambers, 1993).
28. Hobsbawm and Rudé, Captain Swing, p.247.
29. Ibid., p.263.
30. Mingay, The Unquiet Countryside, p.49.
31. P.R.O., MH 12/234.
32. P.R.O., HO 107/1184/15.
33. 1839 Parish Map of Ramsbury, information from B. Croucher.
34. Croucher, The Village in the Valley, p.133.
35. P.R.O., HO 107/1184/15.
36. Roy Alexander, Unpublished papers, John Alexander's apprenticeship certificate, and passenger manifest of St James sworn by the Master F.H. Meyers dated 28 July 1845 on arrival in New York.
37. Roy Alexander, Unpublished papers, letter from George Woolford 17 August 1853.
38. Roy Alexander, Unpublished papers, various correspondence.
39. P.R.O., HO 107/1686.
40. P.R.O., RG 9/725.
41. P.R.O., RG 11/1275 and P.R.O., RG 12/972.
42. P.R.O., HO 107/1686.
43. P.R.O., RG 9/742 and P.R.O., RG 10/1275.

3 LONDON AND THE OLD BAILEY, pp.27-36.

1.   Census of Great Britain, Enumeration Abstract, 1831 (printed by order of the House of Commons, 2 April 1833, 3 Vols), Vol.I, pp.365-76.
2.   George, M., London Life in the Eighteenth Century (Harmondsworth, Middlesex: Penguin Books, 1985), pp.112 and 113.
3.   Ibid., p.114.
4.   Ibid., pp.129 and 130.
5.   Mayhew, H., London Labour and the London Poor (New York: 4 Vols, Dover Publication, 1968), Vol.IV, p.29.
6.   Ibid., p.308.
7.   Davis, H.W.C., The Age of Grey and Peel (London: Oxford University Press, 1967), p.168, by permission of Oxford University Press.
8.   Rudé, George, Protest and Punishment (Oxford: Clarendon Press, 1978), p.14, by permission of Oxford University Press.
9.   Thornbury, Walter, London Recollected (London: 6 Vols, Alderman Press, 1985), Vol.II, p.462.
10. Baker, J.H., 'Criminal Courts and Procedure at Common Law 1550-1800' in J. S. Cockburn (ed.), Crime in England 1550-1800 (London: Methuen, 1977), pp.26-31.
11. Crew, Albert, The Old Bailey (London: Ivor, Nicholson and Watson, 1933), p.13.

12. Griffiths, Arthur, *The Chronicles of Newgate* (London: Bracken Books, 1987), p.4.
13. *Ibid.*, p.274.
14. *Ibid.*, pp.287-9
15. *Ibid.*, p.376.
16. Rose, June, *Elizabeth Fry* (London: Macmillan, 1980), p.69. With permission © June Rose, 1980.
17. Griffiths, Albert, *The Chronicles of Newgate* (London: Bracken Books, 1987), pp.376-9.
18. Rose, June, *Elizabeth Fry*, pp.84-9.
19. Thornbury, *London Recollected*, Vol.II, p.459.
20. Rose, *Elizabeth Fry*, p.92.
21. Griffiths, *The Chronicles of Newgate*, p.389.
22. Rose, *Elizabeth Fry*, pp.98-100.
23. *Ibid.*, p.147.
24. Bryne, Richard, *Prisons and Punishment of London*, pp.37-8.
25. Atkinson, C. M., *Jeremy Bentham* (London: Methuen & Co., 1905), p.38.
26. *Ibid.*, p.39.
27. Bryne, *Prisons and Punishments of London*, p.38.
28. Atkinson, *Jeremy Bentham*, p.144.
29. Griffiths, *The Chronicles of Newgate*, pp.556-7.
30. *Ibid.*, pp.564-5.
31. Shaw, A.G.L., *Convicts and the Colonies* (London: Faber & Faber, 1966), p.43.
32. *Ibid.*, p.49.
33. *Census of Great Britain, Enumeration Abstract*, pp.366 and 367.
34. P.R.O., PCOM 2/202 and A.O.T., CON. 15.
35. The Old Bailey Session Papers, November 1832-October 1833.
36. P.R.O., HO 77/39.
37. *The Old Bailey Session Papers*, case 679, P.R.O., PCOM 2/202, HO 77/39, HO 77/40 and HO 77/41.
38. *Ibid.*, case 1204; P.R.O., PCOM 2/202.
39. *Ibid.*, case 75.
40. *Ibid.*, case 678.
41. P.R.O., PCOM 2/202, HO 77/40.
42. *The Old Bailey Session Papers*, case 891.
43. P.R.O., PCOM 2/202 and HO 77/40.
44. *The Old Bailey Session Papers*, cases 1060,1162 and1209.
45. *Ibid.*, case 784. P.R.O., PCOM 2/202, HO 77/40 and HO 11/9.
46. *Ibid.*, case 22. P.R.O., PCOM 2/202 and HO 77/40.
47. P.R.O., HO 13/62, PCOM. 2/202 and HO 77/40.
48. P.R.O., PCOM. 2/202 and HO 77/42.
49. P.R.O., PCOM 2/202, HO 77/40, HO 77/41 and HO 77/42.
50. *The Old Bailey Session Papers*, November 1840-October 1841, case 1685 and November 1836-October 1837 case 1962; P.R.O., HO 77/48.
51. Thornbury, *London Recollected*, Vol.II, p.249.
52. Wheatley, H.B. (ed.), *John Stow's The Survey of London* (London: J.M. Dent and Sons Ltd. (1912), 1970), p.115.
53. *Census of Great Britain, Enumeration Abstract, 1831* (printed by order of the House of Commons 2 April 1833, 3 Vols), Vol.I, pp.368 and 369.
54. *Census of Great Britain, Enumeration Abstract, 1841* (London: Printed by W. Clowes and Sons for Her Majesty's Stationery Office, 1843, 3 Vols), Vol.I, pp.179 and180.
55. Christchurch, Spitalfields, Marriage Register, June 1828-August 1843, p.255.
56. St Botolph Without Aldgate, Burial Register, 1816-1836, p.105.
57. Christchurch, Spitalfields, Banns Register, 1805-1833, p.51.
58. St Botolph Without Aldgate, Baptism Register, 1822-1829 pp.127, 243 and 296.
59. Census of Great Britain, Enumeration Abstract, 1831, Vol.1, pp.378-83, 1841, Vol.3, pp.108-25.
60. Census of Great Britain, Enumeration Abstract, 1831, Vol.1, pp.368-77.
61. The Old Bailey Session Papers, November 1841-October 1842, case 1250; P.R.O., HO 77/49.

4   SHIPS, pp.37-46.

1. P.R.O., HO 8/27.
2. Hobsbawm and Rudé, *Captain Swing* (London: Lawrence & Wishart (1969), 1970), p.263 and P.R.O., HO 11/8.
3. Bateson, Charles, *The Convict Ships 1787-1868* (Glasgow: Brown, Son & Ferguson Ltd.), pp.360, 361 and 386.
4. *Ibid.*, p.87 and 88.
5. *Ibid.*, p.69.
6. P.R.O., ADM 101/13/9, ADM 101/57/7, ADM. 101/74/6, ADM 101/22/8, ADM 101/65/3, ADM 101/25/5, ADM 101/29/3 and ADM 101/19/6.
7. Bateson, *The Convict Ships 1787-1868*, pp.379-95.
8. A.O.T., CON. 18/6.
9. Robson, L.L., *A History of Tasmania, Vol.1* (Melbourne: Oxford University Press, 1983), p.166.
10. P.R.O. HO 11/9 and PCOM 2/202.
11. Bateson, *The Convict Ships 1787-1868*, pp.362, 363 and 388.
12. P.R.O., PCOM 2/202 and ATO, CON. 18/24.
13. Bateson, *The Convict Ships 1787-1868*, pp.352, 353 and 389.

14. *The Times*, 3 and 4 September 1833.
15. Bateson, *The Convict Ships 1787-1868*, pp.246-8.
16. *Ibid.*, pp.364, 365 and 392 and P.R.O., H.O. 11/12.
17. A.O.T., CON. 19/3.
18. P.R.O., PCOM 2/207.
19. P.R.O., HO 11/13, PCOM 2/207.
20. Bateson, *The Convict Ships1787-1868*, pp.366, 367 and 392.
21. P.R.O., ADM 101/65/3.
22. A.O.T., CON. 19/3.
23. A.O.T., CON. 15/2.
24. Hughes, Robert, *The Fatal Shore*, pp.283, 307 and 308.
25. West, John, *The History of Tasmania*, ed. A.G.L. Shaw (London: Angus & Robertson (1852), 1981), pp.85 and 137, published with permission of the Royal Australian Historical Society, Sydney, Australia.
26. Hughes, *The Fatal Shore*, pp.385 and 392.
27. Hobsbawm and Rudé, *Captain Swing*, p.269 and P.R.O., HO 10/48.
28. Robson, L.L., *A History of Tasmania*, p.168.
29. P.R.O., HO 10/48 and HO 10/49.
30. P.R.O., CO 283/6.
31. Hobsbawm and Rudé, *Captain Swing*, p.273.
32. P.R.O., CO 283/7.
33. Robson, *A History of Tasmania*, p.146.
34. Sweeney, Christopher, *Transported in Place of Death Convicts in Australia* (Melbourne: MacMillan Company of Australia, 1981), p.138. By permission of copyright owner C/-Curtis Brown (Aust) Pty Ltd, Sydney.
35. Bartlett, Anne, 'The Launceston Female Factory', in the *Tasmanian Historical Research Association Papers and Proceedings*, Vol.41, No.2 (Tasmania: Arts; Advisory Board, 1994), pp.114-24.
36. A.O.T., CON. 40/7.
37. A.O.T., CON. 52/1 and Chapel for the Convict Party Marriage Register.
38. P.R.O., CO 280/145 dated 22 July 1842.
39. Bateson, *The Convict Ships 1787-1868*, pp.364-7 and 392.
40. P.R.O., CO 280/145.
41. Hughes, *The Fatal Shore*, pp.523 and 524.
42. A.O.T., CON. 40/8.
43. A.O.T., Christ Church, Longford, Marriage Register.
44. A.O.T., CON. 40/4.
45. A.O.T., St John's Church, Launceston, Marriage Register.

5 LONGFORD TO TABLE CAPE, pp.47-62.

1. P.R.O., ASSI 5/152/2.
2. P.R.O., HO 8/33.
3. Bateson, Charles, *The Convict Ships 1787-1868* (Glasgow: Brown, Son & Ferguson Ltd.), pp.362, 363 and 388.
4. P.R.O., HO 11/9, HO 27/43, HO 10/49 and HO 10/50.
5. Queen Victoria Museum and Art Gallery, Launceston, Sanderson papers.
6. A.O.T., Census 1842, Norfolk Plains, Parish No. 2, return No. 3.
7. P.R.O., CO 283/26, pp.317, 318 and 320, CO 283/31, pp.2033-5 and 2037, CO 283/50, pp.339-42.
8. A.O.T., P.O.L. 20/9/1 pp.226 and 228.
9. Letter from Joseph Aloysius Alexander dated 31 August 1980.
10. P.R.O., CO 283/28, p.629, CO 283/31, p.2033 and C.O. 283/50, p.40.
11. P.R.O., CO 283/22, pp.304 and 529 and Alexandria house deeds.
12. *Cornwall Chronicle*, 4 August 1852, 21 and 25 August 1852 and *Advocate*, 7 November 1925.
13. *Advocate*, 7 November 1925.
14. Queen Victoria Museum and Art Gallery, Launceston, Sanderson papers, P.C.W. 8/9/31.
15. *Cornwall Chronicle*, 28 September, 3 and 5 October 1853 and *Advocate*, 7 November 1925.
16. MacKenzie, J.C., handwritten paper dated 1916 on his 69 years in Tasmania.
17. Stoney, *A Residence in Tasmania* (London: Smith, Elder & Co., 1856), Chap.1, p.2.
18. *Ibid.*, Chap.19, p.239.
19. *Ibid.*, p.242.
20. *Ibid.*, p.243.
21. *Ibid.*, p.244.
22. *Ibid.*, p.245.
23. *Ibid.*, pp.254/5.
24. *Ibid.*, p.256.
25. *Ibid.*, p.257.
26. *Ibid.*, p.266.
27. *Ibid.*, Chap.20, p.273.
28. *Ibid.*, p.274.
29. A.O.T. CB 7/8, pp.18 and 19.
30. West, John, *The History of Tasmania*, ed. A.G.L. Shaw (London: Angus & Robertson (1852), 1981), pp.xi-xxi, published with permission of the Royal Australian Historical Society, Sydney, Australia.

31. Queen Victoria Museum and Art Gallery, Launceston, Sanderson papers. P.R.O., CO 283/24, p.173 and CO 283/28, p.528.
32. P.R.O., CO 283/25, pp.26, 491 and 1046, CO 283/26, pp.451, 452 and 454.
33. P.R.O., CO283/25, p.64 and *Advocate*, 7 November 1925.
34. P.R.O., CO 283/28, p.733.
35. Melbourne R.O. shipping records passenger manifest- Donald McKay December, 1856.
36. Queen Victoria Museum and Art Gallery, Launceston, Sanderson papers- Kathleen Mayne, 18 August 1931.
37. *Cornwall Chronicle*, 7 July 1858.
38. *Advocate*, 7 November 1925.
39. *Launceston Examiner*, 1 March 1860 and P.R.O. CO 283/30, p.390.
40. P.R.O., CO 283/30, p.590, CO 283/32, pp.583, 585 and 586 and *Directory of Tasmania* 1867/8, p.146.
41. P.R.O., CO 283/29, p.1654 and CO 283/32, p.589; Queen Victoria Museum and Art Gallery, Launceston, Sanderson papers dated 16 February 1921; Pioneer Village Museum, Burnie, Tasmania, Rouse papers, letter to Warden of the Launceston Marine Board dated 13 May 1863.
42. Queen Victoria Museum and Art Gallery, Launceston, Sanderson papers dated 16 February 1921.
43. *Advocate*, 7 November 1925.
44. A.O.T. New Norfolk Asylum, H.S.D. 247, Admission No. 1575.
45. *Emu Bay Times*, 11 June 1898.
46. P.R.O., CO 283/30, p.47.
47. P.R.O., CO 283/31, p.2033-5 and 2037 and CO 283/50, p.339-42.
48. *Advocate*, 7 November 1925.

6 EARLY LIFE, pp.65-83.

1. Tasmanian Probate Registry, Will of Matthias Alexander.
2. P.R.O., CO 283/50, p.11.
3. *Advocate*, 17 July 1935.
4. *Directory of Tasmania*, 1867/8, p.146.
5. P.R.O., CO 283/50, p.9.
6. *Launceston Examiner*, 13 October 1880 and *Advocate*, 7 November 1925.
7. *Advocate*, 20 January 1917 and 28 January 1929.
8. Hearn, A.C., *Somerset The Cam* (Somerset: A.C. (Fuzzy) Hearn, 1992), p.23.
9. Handwritten account by Richard Hilder dated 1927.
10. *Launceston Examiner and Mercury*, 28 April 1892.
11. FMA unpublished papers.
12. *Examiner*, 30 October, 25 and 27 December 1855.
13. Pioneer Village Museum, Burnie, Tasmania, Rouse papers, various letters dated 1878.
14. P.R.O., CO 283/29, p.57, CO 283/30, p.21 and CO 283/32, p.589.
15. Hearn, *Somerset The Cam*, pp.15, 19 and 23 and *Launceston Examiner*, 4 October 1878.
16. P.R.O., CO 283/50, p.534.
17. P.R.O., CO 283/50, p.9.
18. Baillier, F.F., *Baillier's, Tasmanian Gazette and Road Guide 1877* (Melbourne: Baillier, 1877), pp.226-7.
19. *Launceston Examiner*, 29 July 1878.
20. *Ibid.*, 16 September 1878.
21. *Advocate*, 7 November 1925
22. P.R.O., CO 283/50, pp.9 and 534, CO 283/52, p.237 and *Launceston Examiner*, 21 August 1878.
23. *Launceston Examiner*, 20 November 1878.
24. *Ibid.*, 13 November 1879.
25. *Ibid.*, 25 December 1879.
26. *Ibid.*, 6 September 1880.
27. *Ibid.*, 17 November 1880.
28. FMA unpublished papers.
29. *Launceston Examiner*, 6 December 1879.
30. *Ibid.*, 7 January 1880.
31. *Ibid.*, 20 November 1879 and 7 January 1880 and FMA unpublished papers.
32. *Launceston Examiner*, 12 June 1879.
33. *Ibid.*, 19 February and 21 March 1881.
34. FMA unpublished papers.
35. *Launceston Examiner*, 24 January 1881.
36. FMA unpublished papers.
37. *Launceston Examiner*, 14 November 1881.
38. *The Australian Handbook 1890*, pp.439-40.
39. *Launceston Examiner*, 24 June 1881.
40. *Ibid.*, 26 September 1882.
41. *Ibid.*, 29 March 1881.
42. *Ibid.*, 24 January 1881.
43. *Ibid.*, 7 September and 27 October 1882.
44. *Ibid.*, 8 April 1882.
45. *Ibid.*, 30 December 1882.
46. *Ibid.*, 16 January 1883.

47. *Daily Telegraph* (Tasmania), 23 August 1883.
48. *Launceston Examiner*, 14 June 1883.
49. *Ibid.*, 8 September and 2 November 1883.
50. *Ibid.*, 25 December 1883.
51. *Ibid.*, 27 May, 27 June, 7 July and 22 August 1884.
52. *Ibid.*, 15 November 1884 and *Daily Telegraph* (Tasmania), 11 November 1884.
53. *Launceston Examiner*, 8 December 1884.
54. *Ibid.*, 1 January 1885.
55. *Daily Telegraph* (Tasmania), 17 April and 6 May 1885.
56. *Ibid.*, 23 October 1885.
57. *Ibid.*,18 March, 29 April, 29 May, 2 July, 8 September, 27 October, 21 November and 25 December 1885.
58. *Ibid.*,17 April and 29 December 1885.
59. *Ibid.*, 29 May 1885.
60. *Ibid.*, 20 October 1885.

7   WARATAH, WYNARD AND MELBOURNE, pp.83-96.

1. Robson, L.L., *A History of Tasmania, Vol. II* (Melbourne: Oxford University Press, 1991), pp.88 and 89, reproduced with permission of Oxford University Press ANZ.
2. *Launceston Examiner*, 25 July 1878.
3. *Ibid.*, 19 November 1881 and 17 March 1883.
4. *Ibid.*, 11 July 1884.
5. *Ibid.*, 19 November 1881.
6. *Daily Telegraph* (Tasmania), 25 October 1883.
7. *Launceston Examiner*, 11 July 1884.
9. *Daily Telegraph* (Tasmania), 21 July 1884.
10. *Launceston Examiner*, 4 and 8 August 1885.
11. FMA private papers, recollections of life at Waratah.
12. *Launceston Examiner*, 28 January 1886.
13. *Launceston Examiner*, 18 February and *Daily Telegraph* (Tasmania), 27 August 1886.
14. *Launceston Examiner*, 16 June 1886.
15. *Launceston Examiner*, 14 September and *Daily Telegraph* (Tasmania), 23 September 1886.
16. *Launceston Examiner*, 29 December 1886 and 1 January 1887.
17. *Ibid.*, 4 June 1887.
18. *Launceston Examiner*, 5 July and *Daily Telegraph* (Tasmania), 6 July 1886.
19. *Daily Telegraph* (Tasmania), 6 July 1886.
20. *Launceston Examiner*, 9 August 1886.
21. *Launceston Examiner*, 26 November 1886.
22. FMA private papers recollections of life at Waratah.
23. *Launceston Examiner*, 31 December 1886.
24. *Daily Telegraph* (Tasmania), 1 December 1886.
25. *Ibid.*, 20 October 1886.
26. *Ibid.*, 12 November 1886.
27. *Ibid.*, 1 December 1886.
28. *Launceston Examiner*, 14 May and *Daily Telegraph* (Tasmania), 19 May 1886.
29. *Daily Telegraph* (Tasmania), 13 and 18 February 1886.
30. *Ibid.*, 24 February 1886.
31. *Ibid.*, 1 December 1886.
32. *Launceston Examiner*, 13 May 1887.
33. *Launceston Examiner*, 7 July and *Daily Telegraph* (Tasmania), 4 July 1887.
34. *Launceston Examiner*, 24 June and *Daily Telegraph* (Tasmania), 28 June 1887.
35. *Daily Telegraph* (Tasmania), 23 June 1887.
36. *Launceston Examiner*, 29 April and *Daily Telegraph* (Tasmania), 22 April 1887.
37. *Launceston Examiner*, 15 July 1887.
38. *Ibid.*, 16 and 29 April 1887.
39. *Ibid.*, 2 June, 13 August, 9 September and 4 October 1887.
40. *Daily Telegraph* (Tasmania), 2 and 30 April 1887.
41. *Launceston Examiner*, 7 October and *Daily Telegraph* (Tasmania), 6 October 1887.
42. *Launceston Examiner*, 25 January, 3, 5 and 21 March, 4, 6 and 28 April, 26 May, 10 September, 22 October and *Daily Telegraph* (Tasmania), 5 and 16 July, 12 September and 13 October 1888.
43. *Launceston Examiner*, 19 March and 18 April and *Daily Telegraph* (Tasmania), 8 August 1888.
44. *Daily Telegraph* (Tasmania), 15 March 1888.
45. *Launceston Examiner*, 3 February 1888.
46. Pink, Kerry, *And Wealth for Toil* (Burnie, Tasmania: *Advocate* Marketing Services Pty Ltd., 1990), p.284 and *Launceston Examiner*, 4 May 1888.
47. *Daily Telegraph* (Tasmania), 3 August 1888.
48. *Ibid.*, 19 March 1888.
49. *Launceston Examiner*, 23 and 29 March and *Daily Telegraph* (Tasmania), 23 March 1888.
50. *Daily Telegraph* (Tasmania), 26 March 1888.

51. *Launceston Examiner*, 20 April and *Daily Telegraph* (Tasmania), 20 April 1888.
52. *Launceston Examiner*, 11 February and *Daily Telegraph* (Tasmania), 5 March 1888.
53. *Launceston Examiner*, 6 September 1888.
54. *Daily Telegraph* (Tasmania), 29 December 1888.
55. FMA unpublished papers.
56. FMA unpublished papers.
57. Davison, G., *The Rise and Fall of Marvellous Melbourne* (Melbourne: Melbourne University Press, 1979), p.229.
58. *The Times*, 2 April 1890.
59. Cannon, M., *The Land Bloomers* (Melbourne: Melbourne University Press (1966), 1967), p.17.
60. *The Times*, 5 April 1890.
61. *Argus*, 3 June 1891.
62. *Ibid.*, 1 June 1891.
63. *Ibid.*, 16 June 1891.
64. *Ibid.*, 23 June 1891.
65. Cannon, *The Land Bloomers*, pp.22 and 28.
66. Davison, *Marvellous Melbourne*, p.247.
67. F MA unpublished papers.
68. *Launceston Examiner*, 11 June 1892.
69. *Launceston Examiner*, 2 May 1894 and FMA unpublished papers.
70. *Hobart Mercury*, 22 June 1894.
71. *Ibid.*
72. Alexander, F.M., *The Use of the Self* (London: Methuen & Co. Ltd., 1932), pp.3-36.

8 FAMILY LIFE IN WYNARD AND ALEXANDER THE RECITER, pp.97-111.

1. *Launceston Examiner*, 17 August 1889, 4 April and 24 December 1990.
2. *Ibid.*, 7 January 1893.
3. *Ibid.*, 4 and 8 November 1890.
4. *Ibid.*, 18 October 1890 and 24 December 1891.
5. *Ibid.*, 26 January 1889, June and 24 December 1890, 15 June and 24 September 1892.
6. *Ibid.*, 12 June 1890, 12 May 1891 and 19 June 1893.
7. *Ibid.*, 6 November and 15 April 1890.
8. *Ibid.*, 4 November 1890.
9. *Ibid.*, 14 and 30 May, 30 September 1890, 18 March, 29 April and 27 October 1892, 20 February and 19 June 1893.
10. *Ibid.*, 31 May, 1 July, 24 and 29 September 1892, 21 March, 16 and 19 June and 29 July 1893.
11. *Ibid.*, April 1890,1891, 1892, 1893 and *Advocate*, 19 October 1931.
12. *Launceston Examiner*, 16 July and 16 November 1889, 22 April 1890, 5 November 1891, 18 March and 29 July 1893.
13. *Ibid.*, 6, 7, and 8 January 1890 and 13 January 1893.
14. *Ibid.*, 28 March 1889.
15. *Ibid.*, 22 March and 20 December 1890 and 23 March 1891.
16. *Ibid.*, 28 December 1891, 4 January, 18, 22 and 23 March 1892.
17. *Ibid.*, 27 December 1892, 4 January, 20, 22,and 24 March, 25 May, 27 and 29 December 1893 and *Wellington Times*, 22 October 1892.
18. *Launceston Examiner*, 22 May, 22 July 1891, 16 September and 10 October 1892, 7, 8 and 26 April, 1893 and *Wellington Times*, 24 December 1891 and 12 and 26 May 1892.
19. *Launceston Examiner*, 13 March 1893.
20. *Ibid.*,10 February 1894.
21. *Ibid.*, 22 February and 15 March 1894.
22. *Ibid.*, 11 and 21 May and 20 June 1894.
23. *Ibid.*,10 May 1889, 17 and 21 February 1891 and 2 June 1893.
24. P.R.O., CO 283/31.
25. P.R.O., CO 283/50.
26. Unpublished Page letters.
27. *Hobart Mercury*, 16 February 1895.
28. *Ibid.*, 21 July 1894.
29. *Ibid.*, 14 August 1894.
30. *Ibid.*, 8 October and 11 December 1894.
31. *Launceston Examiner*, 12 November 1894.
32. *Ibid.*, 12 September 1894.
33. FMA unpublished papers.
34. 'Elocution Entertainment', extract from *Christchurch Press* (New Zealand), 3 April 1895.
35. *New Zealand Times*, 7 and 9 May 1895, *Evening Post*, 7 and 9 May 1895.
36. *Daily Telegraph* (NZ), 14 May 1895, *Hawkes Bay Herald*, 14 May 1895.
37. *Daily Telegraph* (NZ), 9, 10 or 11 May 1895.
38. *Ibid.*, 16 May 1895 and *Hawkes Bay Herald*, 16 May 1895.
39. *Hawkes Bay Herald*, 16 May 1895.
40. *Auckland Star*, 23 May 1895, *New Zealand Herald*, 11 June 1895 and *Evening Star*, 14 June 1895.
41. *New Zealand Herald*, 18 June 1895.
42. *Auckland Star*, 18 June 1895.
43. *Ibid.*, 24 June 1895.

44. *Ibid.*, 27 June 1895.
45. *Launceston Examiner*, 24 and 25 July 1895.
46. *New Zealand Herald*, 21 November 1895.
47. *Argus*, 15 February and 21 March 1896.
48. *Ibid.*, 11 and 18 July 1896.
49. *Ibid.*, 3, 10, 17 and 26 October, 7, 10 and 14 November and 4 December 1896.
50. *Launceston Examiner*, 26 and 30 January 1897.
51. *Ibid.*, 20, 21, 22 and 30 January 1897.
52. *Ibid.*, 1 March 1897, *Wellington Times* (Tasmania), 27 February and 13 March 1897.

9   TEACHING IN MELBOURNE AND SYDNEY, pp.113-30.

1. *Argus*, 13 March 1897.
2. McCullock, Samuel Clyde, *Australian Dictionary of Biography 1851-1890 Vol.5* (Melbourne: Melbourne University Press, 1974), eds. Nairne, B., Serle, G. and Ward, R., pp.143-4.
3. Foster L., *Australian Dictionary of Biography 1891-1939 Vol.11* (Melbourne: Melbourne University Press, 1988), ed. Serle, G., pp.422-3.
4. Johns, F., *Notable Australians and Who is Who in Australasia* (Adelaide: Fred Johns, 1908).
5. *Argus*, 9 May 1897.
6. *Ibid.*, 21 August 1897.
7. *Ibid.*, 25 September 1897.
8. *Ibid.*, September, October and November 1897 and January, February and March 1898.
9. FMA, unpublished programme and costings for 25 March 1898.
10. *Launceston Examiner*, 19 June 1895.
11. *Argus*, May 1898.
12. *Hobart Mercury*, 4 and 5 December 1894.
13. *Argus*, 4 June and 12 August 1898.
14. *Ibid.*, 12 and 14 May 1898
15. *Ibid.*, 24 June 1898.
16. *Adelaide Advertiser*, 21 and 22 July 1898.
17. *Launceston Examiner*, 9 and 14 January and 11 February 1899.
18. *Ibid.*, 8 July 1899.
19. *Argus*, 21 October 1899.
20. *Age*, 28 August 1899.
21. *Melbourne Punch*, 2 September 1899.
22. *Ibid.*, September 1899.
23. *Launceston Examiner*, 2 September 1899.
34. *Argus*, 2 September 1899.
25. *Bendigo Advertiser*, 4 October 1899.
26. *Ibid.*, 5, 6 and7 October 1899.
27. *Argus*, 2 October 1899.
28. *Ibid.*, 11 October 1899.
29. *Ibid.*, 24 October 1899.
30. *Launceston Examiner*, 1 November 1899.
31. *Argus*, 28 and 30 October 1899.
32. *Ibid.*, 23 December 1899.
33. *Sydney Daily Telegraph*, 17 March and 21 April 1900.
34. FMA Sydney Booklet.
35. *Sydney Daily Telegraph*, 21 July 1900.
36. *Ibid.*, 4 August 1900.
37. *Ibid.*, 18 August 1900.
38. *Ibid.*, 2 September 1900.
39. *Ibid.*, 17 September 1900.
40. *Evening News* (Australia), *Sydney Daily Telegraph*, *Sydney Morning Herald*, and *Sydney Mail*, 3,15 and 17 September and 1 October 1900.
41. *Sydney Morning Herald*, 6 January 1948.
42. *Sydney Daily Telegraph* and *Sydney Morning Herald*, 31 December 1900.
43. R. Young unpublished letters.
44. CRS B5179 (b) Dept of Defence, Central Army Records Office, Muster Roll of the Fifth Contingent for Service in South Africa, p.14.
45. *Argus*, 15 January and 4 February 1901.
46. *Ibid.*, 5 and 16 February 1901.
47. *Ibid.*, 19 June 1901.
48. *Ibid.*, 17-21 July 1901.
49. *Ibid.*, 2 October 1901.
50. *Ibid.*, 19, 21 and 28 April 1901.
51. Official Records of the Australian Military Contingents to the War in South Africa, ed. by P.L. Murray, pp.274-7 and 297.
52. *Argus*, 4 May 1901.
53. *Ibid.*, 10 and 17 January 1903 and letter AR to FMA, 28 January 1905.
54. *Sydney Daily Telegraph* and *Sydney Morning Herald*, 19 June 1901.
55. *Sydney Daily Telegraph*, 9 and 16 February and 2 March 1901.

56. *Sydney Daily Mail*, 6 July and FMA Scrapbook, *Sydney Morning Herald* and *Evening News* (Australia), 28 June 1901.
57. *Sydney Daily Telegraph*, 25, 26 September, 1,2,4 and 5 October 1901.
58. *Ibid.*, 16 and 22 November 1901.
59. Johns, F., *Who is Who in Australia* (Adelaide: Fred Johns, 1903), p.230.
60. *Sydney Daily Telegraph*, 30 November 1901.
61. FMA Sydney Dramatic and Operatic Conservatorium Prospectus, *Sydney Daily Telegraph*, 4, 11, 18 and 25 January 1902 and *Sydney Morning Herald*, 18 January 1902.
62. *Coota Liberal*, 6 August 1902.
63. *Daily Free Press* (Australia), 17 June 1902.
64. *National Advocate* (Australia), 17 June 1902
65. *Bathurst Daily Times* and *Bathurst Daily Free Press*, 18 June 1902.
66. *Orange Leader* 18 June 1902.
67. *Cowra Free Press* (Australia), 7 August 1902.
68. FMA Scrapbook.
69. *Sydney Daily Telegraph*, 24 October 1902.
70. *Sydney Morning Herald*, 29 November 1902 and *Sydney Daily Telegraph*, numerous throughout 1903.
71. *Wagga Wagga Express*, 12 July 1903.
72. *Sydney Daily Telegraph*, 5 and 12 December 1903.
73. *Ibid.*, 12 December 1903.
74. *Ibid.*, 13 February 1904.
75. *Argus*, 10 and 17 January 1903 and AR letter to FMA 28 January 1905.
76. *Ibid.*, 14 March 1903.
77. *Ibid.*, 16 April 1904.
78. *Launceston Examiner*, 29 February and 2 March 1904.

10   LONDON AND MELBOURNE, pp.133-50.

1. *Sydney Daily Telegraph*, 12, 13 and 14 April 1904.
2. *Ibid.*, 16, 19 and 22 April 1904.
3. *Hobart Mercury*, 25 April 1904.
4. *The Times*, 19 May 1904.
5. *Ibid.*, 23 May 1904.
6. *Ibid.*, 8, 13 and 15 June 1904.
7. Mitchell, B.R., and Deane, P., *Abstract of British Historical Statistics* (Cambridge, 1962), p.60, and Mitchell B.R., *British Historical Statistics* (Cambridge, 1988), p.104 in Thompson, F.M.L. (ed.), *The Cambridge Social History of Britain 1750-1950, Vol.2* (Cambridge: Cambridge University Press, 1990), pp.133-135.
8. *Evening Standard Theatre Guide*, 1994.
9. FMA Scrapbook, advertising pamphlets produced circa 1907 and 1910.
10. *Morning Post*, 7 March 1907.
11. *Pall Mall Gazette*, 14 March 1908.
12. Alexander, F.M., *Conscious Control in Relation to Human Evolution in Civilization* (London: Methuen & Co. Ltd., 1912), p.x.
13. FMA Scrapbook, Alexander Leeper, Report on Physical Culture, extracts printed 8 March 1909.
14. The Medical Directory, 77th Edition (London: J. & A. Churchill Ltd., 1921), p.321.
15. *Pall Mall Gazette*, 19 October 1909.
16. Alexander, F.M., *Why We Breathe Incorrectly* (London: November 1909).
17. Alexander, F.M., *A Protest* (London: April 1910).
18. FMA private papers.
19. FMA Scrapbook, Alexander Leeper, Report on Physical Culture, extracts printed 8 March 1909.
20. Alexander, F.M., *Man's Supreme Inheritance* (London: Methuen & Co. Ltd., 1910), p.x.
21. *Sydney Daily Telegraph*, 16 March 1911.
22. *Sydney Morning Herald*, 18 March 1911.
23. *Argus*, 20 and 24 March 1911.
24. *Hobart Mercury*, 27, 28 and 30 March 1911.
25. *The Times*, 3 and 5 May 1911.
26. Electoral Roll for St Kilda, 1912.

11   THE FIRST WORLD WAR, pp.151-69.

1. Newnham College Register 1871-1923, Vol.1.
2. *Ibid.*
3. Froebel Archive for Childhood Studies, Froebel College, Roehampton.
4. *The Medical Directory*, 77th Edition (London: J. & A. Churchill Ltd., 1921), p.297, and *The Medical Directory*, 102nd Edition (London: J. & A. Churchill Ltd., 1946), p.271.
5. Butler, K.T. and McMorran, H.I. (eds.), *The Girton College Register 1869-1946* (Cambridge: printed privately for Girton College, 1948), p.1907, the late Miss M. Goldie and Tasker, I., *Connecting Links* (London: Sheildrake Press, 1978).
6. Mechin, G., 1914 Diary.
7. *Ibid.*
8. *Ibid.*

9. Gilbert, M., *First World War* (London: Weidenfeld and Nicolson, 1994), pp.36 and 43.
10. *Ibid.*, p.57, and Keegan, J., *The First World War* (London: Hutchinson, 1998), p.108.
11. Keegan, J., *The First World War*, pp.112 and 113.
12. Laffin, J., *A Western Front Companion 1914-1918* (Stroud, Gloucestershire: Alan Sutton Publishing Ltd., 1994), p.104 and Gilbert, *First World War*, pp.72-75.
13. Gilbert, *First World War*, pp.84 and 157.
14. *Ibid.*, p.245, and Laffin, *A Western Front Companion*, pp.38, 41 and 44.
15. Laffin, *A Western Front Companion*, p.41.
16. Gilbert, *First World War* (London: Weidenfeld and Nicolson, 1994), pp.92-99.
17. Keegan, J., *The First World War*, pp.143 and 146.
18. Gilbert, M., *First World War* (London: Weidenfeld and Nicolson, 1994), pp.102, 104, 105, 110, 119 and 125.
19. Keegan, J., The First World War, pp. 214 and 215, and Liddell Hart, B.H., *History of the First World War* (London: Papermac (Faber & Faber, 1930), 1997), pp.183 and 185.
20. Gilbert, M., *First World War* (London: Weidenfeld and Nicolson, 1994), pp.213 and 226.
21. *Ibid.*, p.226.
22. *Advocate*, 19 November 1985.
23. Gilbert, *First World War*, p.138.
24. *This England* magazine, Autumn 1996, pp.12 and 13.
25. Gilbert, *First World War*, pp.202-3.
26. *Who's Who in America 1930-1931*, Vol.16, ed. Marquis, A.N., (Chicago: The A N Marquis Co., 1930), p.680.
27. Gilbert, *First World War*, pp.251-252.
28. *Ibid.*, p.237.
29. *Ibid.*, pp.232 and 234, and Keegan, The First World War, pp.300-8.
30. Gilbert, M., *First World War*, pp.224-5.
31. *Ibid.*, p.224.
32. Laffin, *A Western Front Companion*, pp.38 and 44.
33. Liddell Hart, *History of the First World War*, p.226.
34. Keegan, J., *The First World War*, pp.317 and 318.
35. *Ibid.*, p.321, Gilbert, *First World War*, p.299, and Liddell Hart, *History of the First World War*, p.247.
36. Gilbert, M., *First World War*, pp.198, 266 and 286.
37. *Ibid.*, p.253.
38. *Ibid.*, p.300.
39. Alexander, F.M., *Man's Supreme Inheritance*, 2nd edition (London: Chaterson Ltd., 1943 (printed in USA 1918)), pp.159 and 174.
40. Gilbert, *First World War*, p.274.
41. FMA private papers.
42. Tasker, I., *Connecting Links* (London: Sheildrake Press, 1978).
43. Gilbert, *First World War*, pp.279 and 328, and Liddell Hart, *History of the First World War*, pp.308-10.
44. Liddell Hart, *History of the First World War*, pp.319-321, and Keegan, *The First World War*, pp.351 and 352.
45. Keegan, J., *The First World War*, pp.353-5.
46. *Ibid.*, pp.355-7.
47. *Ibid.*, pp.358-69.
48. Liddell Hart, *History of the First World War*, p.323, and Brittain, Vera, *Testament of Youth* (London: Virago Press Ltd. 1978, first published Victor Gollancz Ltd., 1933), p.356.
49. Gilbert, *First World War*, pp.336 and 337.
50. *Ibid.*, pp.363-5, 367, 369-70 and 377, and Keegan, *The First World War*, p.394.
51. Keegan, *The First World War*, pp.395-7, and Liddell Hart, *History of the First World War*, 1997), pp.337-48.
52. Liddell Hart, *History of the First World War*, p.366.
53. *New York Evening Post*, 5 January, *New York Times*, 20 January and *Richmond Times Dispatch*, Virginia, 25 January 1918.
54. *New York Herald*, February, *St Louis Globe*, 16 February, *New York Times*, 17 February, *Indianapolis Star*, 17 February, *Boston Evening Transcript*, 23 February, *Philadelphia Telegraph*, 2 March, *Boston Herald*, 16 March, *Brooklyn Daily Eagle*, 16 March, *Pittsburg Dispatch*, 18 March, *Chicago Daily News*, 18 March, *Springfield Republican*, March and *Springfield Union*, 24 March 1918.
55. *New Republic*, 11 and 22 May 1918.
56. *Dial*, 6 June, *Washington Herald*, 9 June, *Baltimore Sun*, 22 June, *St Louis Republican*, 22 June, *Chicago Evening Post*, 6 July, University of Chicago Press, July and *Indianapolis Times*, 29 July.
57. *Chicago Tribune*, 9 February 1919.
58. *New Republic*, May 1918 and *Dial*, June 1918.
59. Tasker, I., *Connecting Links* (London: Sheildrake Press, 1978).
60. Liddell Hart, *History of the First World War*, pp.367-71.
61. Gilbert, M., *First World War*, p.247.
62. *Ibid.*, p.427 and Keegan, *The First World War*, pp.437-40.
63. Gilbert, *First World War*, p.499.
64. *Ibid.*, p.541, and Keegan, *The First World War*, pp.451-3.
65. Gilbert, *First World War*, p.351.
66. Laffin, *A Western Front Companion 1914-1918*, pp.181, 192 and 197.
67. Gilbert, *First World War*, p.222.
68. Chapman, Guy (ed.), *Vain Glory* (London: Cassell & Co. Ltd., 1937), pp.706 and 707. Attempts to trace the copyright holder of this book have been unsuccessful.
69. Pepys, Samuel, jun, *A Last Diary of the Great War* (London: John Lane, 1919), pp.268-71.

12. THE 1920s, pp.170-185.

1. Laffin, J., *A Western Front Companion 1914-1918* (Stroud, Gloucestershire: Alan Sutton Publishing Ltd., 1994), pp.44 and 45.
2. Gilbert, M., *First World War* (London: Weidenfeld and Nicolson, 1994), p.540.
3. Letter Robinson to FMA, 1 March 1919.
4. *The National Cyclopaedia of American Biography being the History of the United States, Vol. XXVII* (James T. White & Co., 1940), pp.194 and 195.
5. Matunck, R.I., *Forward and Up at Fifty*, Carla Atkinston, a pamphlet dated summer 1943.
6. Erika Whittacker née Schumann.
7. FMA Diary 1922.
8. *The Medical Directory, 77th Edition* (London: J. & A. Churchill Ltd., 1921), p.883 and *The Medical Directory*, 102nd Edition (London: J. & A. Churchill Ltd., 1946), p.937.
9. Alexander, F.M., *Universal Constant in Living* (New York: E.P. Dutton & Co. Inc., 1942), p.210.
10. *The Medical Directory, 77th Edition*, p.891.
11. *New Republic*, 24 January 1923.
12. *London Gazette*, 11 December 1923, pp.8696 and 8698 and 24 January 1924, p.938.
13. Methuen receipts 1924.
14. Tasker, I., *Connecting Links* (London: Sheildrake Press, 1978).
15. Bexley Local Studies and Archive Centre, Catalogue of freehold estate William Steele Esq., 1761.
16. P.R.O. IR 58/6248.
17. Bexley Local Studies and Archive Centre, Lamorbey Electoral Roll, 1924.
18. Bexley Local Studies and Archive Centre, Bexley Rate Book, Upton Road, 8 April 1925.
19. *The Times*, *Daily Telegraph* and *Daily Graphic*, 26 July 1923, *Daily News*, 27 July 1923 and *Daily Express*, 28 July 1923.
20. *British Medical Journal*, 24 May 1924.
21. *Lancet*, 17 and 21 June 1924.
22. *Literary Guide*, October 1925.
23. Dale, Dr. H.H., 'Introductory note in Memoriam Rudolf Magnus' (1873-1927), *Lane Lectures on Experimental Pharmacology and Medicine* (California: Stanford University Press, 1930), pp.241-247.
24. *Chambers Biographical Directory Vol.2* (Edinburgh: W. and R. Chambers, 1974), p.173.
25. *British Medical Journal*, 25 December 1926.
26. *Ibid.*, 29 May 1926
27. *Journal of School of Hygiene and Physical Education*, March 1927.
28. *London Evening Standard*, 17 March 1928.
29. *British Medical Journal*, 17 March and 5 May 1928.
30. *The Times Educational Supplement*, 28 April, 12 and 19 May and 14 July 1928.
31. *Who's Who*, 1948 (London: Adam & Charles Black, 1948).
32. *The Medical Directory, 102nd Edition* (London: J. & A. Churchill Ltd., 1946), p.192.
33. Alexander, F.M., *The Use of the Self* (London: Methuen & Co. Ltd., 1932), p.vii.
34. *The Statesman*, Calcutta, 25 May 1928.
35. *British Medical Journal*, letters dated 13 and 23 October and 9 November 1928.
36. *Ibid.*, 16 November 1929.
37. *Ibid.*, *The Medical Directory, 92nd Edition* (1936), p.695 and *The Medical Directory*, 102nd Edition, p.636, and *British Medical Journal*, 7 December 1929.
38. *Brooklyn Citizen*, 27 June 1929.
39. Letter by FMA dated 22 July 1930 published in *A New Technique* (London: Watts & Co., 1935).
40. The late Miss M. Goldie.
41. 'Alexander Times', 1929.
42. *Ibid.*, 1931, and Tasker, *Connecting Links*, 1978.
43. Alexander, *The Use of the Self*, pp.125-33.
44. *Women's Employment*, June 1931.
45. *London Gazette*, 11 March 1927, pp.1665, 1669 and 1670.

13 THE DEVELOPMENT OF THE WORK, pp.186-99.

1. Whittaker, Erika, FM Alexander Memorial Lecture, 26 October 1985.
2. Letter McInnes to Tasker dated 10 December 1939.
3. AUSTAT Journal Vol.1, No.2, 1987.
4. Westfeldt, L., *F. Matthias Alexander The Man and his Work* (London: George Allen & Unwin Ltd., 1964), pp.1, 31-3 and 46.
5. Interview Margaret Goldie 1995.
6. *Alexander Journal* No.11 Spring 1991 and *National Trust Magazine* No.76 Autumn 1995.
7. The Life of Countess Catherine 'Kitty' Meyrick Wieloposka as told at interview to Joe Armstrong.
8. *Alexander Journal* No.9 Summer 1988; Pat McDonald Memorial Lecture, 1963.
9. Old Vic programme dated 5 December 1933.
10. Old Vic programme dated 13 November 1934.
11. Whittaker, Erika, 'The First Training Course', *Alexander Review* (Australia), Vol.2, No.3, September 1987.
12. Letter Matheson Lang to FMA dated 26 November 1909.
13. Rudolf Steiner Hall programme dated 3 December 1935.
14. Alexander, F.M., *The Use of the Self* (London: Methuen & Co. Ltd., 1932), p.x.
15. *The Statesman* (Calcutta), 17 February 1932.

16. The *Student Movement*, May 1932.
17. *British Medical Journal*, 4,18 and 25 June and 9 July 1932.
18. *Medical World*, 7 October 1932 and *The Listener*, 14 December 1932.
19. Alexander, F.M., *The Universal Constant in Living* (New York: E.P. Dutton & Co. Inc., 1942), p.viii.
20. Letter Norman Coaker to Tasker and Tasker, I., *Connecting Links* (London: Sheldrake Press, 1978), p.24.
21. Tasker, *Connecting Links*, p.24.
22. *Ibid.*, p. 23.
23. *Ibid.*, p.24 and various letters from pupils.
24. The *Star* (South Africa), 7 June 1938.
25. AUSTAT Journal Vol.1, No.2, 1987.
26. Westfeldt, *F. Matthias Alexander The Man and his Work*, p.95.
27. *Alexander Journal*, No.11 Spring 1991.
28. Notes written by George Trevelyan, October 1936.
29. Fenton, J., *Bushlife in Tasmania* (Launceston, Tasmania: Regal Publications (1989), originally published by Hazell, Watson and Viney Ltd., London in 1891), p.x.
30. Pink, Kerry, *And Wealth for Toil* (Burnie, Tasmania: *Advocate* Marketing Services Pty Ltd., 1990), pp.263, 264 and 284.
31. Interview with Terry J. McKenna, grandson of Ben McKenna 1987 and letter dated 17 September 2000.
32. Shaw, George Bernard, Preface in *London Music in 1883-1889 as heard by Corno di Bassetto* (London: Constable, 1937).
33. *British Journal of Physical Medicine,* February 1935 and *British Medical Journal*, 27 June 1936.
34. The *New Era*, February 1936.
35. FMA Scrapbook; the lecture given on 17 October 1936 was published in 'Labour Management', the Journal of the Institute.
36. *British Medical Journal*, 20 November 1937.
37. *British Medical Journal*, 29 May 1937.
38. *Brooklyn Citizen*, 27 January 1937.
39. *Ibid.*, 29 March 1938.
40. Methuen & Co. receipts January to June 1938.
41. Fred Watts printing bills period to 31 Dec. 1938 dated 23 Feb. 1939.
42. Whittaker, FM Alexander Memorial Lecture.
43. Alexander, F.M., *Man's Supreme Inheritance*, 2nd edition (London: Chaterson Ltd.,1943, printed in USA (1918)), p.137.

14   THE SECOND WORLD WAR, pp.201-17.

1. Evans, Joan (née Mechin), 70th Birthday Invitation and Menu Card.
2. Letter FMA to Tasker dated 29 January 1939
3. Evans, Joan, 1939 Diary.
4. *British Medical Journal*, 17 June, 1 and 15 July and 19 August 1939.
5. *Brooklyn Citizen*, dated 7 April 1939.
6. Herrick, C. Judson, *George Ellett Coghill Naturalist and Philosopher* (Chicago, Illinois: The University of Chicago Press, 1949), pp.7-74. Published with permission from The University of Chicago, copyright 1949 by University of Chicago.
7. *Ibid.*, pp.109-10.
8. *Ibid.*, pp.117 and 118.
9. *Ibid.*, pp.134 and 135.
10. *Ibid.*, p.107.
11. *Ibid.*, p.123.
12. *Brooklyn Citizen*, 7 April, 1 and 12 May 1939.
13. Letter FMA to Tasker dated 1 and 3 September 1939.
14. *Ibid.*, dated 14 October 1939.
15. *Ibid.*, dated 16 December 1939 and 29 March 1940.
16. *Ibid.*, dated 27 December 1939.
17. *Literary Guide*, March 1940.
18. *Medical Press and Circular*, 3 April 1940.
19. Letter FMA to Tasker dated 23 May 1940.
20. *Ibid.*, dated 22 June 1940.
21. *Ibid.*, dated 28 June 1940.
22. Evans, Joan, 1940 Diary.
23. P.R.O., ADM 199/2208 and the late Miss E.A.M. Goldie recollections of the journey.
24. P.R.O., ADM 199/2208.
25. Gilbert, M., *Second World War* (London: Phoenix Giant (Weidenfeld and Nicolson, 1989), 1996), p.108.
26. Letter FMA to Tasker dated 10 July 1940.
27. P.R.O., ADM 199/2208.
28. *Ibid.*, and letter FMA to Carrington dated 10 July 1940.
29. FMA/Barlow dated 28 July, 17 August and one undated July/early August 1940.
30. Bexley Local Studies and Archive Centre, Post 22 Log Book of Air Raid Incidents in Birchwood Ward (Area 4), Official Record for Major H. Allen; List of Incidents up to December 1943, dated January 1944, Westminster Archives, Bomb incidents, 7 September 1940 HE bomb in Carlisle Place.
31. Carrington, W., *The Foundations of Human Well* (London: STAT Books, 1994) and letters FMA to Carrington dated 11 October 1940 and 22 February 1941.
32. Letter FMA to Tasker dated 15 September 1940.
33. Letters FMA to Barlow dated 27 September and 10 October 1940 and FMA to Tasker dated 15 and 22 October 1940.

34. *The Villager*, 27 March 1980, p.3, 'Historic Homes of Stow' by Kathy Olohan.
35. Letters various FMA to Tasker, Carrington & Barlow.
36. *Boston Evening Transcript*, 29 January 1941.
37. Bexley Local Studies and Archive Centre, Post 22 Log Book of Air Raid Incidents in Birchwood Ward (Area 4), Official Record for Major H. Allen.
38. Gilbert, *Second World War*, p.148.
39. Bexley Local Studies and Archive Centre, Post 22 Log Book of Air Raid Incidents in Birchwood Ward (Area 4), Official Record for Major H. Allen; List of Incidents up to December 1943, dated January 1944, including cuttings from *Kentish Times* newspaper.
40 Letters FMA to Barlow dated 24 August, 10, 18 and 27 September 1940.
41. Letters FMA to Carrington dated 30 October and 5 December 1940.
42. Letters FMA to Tasker dated 3 February, 7 April and 22 May, Carrington dated 24 January and 22 February and Joan Mechin dated 22 March 1941.
43. Bexley Local Studies and Archive Centre, List of Incidents up to December 1943, dated January 1944; Westminster Archives, Bomb incidents, 17 Ashley Place 17 April 1941; and letters FMA to Tasker dated 3 June and 3 August, Joan Mechin dated 30 June and Barlow dated 10 and 26 May 1941.
44. Gilbert, *Second World War*, p.179.
45. Mechin, Joan, 1941 Diary, letter FMA to Joan Mechin dated 30 June and to Tasker dated 3 July 1941.
46. Alexander, F.M., *Universal Constant in Living* (London: Methuen & Co. Ltd., 1942), pp.xxi-xxviii.
47. *Chambers Biographical Directory Vol. 2* (Edinburgh: W. and R. Chambers, 1974), p.1173.
48. *The Times*, 24 November 1988 and the *Guardian*, 25 November 1988.
49. Letters FMA to Tasker dated 3 and 22 July and 3 August and Barlow dated 10 and 26 May 1941.
50. WHO magazine, September 1941.
51. Letters FMA to Barlow dated 28 October and 8 December 1941.
52. *Ibid.*, dated 17 November 1941 and to Carrington dated 25 November 1941.
53. Extract from *The Second World War* by John Keegan, p.261, originally published by Hutchinson. Reprinted by permission of The Random House Group Limited © John Keegan/1990.
54. Letters FMA to Barlow dated 16 February and 27 March 1942.
55. Letters FMA to Barlow dated 18 January, 2 June and 20 July 1942, to Douglas various letters dated June 42-February 43 and Tasker dated 27 July 1942.
56. Letters FMA to Tasker dated 27 July, Barlow dated 21 September, 11 October and 1 December, Carrington dated 11 November and Joan Mechin dated 10 November 1942.
57. Letters FMA to Barlow dated 28 December 1942 and 19 May 1943.
58. Extract from *The Second World War*, by John Keegan, p.121, originally published by Hutchinson. Reprinted by permission of The Random House Group Limited © John Keegan/1990.
59. Letter FMA to Douglas dated 13 July 1943.

15 THE SOUTH AFRICAN CASE, pp.218-33.

1. Keegan, J., *The Second World War* (London: Hutchinson, 1989), pp.187 and 234-7.
2. *Ibid.*, p.346.
3. Letter FMA to Douglas dated 4 August 1943.
4. *The Commercial Law Report* (Cape Town and Johannesburg: Juta & Co. Ltd., November 1949), article by Norman Coaker, pp.655 and 656.
5. *Star*, 19 April 1943.
6. *Ibid.*, 30 June 1943.
7. Letter FMA to Annie Alexander dated 11 September 1943.
8. Keegan, *The Second World War*, pp.299-301 and 353 and Gilbert, M., *Second World War* (London: Phoenix Giant (Weidenfeld and Nicolson, 1989), 1996), pp.473 and 481-2.
9. Letter FMA to Douglas dated 19 January and 25 March and Carrington dated 3 June 1944.
10. Letter Douglas to FMA dated 16 November 1943.
11. Letters FMA to Douglas dated 15 November 1943 and 5 January 1944.
12. Letter Coaker to Messrs. Hardy Philip and Scott-Brown dated 19 July 1944.
13. Gilbert, *Second World War*, pp.496, 526 and 531.
14. Keegan, *The Second World War*, p.438.
15. Gilbert, *Second World War*, pp.539-41.
16. Letters FMA to Douglas dated August and September 1944.
17. Bexley Local Studies and Archive Centre, Post 22 Log Book of Air Raid Incidents in Birchwood Ward (Area 4). Official Record for Major H. Allen, and List of Incidents in Sidcup area.
18. Letter Cripps to FMA dated 8 September 1944.
19. Detailed in the Evidence given to the Commission in London.
20. Letters Lytton to FMA dated 22 September 1944 and FMA to Douglas dated 13 October 1944.
21. Letter FMA to the South African High Commissioner dated 9 October 1944.
22. P.R.O. AIR 27/2121 No. 614 Squadron Form 540.
23. Walter Carrington.
24. Letter FMA to Douglas dated November 1944.
25. Gilbert, *Second World War*, pp.593, 596, 602, 604 and 618.
26. Bexley Local Studies and Archive Centre, Post 22 Log Book of Air Raid Incidents in Birchwood Ward (Area 4). Official Record for Major H. Allen, pp.93-9.
27. Gilbert, *Second World War*, pp.589 and 653.
28. Letter FMA to Jones dated February 1945.

29. Bexley Local Studies and Archive Centre, Borough of Bexley - 19 May 1945, Schedule of Properties rendered Uninhabitable by Enemy Action.
30. Letter FMA to Jones dated 20 May 1945.
31. Letter FMA to Douglas dated 15 April 1945.
32. Letter FMA to Jones dated 16 July 1945.
33. *Ibid.*,
34. Letter FMA to Douglas dated 26 July 1945.
35. Letter FMA to Jones dated 6 October 1945.
36. Detailed in the Evidence given to the Commission in London.
37. Letter Heaton-Nichols to Cripps dated 22 February 1945.
38. Sherrington, Charles, *The Endeavour of Jean Fernel* (Cambridge: Cambridge University Press, 1946), p.89.
39. Letter Skinner to FMA dated 27 May 1946.
40. *Medical Press*, 30 October 1946, CCXVI No. 5608.
41. Letters FMA to Douglas dated 8 February and 5 March 1946.
42. Letter FMA to Jones dated 3 March 1947.
43. *The Medical Directory, 102nd Edition* (London: J. & A. Churchill Ltd., 1946), and Detailed in the Evidence given to the Commission in London.
44. Detailed in the Evidence given to the Commission in London.
45. Letter FMA to Jones dated 11 November 1947.
46. Correspondence between Lytton and Horder, July to September 1947.
47. Barlow's evidence at the trial in South Africa.
48. The late Miss Irene Tasker's Diary 1942.
49. Mandela, Nelson, *Long Walk To Freedom* (London: Little, Brown and Company, 1994), pp.189, 211, 219, 336 and 337, with permission from Little Brown publishers.
50. *Ibid.*, pp.348 and 361.
51. *Ibid.,* p.459.
52. *Ibid.*, p.84.
53. *Ibid.*, p.198.
54. *Ibid.*, p.220.
55. Barlow, Dr. Wilfred, *More Talk of Alexander* (London: Victor Gollancz Ltd., 1978), pp.38-52.
56. *Star*, 18 February 1948.
57. *Ibid.*, 24 February 1948.
58. *Ibid.*, 19 February 1948.
59. Letter FMA to Jones dated 20 June 1950.
60. Ludovici, Anthony, unpublished account of the trial, written in 1948, p.299.

16   FINAL YEARS, pp.234-40.

1. *British Journal of Physical Medicine*, May/June and November/December 1948.
2. Letter dated 24 December 1948, Neil to Carrington.
3. Barlow, Dr. Wilfred, *More Talk of Alexander* (London: Victor Gollancz Ltd., 1978), p.191.
4. Barlow, *More Talk of Alexander*, pp.190-203.
5. *Daily Telegraph*, 21 October 1950.
6. *Ibid.*, 28 October 1950 and letter FMA to Douglas dated 20 November 1950.
7. Text of FMA's talk at St Dunstan's Home.
8. *British Medical Journal*, 18 August 1951.
9. *Sunday Chronicle*, 30 March and 6 April 1952.
10. *Observer*, 2 March 1952.
11. *Lancet*, 3 May 1952.
12. Letter FMA to Douglas dated 22 October 1953.
13. *News Chronicle*, 26 February 1953.
14. *Lancet*, 6 June 1953.
15. *Sunday Graphic*, 7 March 1954.
16. *London Evening News*, 8 March 1954.
17. Morgan, L., *Inside Yourself* (London: Hutchinson 1954), foreword.
18. Barlow, *More Talk of Alexander*, pp.29-37.
19. *New Statesman and Nation*, 22 May and 5 June 1954.
20. *Boston Evening News* (England), 14 September 1954.
21. *Lancet*, 16 January 1954.
22. *Manchester Guardian*, 9 June 1954 and 7 and 21 May 1955.

BIBLIOGRAPHY

PRINTED SOURCES

Alexander, F.M., *A Protest* (London: April 1910).

Alexander, F.M., *Man's Supreme Inheritance* (London: Methuen & Co., Ltd., 1910).

Alexander, F.M., *Man's Supreme Inheritance* (Addenda) (London: Methuen & Co. Ltd., 1911).

Alexander, F.M., *Man's Supreme Inheritance*, 2nd edition (London: Methuen & Co. Ltd., 1939 (1918)).

Alexander, F.M., *Man's Supreme Inheritance*, 2nd edition (London: Chaterson Ltd., 1943 (printed in USA 1918)).

Alexander, F.M., *Conscious Control in Relation to Human Evolution in Civilization* (London: Methuen & Co. Ltd., 1912).

Alexander, F.M., *Constructive Conscious Control of the Individual* (New York: Dutton & Company, 1923).

Alexander, F.M., *Cultivating the Singing and Speaking Voice by New and Approved Methods* (Sydney: John Andrew & Co., 1900).

Alexander, F.M., *The Use of the Self* (London: Methuen & Co. Ltd., 1932).

Alexander, F.M., *Universal Constant in Living* (London: Methuen & Co. Ltd., 1942).

Alexander, F.M., *Universal Constant in Living* (New York: E.P. Dutton & Co. Inc., 1942).

Alexander, F.M., *Why We Breath Incorrectly* (London: November 1909).

Alexander, F.M., *A New Technique* (London: Watts & Co., 1935).

Alexander, F.M., The Trust Fund, *Penhill House* (London: Watts & Co., 1934).

Atkinson, C.M., *Jeremy Bentham* (London: Methuen & Co., 1905).

Barlow, Dr. Wilfred, *The Alexander Principle* (London: Victor Gollancz Ltd., 1973).

Barlow, Dr. Wilfred, *More Talk of Alexander* (London: Victor Gollancz Ltd., 1978).

Bartlett, A., *The Launceston Female Factory*, Tasmanian Historical Research Association Papers and Proceedings, Vol.41, No.2 (Tasmania: Arts Advisory Board, 1994).

Bateson, C., *The Convict Ships 1787-1868* (Glasgow: Brown, Son & Ferguson Ltd. (1959), 1969).

Baillier, F.F., *Baillier's Tasmanian Gazette and Road Guide 1877* (Melbourne: Baillier 1877).

Brewer, J. and Styles, J. (ed.), *An Ungovernable People. The English and their Law in the Seventeenth Century* (London: Hutchinson & Co. (Publishers) Ltd., 1980).

Brittain, Vera, *Testament of Youth* (London: Virago Press Ltd. 1978, first published Victor Gollancz Ltd., 1933).

Bryne, R., *Prisons and Punishment of London* (London: Harrap, 1989).

Butler, K.T. & McMorran, H. I. (ed.), *The Girton College Register 1869-1946* (Cambridge: printed privately for Girton College, 1948).

Cannon, Michael, *The Land Boomers* (Australia: Melbourne University Press (1966), 1967).

Carrington, W., *The Foundations of Human Well* (London: STAT Books, 1994).

Census of Great Britain (1831), Enumeration Abstract.

Census of Great Britain (1841), Enumeration Abstract.

Chambers Biographical Directory, Vol. 2 (Edinburgh: W & R Chambers, 1974).

Chambers, J., *The Wiltshire Machine Breakers*, Vol.1 The Riots & Trials (Herts: Jill Chambers, 1993).

Chambers, J., *The Wiltshire Machine Breakers*, Vol.2 The Rioters (Herts: Jill Chambers, 1993).

Chandler, J.H. (ed.), *Wiltshire Dissenters' Meeting House Certificates 1689-1852* (Devizes: Wiltshire Record Society, 1985).

Chapman, Guy (ed.), *Vain Glory* (London: Cassell & Co. Ltd., 1937).

Cockburn, J.S. (ed.), *Crime in England 1550-1800* (London: Methuen, 1977).

Crew, A., *The Old Bailey* (London: Ivor, Nicholson & Watson, 1933).

Croucher, B., *The Village in the Valley* (Wiltshire: Barbara Croucher, 1986).

Dale, Dr. H.H., *Introductory note in Memoriam Rudolf Magnus (1873-1927)*, Lane Lectures on Experimental Pharmacology and Medicine, (California: Stanford University Press, 1930).

Davis, H.W.C., *The Age of Grey and Peel* (London: Oxford University Press (1929), 1987).

Davison, G., *The Rise and Fall of Marvellous Melbourne* (Melbourne: Melbourne University Press (1978), 1979).

Directory of Tasmania, 1867/68.

Fenton, J., *Bushlife in Tasmania* (Launceston, Tasmania: 1989, originally published by Hazell, Watson & Viney Ltd., London, 1891).

George, M.D., *London Life in the Eighteenth Century* (Harmondsworth, Middlesex: Penguin Books (1925) 1985).

Gray, John, *Your Guide to the Alexander Technique* (London: Victor Gollancz Ltd., 1990).

Griffiths, A., *The Chronicles of Newgate* (London: Bracken Books (1883) 1987 facsimile reprint of 1884 edition).

Gilbert, M., *First World War* (London: Weidenfeld and Nicolson, 1994).

Gilbert, M., *Second World War* (London: Phoenix Giant (Weidenfeld and Nicolson, 1989), 1996).

Hammond, J.L. & Barbara, *The Village Labourer* (London: Longmans, Green & Co. (1911), 1966).

Hearn, A.C., *Somerset The Cam* (Somerset: A.C. (Fuzzy) Hearn, 1992).

Herrick, C. Judson, *George Ellett Coghill Naturalist and Philosopher* (Chicago, Illinois: The University of Chicago Press, 1949).

Hobsbawm, E.J., *The Age of Empire 1875-1914* (England: Abacus (Weidenfeld & Nicolson Ltd., 1987), 1996).

Hobsbawm, E.J., and Rudé, G., *Captain Swing* (London: Lawrence & Wishart (1969), 1970).

Hocking, C., *Dictionary of Disasters at Sea During the Age 1824-1962* (London: Lloyds Register of Shipping, 1969).

Hughes, R., *The Fatal Shore* (London: Collins Harvill, 1987).

Huxley, Aldous, *Eyeless In Gaza* (London: Chatto & Windus, 1936).

Johns, F., *Notable Australians & Who is Who in Australasia* (Adelaide: Fred Johns, 1908).

Jones, Frank Pierce, *Body Awareness In Action* (New York: Schocken Books, 1976).

Keegan, J., *The First World War* (London: Hutchinson, 1998).

Keegan, J., *The Second World War* (London: Hutchinson, 1989).

Laffin, J., *A Western Front Companion 1914-1918* (Stroud, Gloucestershire: Alan Sutton Publishing Ltd., 1994).

Laslett, P., *The World We have Lost—Further Explored* (London: Methuen (1965), 1983).

Liddell Hart, B.H., *History of the First World War* (London: Papermac (Faber & Faber, 1930), 1997).

Lucas, E.V., *A Wanderer in London* (London: Methuen (1906), 1911).

Magnus, Philip, *King Edward the Seventh* (London: John Murray, 1964).

Maisel, E., *The Alexander Technique* (Great Britain: Thames & Hudson (1974), 1990 (USA, 1969)).

Mayhew, H., *London Labour and the London Poor* (New York: 4 Vols., Dover Publications (1861-1862), Vol.IV, 1968).

Mandela, Nelson, *Long Walk To Freedom* (London: Little, Brown and Company, 1994).

Mingay, G.E. (ed.), *The Unquiet Countryside* (London: Routledge, 1989).

Mitchell, B.R. and Deane, P., *Abstract of British Historical Statistics* (Cambridge, 1962).

Mitchell, B.R., *British Historical Statistics* (Cambridge, 1988).

Morgan, L., *Inside Yourself* (London: Hutchinson, 1954).

Moulton, J.L., *Battle for Antwerp* (London: Ian Allan, 1978).

Nairne, B., Serle, G. & Ward, R. (ed.), *Australian Dictionary of Biography 1851-1890 Vol 5* (Melbourne: Melbourne University Press, 1974).

Nairne, B., Serle, G., & Ward, R. (ed.), *Australian Dictionary of Biography 1891-1939 Vol 7* (Melbourne: Melbourne University Press, 1979).

Newnham College Register, Vol.1, 1871-1923.

Old Bailey Session Papers, (Nov. 1832-Oct. 1833, Nov. 1840-Oct. 1841, Nov. 1841-Oct. 1842).

Pepys, Samuel, jun., *A Last Diary of the Great War* (London: John Lane, 1919).

Pink, Kerry, *And Wealth for Toil* (Burnie, Tasmania: Advocate Marketing Services Pty Ltd., 1990).

Poll for Electing of the Knights of the Shire for the County of Wilts, A True Copy (London: 1705).

Poll of the Freeholders of Wiltshire for Electing a Knight of the Shire Taken at Wilton on 18, 19, 20 & 21 August 1772 (Salisbury: 1772).

Poll for the Election of Two Knights for the County of Wilts to Serve in Parliament 1818 (Salisbury: 1818).

Ramsay, G.D. (ed.), *Two Sixteenth Century Taxation Lists 1545 and 1576—Taxpayers for the Subsidy of 1576* (Devizes: Wiltshire Record Society, 1954).

Robson, L.L., *A History of Tasmania, Vol.I* (Melbourne: Oxford University Press, 1983).

Robson, L.L., *A History of Tasmania, Vol. II* (Melbourne: Oxford University Press, 1991).

Robson, L.L., *The Convict Settlers of Australia* (Hong Kong: Melbourne University Press, 1983).

Rose, J., *Elizabeth Fry* (London: Macmillan, 1980).

Rudé, G., *Protest and Punishment* (Oxford: Clarendon Press, 1978).

Sandell, R.E. (ed.), *Abstracts of Wiltshire Inclosure Awards and Agreements* (Devizes: Wiltshire Record Society, 1971).

Serle, G., (ed.), *Australian Dictionary of Biography 1891-1939 Vol.11* (Melbourne: Melbourne University Press, 1988).

Shaw, A.G.L., *Convicts and the Colonies* (London: Faber & Faber, 1966).

Shaw, George Bernard, *Preface in London Music in 1883-1889 as heard by Corno di Bassetto* (London: Constable, 1937).

Sherrington, Charles, *The Endeavour of Jean Fernel* (Cambridge: Cambridge University Press, 1946).

Smith, Joanna, *Edwardian Children* (London: Hutchinson & Co., 1983).

Stoney, Capt. H. Butler, *A Residence in Tasmania* (London: Smith, Elder & Co., 1856).

Sweeney, C., *Transported in Place of Death Convicts in Australia* (Melbourne: MacMillan Company of Australia, 1981).

Tasker, I., *Connecting Links* (London: Sheildrake Press, 1978).

The Australian Handbook 1879 (London, Melbourne, Sydney & Brisbane: Gordon & Gotch, 1879).

The Australian Handbook 1890 (London, Melbourne, Sydney & Brisbane: Gordon & Gotch 1890).

The Medical Directory, 77th Edition (London: J. & A. Churchill Ltd., 1921).

The Medical Directory, 92nd Edition (London: J. & A. Churchill Ltd., 1936).

The Medical Directory, 102nd Edition (London: J. & A. Churchill Ltd., 1946).

The National Cyclopaedia of American Biography being the History of the United States, Vol. XXVII (James T. White & Co., 1940), pp.194-5.

The Victoria History of the Counties of England, A History of Berkshire, Vol.4, ed. by William Page (The University of London, Institute of Historical Research, reprinted from the original edition of 1924 by Dawson of London, 1972).

The Victoria History of the Counties of England, A History of Wiltshire, Vol.1, ed. by R.B. Pugh & Elizabeth Crittall (The University of London, Institute of Historical Research, Oxford University Press, 1957).

The Victoria History of the Counties of England, A History of Wiltshire, Vol.2, ed. by R.B. Pugh & Elizabeth Crittall (The University of London, Institute of Historical Research, Oxford University Press, 1955).

The Victoria History of the Counties of England, A History of Wiltshire, Vol.3, ed. by R.B. Pugh (The University of London, Institute of Historical Research, Oxford University Press, 1956).

The Victoria History of the Counties of England, A History of Wiltshire, Vol.4, ed. by R.B. Pugh (The University of London, Institute of Historical Research, Oxford University Press, 1959).

The Victoria History of the Counties of England, A History of Wiltshire, Vol.5, ed. by R.B. Pugh (The University of London, Institute of Historical Research, Oxford University Press 1957).

The Victoria History of the Counties of England, A History of Wiltshire, Vol.12, ed. by D.A. Crowley (The University of London, Institute of Historical Research, Oxford University Press, 1983).

Thompson, F.M.L. (ed.), *The Cambridge Social History of Britain 1750-1950* (Cambridge: Cambridge University Press, 1990).

Thorn, C. & F. (ed.), *Domesday Book Vol 6 Wiltshire* (Chichester: Phillimore, 1979).

Thornbury, W., *London Recollected* (London: 6 Vols., Alderman Press, Vol.II (1872-8), 1985).

West, J., *The History of Tasmania*, ed. A.G.L. Shaw (London: Angus & Robertson (1852), 1981).

Westfeldt, L., *F. Matthias Alexander The Man and his Work* (London: George Allen & Unwin Ltd. (1964).

Wheatley, H.B. (ed.), *John Stow's The Survey of London* (London: J.M. Dent & Sons Ltd. (1912), 1970).
Wiltshire Poll Book 1819.
Wiltshire Dissenters' Meeting House Certificates (Wiltshire Record Society).
Who was Who, 1916-1928, Vol.2 (London: Adam & Charles Black, 1928).
Who's Who, 1916 (London: Adam & Charles Black, 1916).
Who's Who, 1948 (London: Adam & Charles Black, 1948).
Who's Who in America, 1930-1931, Vol.16, ed, Marquis, A.N. (Chicago: The A N Marquis Co., 1930).
Wrigley and Schofield, *The Population History of England 1541-1871 A Reconstruction* (London: Edward Arnold, 1981).

NEWSPAPERS AND MAGAZINES

UNITED KINGDOM
Birmingham Post
British Journal of Physical Medicine
British Medical Journal
Bolton Evening News
Christian World
Daily Express
Daily Graphic
Daily Mail
Daily News
Daily Telegraph
Devizes and Wiltshire Gazette
Field
Journal of Massage and Medical Gymnastics
Journal of School Hygiene & Physical Education
Kentish Times
Lancet
Listener
Literary Guide
London Evening News
London Evening Standard
Manchester Guardian, later Guardian
Medical Press and Circular
Medical World
Morning Leader
Morning Post
National Trust Magazine
New Era
New Statesman and Nation
News Chronicle
Observer
Occult
Onlooker
Pall Mall Gazette
Salisbury and Winchester Journal
Student Movement
Sunday Chronicle
Sunday Graphic
The Times
The Times Educational Supplement
Theosophist
This England
Westminster Gazette
Women's Employment

UNITED STATES
Atlantic Monthly
Baltimore Sun
Boston Evening News
Boston Evening Transcript
Boston Herald
Brooklyn Citizen
Brooklyn Daily Eagle
Chicago Daily News
Chicago Evening Post
Chicago Tribune
Dial
Indianapolis Star
Indianapolis Times
New Republic
New York Evening Post
New York Evening Mail

New York Herald
New York Times
New York Tribune
Pittsburgh Dispatch
Philadelphia Telegraph
Richmond Times Dispatch
St Louis Globe
St Louis Republican
Springfield Republican
Springfield Union
The Village, Mass.
University of Chicago Press
Washington Herald
WHO

AUSTRALIA & NEW ZEALAND
Adelaide Advertiser (Australia)
Advocate (Tasmania)
Age (Australia)
Argus (Australia)
Armidale Express (Australia)
Auckland Star (New Zealand)
Bathurst Daily Times (Australia)
Bathurst Daily Free Press, (Australia)
Bendigo Advertiser (Australia)
Christchurch Press (New Zealand), Elocution Entertainment
Coota Liberal (Australia)
Cornwall Chronicle (Tasmania)
Cowra Free Press (Australia)
Daily Free Press (Australia)
Daily Telegraph (New Zealand)
Daily Telegraph (Tasmania)
Emu Bay Times (Tasmania)
Evening News (Australia)
Evening Post (New Zealand)
Evening Star (New Zealand)
Hawkes Bay Herald (New Zealand)
Hobart Mercury (Tasmania)
Launceston Examiner (Tasmania)
Maitland Daily Mercury (Australia)
Melbourne Punch (Australia)
National Advocate (Australia)
New Zealand Herald
New Zealand Times
Orange Leader (Australia)
Sydney Daily Mail (Australia)
Sydney Daily Telegraph (Australia)
Sydney Morning Herald (Australia)
Wagga Wagga Express (Australia)
Wellington Times (Tasmania)

INDIA
The Statesman (Calcutta)

SOUTH AFRICA
Advancement of Science Journal
Manpower
Cape Times
Star
The Commercial Law Report (Cape Town & Johannesburg: Juta & Co. Ltd., November 1949)
The Transvaal Teachers' Association Journal

Sources

MANUSCRIPT SOURCES

PUBLIC RECORD OFFICE:
ADM 101/13/9, Surgeon's Journal, H.M.S. Buffalo.
ADM 101/19/6, Surgeon's Journal, The Diane.
ADM 101/22/8, Surgeon's Journal, The Edward.
ADM 101/25/5, Surgeon's Journal, The Emma Eugenia.
ADM 101/29/3, Surgeon's Journal, The George Hibbert.
ADM 101/57/7, Surgeon's Journal, The Numa.
ADM 101/65/3, Surgeon's Journal, The Royal Admiral.
ADM 101/74/6, Surgeon's Journal, The William Bryan.
ADM 199/2208, Royal Navy War Diary.
AIR 27/2121, No. 614 Squadron Form 540.
ASSI 24/18/3, Wiltshire Assizes Records.
ASSI 5/152/2, Berkshire Assizes Records.
CO 280/145, Governor's Dispatches.
CO 283/6, Hobart Gazette 1835.
CO 283/7, Hobart Gazette 1836.
CO 283/22, Hobart Gazette 1852.
CO 283/23, Hobart Gazette 1853.
CO 283/24, Hobart Gazette 1854.
CO 283/25, Hobart Gazette 1855.
CO 283/26, Hobart Gazette 1856.
CO 283/28, Hobart Gazette 1858.
CO 283/29, Hobart Gazette 1859.
CO 283/30, Hobart Gazette January - June 1860.
CO 283/31, Hobart Gazette July - December 1860.
CO 283/32, Hobart Gazette January - June 1861.
CO 283/50, Hobart Gazette January - June 1870.
CO 283/51, Hobart Gazette July - December 1870.
CO 283/52, Hobart Gazette January - June 1871.
E 179/348, Hearth Tax Records.
HO 8/27, Prison Hulk Quarterly Returns, The York.
HO 8/33, Prison Hulk Quarterly Returns, The York.
HO 10/32, General Muster of Convicts in New South Wales & Tasmania 1837.
HO 10/39, Register of Convicts in Tasmania on 31 Oct. 1846 with statement of condition on that day including the names of all who were convicts in January 1842.
HO 10/48, Tasmanian Nominal Return of Convicts, year ending 31 Dec. 1832.
HO 10/49, Tasmanian Nominal Return of Convicts, year ending 31 Dec. 1833.
HO 10/50, Tasmanian Nominal Return of Convicts, year ending 31 Dec. 1835.
HO 10/51, Tasmanian Nominal Return of Convicts, year ending 31 Dec. 1841.
HO 11/8, Convict Transportation Records 1831-1832.
HO 11/9, Convict Transportation Records, 1833-1834.
HO 11/12, Convict Records 1839-1841.
HO 11/13, Convict Records 1842-1843.
HO 13/62, Pardons & Reprieves.
HO 27/42, Criminal Registers.
HO 27/43, Criminal Registers.
HO 77/39, Newgate Calendars 1832.
HO 77/40, Newgate Calendars 1833.

HO 77/41, Newgate Calendars 1834.
HO 77/42, Newgate Calendars 1835.
HO 77/48, Newgate Calendars 1841.
HO 77/49, Newgate Calendars 1842.
HO 107/1184, 1841 Census.
HO 107/1686, 1851 Census.
IR 17/10/23, Apprenticeship Records.
IR 23/96, Land Tax Records.
IR 38/224, Ramsbury Tithe Maps & assessments.
IR 58/6248, 1910 Property Census.
MH 12/234, Poor Law Records.
PCOM 2/202, Register of Newgate Prisoners, 1832-1834.
PCOM 2/206, Register of Newgate Prisoners, 1840-1842.
PCOM 2/207, Register of Newgate Prisoners, 1842-1844.
RG 9, 1861 Census.
RG 10, 1871 Census.
RG 11, 1881 Census.
RG 12, 1891 Census.

GUILDHALL LIBRARY, CITY OF LONDON
London Gazette, 1920-1939.

BEXLEY LOCAL STUDIES AND ARCHIVE CENTRE
Catalogue of freehold estate William Steele Esq., 1761.
Lamorbey & Christchurch Electoral Rolls 1924,1929,1938, 1946-1956.
Bexley Rate Books various, Upton Road, 11 April & October 1924, 8 April 1925 & 6 October 1926.
Post 22 Log Book of Air Raid Incidents in Birchwood Ward (Area 4). Official Record for Major H. Allen.
List of Incidents upto December 1943, dated January 1944, Sidcup/Bexley area.
Schedule of Properties rendered Uninhabitable by Enemy Action, Sidcup/Bexley area.

WESTMINSTER ARCHIVES
Bomb incidents, 1940 &1941.

WILTSHIRE AND SWINDON RECORD OFFICE
W.S.R.O. 1883/27, Axford Enclosure Agreement 1727.
W.S.R.O. 1792/38L, 1839 Map of Ramsbury by U. B. Vine.
W.S.R.O. A1 345/339A, Land Tax Assessments 1783-1804.
W.S.R.O. 2027H, Ramsbury Church Pew List circa early 18th century.
W.S.R.O. 3035/10, Ramsbury Church Pew List circa 1780s.
W.S.R.O. Wills, Sarum Peculiar & Prebendal Courts, 1462-1800.
W.S.R.O. Wills, Dean of Old Sarum 1500-1801, & Sarum Consistory 1526-1799.
W.S.R.O. 1833/165-7 Ramsbury Leases 1625-1796.

AUSTRALIAN RECORD OFFICES & MUSEUMS

ARCHIVES OFFICE OF TASMANIA (AOT)
CON 14, Indents of Male Convicts, 1827, 1831, 1839, 1841-1853.
CON 15, Indents of Female Convicts, 1839, 1842-1853.

CON 18, Description Lists of Male Convicts, (included some females prior to 1841).

CON 19, Description Lists of Female Convicts, 1841-1853.

CON 31, Male Convict Conduct Records, 1803-1843.

CON 40, Female Convict Conduct Records, 1803-1843.

CON 52, Registers of Applications for Permission to Marry, 1834-1857.

POL 20/9/1, Returns of Crews & Passengers departing from Launceston, 1848-1854.

CB 7, Description Lists of Immigrants to Tasmania.

HSD 247, New Norfolk Asylum Admission Book.

Chapel for the Convict Party Marriage Register.

Christ Church, Longford, Marriage Register.

St John's Church, Launceston, Marriage Register.

Tasmanian Census, 1842, Norfolk Plains, Parish No. 2.

AUSTRALIAN ARCHIVES OFFICE, MELBOURNE

B5179, Muster Roll of the Fifth Contingent for Service in South Africa.

Official Records of the Australian Military Contingents to the War in South Africa, ed. by Lt. Col. P. L. Murrey.

MELBOURNE RECORD OFFICE

Manifest of ships arrivals December 1856.

Electoral Roll St Kilda 1912.

PIONEER VILLAGE MUSEUM, BURNIE, TASMANIA

Rouse Papers, May 1863 & 1878.

Various Alexander family letters.

QUEEN VICTORIA MUSEUM AND ART GALLERY, LAUNCESTON, TASMANIA

SANDERSON PAPERS.

TASMANIAN PROBATE REGISTRY

Will of Matthias Alexander, senior.

Will of Joseph Alexander, senior.

PRIVATE COLLECTIONS:

Alexander, F.M., recital programme costings, 25 March 1898.

Alexander, F.M., Diary 1922.

Alexander, F.M., handwritten records held by author, Alexander family and teachers.

Alexander, F.M., Sydney Dramatic & Operatic Conservatorium Prospectus.

Alexander, Amy Maria, Australian postcard collection, July 1904 - January 1911.

Alexander, Amy Maria, English postcard collection, May - October 1911.

Alexander, Roy, John Alexander's Apprenticeship Certificate.

Alexander, Roy, copy of Manifest of *St James*.

Alexander Journal, No.9 dated Summer 1988, Pat McDonald Memorial Lecture, 1963.

Alexander Journal, No.11 Spring 1991.

Alexander Times, 1929

Alexandria, Wynyard, Tasmania, House Deeds.

AUSTAT Journal Vol.1 No.2 1987.

Croucher, Barbara, Map & Listings of Ramsbury 1839.

Evans, Joan (née Mechin), 70th Birthday Invitation & Menu Card.

Evans, Joan (née Mechin), 1939 Diary.

Evans, Joan (née Mechin), 1940 Diary.

Evans, Joan (née Mechin), 1941 Diary.

Evidence given to the Commission in London, July 1947.

Hilder, Richard, handwritten account dated 1927.

Leeper, Alexander, a Report on Physical Culture dated March 1909.

Ludovici, Anthony, unpublished account of the Alexander Libel Action, written in 1948.

MacKenzie, J.C., handwritten account 1916 on 69 years in Tasmania.

Mechin, B.G., Diary 1914.

Matunck, R.I., *Forward and Up at Fifty*, Carla Atkinson, a Pamphlet dated summer 1943. Methuen & Co. receipts January to June 1938.

Old Vic programme dated 5 December 1933.

Old Vic programme dated 13 November 1934.

Rudolf Steiner Hall programme dated 3 December 1935.

Tasker, I., 1942 Diary.

Text of F.M. Alexander's talk at St Dunstan's Home.

The Life of Countess Catherine 'Kitty' Meyrick Wieloposka as told at interview to Joe Armstrong.

Trevelyan, George, Notes dated October 1936.

Watts, Fred, printing bills period to 31 December 1938 dated 23 February 1939.

Whittaker, Erika, FM Alexander Memorial Lecture 26 October 1985.

Whittaker, Erika, 'The First Training Course' published in the *Alexander Review* (Australia) Vol.2 No.3 September 1987.

LETTERS:

Alexander, Betsy, to FMA, 26 April 1904-9 May 1905.

Alexander, A.R., to FMA, 27 April 1904-18 May 1905.

Alexander, A.R., to Joan Mechin, 1941.

Alexander, Agnes, Amy & May to FMA, 1904 & 1923.

Alexander, Edith, to FMA, 30 March 1917-31 January 1920.

Alexander, F.M., to Annie Alexander, 11 September 1943.

Alexander, F.M., to Wilfred and Marjory Barlow, 10 July 1940-7 June 1943.

Alexander, F.M., to Joan Mechin, 22 September 1940-10 November 1942.

Alexander, F.M., to Irene Tasker, 1936-1948.

Alexander, F.M., to Walter Carrington, 1940-1947.

Alexander, F.M., to Mungo Douglas, 1942-1953.

Alexander, F.M., to Frank Pierce Jones, 1943-1953.

Alexander, F.M., to the South African High Commissioner dated 9 October 1944.

Alexander, Roy, large collection from many members of the Alexander family in USA & from George Woolford and various others in Ramsbury sent to America in 1850s.

Coaker to Messrs. Hardy Philip and Scott-Brown dated 19 July 1944.

Cripps to FMA dated 8 September 1944.

Heaton-Nichols to Cripps dated 22 February 1945.

Lytton to FMA dated 22 September 1944.

Lytton and Horder, July to September 1947.

Matheson Lang to FMA dated 26 November 1909.

McInnes to Tasker dated 10 December 1939.

Page various to FMA, 1938.

Skinner to FMA dated 27 May 1946.

Tasker, I. to FMA, 1937.

Vicary, Owen to FMA, 1920.

Young, Robert to FMA, 26 April 1904 - 4 April 1905.

INDEX

Compiled by Auriol Griffith-Jones

Note: Women are indexed under their maiden names (where known). *Italic* page numbers refer to illustrations; **bold** page numbers refer to the Family Trees

Alexander, Henrietta (Harriet), b.1862, m.James King Percy, 59, 60, 61, 77, **255**

Alexander, Henry, 1817-1912, m.Esther Bright, 12, 250, **255**

Alexander, Henry, 1868-1936, m.Alice Stensland, 25, **254**

Alexander, Hezekiah, 1815-c.1894, to America, 23, **254**

Alexander, Horace, b. & d. 1883, 73, 80, **256**

Alexander, Jabez, 1844-6 in America, 23, **254**

Alexander, Jabez, b.1848, in America, 24, **254**

Alexander, James, b.1794, m.Sarah Pearce, 10, 23, **253**

Alexander, Jane, 1808-93, m.(1) John Woodley, (2) George Chivers, 12, 249, **255**

Alexander, Jane, 1834-75+, m.Samuel Darknell, America, **254**

Alexander, Jane, 1859-1917, m.Elmer Gould, **254**

Alexander, Jane, b.1711, 8-9

Alexander, Janet, b.c.1866, 65

Alexander, Jim, fl.1987, 68, 69

Alexander, John, 1674-1758, m.Elizabeth Brackstone, 8, 9, **252**

Alexander, John, 1761-1842, m.Hannah Smith, 9, 10-11, **252**, **253**

Alexander, John, 1812-98, 12, 61-2, **255**; to California, 50, 51; land at Table Cape in Tasmania, 51-2, 53, 54, 56, 59; m.Margaret Bourke, 47; m.Martha Coleman, 47, 49, 57; m.Mary Ann Crowther (Thewlis), 50, 62

Alexander, John, 1817-95, America, **254**

Alexander, John, 1843-1936 (father of FM), 49, 68-9, 70, 71, 73, 77-8, 79-80, **256**, **258**, **259**; and Ben McKenna, 196-7, 196; death, 197, 197; as horseman, 78, 93, 100-1, 111, 195-6; m.Betsy Brown (q.v.), 69; Methodism, 77-8; remains in Wynyard, 111, 135, 155

Alexander, John, b.1709 (dsp), 8

Alexander, John, b.1792, m.(1) Phoebe Pike, (2) Harriet Pike, 10, 13, 23, **253**, **254**

Alexander, John Charles (Hezekiah), b.1845, 49, 61-2, **255**

Alexander, John, d.1722, m.Elizabeth, **252**

Alexander, John, s. of Josiah and Hannah, 25, **255**

Alexander, Joseph, 1806-78, 12, 13, 20, **255**; Emily Hotel (Stanley), 57, 59; m.(1) 1824 Elizabeth Brown, 13-14, 22; m.(2) Mary Dyer, 57; m.(3) Harriet Gee, 59, 77, 143; and Swing Riots, 19, 21, 22; in Tasmania, 43-4, 49, 53, 56; transported to Australia (1831), 3, 22, 37, 43-4; at Wynyard, 60, 73

Alexander, Joseph, 1826-97, to America, 23-5, 24, 25, 26, **254**

Alexander, Joseph, b.1798, Ramsbury and Chipping Lambourn, 10-11, **253**

Alexander, Joseph, b.1854, m.Delphine Van Hook, **254**

Alexander, Joseph Redding, b.1841, m.Sarah Dowling, 49, 53, 59, 65, **256**

Alexander, Josiah, 1828-49, m.Hannah Ward, 14, 25, **255**

Alexander, Maria, 1804-70, m.(1) Ambrose Woolford (2) George Brown, 12, 13, 249, **255**

Alexander, Martha Ann, b.1844, m.(1) John Jones, (2) Alexander Shekleton, 49, 61, **255**

Alexander, Martha Matilda, b.1865, 59, **257**

Alexander, Martin Redding, 1849-1906, m.Maria Bramich, 50, 53, 67, 68, 92, **256**

Alexander, Mary Ann, 1830-1908, m.(1) Thomas Watts (2) William Watts, 14, 23, 26, 59, **255**

Alexander, Mary Ann, 1847-1940, m.(1) John Stark, (2) John Wells, (3) Thomas Senior, 49-50, 53, 65-6, 111, **256**

Alexander, Mary Ann, 1850-1932, m.(1) William Eastlick, (2) A.F. Nelson, **254**

Alexander, Matthias, 1810-65 (grandfather of FM), 13-14, **252**, **256**, **258**; brothers and sisters of, 249-51; death, 62, 65; m.Ann Eden Thewlis, 56, 57-9, 62, 65; m.Mary Reading, 45, 47, 49, 50; and Swing Riots, 19, 21; at Table Cape, 53-4; transported to Australia (1831), 3, 22, 37, 40, 43-4

Alexander, Matthias, b.1845, m.(1) Elizabeth Law, (2) Catherine Atkinson, (3) Mary Hartlett, 49, 53, 66-8, **256**

Alexander, Matthias, b.1870s, 88

Alexander, Mattie, 1865-95, m.Arlington Howard, **254**

Alexander, Maud, 1894-1985, m.Charles Smart, **254**

Alexander, Max, b.1916, 172, 173, 175, 190, 204, 212, **256**; as teacher, 191, 198, 201, 229, 235

Alexander, May, 1881-1946, 73, 93, 101-2, 135, 140-1, 140, **256**; children, 144, 147, 149, 185; death (1946), 228; to England, 155, 157; m.Norman Cleland, 137, 141, 143, 185, 186

Alexander, Phoebe, 1823-1875+, m.David Martin, America, **254**

Alexander, Rebecca, fl.1758, m.Ben Hobbs, 9

Alexander, Richard Thomas, 1876-c.1948 (Dick), 73, 75, 93, 111, 238, **256**; horse-racing, 101, 107; to New Zealand, 111, 135, 143, 155

Alexander, Roy Joseph, 1897-1988, m.Jeannette Quick, **254**

Alexander, Sarah Ann, b.1863, 59

Alexander, Stanley Gordon, 1892-3, 73, 77, 102, 110, **256**

Alexander, Susannah, 1824-93, m.William Ponting, 12, 23, 249, 250, **255**

Alexander, Thomas, s. of Josiah and Hannah, 25

Alexander, William, 1829-82, America, **254**

Alexander, William, 1870-1943, m.Florence Perkins, **254**

Alexander, William Adolphus, 1828-89, m.Mary Thornton, 12, 23, 251, **255**

Alexander, William, b.c.1725, 8

Alexander Technique (the Work), 194, 202-4, 237, 245; actors as pupils, 139, 142, 143, 144, 194; affiliated societies, 244; Alexander Society formed (1937), 199; Coghill's contribution to, 202-4; early development of methods, 114-15, 128; early supporters, 153, 154-5; and education, 246, 247-8; FM's legacy (by John Gray), 243-8; independent teaching of, 234-5, 243-4; interest in America, 181-2, 198, 212-13; interpretation of FM's writing, 220; and Jokl trial, 230-3; Jokl's attack on, 220-1; medical establishment interest in, 178-81, 220; medical support for methods, 113, 115, 121-2, 128, 185, 197-8, 228-9; NHS recognition of, 245; publications on, 247; pupils in London, 149-50, 195, 204, 205, 208; pupils in New York, 159-60, 164, 169, 170-2; qualified teachers, 194, 243-4; scientific corroboration, 202-4, 213, 244; teacher training courses, 184, 186-8, 189, 194-5, 227-8

Alexandria, Tasmania, 55, 57, 59, 62

American Center for Alexander Teachers (1964), 244

American Unitarian Association, 209, 216

Amphitrite transport ship, 40-1

Anderson, William, surgeon on Eliza, 37

Annetts, James, Swing rioter, 20

Appleford, Elizabeth, 1722-84, m.David Pike, 11-12, **252**

Appleford family, Ramsbury and Axford, 7, 11, 14

Appleford, Mary, fl.1762, m.Thomas Griffin, 11

Appleford, Simon, fl.1678, Axford, 11

Appleford, Stephen, d.1764, 11, **252**

Appleford, Stephen, fl.1567, of Ramsbury and Axford, 7

Archer, William, review of Man's Supreme Inheritance, 146

Army and Navy Mansions, Victoria Street, London, 139, 149, 150

Arthur, Colonel Sir George, Lieutenant Governor of Tasmania, 40, 43, 44, 45

Ashe, Oscar, theatre manager, 142, 144

Ashley Gardens (No. 118), London, 153

Ashley Place (No. 16), London, 150, 178, 211-12; and independent teachers, 235, 243; school at, 175, 182-4, 191, 204; teacher training courses, 186-8, 189, 194-5, 227-8; teaching from, 150, 151, 155, 157, 172, 182, 194, 199, 218; wartime pupils, 208, 219

Atherton, William, Ramsbury, 47

Atkinson, Carla, pupil in America, 170-2, 171, 173, 174, 201